結界師（けっかいし）

KEKKAISHI

16

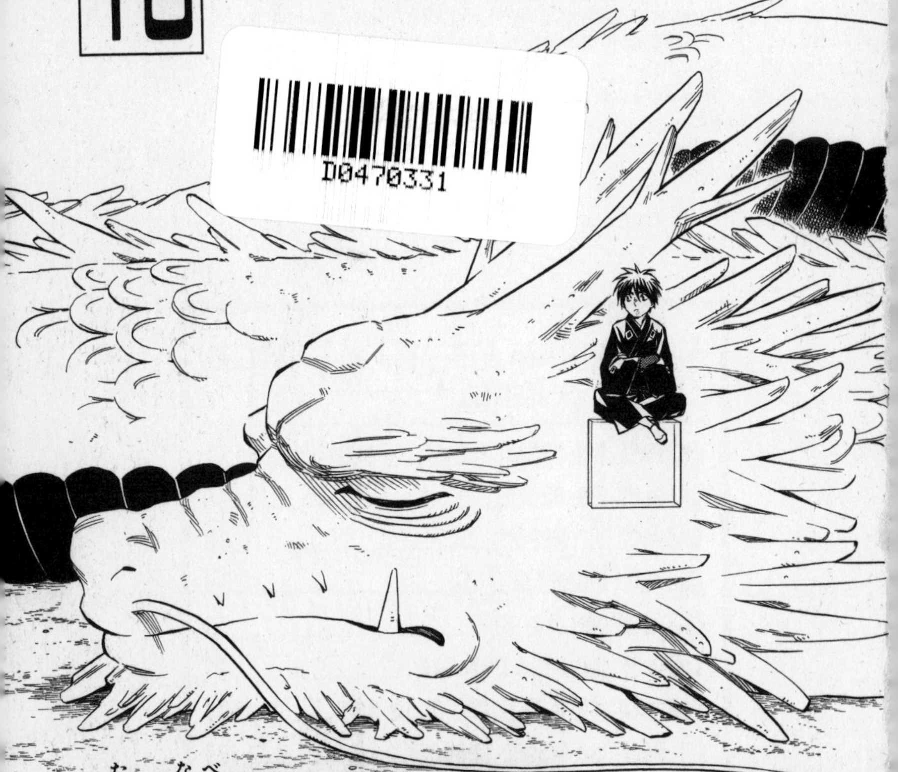

田辺（たなべ）イエロウ

YELLOW TANABE PRESENTS

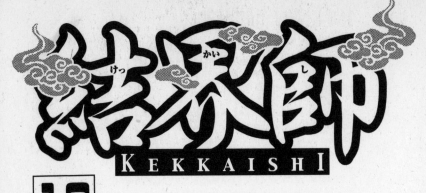

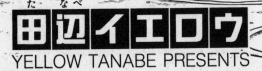

THE STORY THUS FAR

Yoshimori Sumimura and Tokine Yukimura have an ancestral duty to protect the Karasumori Forest from supernatural beings called ayakashi. People with their gift for terminating ayakashi are called kekkaishi, or "barrier masters."

Ichiro Ogi, the eighth member of the Shadow Organization's Council of Twelve, accuses Masamori of botching the battle against the Kokuboro. The council's ninth member, Okuni, is assigned to oversee an inspection of the Karasumori Site and its guardians.

But just before Okuni arrives, mysterious black boxes are delivered to both the site and the headquarters of Masamori's night troops. Two young night troopers escape imprisonment in one of the boxes, which acts as a portal, and now Tokine has entered a box to further unravel its mysteries.

Meanwhile, out of a huge cocoon hidden inside the Karasumori school, a huge ayakashi emerges and proceeds to wreak havoc. If it grows to full size, it will be unstoppable!

KEKKAISHI VOL. 16
TABLE OF CONTENTS

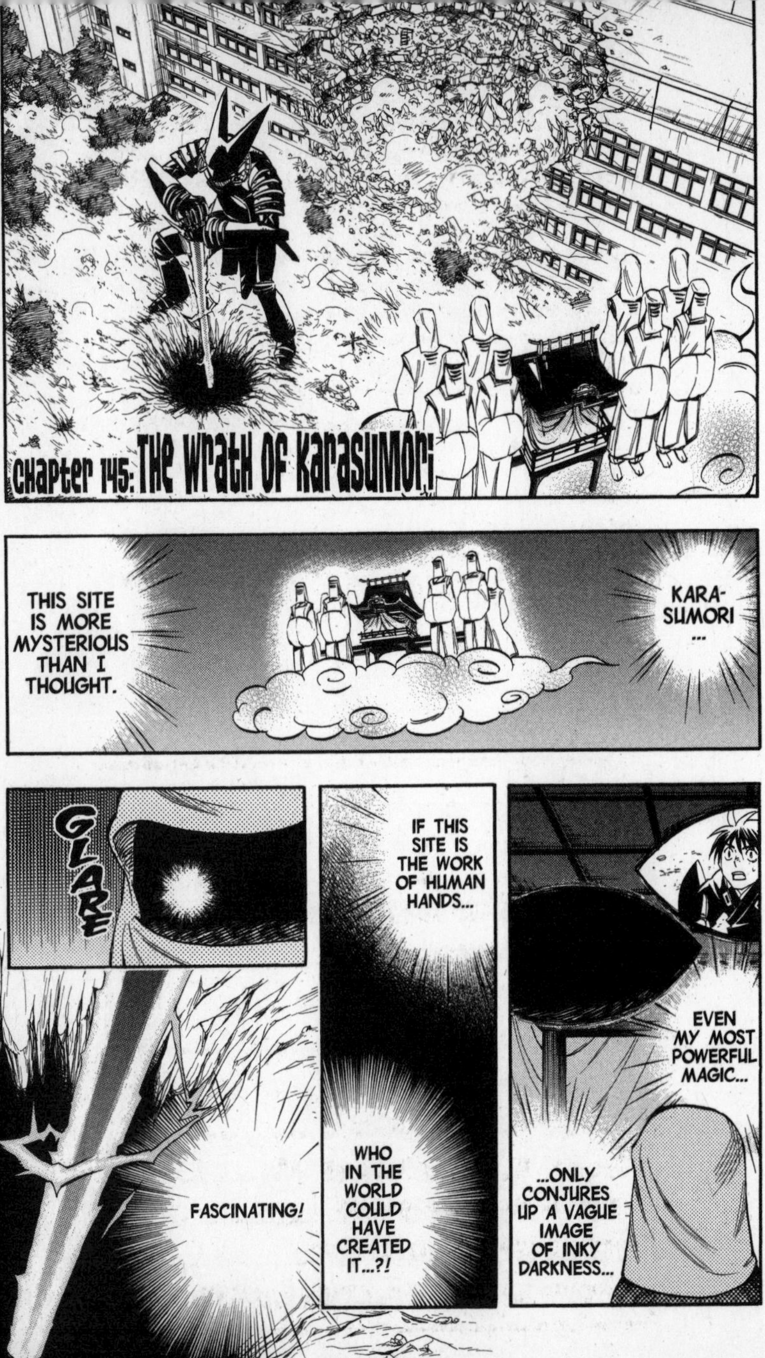
Chapter 145: The Wrath of Karasumori
KARA-SUMORI...
THIS SITE IS MORE MYSTERIOUS THAN I THOUGHT.
EVEN MY MOST POWERFUL MAGIC...
...ONLY CONJURES UP A VAGUE IMAGE OF INKY DARKNESS...
IF THIS SITE IS THE WORK OF HUMAN HANDS...
WHO IN THE WORLD COULD HAVE CREATED IT...?!
GLARE
FASCINATING!

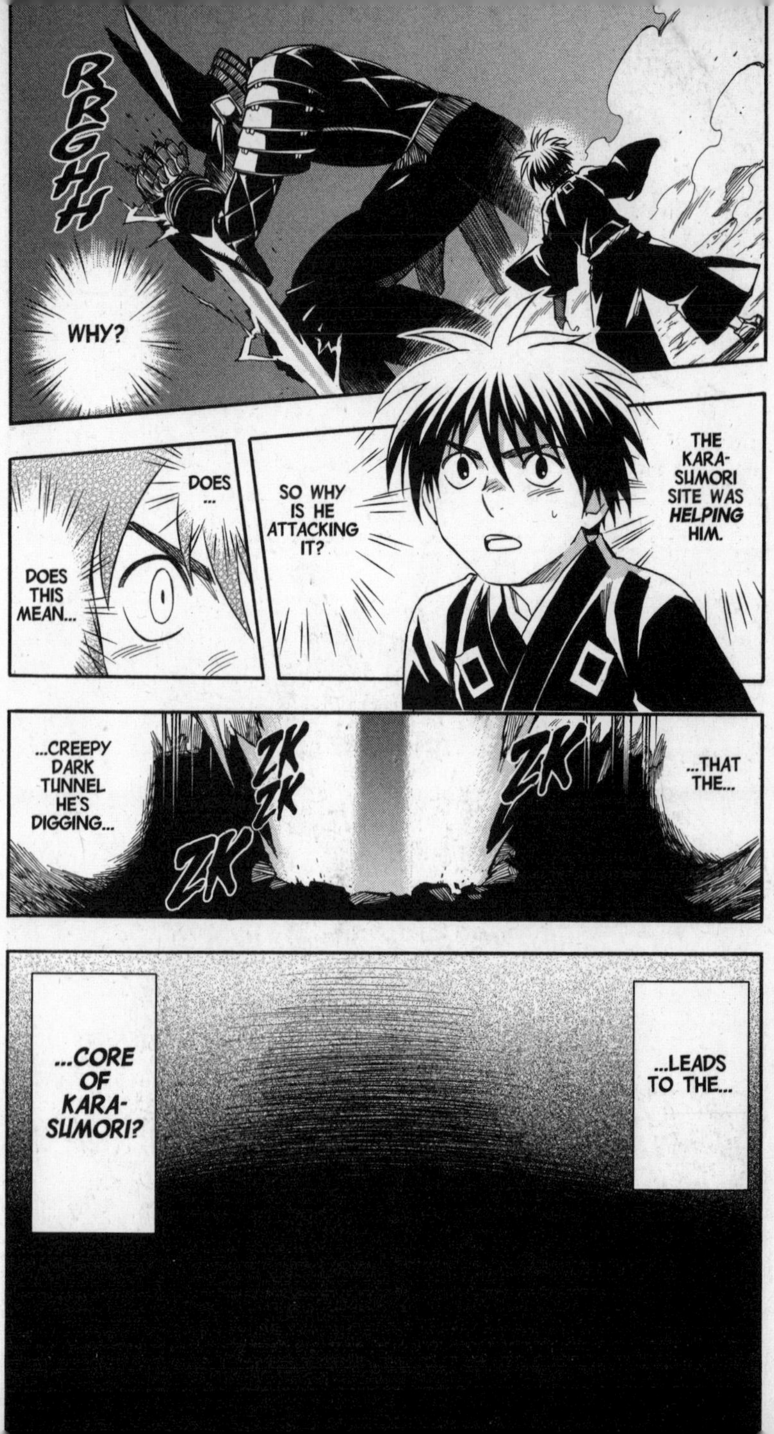
RRGHH
WHY?
THE KARA-SUMORI SITE WAS HELPING HIM.
SO WHY IS HE ATTACKING IT?
DOES...
DOES THIS MEAN...
...THAT THE...
ZK
ZK ZK
ZK
...CREEPY DARK TUNNEL HE'S DIGGING...
...LEADS TO THE...
...CORE OF KARA-SUMORI?

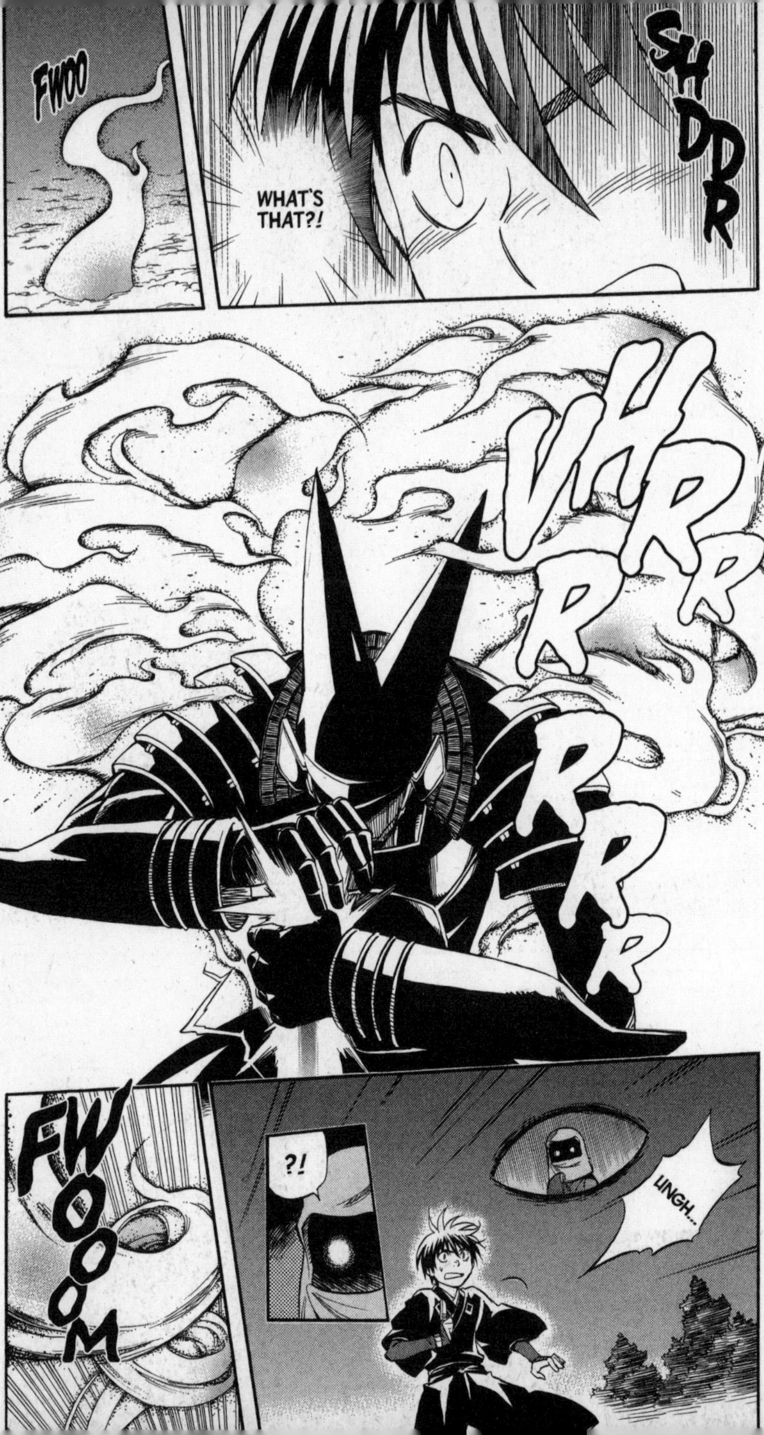
SHDDR
WHAT'S THAT?!
FWOO
VHRRRRRR
?!
UNGH...
FWOOOM

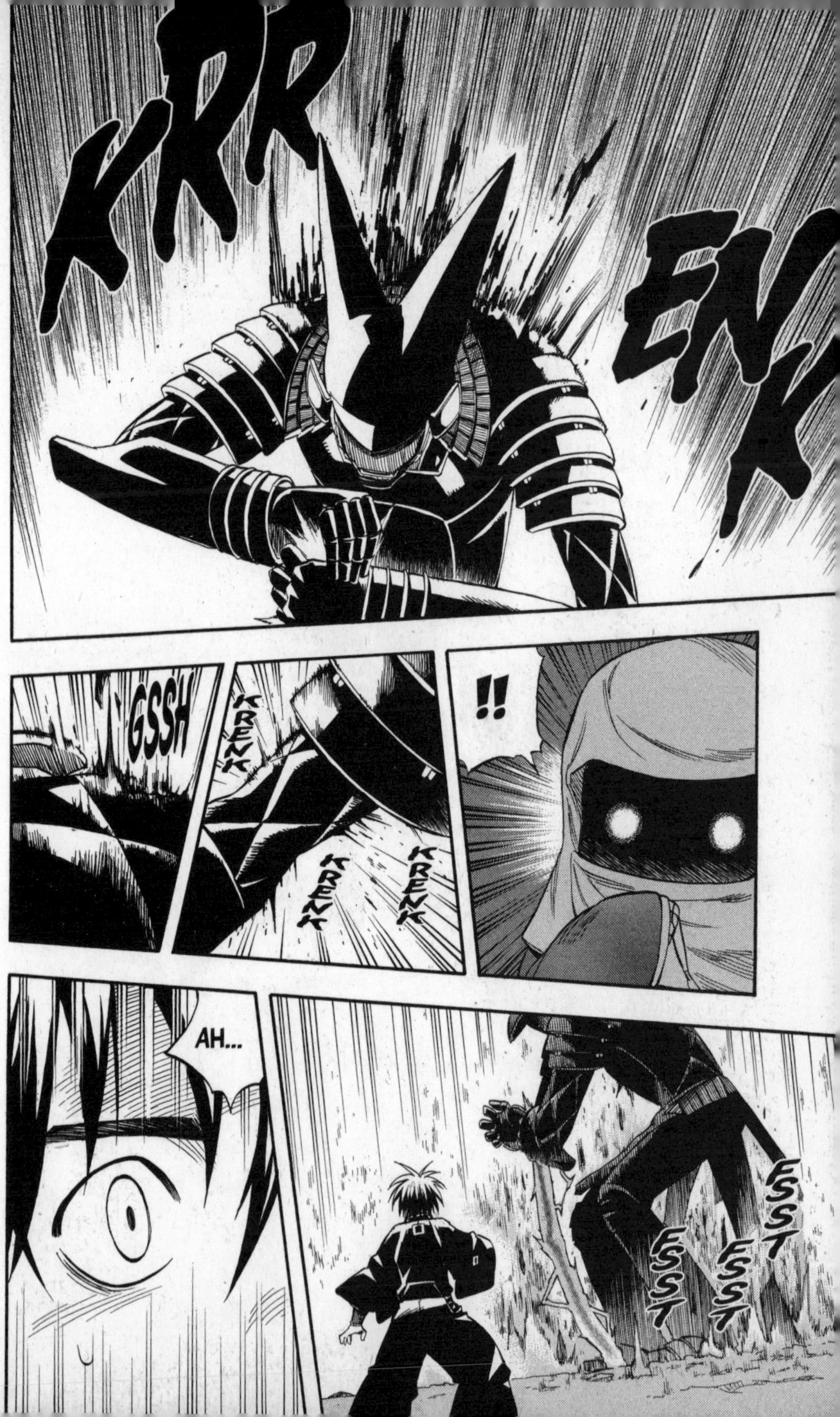
KRR
ENK
!!
KRENK
KRENK
KRENK
GSSH
ESST
ESST
ESST
AH...

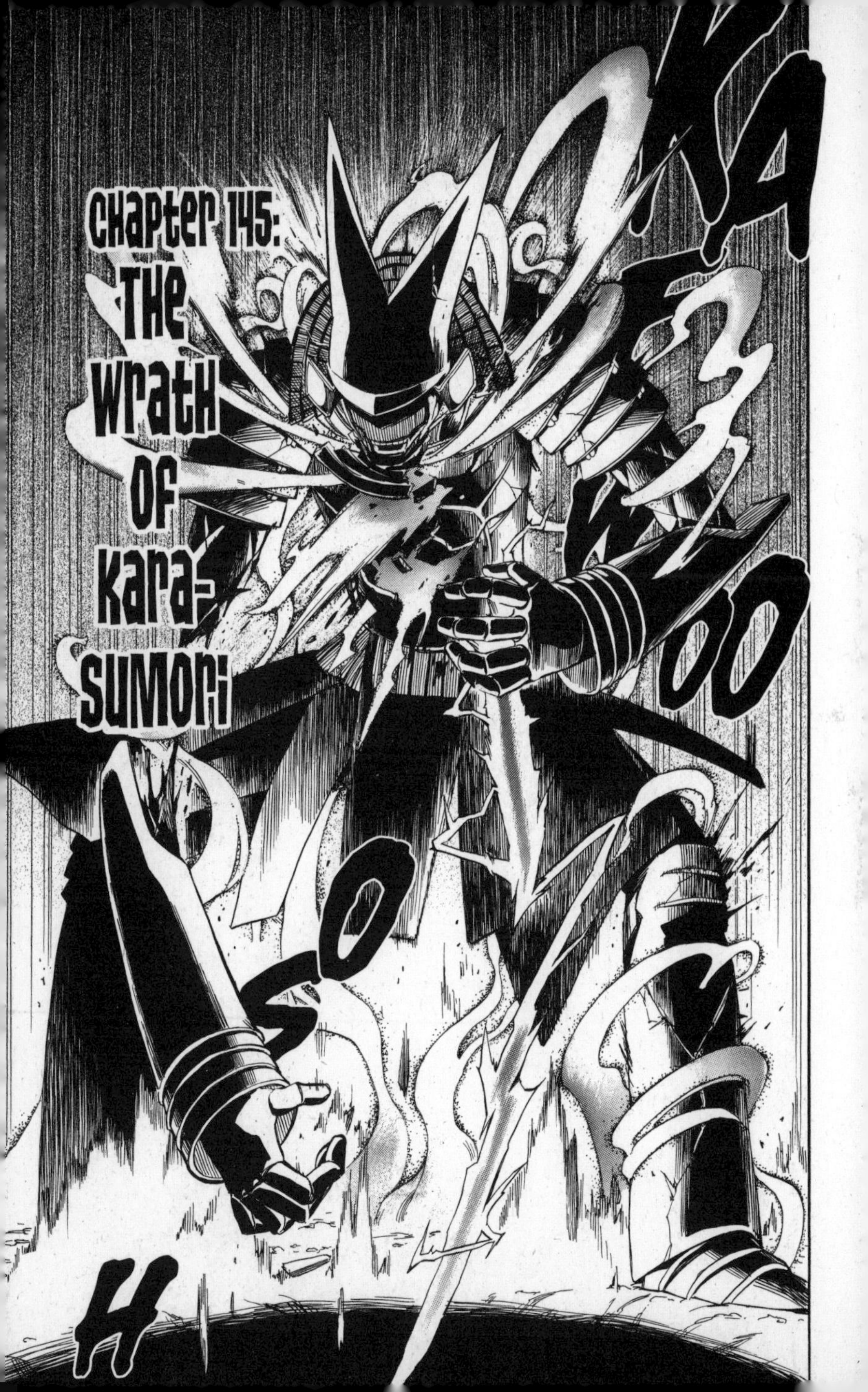
Chapter 145: The Wrath of Karasumori

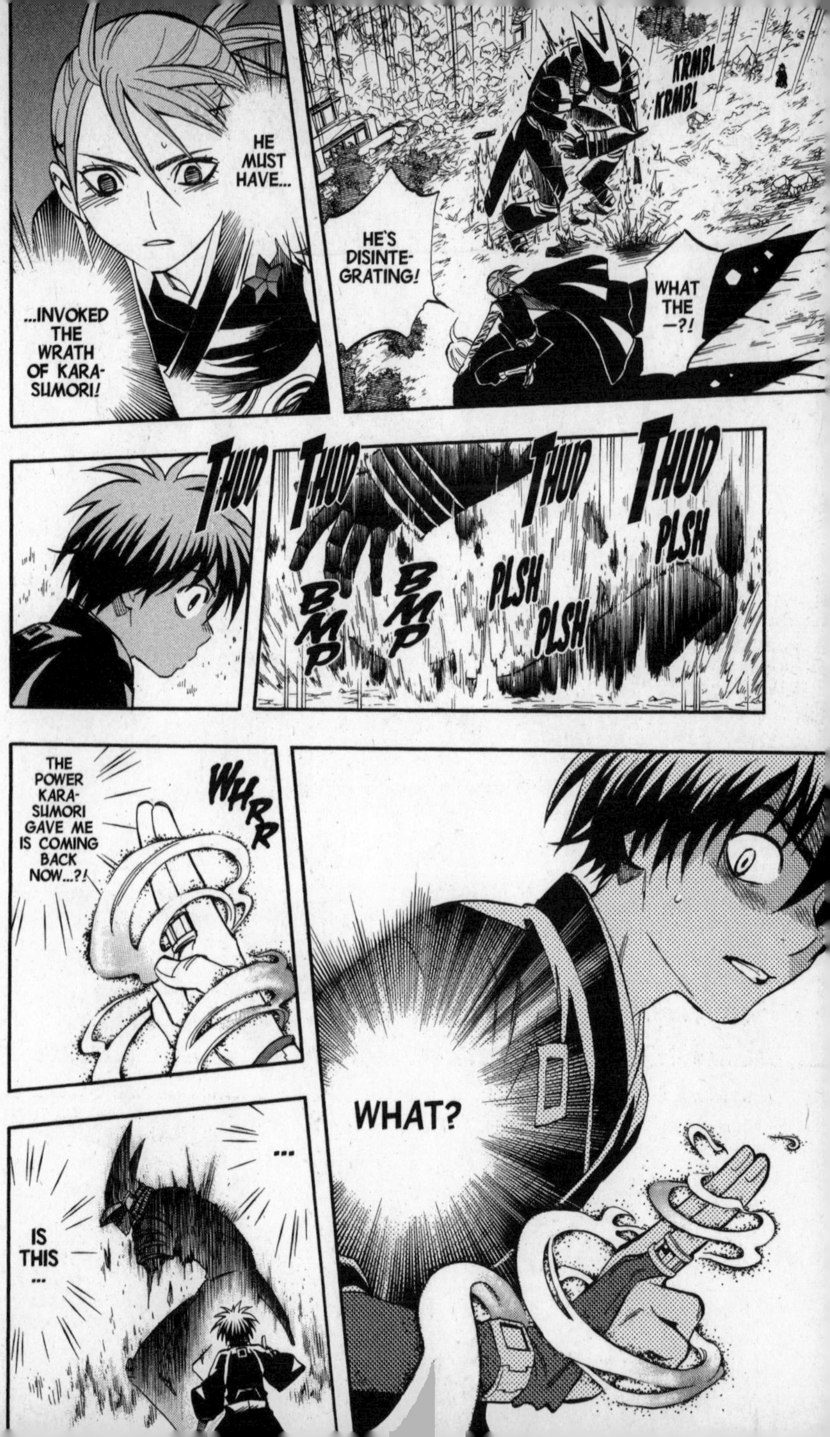
KRMBL
KRMBL
WHAT THE—?!
HE'S DISINTE-GRATING!
HE MUST HAVE...
...INVOKED THE WRATH OF KARA-SUMORI!
THUD
THUD
THUD
THUD
PLSH
PLSH
PLSH
BMP
BMP
WHAT?
WHRR
THE POWER KARA-SUMORI GAVE ME IS COMING BACK NOW...?!
...
IS THIS ...

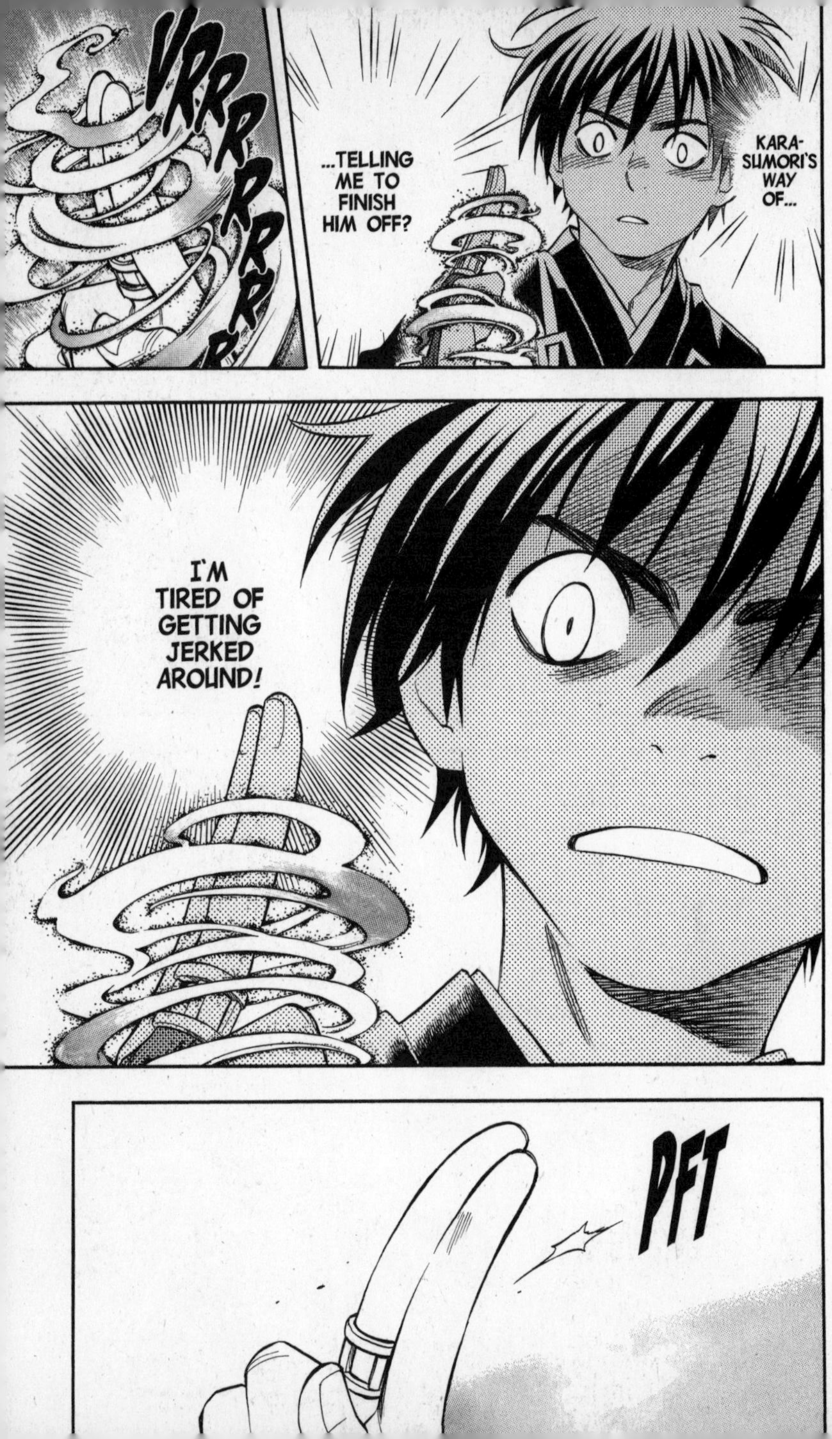
KARA-SUMORI'S WAY OF...
...TELLING ME TO FINISH HIM OFF?
VRRRRRRRR
I'M TIRED OF GETTING JERKED AROUND!
PFT

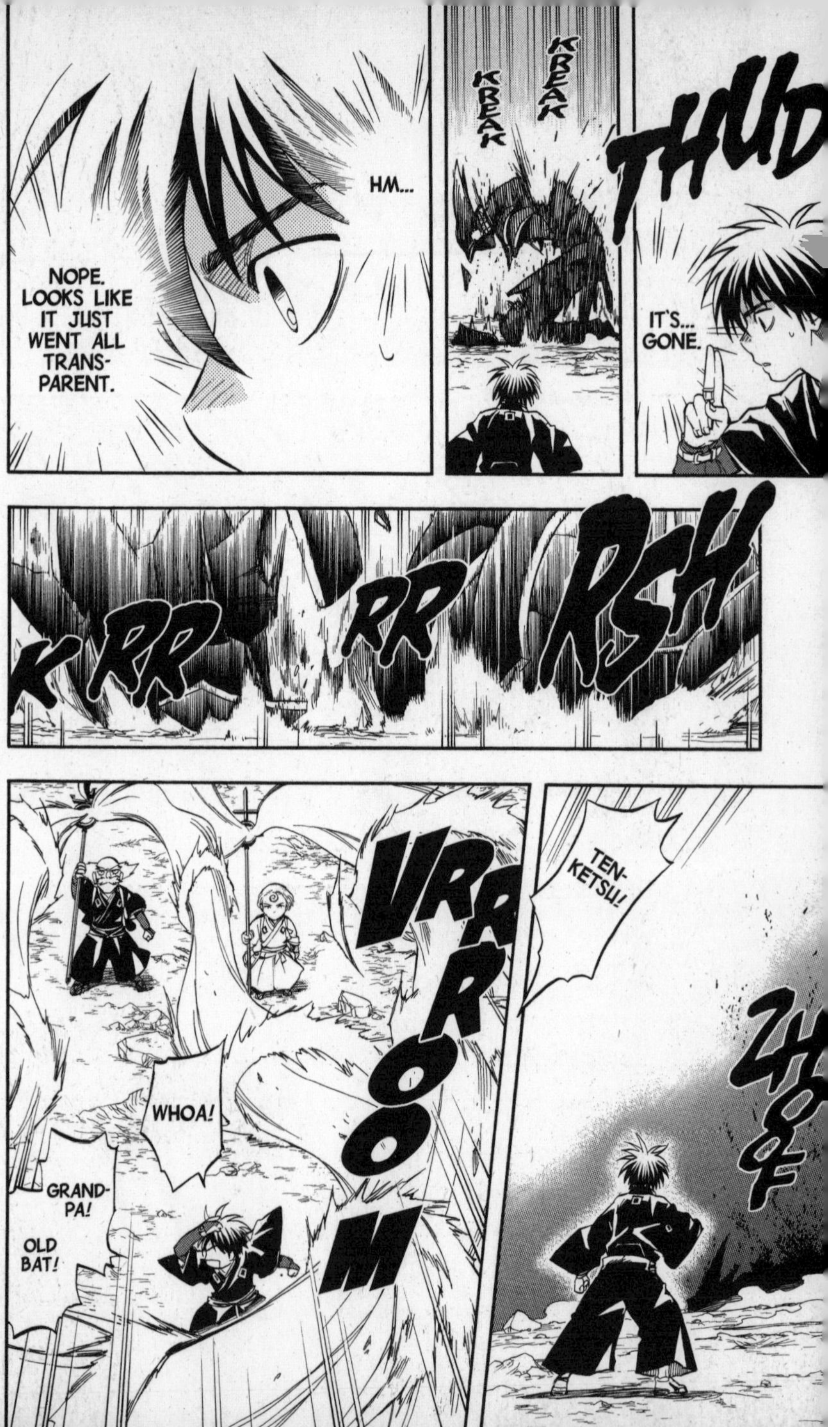
THUD
IT'S... GONE.
KREAK
KREAK
HM...
NOPE. LOOKS LIKE IT JUST WENT ALL TRANS-PARENT.
K RR RR RSH
TEN-KETSU!
ZHOOF
VRRROOOM
WHOA!
GRAND-PA!
OLD BAT!

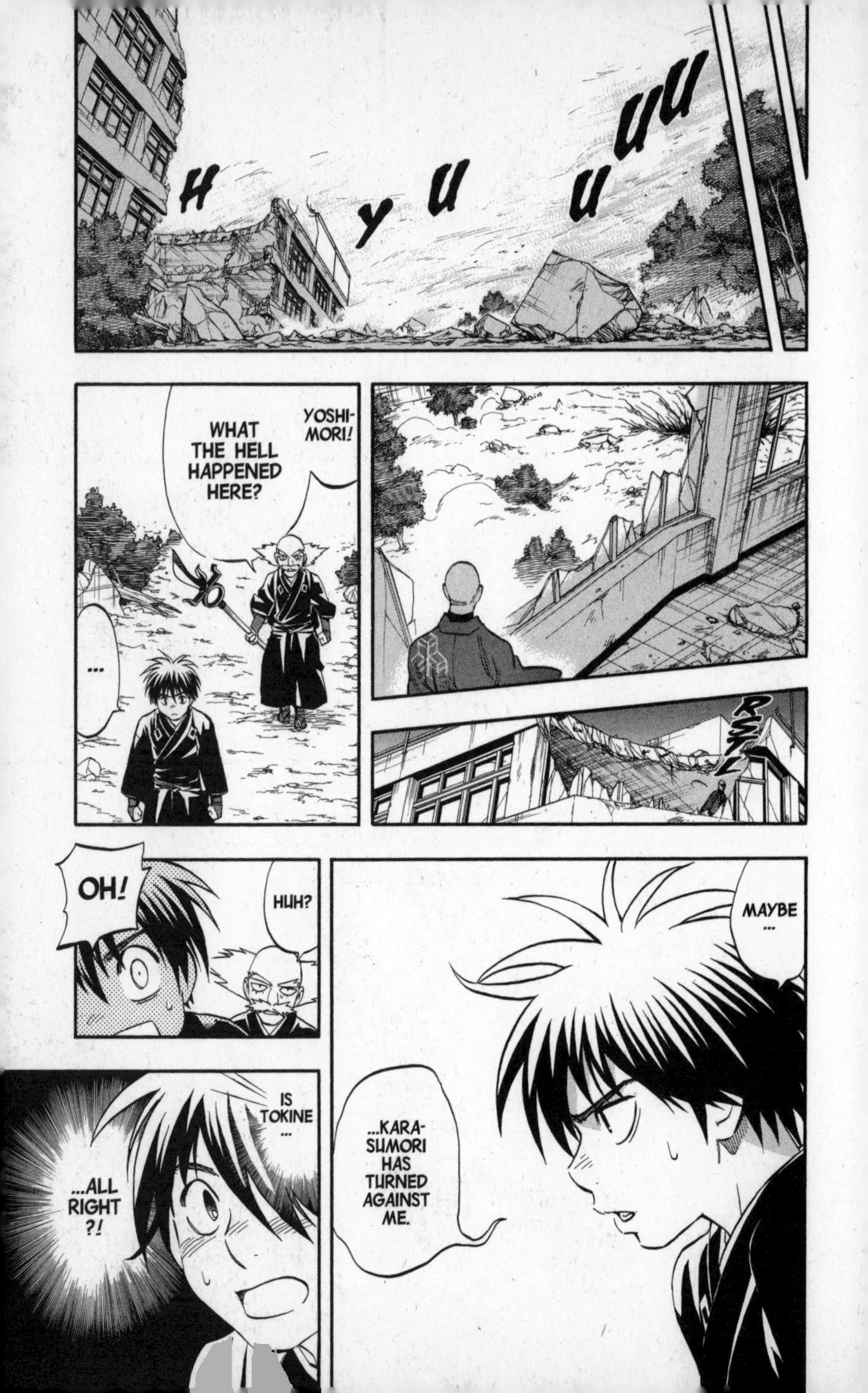
HYUUUUU
YOSHI-MORI!
WHAT THE HELL HAPPENED HERE?
...
MAYBE ...
...KARA-SUMORI HAS TURNED AGAINST ME.
HUH?
OH!
IS TOKINE ...
...ALL RIGHT?!

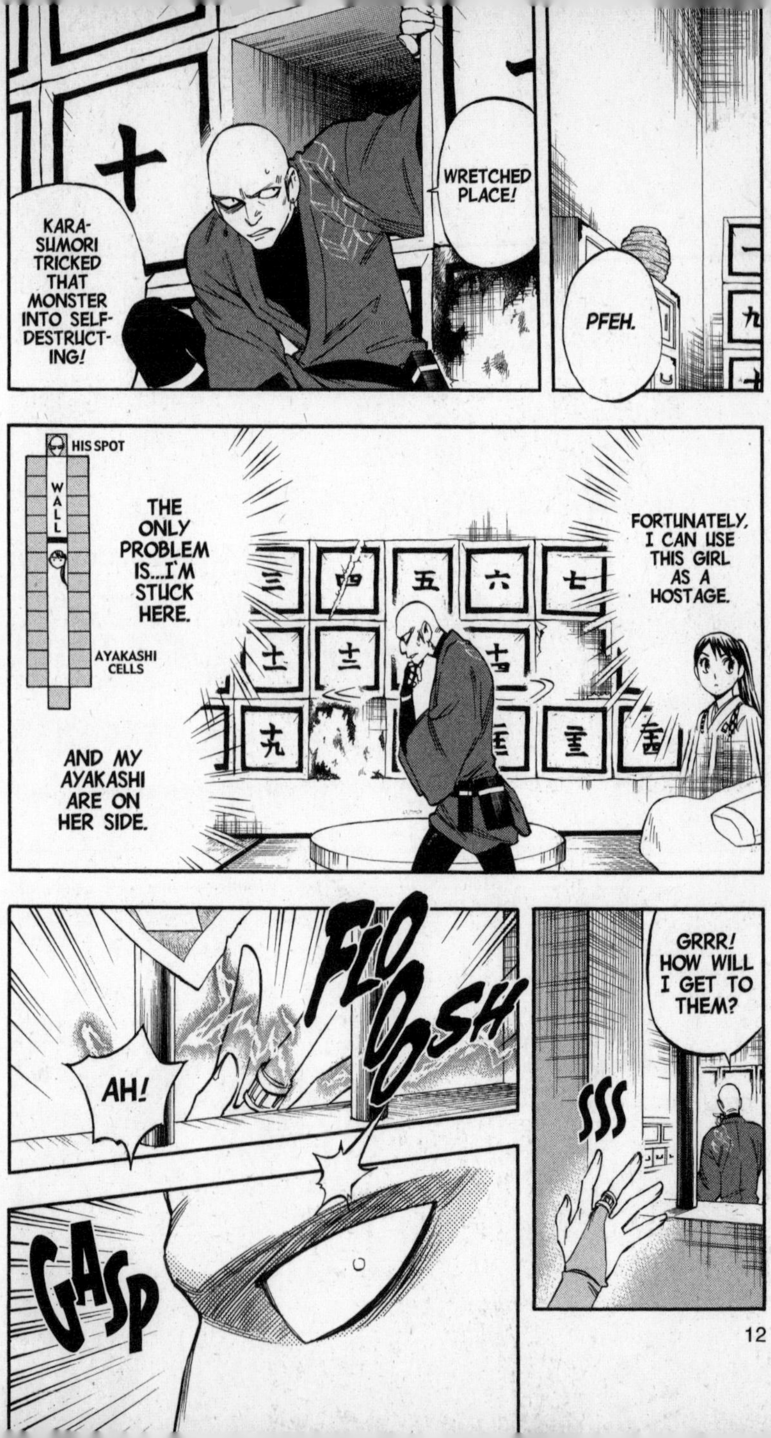
PFEH.
WRETCHED PLACE!
KARASUMORI TRICKED THAT MONSTER INTO SELF-DESTRUCTING!
FORTUNATELY, I CAN USE THIS GIRL AS A HOSTAGE.
THE ONLY PROBLEM IS...I'M STUCK HERE.
HIS SPOT
WALL
AYAKASHI CELLS
AND MY AYAKASHI ARE ON HER SIDE.
GRRR! HOW WILL I GET TO THEM?
SSS
FLOOOSH
AH!
GASP

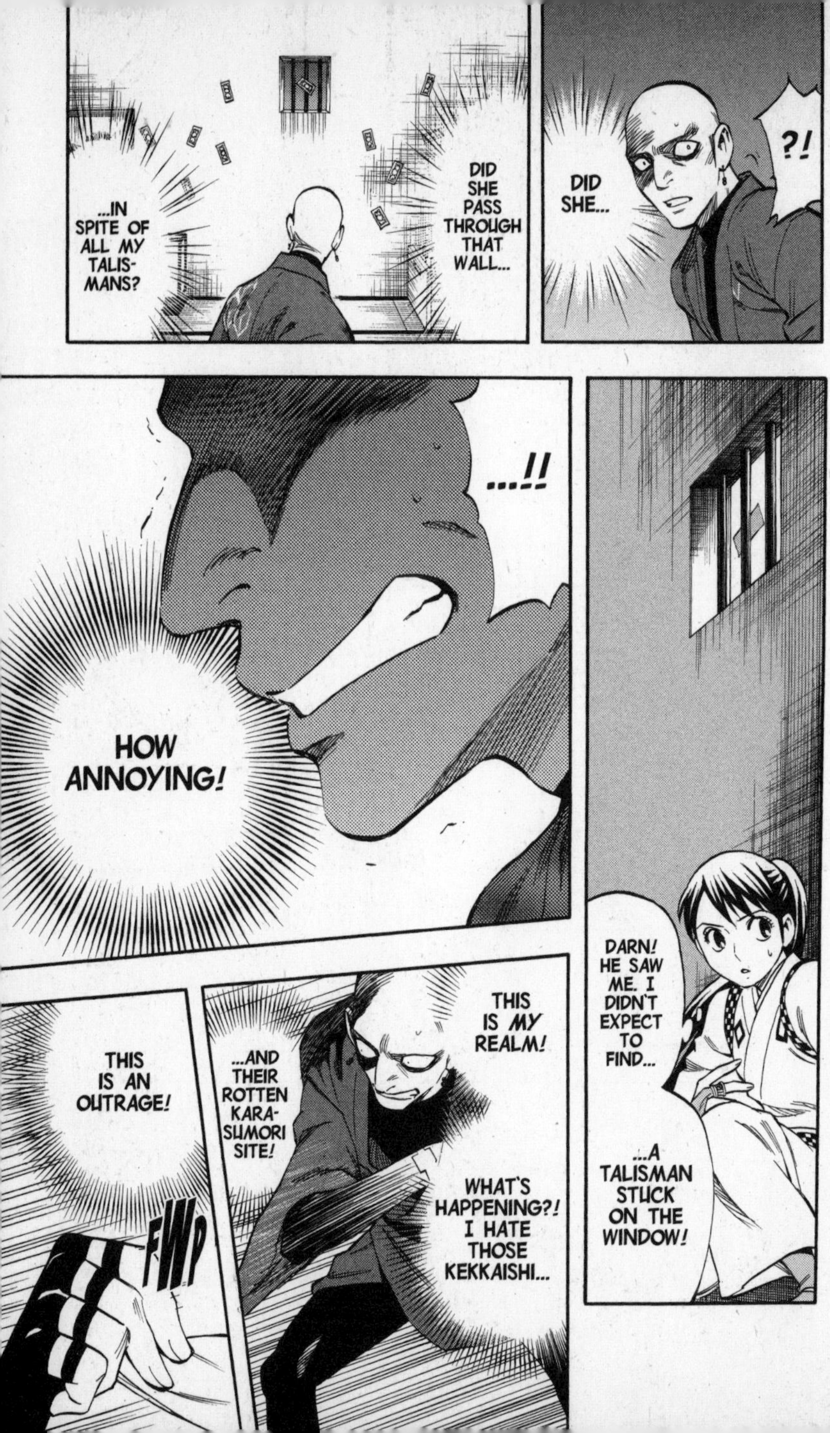
?!
DID SHE...
DID SHE PASS THROUGH THAT WALL...
...IN SPITE OF ALL MY TALISMANS?
DARN! HE SAW ME. I DIDN'T EXPECT TO FIND...
...A TALISMAN STUCK ON THE WINDOW!
...!!
HOW ANNOYING!
WHAT'S HAPPENING?! I HATE THOSE KEKKAISHI...
...AND THEIR ROTTEN KARASUMORI SITE!
THIS IS MY REALM!
THIS IS AN OUTRAGE!
FWP

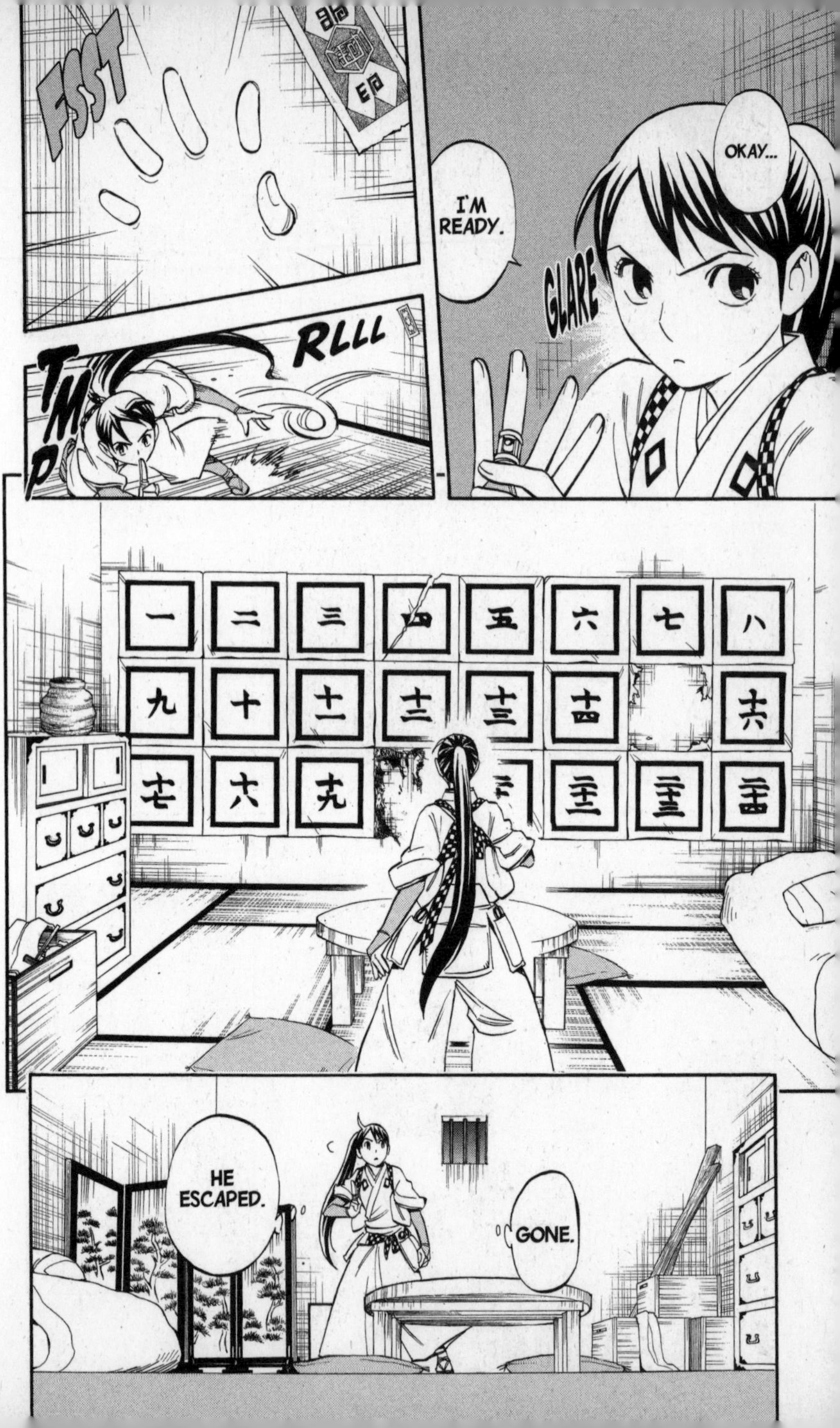
OKAY...
I'M READY.
GLARE
FSST
RLLL
TMP
GONE.
HE ESCAPED.

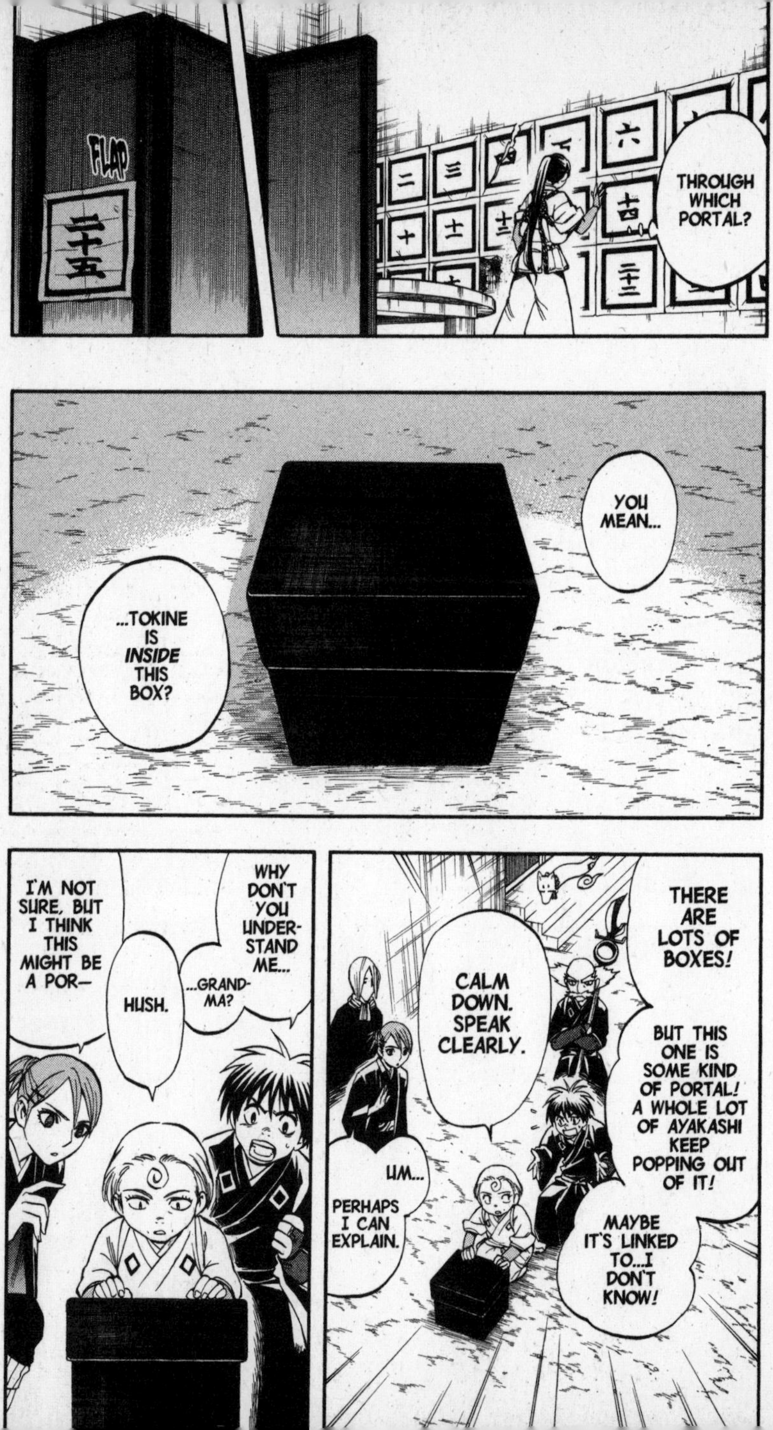
THROUGH WHICH PORTAL?
FLAP
YOU MEAN...
...TOKINE IS *INSIDE* THIS BOX?
THERE ARE LOTS OF BOXES!
BUT THIS ONE IS SOME KIND OF PORTAL! A WHOLE LOT OF AYAKASHI KEEP POPPING OUT OF IT!
CALM DOWN. SPEAK CLEARLY.
MAYBE IT'S LINKED TO...I DON'T KNOW!
UM...
PERHAPS I CAN EXPLAIN.
WHY DON'T YOU UNDER-STAND ME...
...GRAND-MA?
HUSH.
I'M NOT SURE, BUT I THINK THIS MIGHT BE A POR—

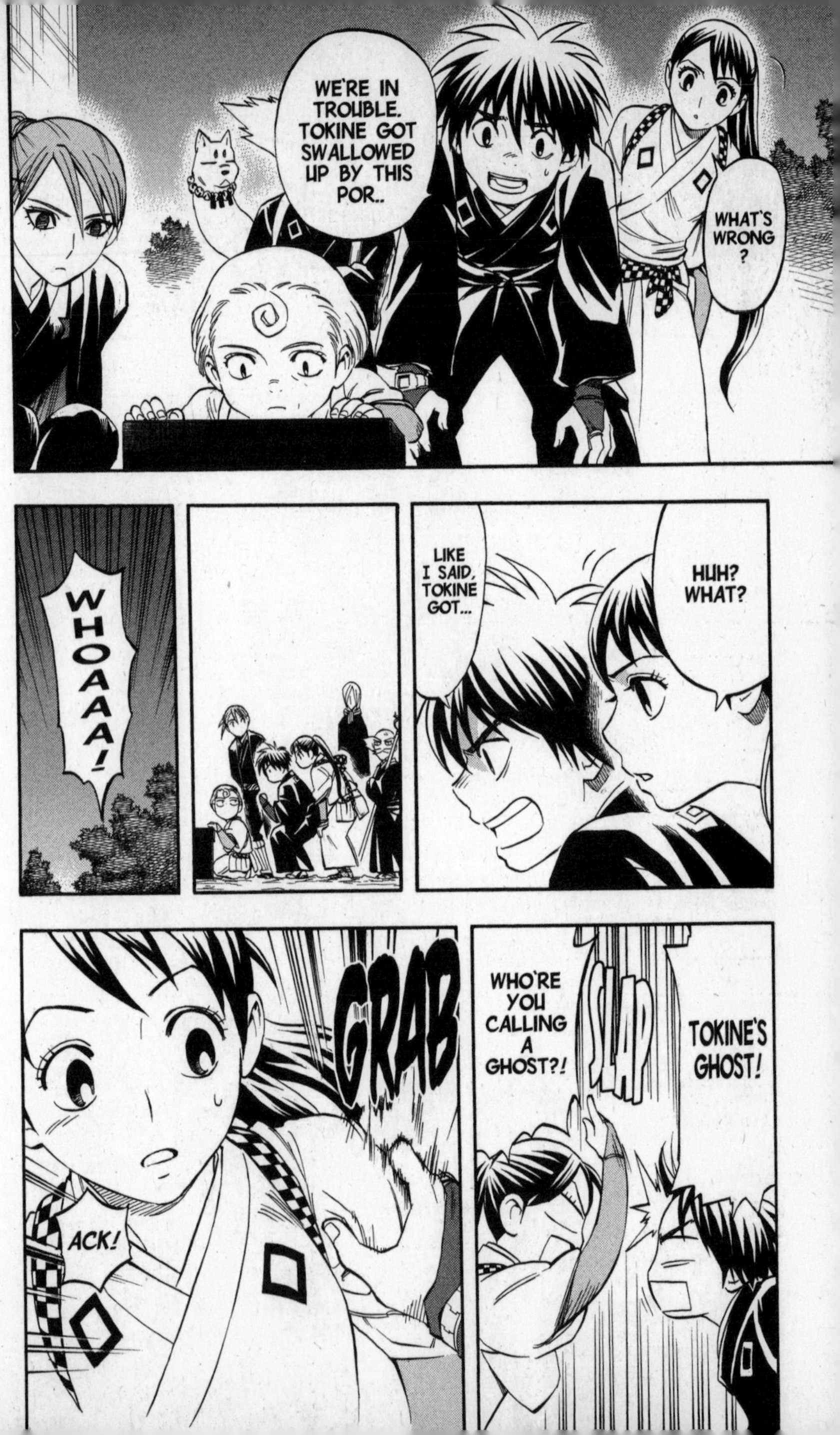
WE'RE IN TROUBLE. TOKINE GOT SWALLOWED UP BY THIS POR..
WHAT'S WRONG ?
HUH? WHAT?
LIKE I SAID, TOKINE GOT...
WHOAAAA!
TOKINE'S GHOST!
SLAP
WHO'RE YOU CALLING A GHOST?!
GRAB
ACK!

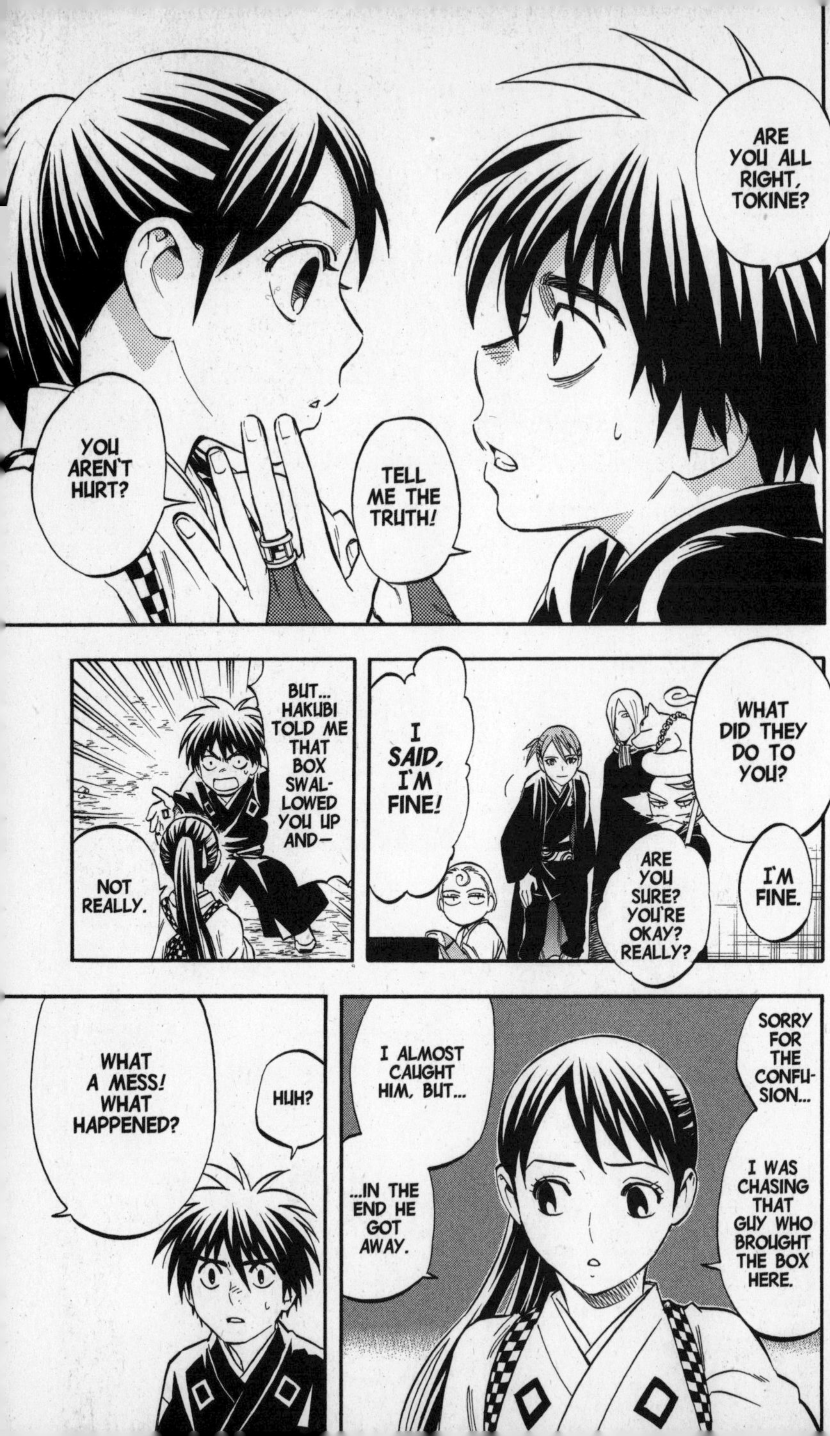
ARE YOU ALL RIGHT, TOKINE?
TELL ME THE TRUTH!
YOU AREN'T HURT?
WHAT DID THEY DO TO YOU?
I'M FINE.
ARE YOU SURE? YOU'RE OKAY? REALLY?
I *SAID*, I'M FINE!
BUT... HAKUBI TOLD ME THAT BOX SWAL-LOWED YOU UP AND—
NOT REALLY.
SORRY FOR THE CONFU-SION...
I WAS CHASING THAT GUY WHO BROUGHT THE BOX HERE.
I ALMOST CAUGHT HIM, BUT...
...IN THE END HE GOT AWAY.
HUH?
WHAT A MESS! WHAT HAPPENED?

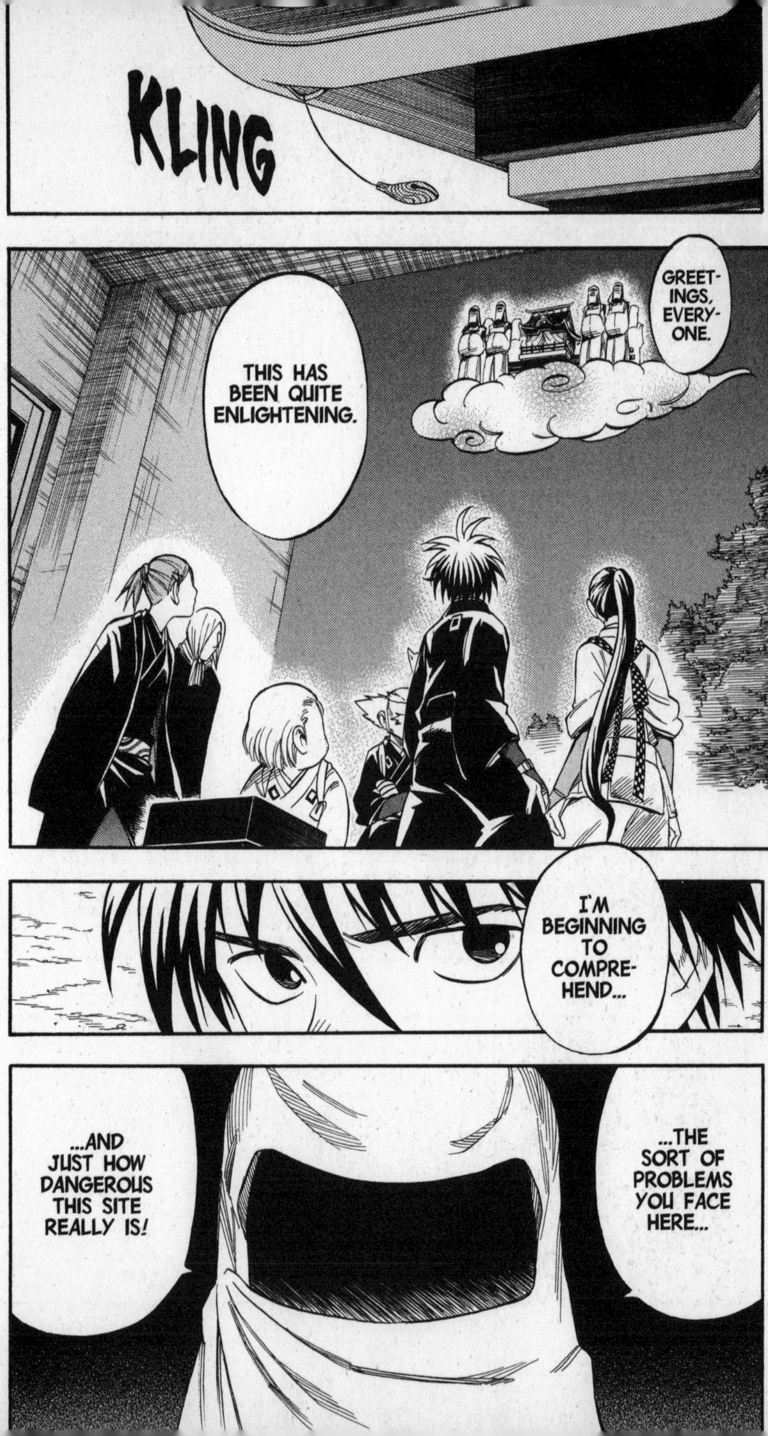
KLING
GREETINGS, EVERYONE.
THIS HAS BEEN QUITE ENLIGHTENING.
I'M BEGINNING TO COMPREHEND...
...THE SORT OF PROBLEMS YOU FACE HERE...
...AND JUST HOW DANGEROUS THIS SITE REALLY IS!

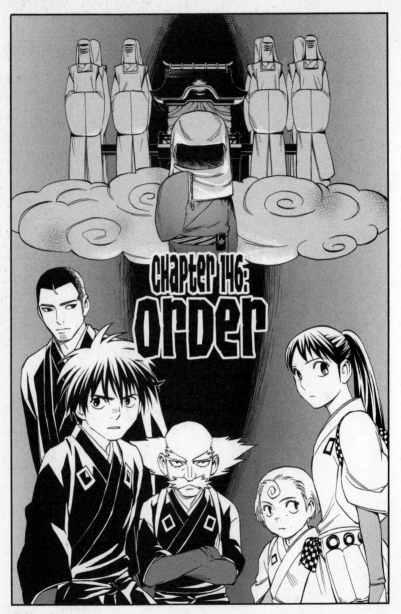

CHAPTER 146:
ORDER

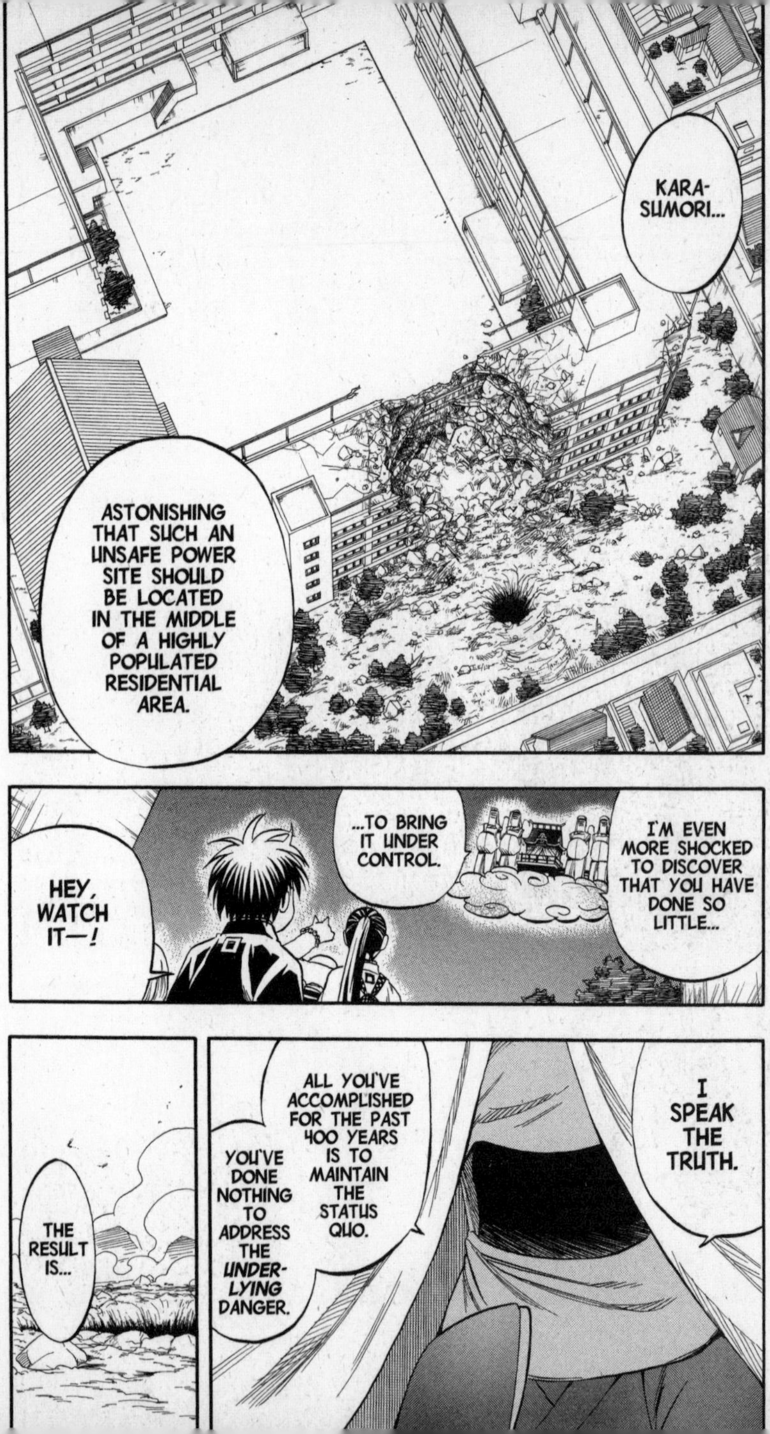
KARA-SUMORI...
ASTONISHING THAT SUCH AN UNSAFE POWER SITE SHOULD BE LOCATED IN THE MIDDLE OF A HIGHLY POPULATED RESIDENTIAL AREA.
I'M EVEN MORE SHOCKED TO DISCOVER THAT YOU HAVE DONE SO LITTLE...
...TO BRING IT UNDER CONTROL.
HEY, WATCH IT—!
I SPEAK THE TRUTH.
ALL YOU'VE ACCOMPLISHED FOR THE PAST 400 YEARS IS TO MAINTAIN THE STATUS QUO.
YOU'VE DONE NOTHING TO ADDRESS THE *UNDERLYING* DANGER.
THE RESULT IS...

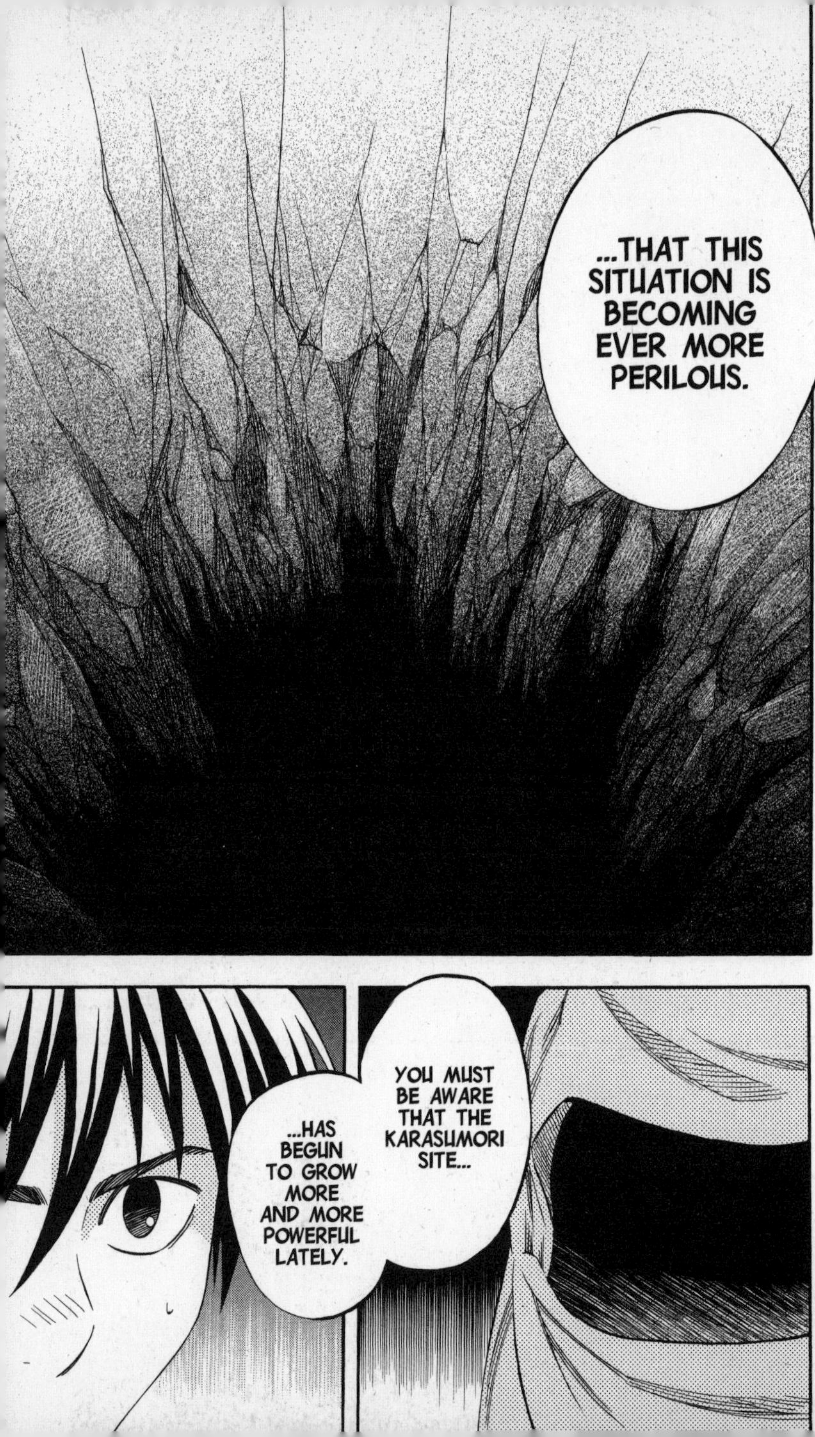
...THAT THIS SITUATION IS BECOMING EVER MORE PERILOUS.
YOU MUST BE AWARE THAT THE KARASUMORI SITE...
...HAS BEGUN TO GROW MORE AND MORE POWERFUL LATELY.

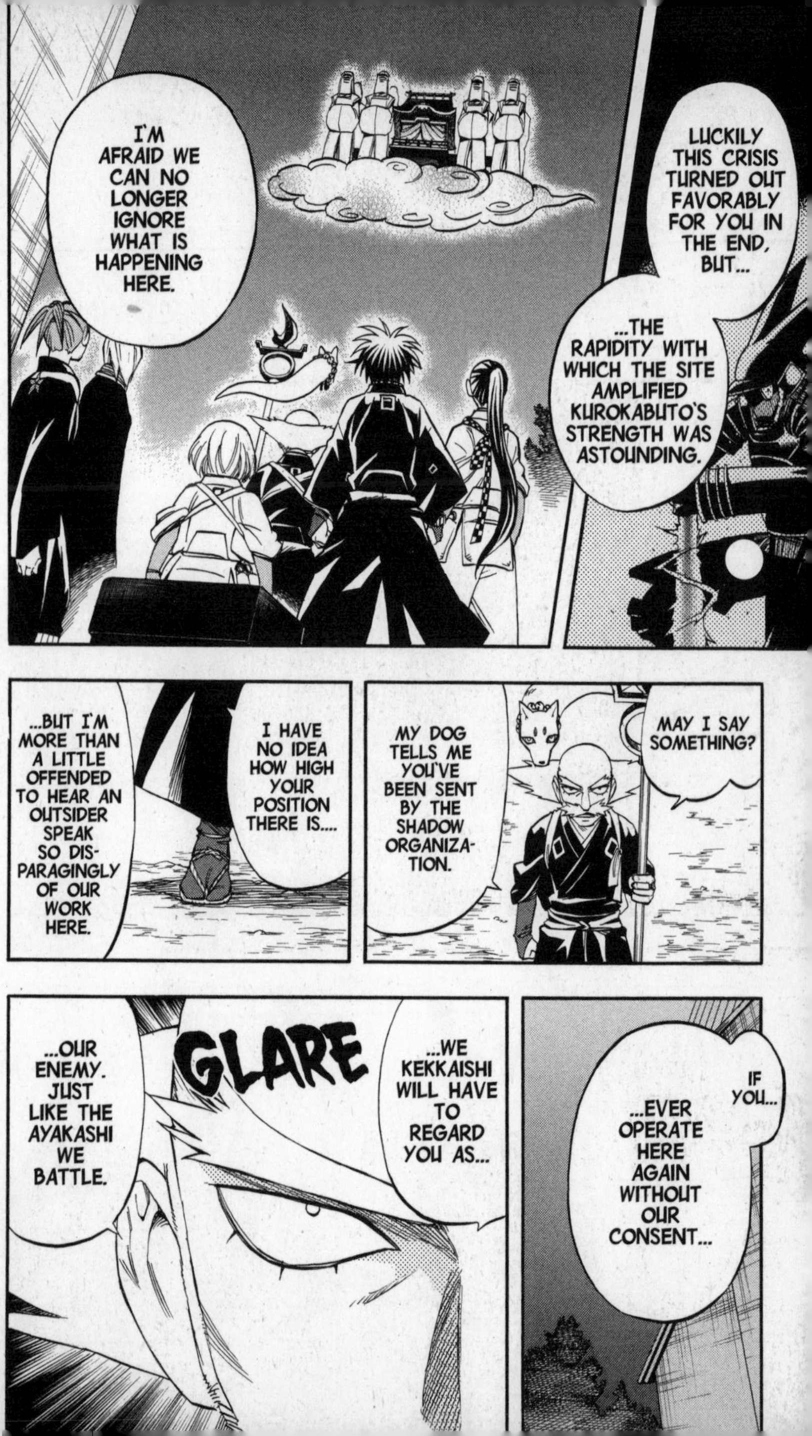
LUCKILY THIS CRISIS TURNED OUT FAVORABLY FOR YOU IN THE END, BUT...
...THE RAPIDITY WITH WHICH THE SITE AMPLIFIED KUROKABUTO'S STRENGTH WAS ASTOUNDING.
I'M AFRAID WE CAN NO LONGER IGNORE WHAT IS HAPPENING HERE.
MAY I SAY SOMETHING?
MY DOG TELLS ME YOU'VE BEEN SENT BY THE SHADOW ORGANIZA-TION.
I HAVE NO IDEA HOW HIGH YOUR POSITION THERE IS....
...BUT I'M MORE THAN A LITTLE OFFENDED TO HEAR AN OUTSIDER SPEAK SO DIS-PARAGINGLY OF OUR WORK HERE.
IF YOU...
...EVER OPERATE HERE AGAIN WITHOUT OUR CONSENT...
...WE KEKKAISHI WILL HAVE TO REGARD YOU AS...
GLARE
...OUR ENEMY. JUST LIKE THE AYAKASHI WE BATTLE.

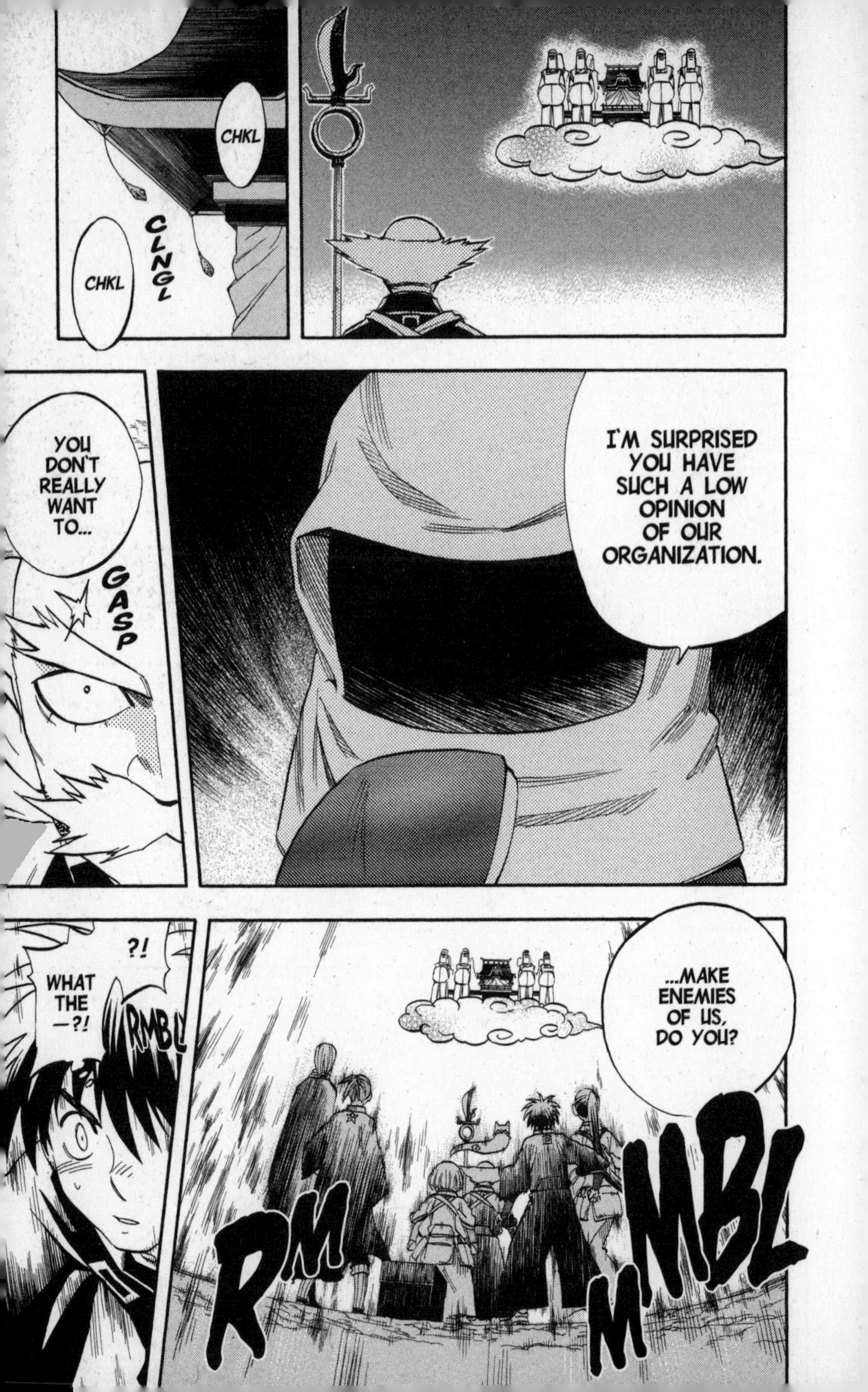
CHKL
CLNGL
CHKL
I'M SURPRISED YOU HAVE SUCH A LOW OPINION OF OUR ORGANIZATION.
YOU DON'T REALLY WANT TO...
GASP
...MAKE ENEMIES OF US, DO YOU?
RMMBL
?!
WHAT THE —?!
RMBL

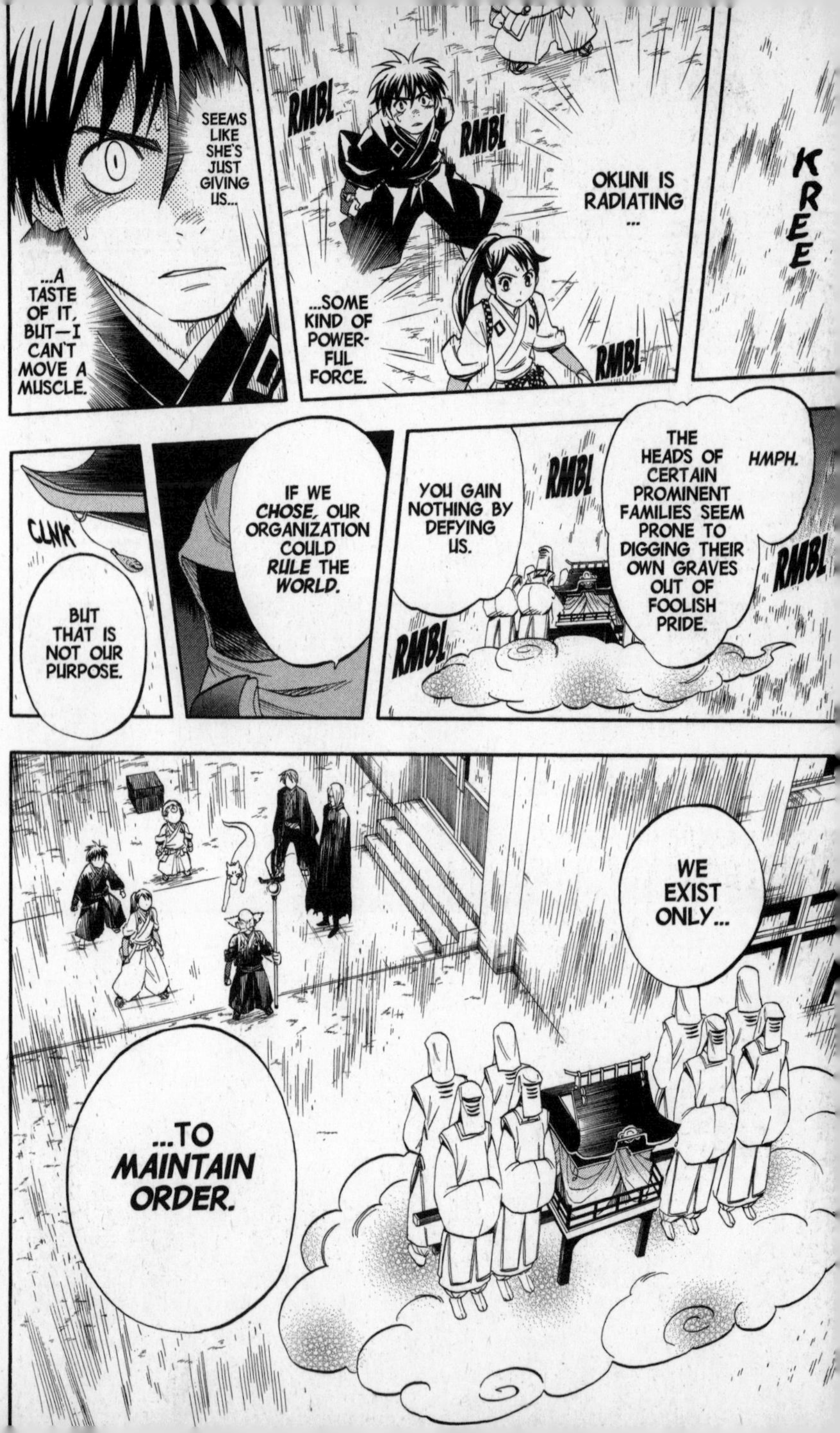

KREE
OKUNI IS RADIATING...
RMBL
RMBL
...SOME KIND OF POWERFUL FORCE.
RMBL
SEEMS LIKE SHE'S JUST GIVING US...
...A TASTE OF IT, BUT—I CAN'T MOVE A MUSCLE.
HMPH.
THE HEADS OF CERTAIN PROMINENT FAMILIES SEEM PRONE TO DIGGING THEIR OWN GRAVES OUT OF FOOLISH PRIDE.
RMBL
RMBL
YOU GAIN NOTHING BY DEFYING US.
RMBL
IF WE CHOSE, OUR ORGANIZATION COULD RULE THE WORLD.
CLINK
BUT THAT IS NOT OUR PURPOSE.
WE EXIST ONLY...
...TO MAINTAIN ORDER.

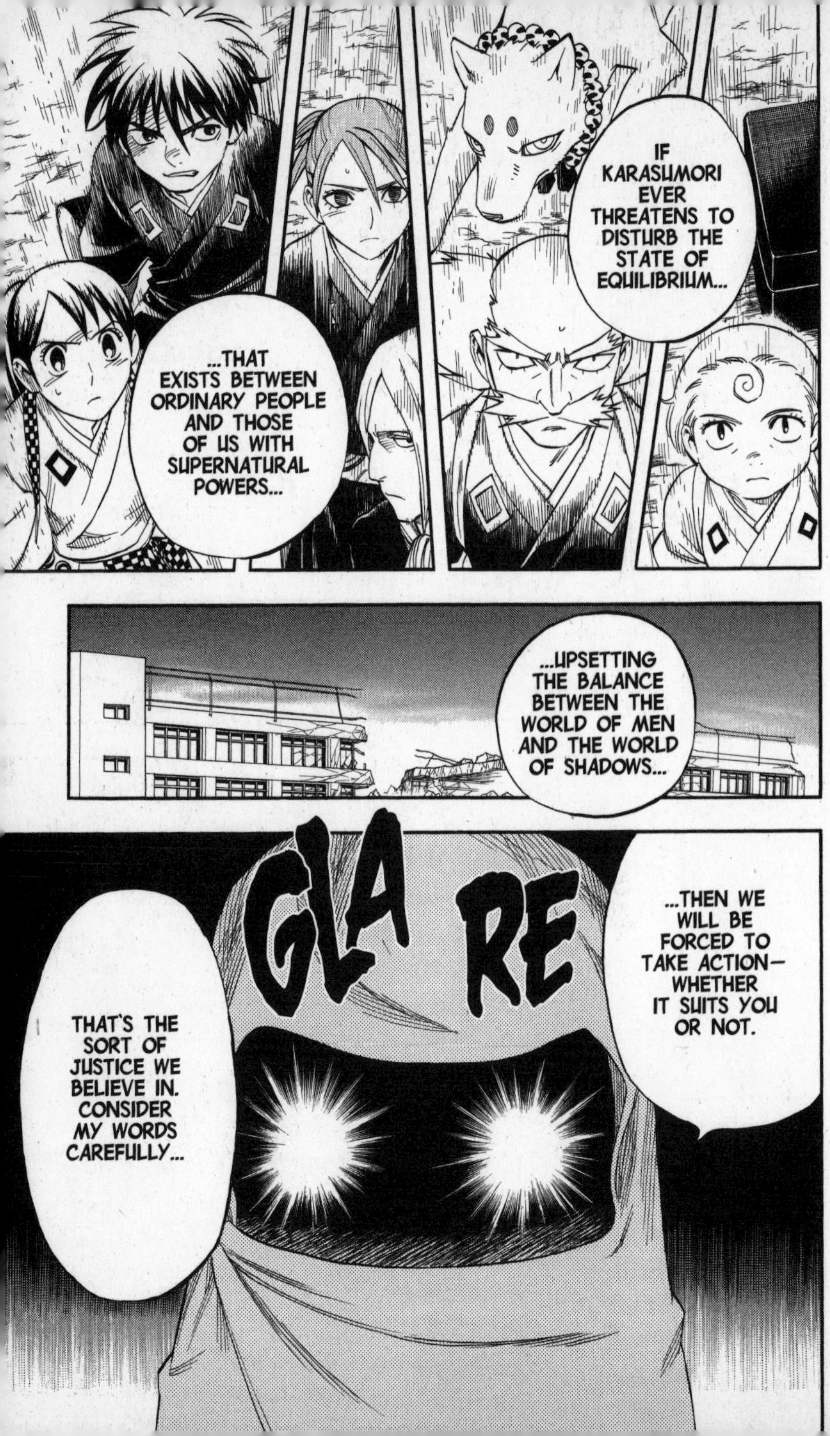
IF KARASUMORI EVER THREATENS TO DISTURB THE STATE OF EQUILIBRIUM...
...THAT EXISTS BETWEEN ORDINARY PEOPLE AND THOSE OF US WITH SUPERNATURAL POWERS...
...UPSETTING THE BALANCE BETWEEN THE WORLD OF MEN AND THE WORLD OF SHADOWS...
...THEN WE WILL BE FORCED TO TAKE ACTION—WHETHER IT SUITS YOU OR NOT.
GLARE
THAT'S THE SORT OF JUSTICE WE BELIEVE IN. CONSIDER MY WORDS CAREFULLY...

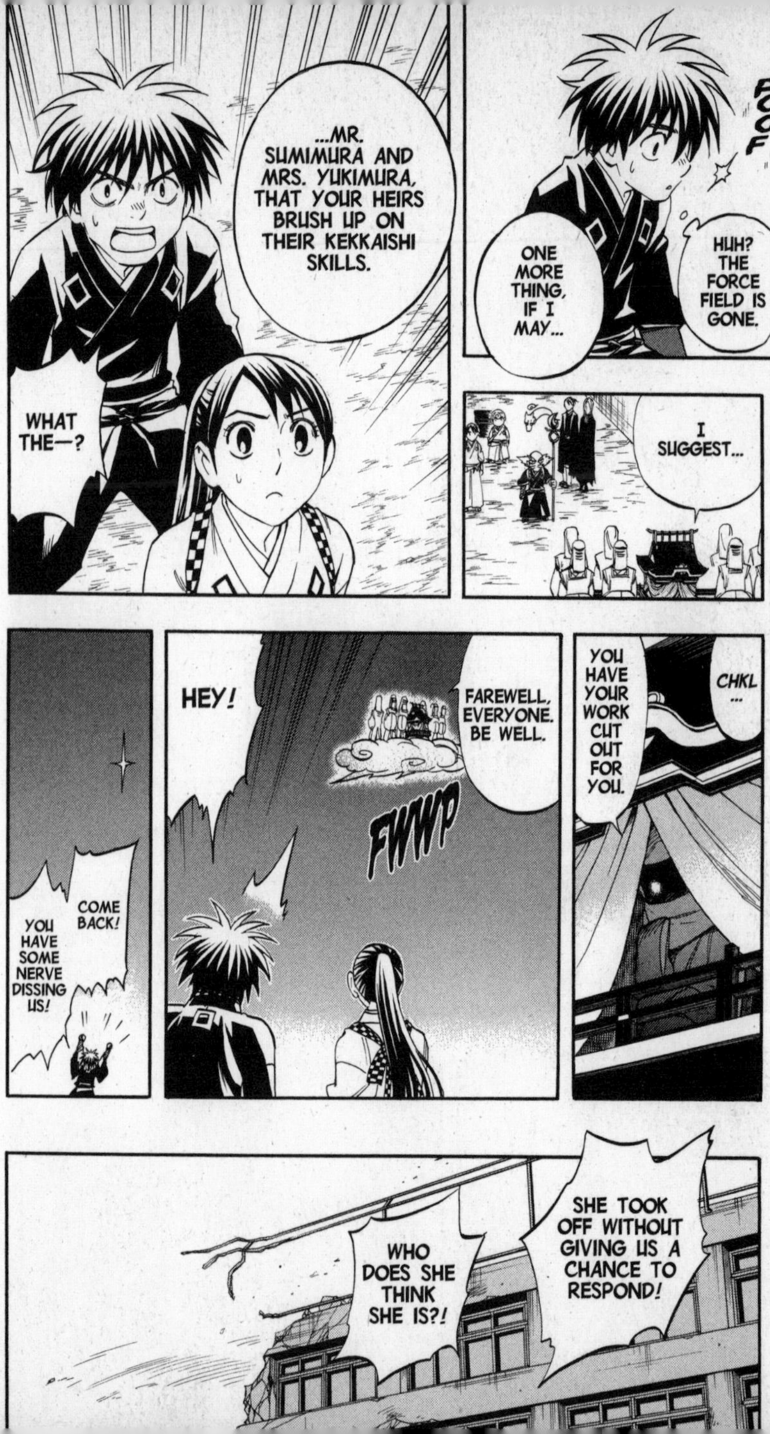
POOF
HUH? THE FORCE FIELD IS GONE.
ONE MORE THING, IF I MAY...
I SUGGEST...
...MR. SUMIMURA AND MRS. YUKIMURA, THAT YOUR HEIRS BRUSH UP ON THEIR KEKKAISHI SKILLS.
WHAT THE—?
CHKL...
YOU HAVE YOUR WORK CUT OUT FOR YOU.
FAREWELL, EVERYONE. BE WELL.
HEY!
FWWP
COME BACK!
YOU HAVE SOME NERVE DISSING US!
SHE TOOK OFF WITHOUT GIVING US A CHANCE TO RESPOND!
WHO DOES SHE THINK SHE IS?!

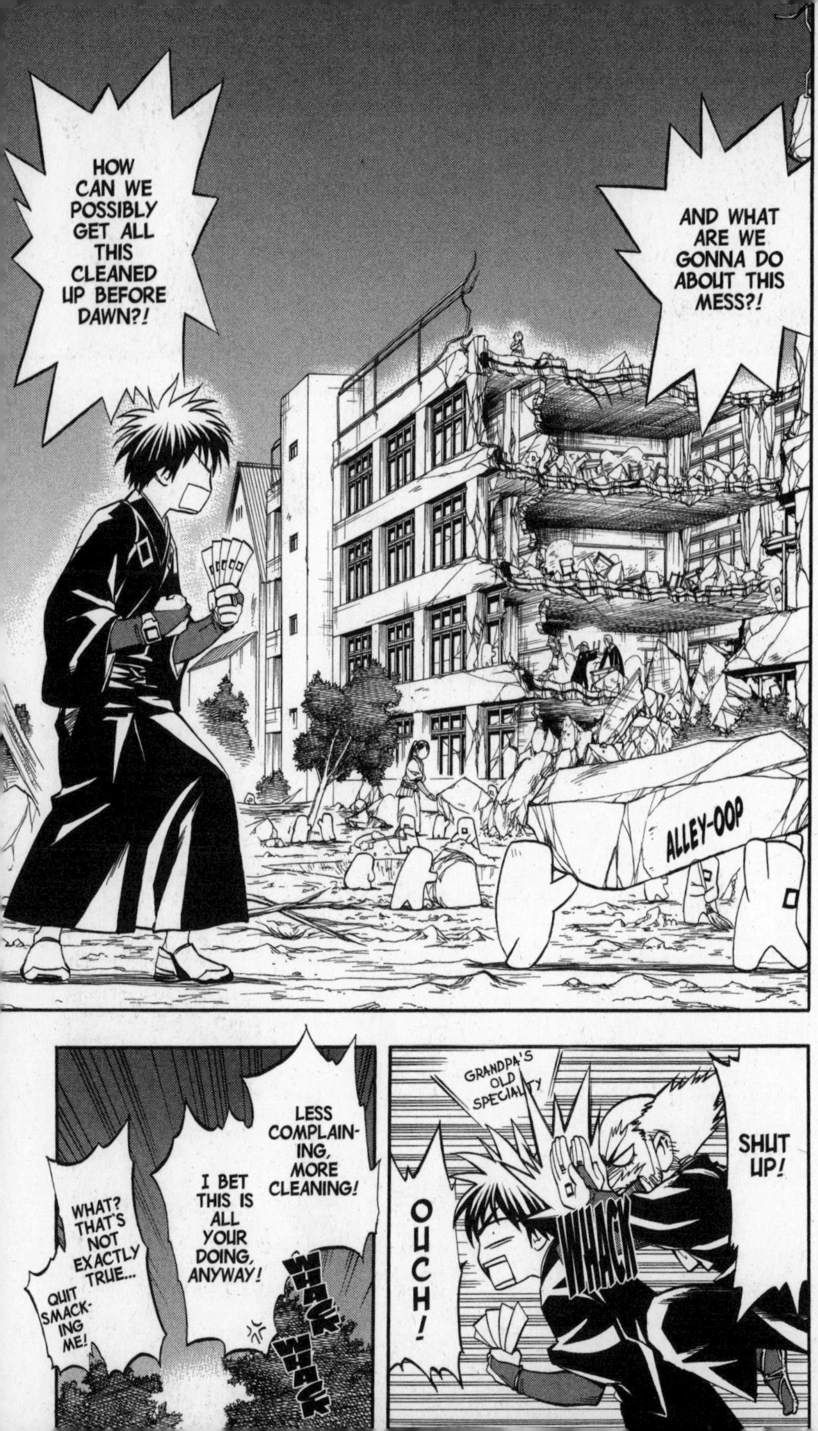
AND WHAT ARE WE GONNA DO ABOUT THIS MESS?!
HOW CAN WE POSSIBLY GET ALL THIS CLEANED UP BEFORE DAWN?!
ALLEY-OOP
SHUT UP!
GRANDPA'S OLD SPECIALTY
WHACK
OUCH!
LESS COMPLAIN-ING, MORE CLEANING!
I BET THIS IS ALL YOUR DOING, ANYWAY!
WHACK WHACK
WHAT? THAT'S NOT EXACTLY TRUE...
QUIT SMACK-ING ME!

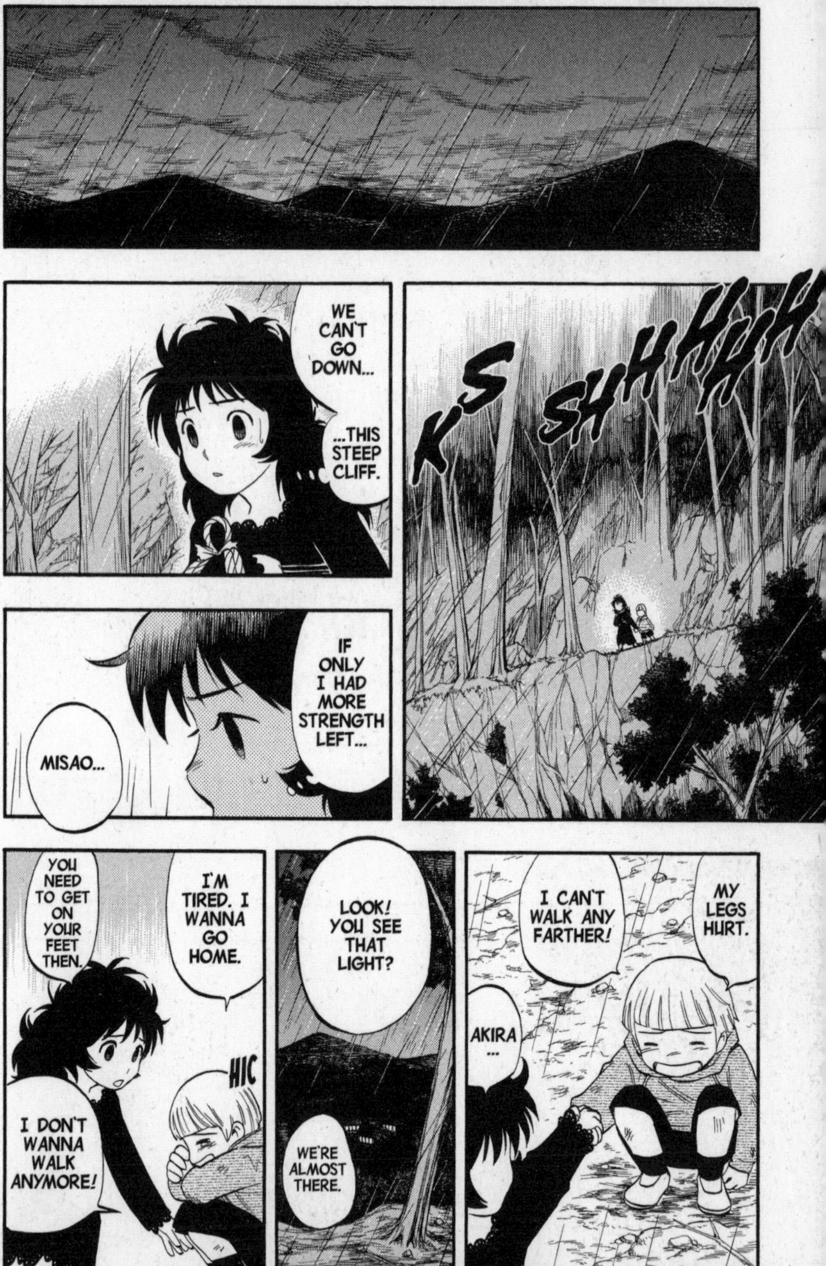
KSHHHHHH
WE CAN'T GO DOWN...
...THIS STEEP CLIFF.
IF ONLY I HAD MORE STRENGTH LEFT...
MISAO...
MY LEGS HURT.
I CAN'T WALK ANY FARTHER!
AKIRA...
LOOK! YOU SEE THAT LIGHT?
WE'RE ALMOST THERE.
I'M TIRED. I WANNA GO HOME.
YOU NEED TO GET ON YOUR FEET THEN.
HIC
I DON'T WANNA WALK ANYMORE!

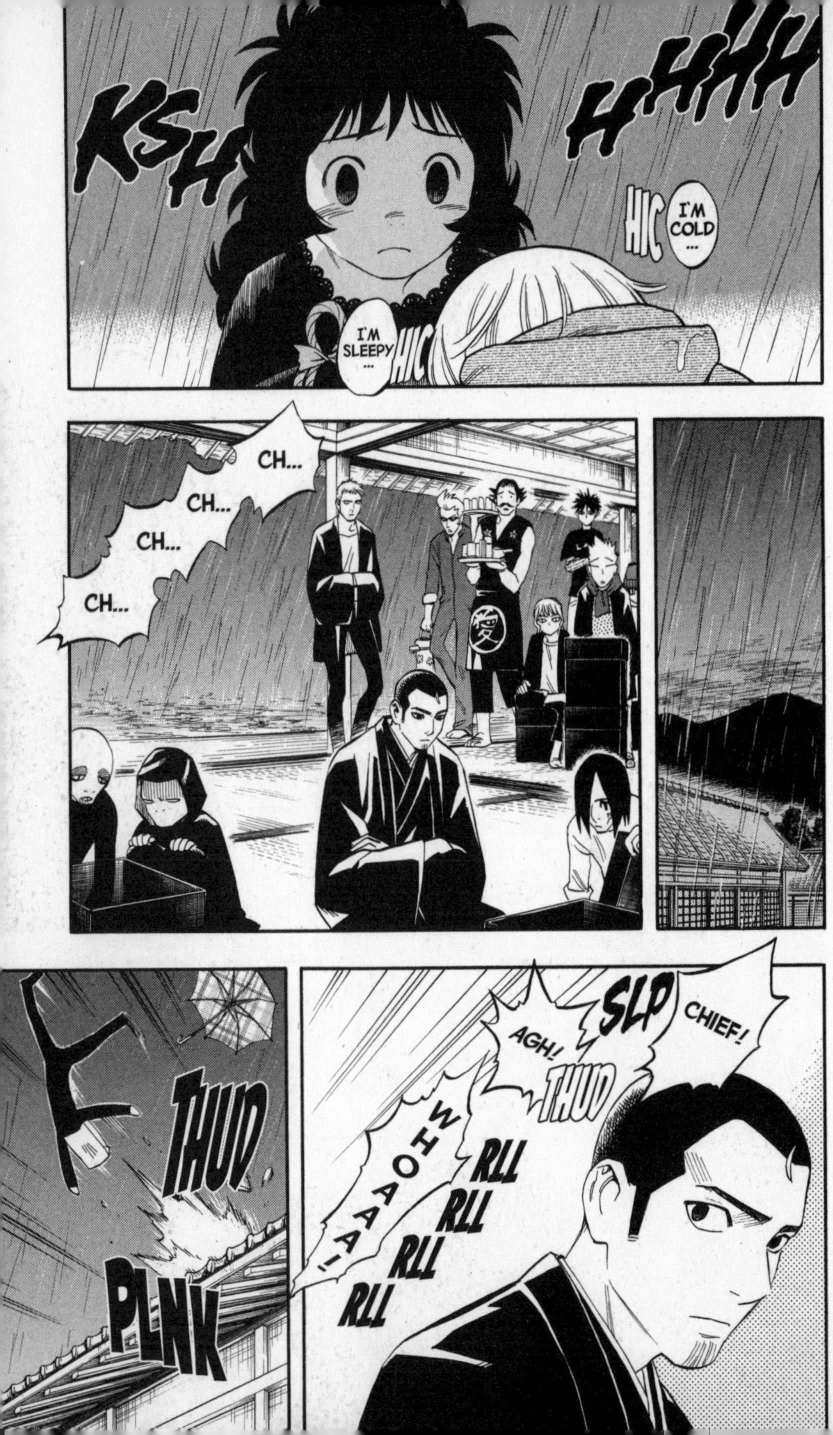
KSH HHHH
HIC
I'M COLD ...
I'M SLEEPY ...
HIC
CH...
CH...
CH...
CH...
CHIEF!
SLP
AGH!
THUD
RLL RLL RLL RLL
WHOAAAA!
THUD
PLNK

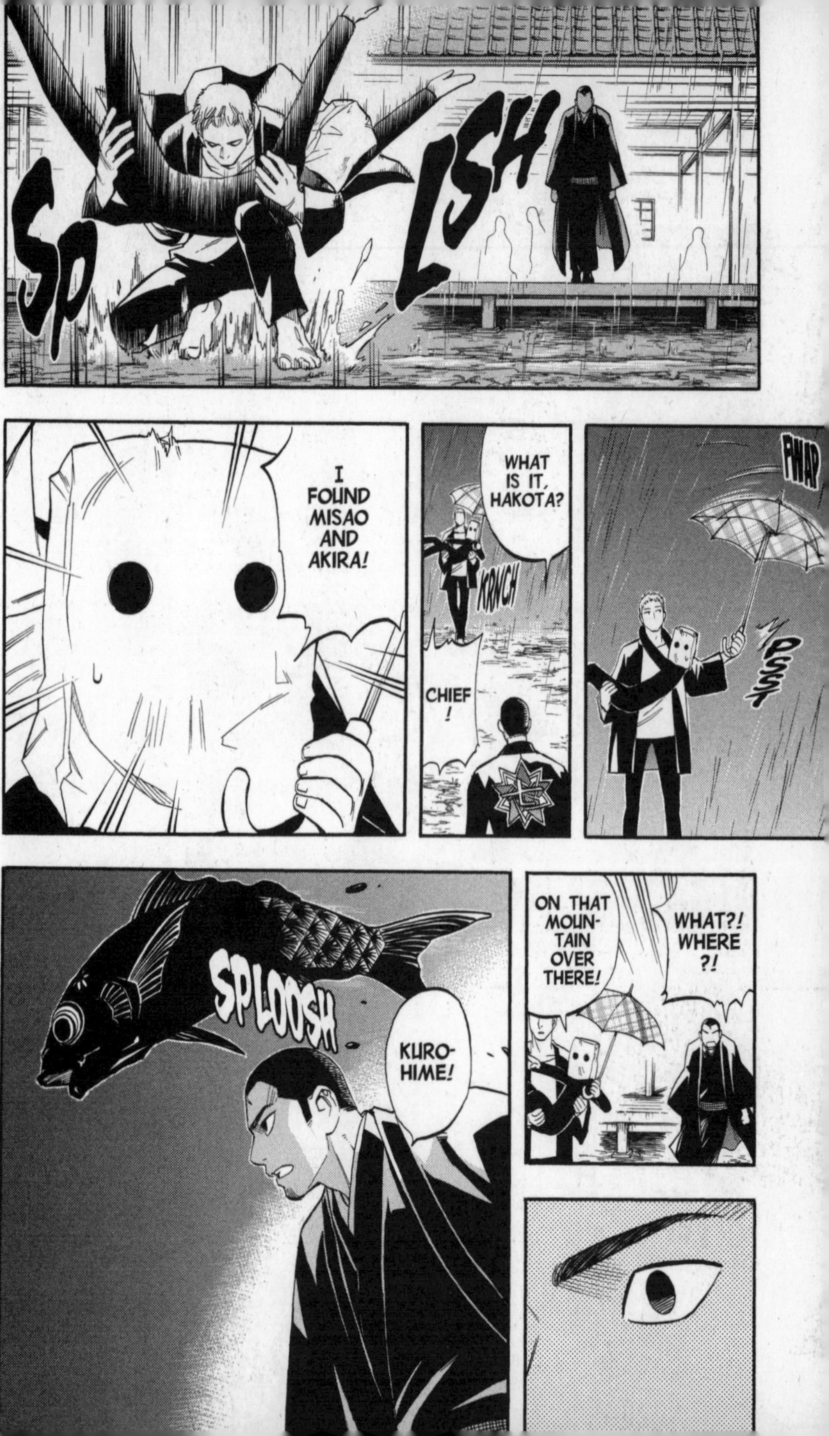
SPLSH
FWAP
PSSST
WHAT IS IT, HAKOTA?
KRNCH
CHIEF!
I FOUND MISAO AND AKIRA!
WHAT?! WHERE?!
ON THAT MOUN-TAIN OVER THERE!
SPLOOSH
KURO-HIME!

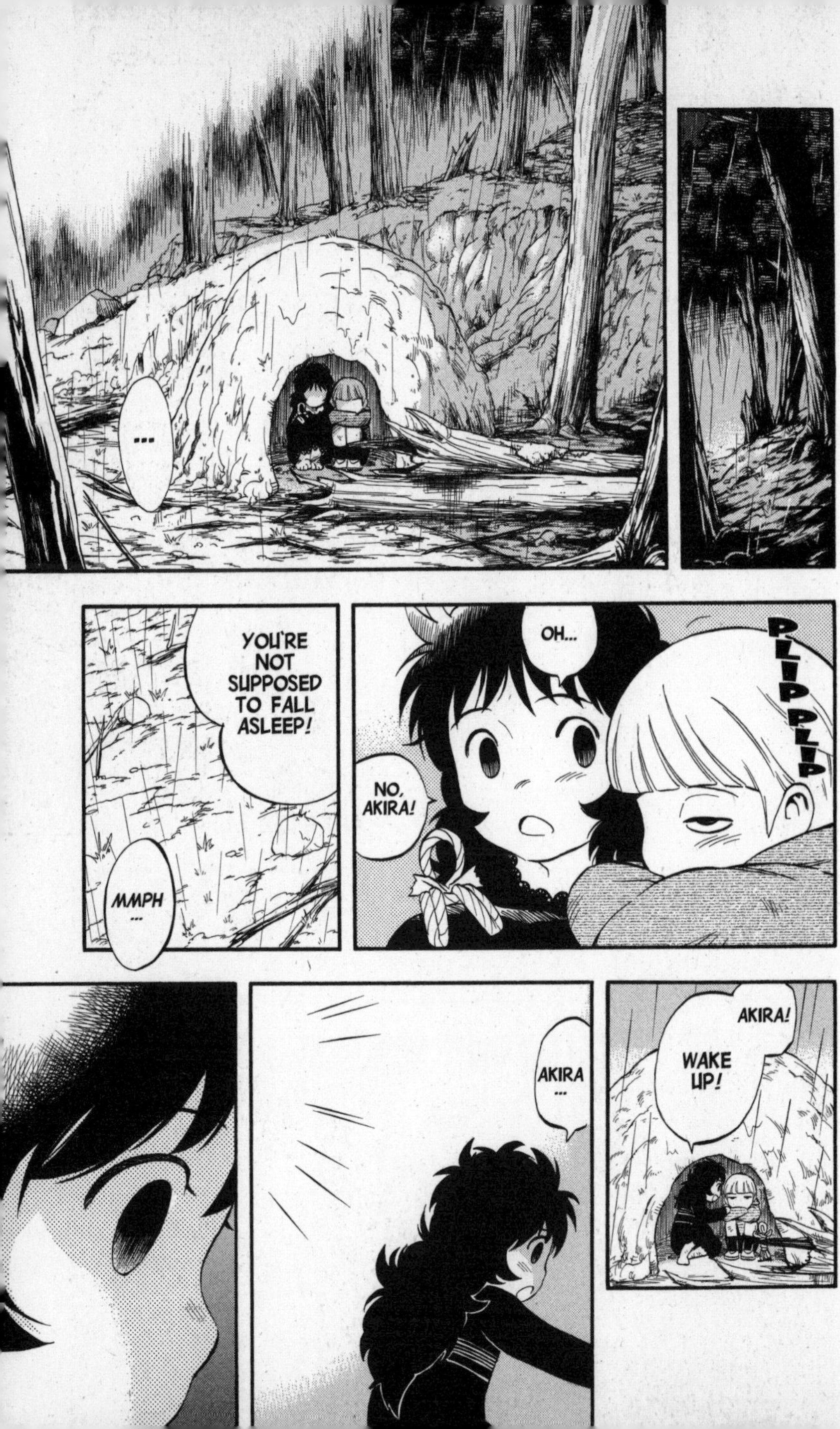
...
OH...
NO, AKIRA!
PLIP PLIP
YOU'RE NOT SUPPOSED TO FALL ASLEEP!
MMPH ...
AKIRA!
WAKE UP!
AKIRA ...

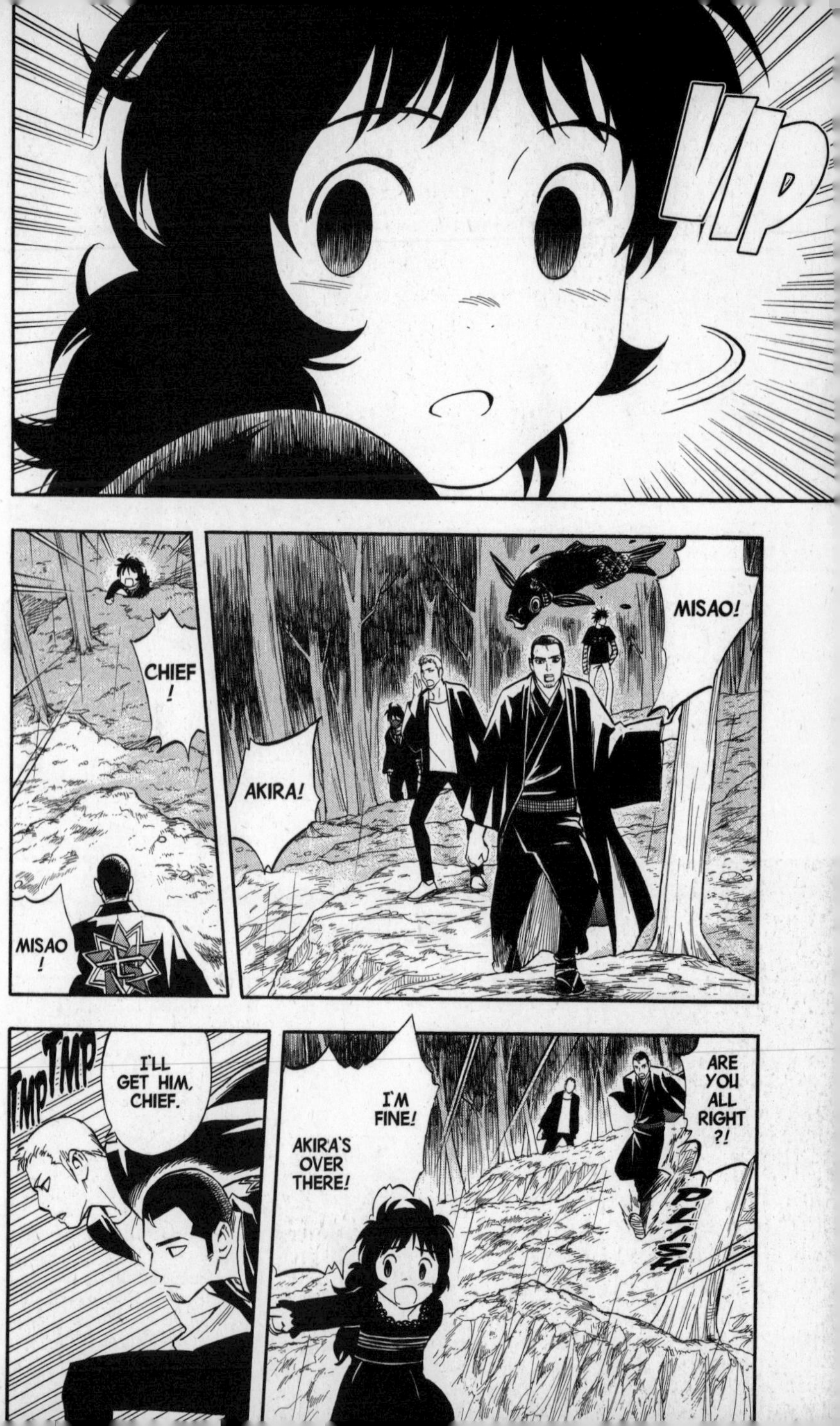
WIP
MISAO!
AKIRA!
CHIEF!
MISAO!
ARE YOU ALL RIGHT?!
PLISH
I'M FINE!
AKIRA'S OVER THERE!
TMP TMP
I'LL GET HIM, CHIEF.

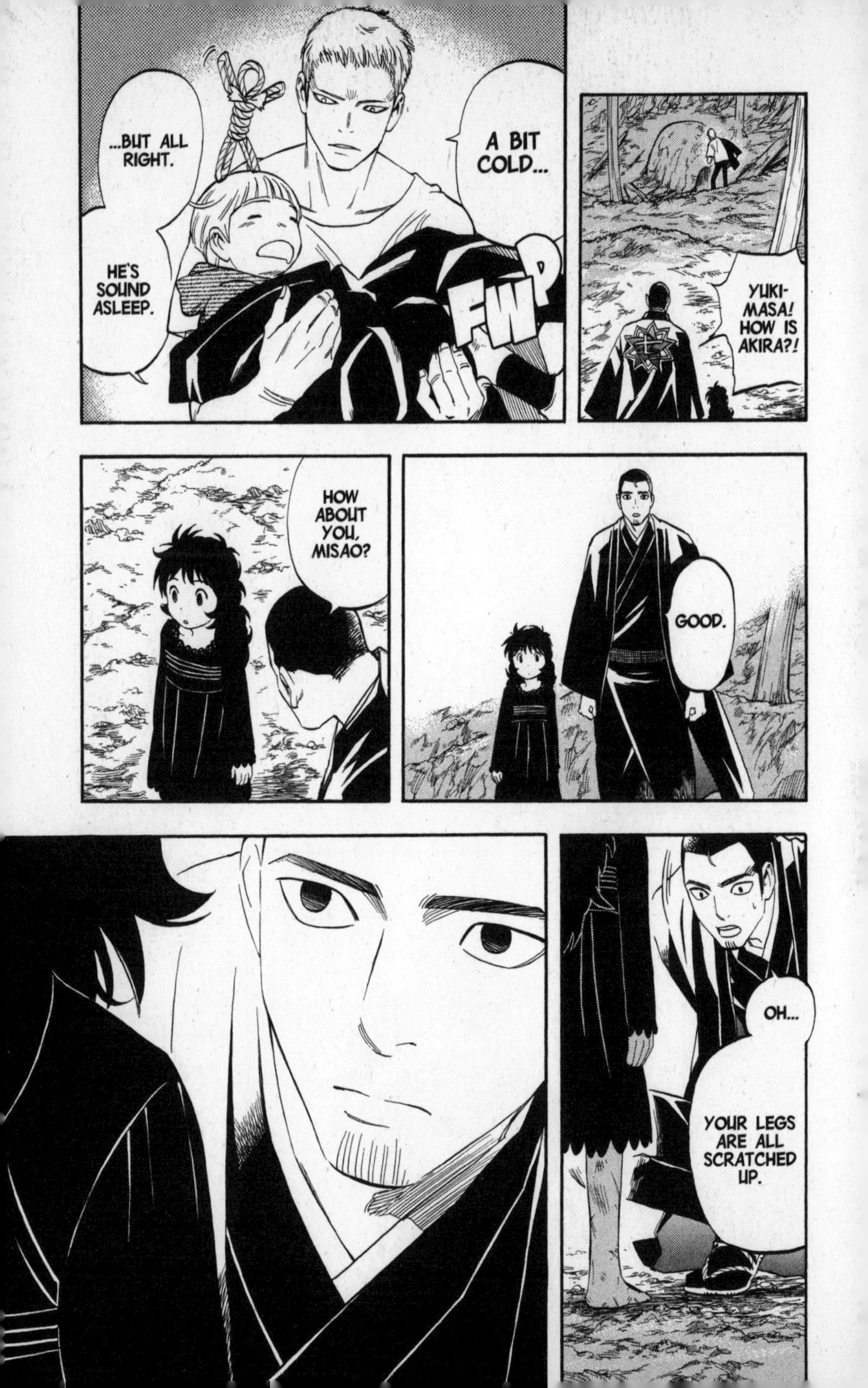
YUKI-MASA! HOW IS AKIRA?!
A BIT COLD...
...BUT ALL RIGHT.
FWP
HE'S SOUND ASLEEP.
GOOD.
HOW ABOUT YOU, MISAO?
OH...
YOUR LEGS ARE ALL SCRATCHED UP.

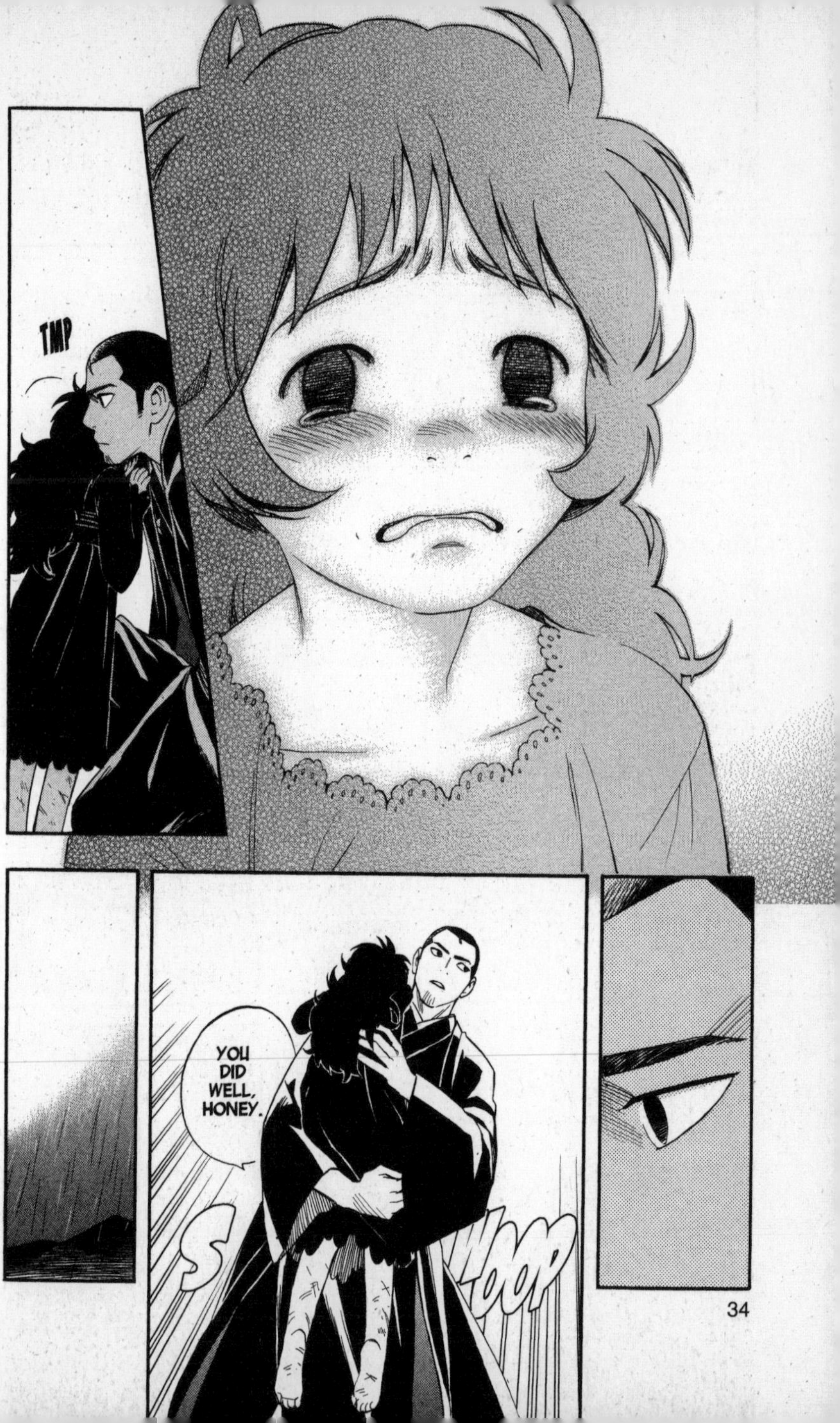
TMP
YOU DID WELL, HONEY.
SWOOP

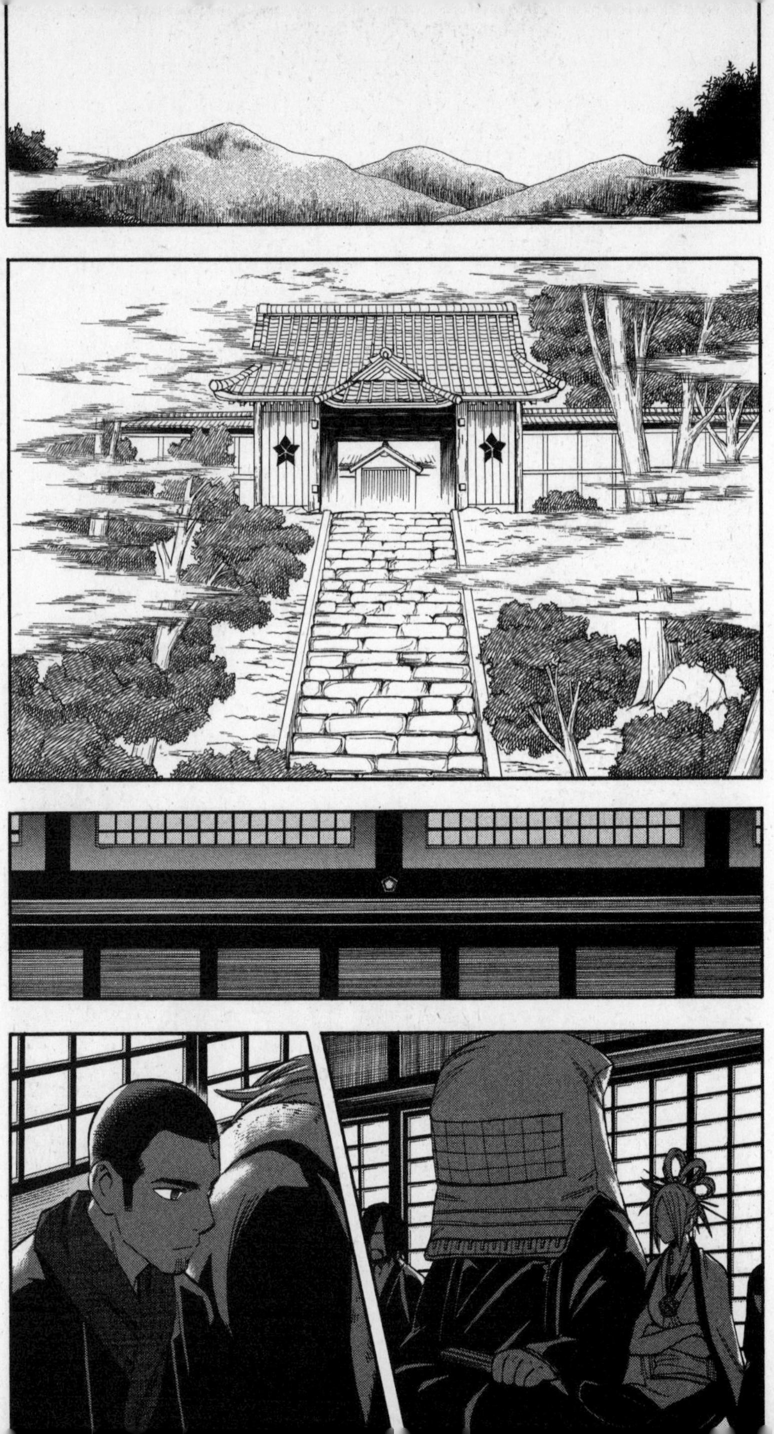

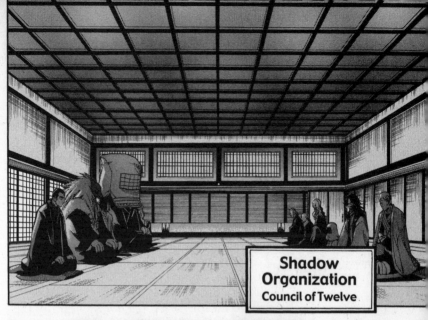

Shadow Organization
Council of Twelve

LADIES AND GENTLE-MEN...

I AM HERE TO REPORT TO YOU ON THE INVESTIGA-TION...

...I RECENTLY CONDUCTED AT THE KARASUMORI SITE.

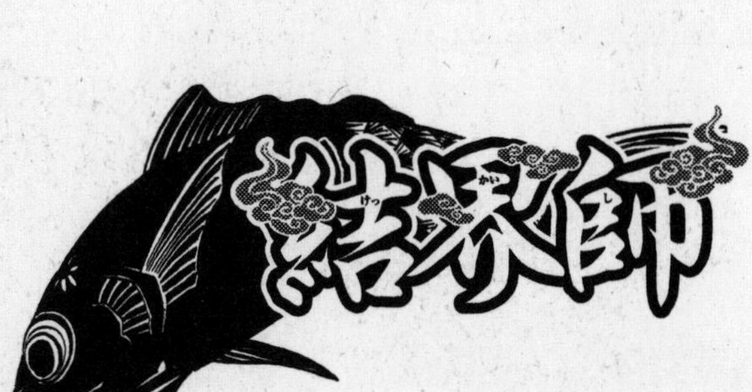
結界師

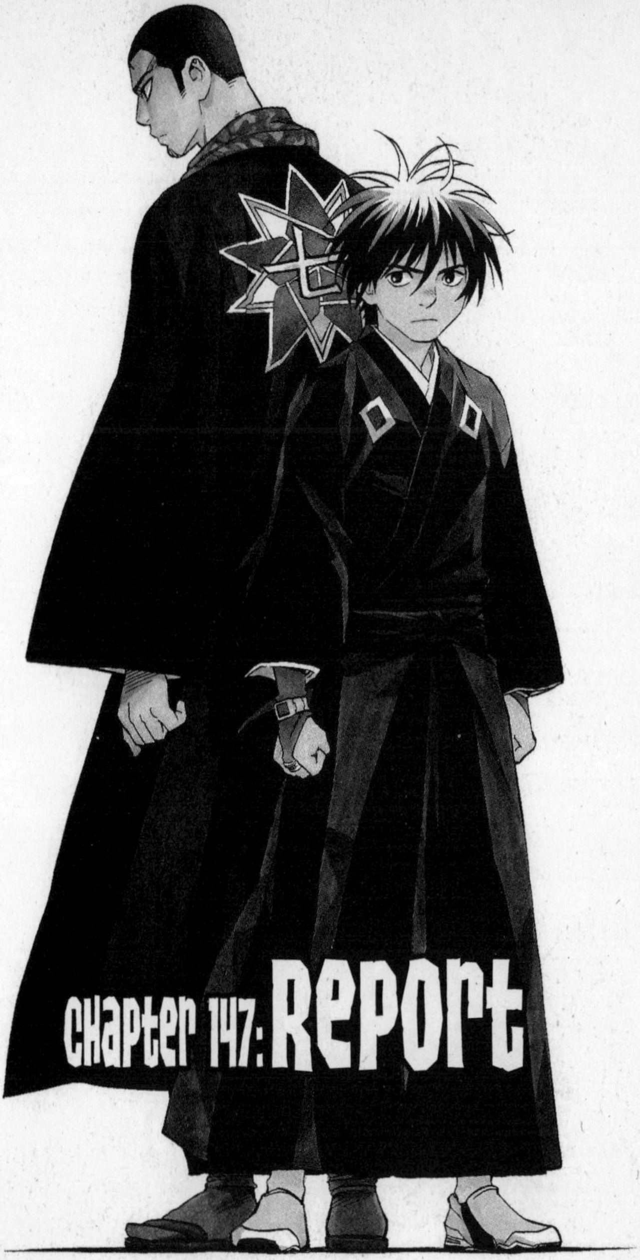
Chapter 147: Report

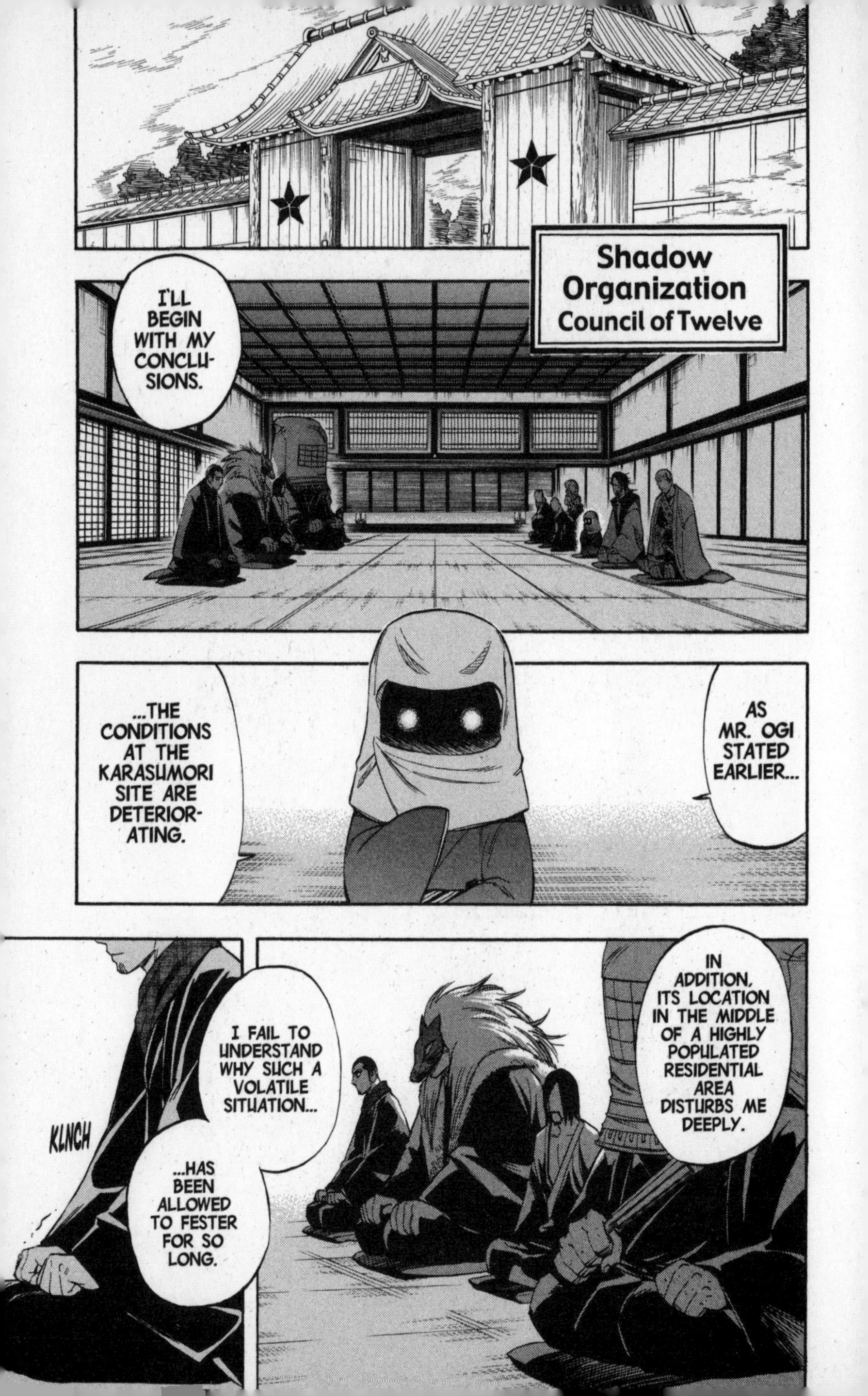
Shadow Organization Council of Twelve
I'LL BEGIN WITH MY CONCLUSIONS.
AS MR. OGI STATED EARLIER...
...THE CONDITIONS AT THE KARASUMORI SITE ARE DETERIORATING.
IN ADDITION, ITS LOCATION IN THE MIDDLE OF A HIGHLY POPULATED RESIDENTIAL AREA DISTURBS ME DEEPLY.
I FAIL TO UNDERSTAND WHY SUCH A VOLATILE SITUATION...
...HAS BEEN ALLOWED TO FESTER FOR SO LONG.
KLNCH

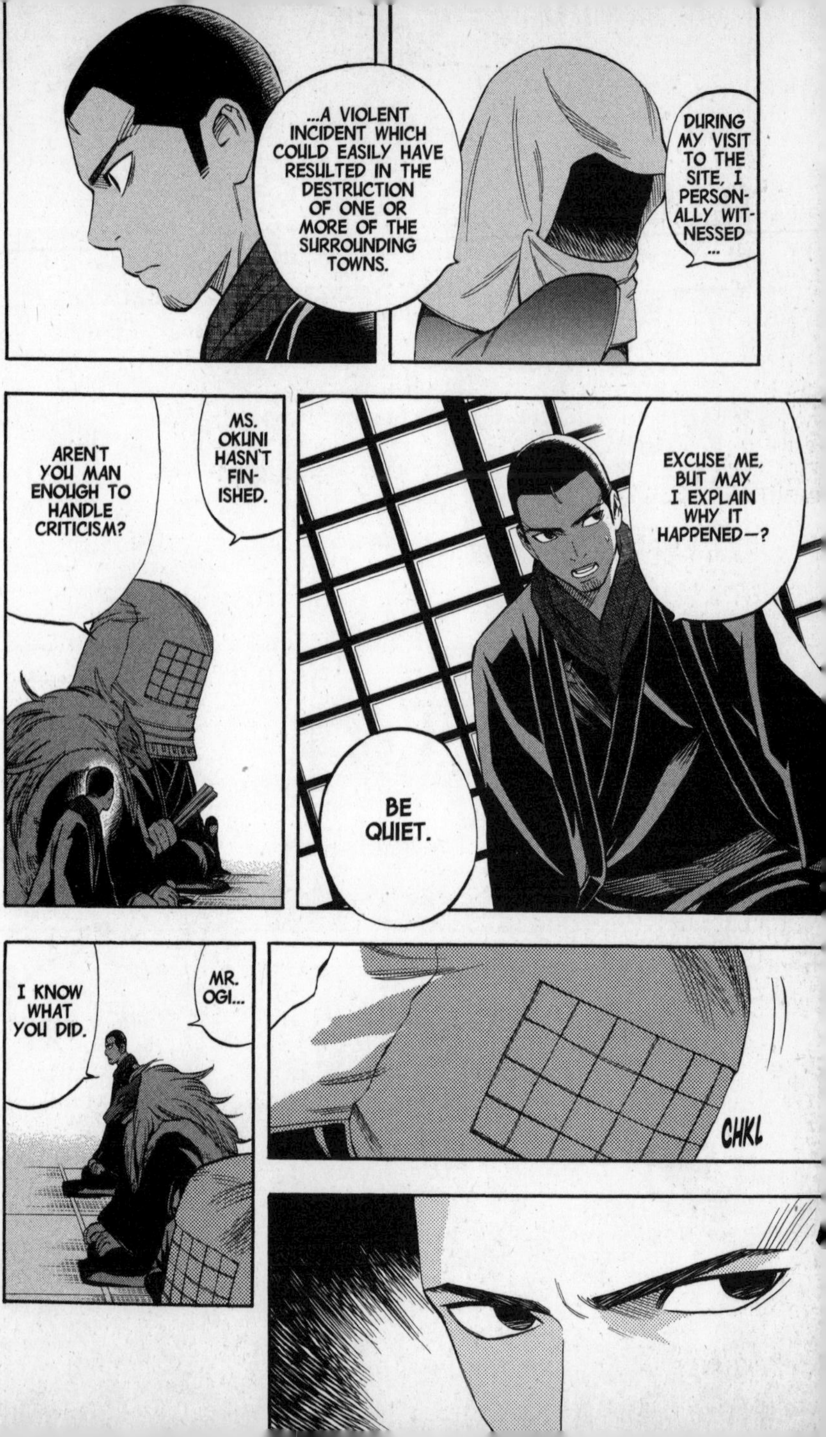
DURING MY VISIT TO THE SITE, I PERSONALLY WITNESSED...
...A VIOLENT INCIDENT WHICH COULD EASILY HAVE RESULTED IN THE DESTRUCTION OF ONE OR MORE OF THE SURROUNDING TOWNS.
EXCUSE ME, BUT MAY I EXPLAIN WHY IT HAPPENED—?
BE QUIET.
MS. OKUNI HASN'T FINISHED.
AREN'T YOU MAN ENOUGH TO HANDLE CRITICISM?
CHKL
MR. OGI...
I KNOW WHAT YOU DID.

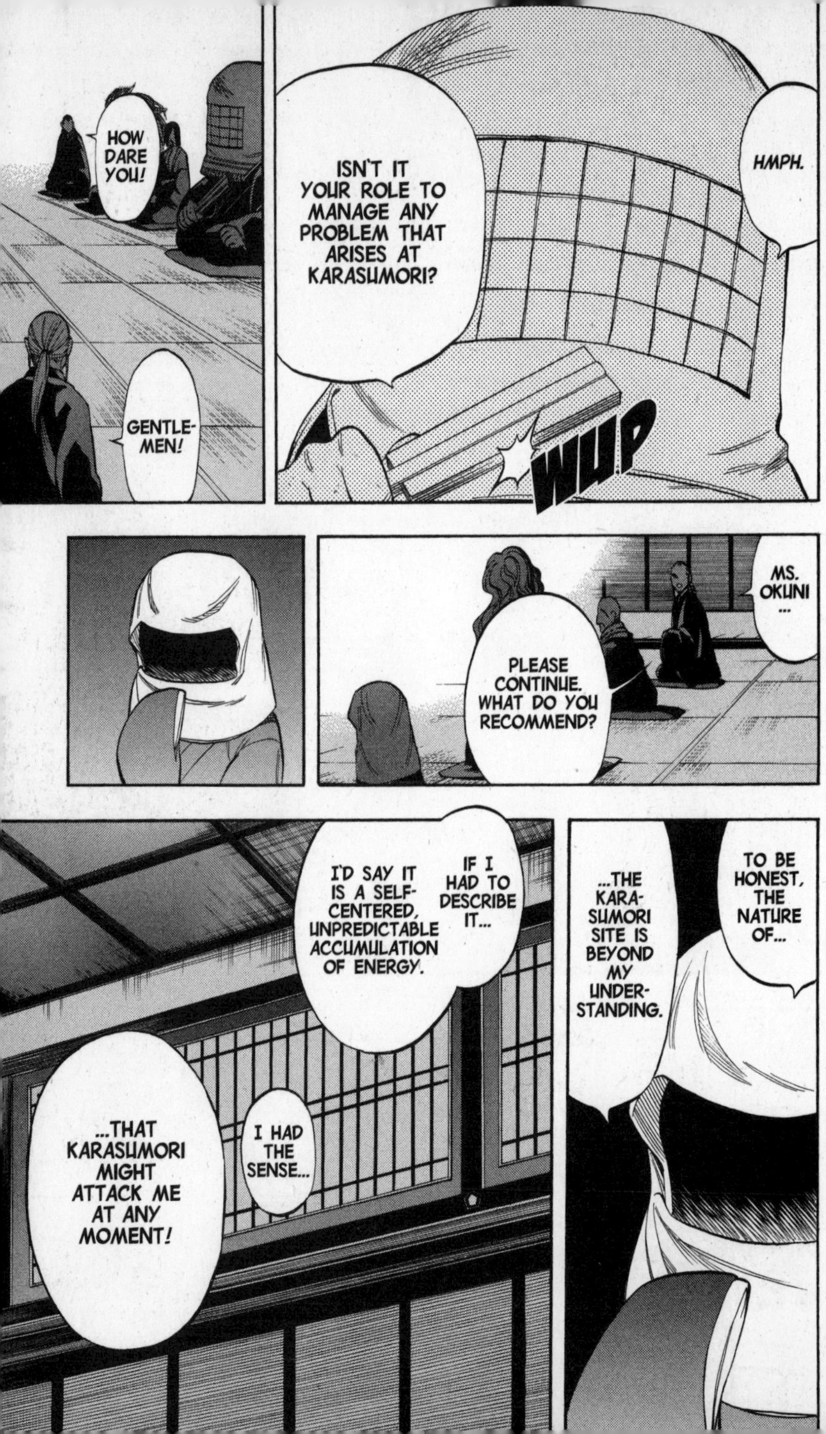
HMPH.
ISN'T IT YOUR ROLE TO MANAGE ANY PROBLEM THAT ARISES AT KARASUMORI?
WUP
HOW DARE YOU!
GENTLE-MEN!
MS. OKUNI...
PLEASE CONTINUE. WHAT DO YOU RECOMMEND?
TO BE HONEST, THE NATURE OF...
...THE KARA-SUMORI SITE IS BEYOND MY UNDER-STANDING.
IF I HAD TO DESCRIBE IT...
I'D SAY IT IS A SELF-CENTERED, UNPREDICTABLE ACCUMULATION OF ENERGY.
I HAD THE SENSE...
...THAT KARASUMORI MIGHT ATTACK ME AT ANY MOMENT!

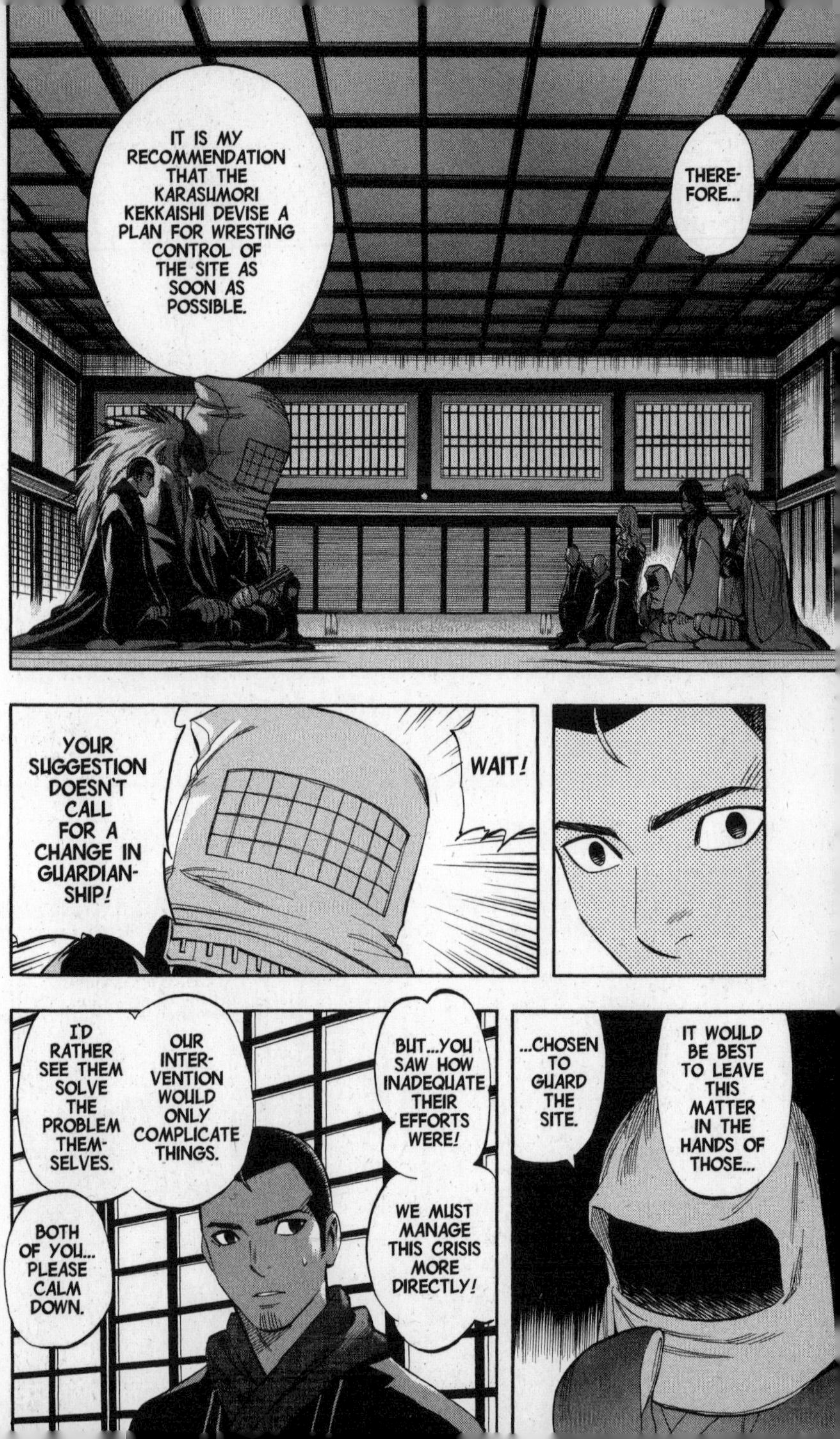
THERE-FORE...
IT IS MY RECOMMENDATION THAT THE KARASUMORI KEKKAISHI DEVISE A PLAN FOR WRESTING CONTROL OF THE SITE AS SOON AS POSSIBLE.
WAIT!
YOUR SUGGESTION DOESN'T CALL FOR A CHANGE IN GUARDIAN-SHIP!
IT WOULD BE BEST TO LEAVE THIS MATTER IN THE HANDS OF THOSE...
...CHOSEN TO GUARD THE SITE.
BUT...YOU SAW HOW INADEQUATE THEIR EFFORTS WERE!
WE MUST MANAGE THIS CRISIS MORE DIRECTLY!
OUR INTER-VENTION WOULD ONLY COMPLICATE THINGS.
I'D RATHER SEE THEM SOLVE THE PROBLEM THEM-SELVES.
BOTH OF YOU... PLEASE CALM DOWN.

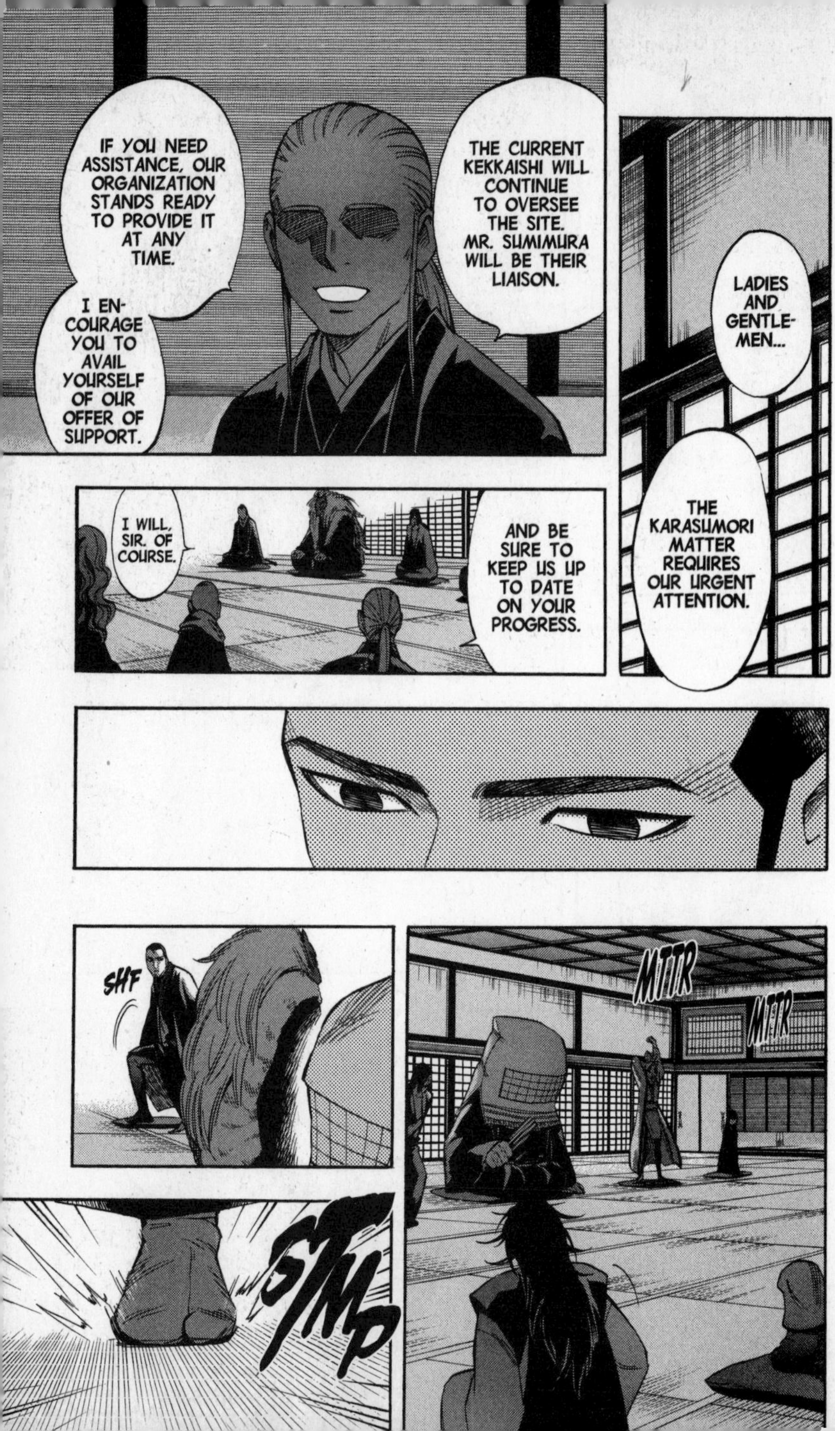
LADIES AND GENTLEMEN...
THE KARASUMORI MATTER REQUIRES OUR URGENT ATTENTION.
THE CURRENT KEKKAISHI WILL CONTINUE TO OVERSEE THE SITE. MR. SUMIMURA WILL BE THEIR LIAISON.
IF YOU NEED ASSISTANCE, OUR ORGANIZATION STANDS READY TO PROVIDE IT AT ANY TIME.
I ENCOURAGE YOU TO AVAIL YOURSELF OF OUR OFFER OF SUPPORT.
AND BE SURE TO KEEP US UP TO DATE ON YOUR PROGRESS.
I WILL, SIR. OF COURSE.
MTTR
MTTR
SHF
GMP

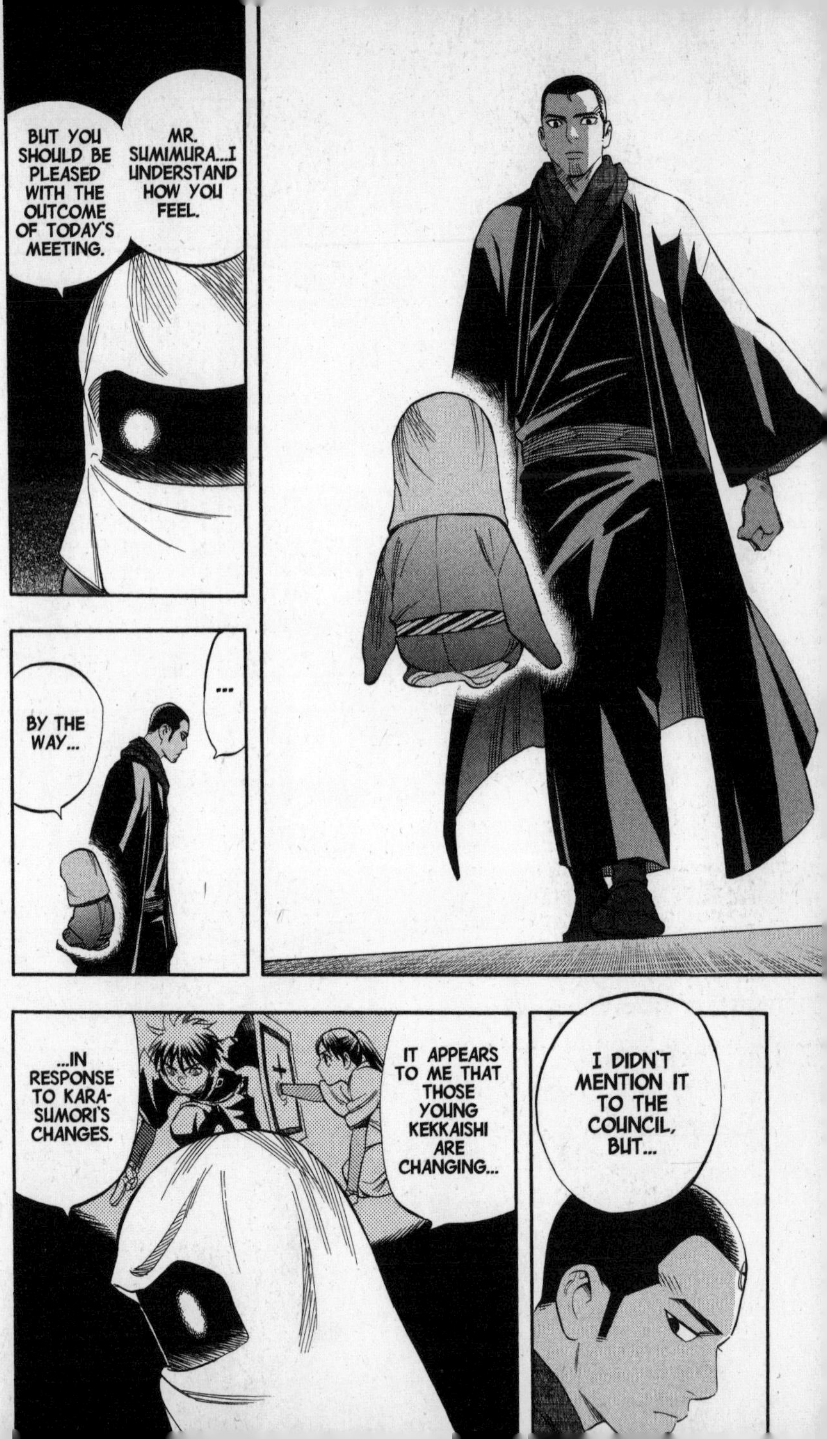
MR. SUMIMURA...I UNDERSTAND HOW YOU FEEL.
BUT YOU SHOULD BE PLEASED WITH THE OUTCOME OF TODAY'S MEETING.
...
BY THE WAY...
I DIDN'T MENTION IT TO THE COUNCIL, BUT...
IT APPEARS TO ME THAT THOSE YOUNG KEKKAISHI ARE CHANGING...
...IN RESPONSE TO KARA-SUMORI'S CHANGES.

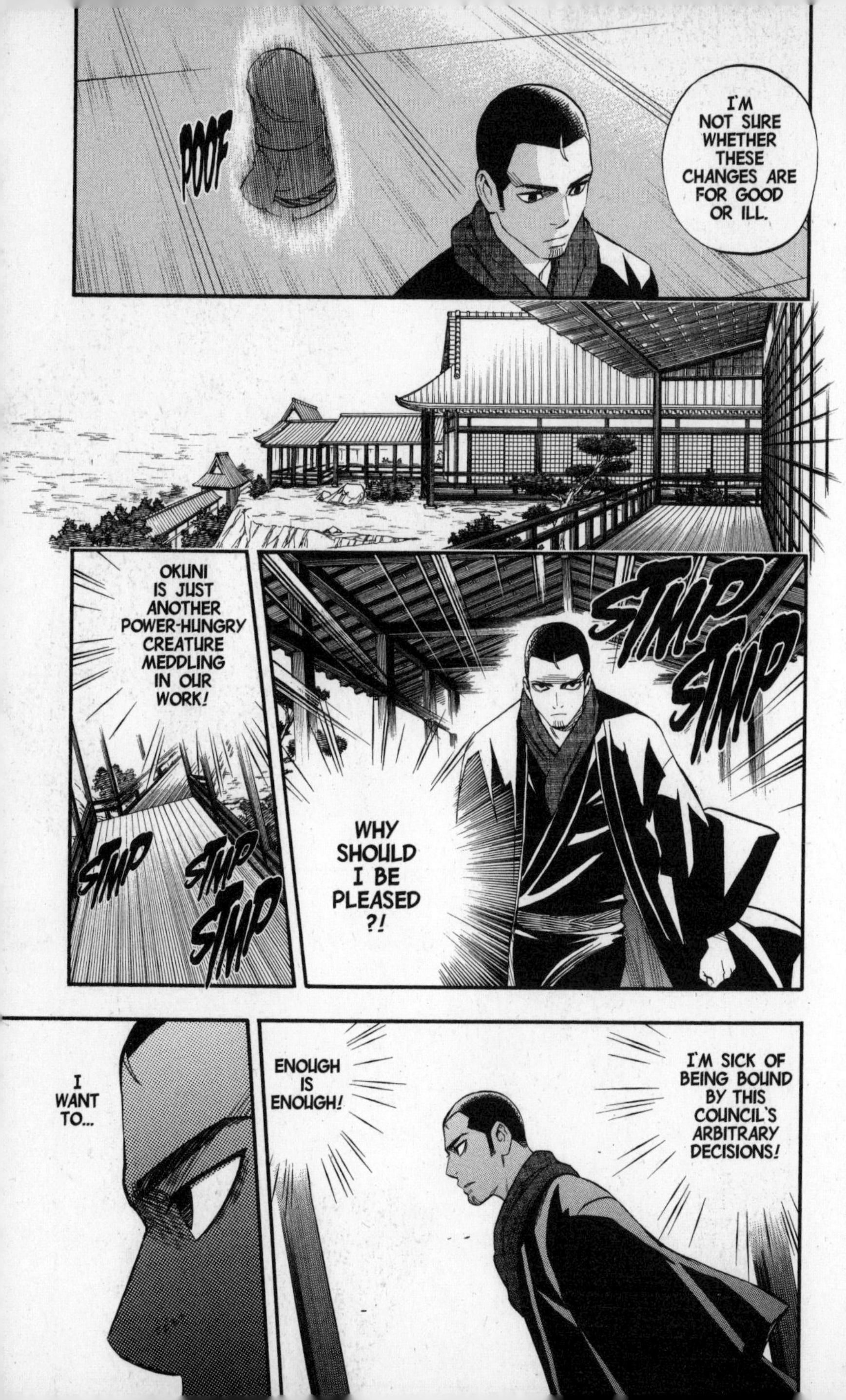
I'M NOT SURE WHETHER THESE CHANGES ARE FOR GOOD OR ILL.
POOF
STMP
STMP
WHY SHOULD I BE PLEASED?!
OKUNI IS JUST ANOTHER POWER-HUNGRY CREATURE MEDDLING IN OUR WORK!
STMP
STMP
STMP
I'M SICK OF BEING BOUND BY THIS COUNCIL'S ARBITRARY DECISIONS!
ENOUGH IS ENOUGH!
I WANT TO...

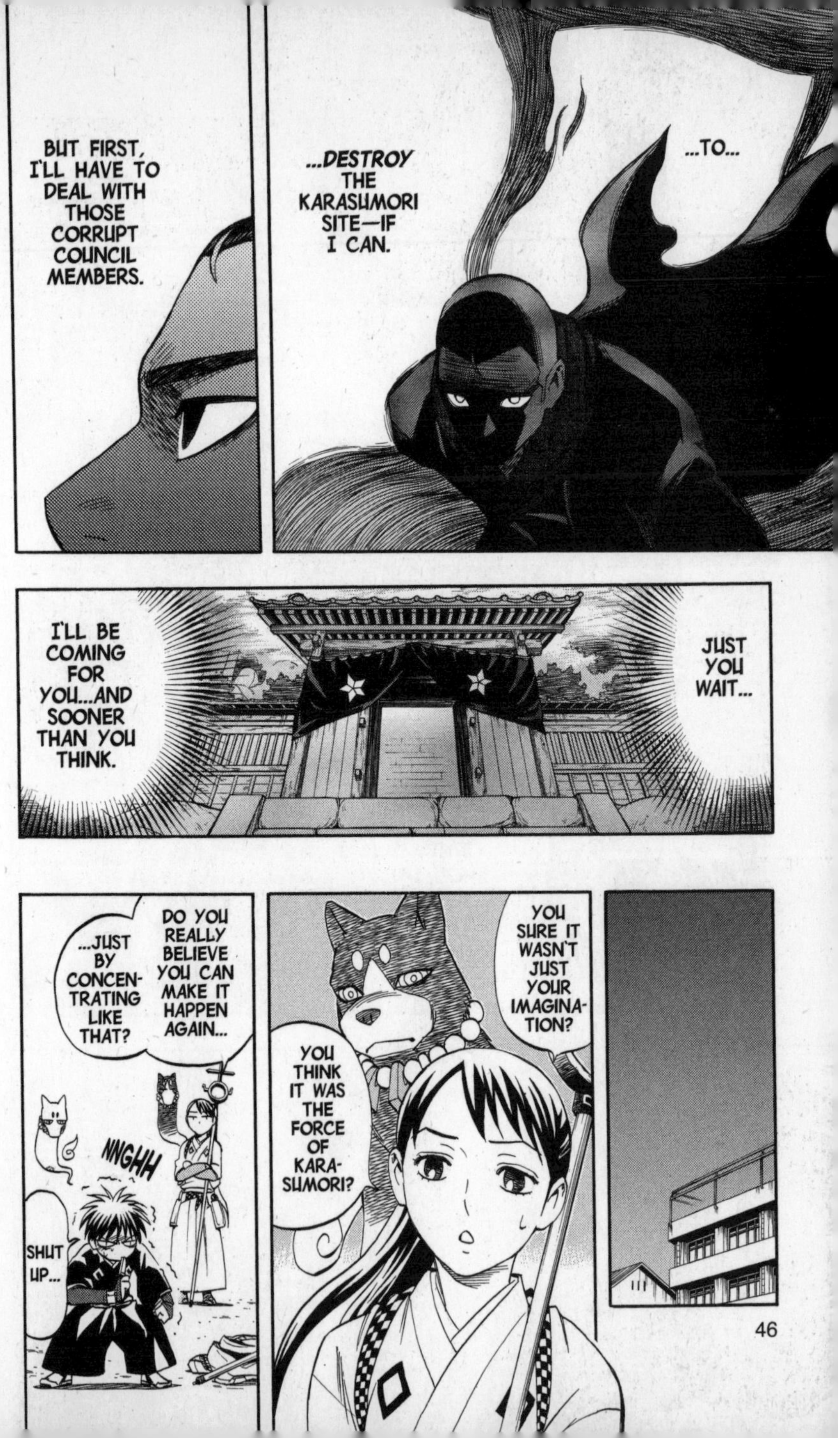
...TO...
...DESTROY THE KARASUMORI SITE—IF I CAN.
BUT FIRST, I'LL HAVE TO DEAL WITH THOSE CORRUPT COUNCIL MEMBERS.
JUST YOU WAIT...
I'LL BE COMING FOR YOU...AND SOONER THAN YOU THINK.
YOU SURE IT WASN'T JUST YOUR IMAGINA-TION?
YOU THINK IT WAS THE FORCE OF KARA-SUMORI?
DO YOU REALLY BELIEVE YOU CAN MAKE IT HAPPEN AGAIN...
...JUST BY CONCEN-TRATING LIKE THAT?
NNGHH
SHUT UP...

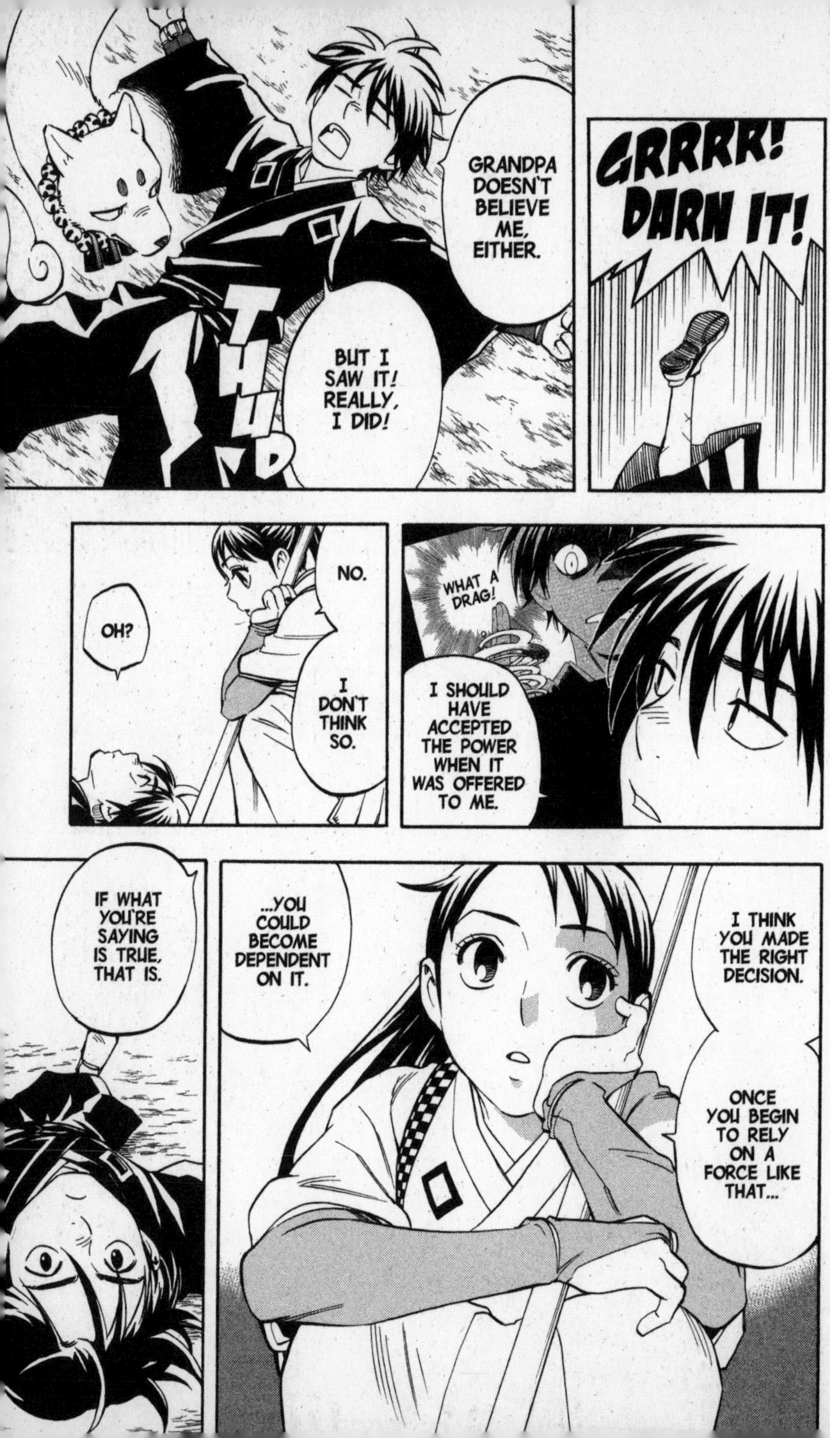
GRRRR! DARN IT!
GRANDPA DOESN'T BELIEVE ME, EITHER.
BUT I SAW IT! REALLY, I DID!
THUD
WHAT A DRAG!
I SHOULD HAVE ACCEPTED THE POWER WHEN IT WAS OFFERED TO ME.
NO.
I DON'T THINK SO.
OH?
I THINK YOU MADE THE RIGHT DECISION.
ONCE YOU BEGIN TO RELY ON A FORCE LIKE THAT...
...YOU COULD BECOME DEPENDENT ON IT.
IF WHAT YOU'RE SAYING IS TRUE, THAT IS.

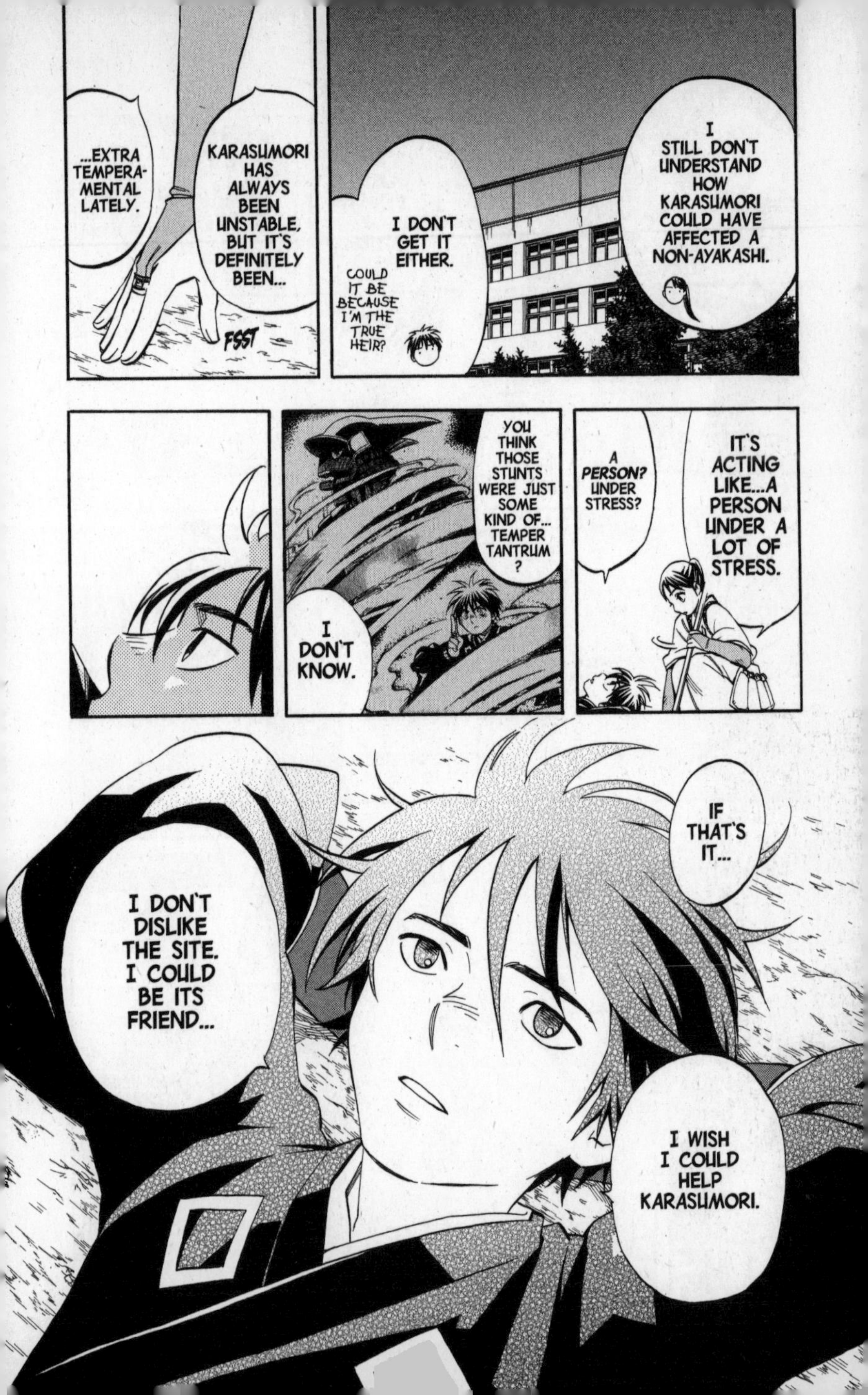
I STILL DON'T UNDERSTAND HOW KARASUMORI COULD HAVE AFFECTED A NON-AYAKASHI.
I DON'T GET IT EITHER.
COULD IT BE BECAUSE I'M THE TRUE HEIR?
KARASUMORI HAS ALWAYS BEEN UNSTABLE, BUT IT'S DEFINITELY BEEN...
...EXTRA TEMPERA-MENTAL LATELY.
FSST
IT'S ACTING LIKE...A PERSON UNDER A LOT OF STRESS.
A *PERSON?* UNDER STRESS?
YOU THINK THOSE STUNTS WERE JUST SOME KIND OF... TEMPER TANTRUM?
I DON'T KNOW.
IF THAT'S IT...
I DON'T DISLIKE THE SITE. I COULD BE ITS FRIEND...
I WISH I COULD HELP KARASUMORI.

I'M
SURPRISED
YOU WOULD
COME TO
SEE ME.

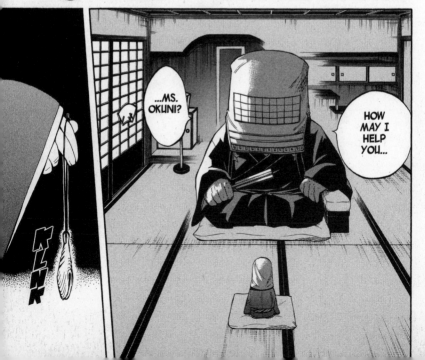

...MS.
OKUNI?

HOW
MAY I
HELP
YOU...

KLNK

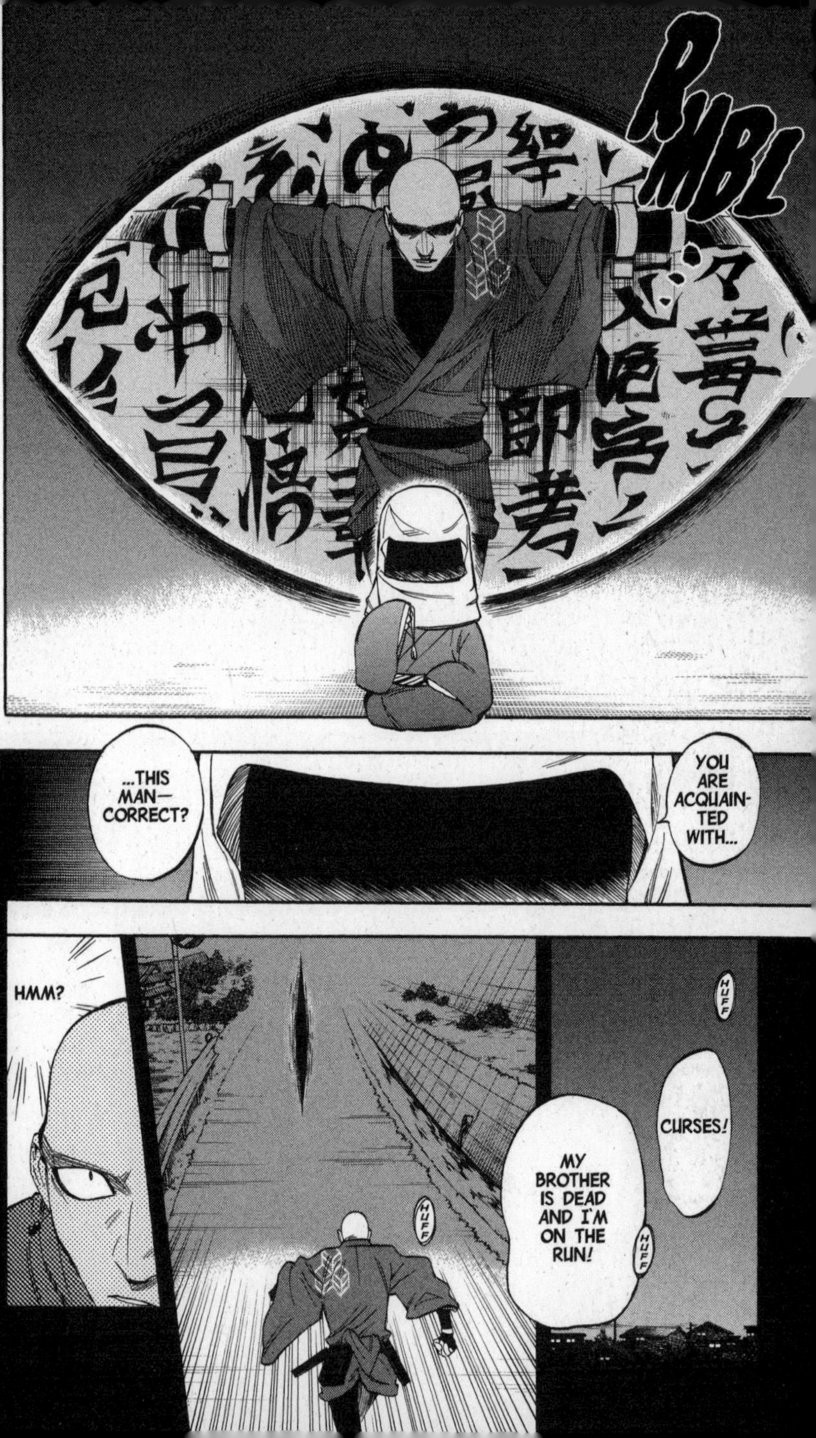
RMBL
YOU ARE ACQUAIN-TED WITH...
...THIS MAN—CORRECT?
HUFF
CURSES!
MY BROTHER IS DEAD AND I'M ON THE RUN!
HUFF
HUFF
HMM?

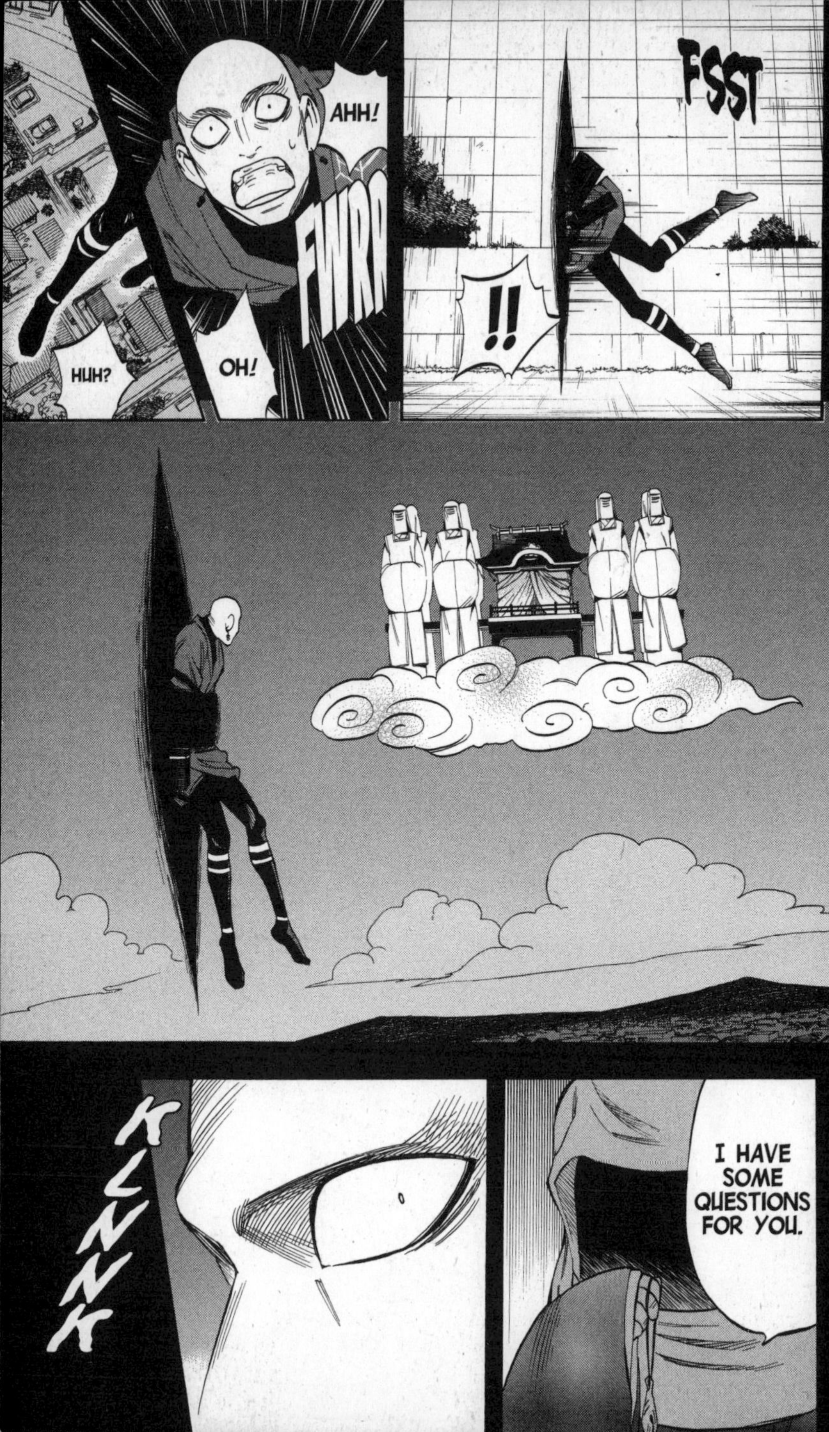
FSST
!!
AHH!
FWRR
OH!
HUH?
I HAVE SOME QUESTIONS FOR YOU.
KLNNK

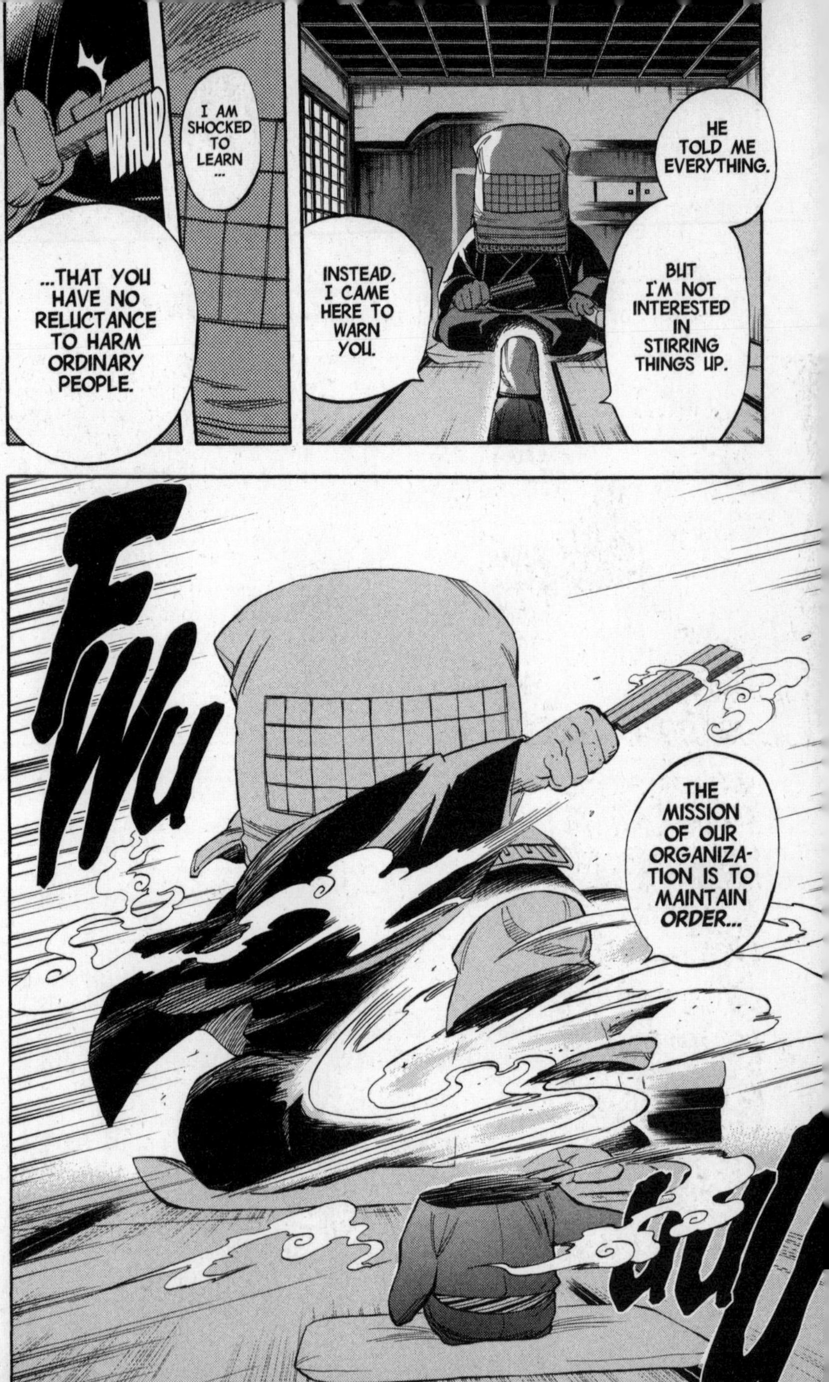
HE TOLD ME EVERYTHING.
BUT I'M NOT INTERESTED IN STIRRING THINGS UP.
INSTEAD, I CAME HERE TO WARN YOU.
WHUP
I AM SHOCKED TO LEARN ...
...THAT YOU HAVE NO RELUCTANCE TO HARM ORDINARY PEOPLE.
THE MISSION OF OUR ORGANIZA-TION IS TO MAINTAIN ORDER...
FWU

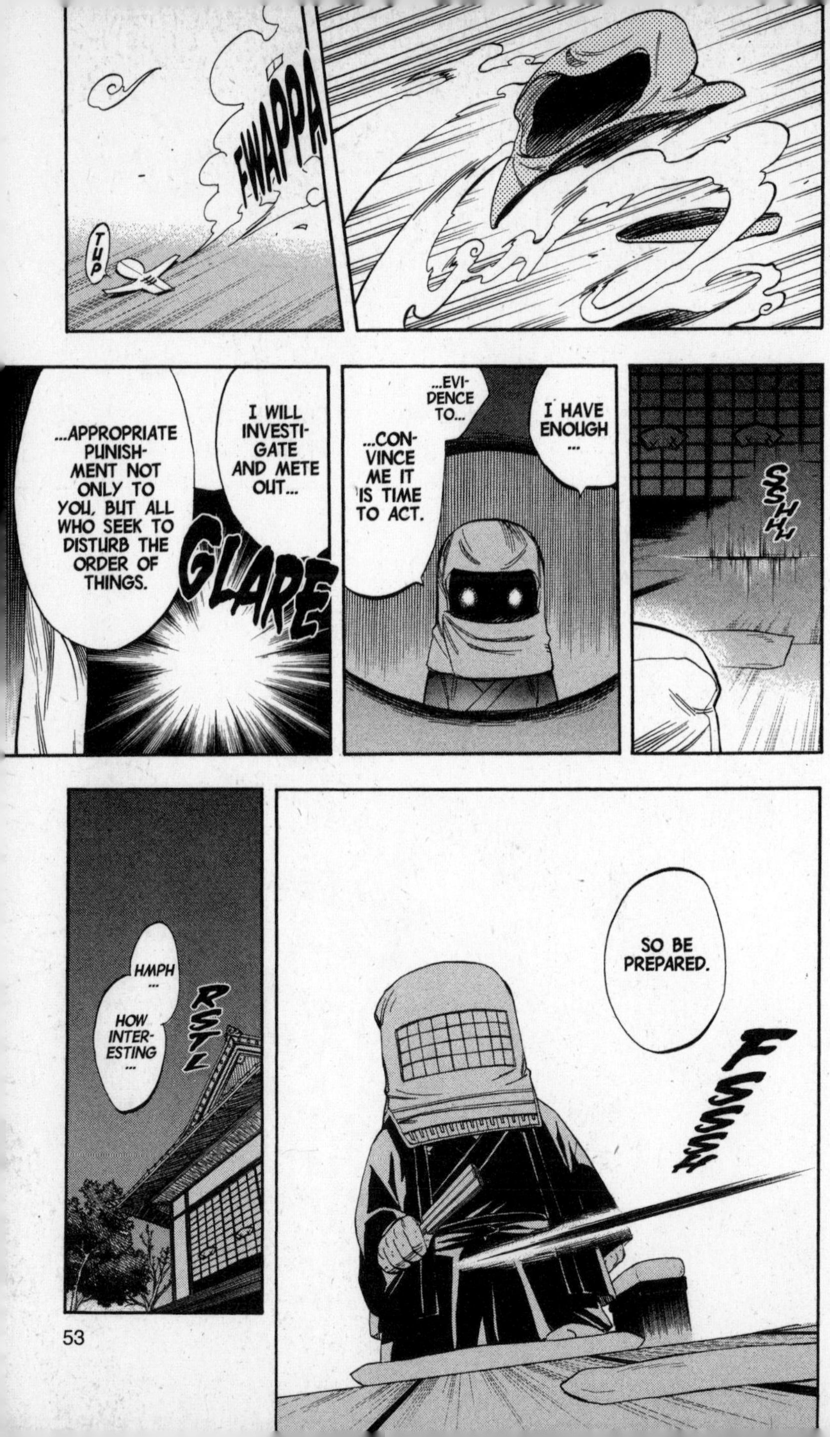
FWAPPA
TUP
SSHH
I HAVE ENOUGH ...
...EVIDENCE TO...
...CONVINCE ME IT IS TIME TO ACT.
I WILL INVESTIGATE AND METE OUT...
...APPROPRIATE PUNISHMENT NOT ONLY TO YOU, BUT ALL WHO SEEK TO DISTURB THE ORDER OF THINGS.
GLARE
SO BE PREPARED.
FSSSSH
HMPH ...
HOW INTERESTING ...
RSTL

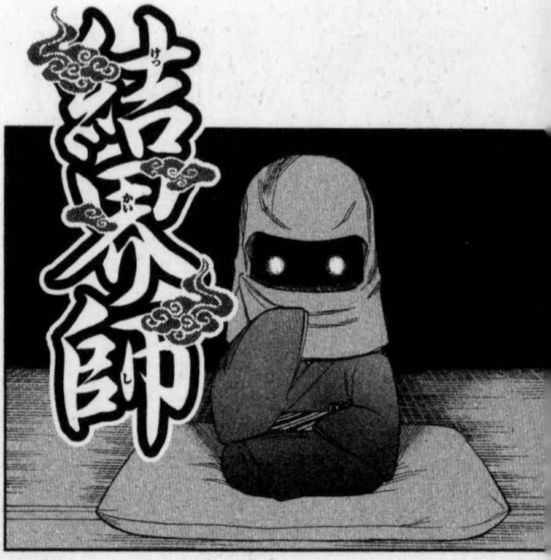
結界師

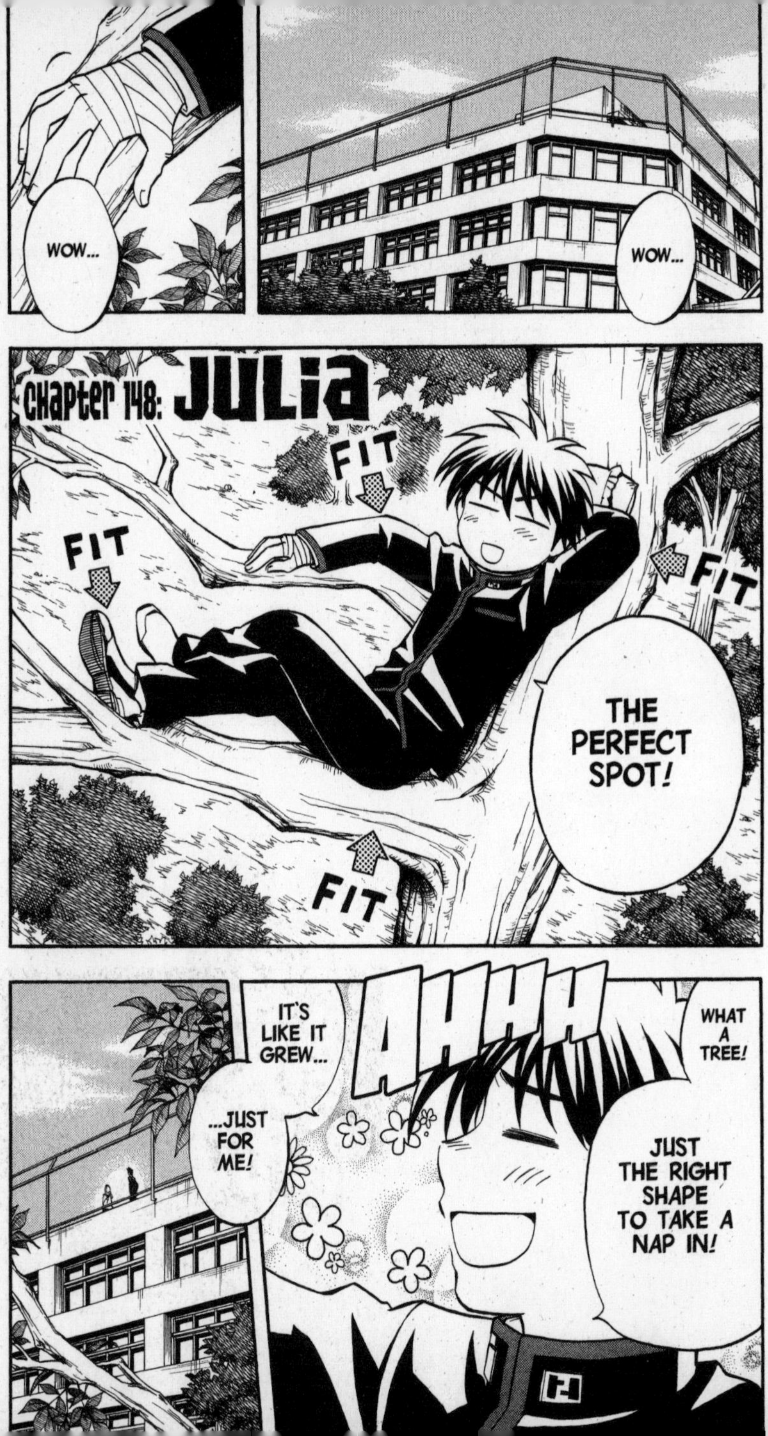
WOW...
WOW...
Chapter 148: Julia
FIT
FIT
FIT
FIT
THE PERFECT SPOT!
WHAT A TREE!
AHHH
JUST THE RIGHT SHAPE TO TAKE A NAP IN!
IT'S LIKE IT GREW...
...JUST FOR ME!

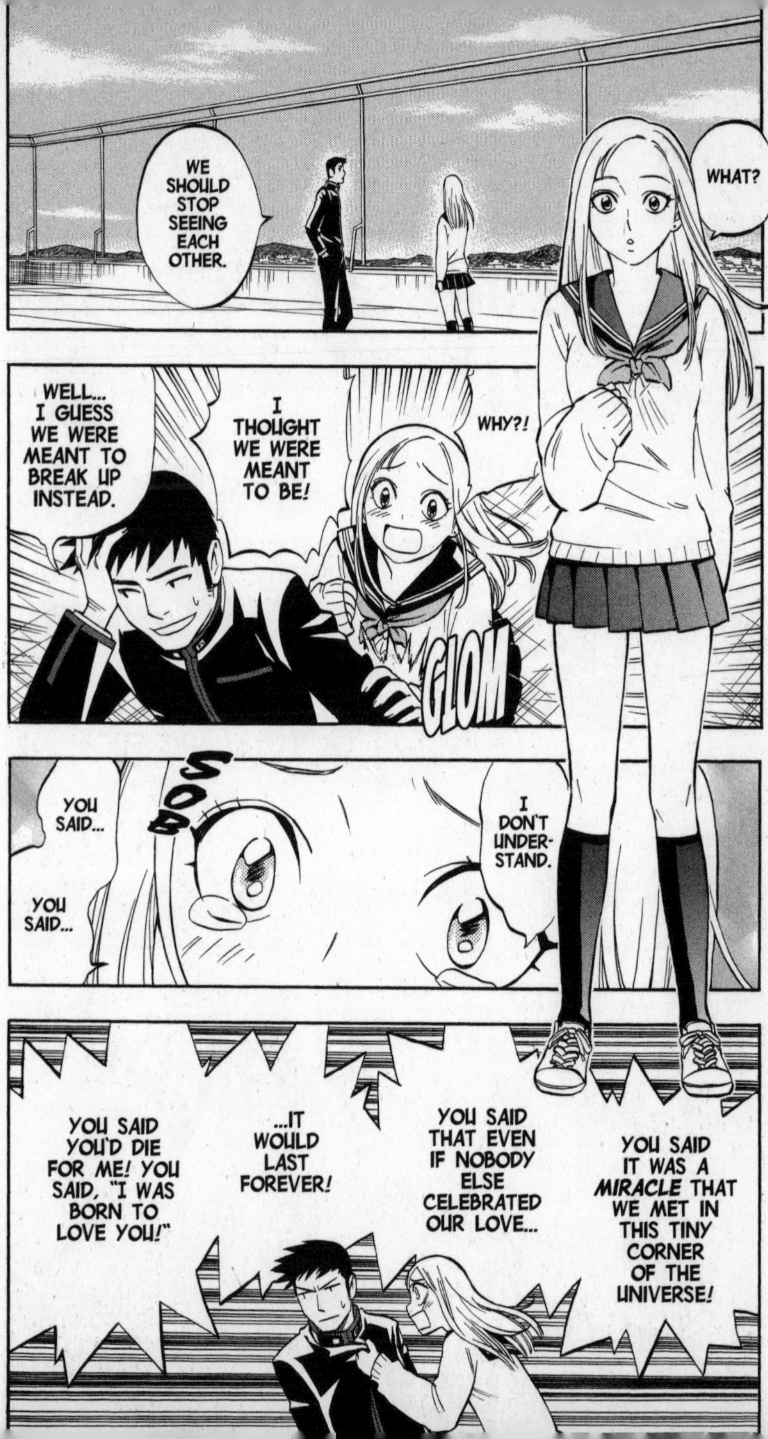
WE SHOULD STOP SEEING EACH OTHER.
WHAT?
WHY?!
I THOUGHT WE WERE MEANT TO BE!
GLOM
WELL... I GUESS WE WERE MEANT TO BREAK UP INSTEAD.
I DON'T UNDER-STAND.
SOB
YOU SAID...
YOU SAID...
YOU SAID IT WAS A *MIRACLE* THAT WE MET IN THIS TINY CORNER OF THE UNIVERSE!
YOU SAID THAT EVEN IF NOBODY ELSE CELEBRATED OUR LOVE...
...IT WOULD LAST FOREVER!
YOU SAID YOU'D DIE FOR ME! YOU SAID, "I WAS BORN TO LOVE YOU!"

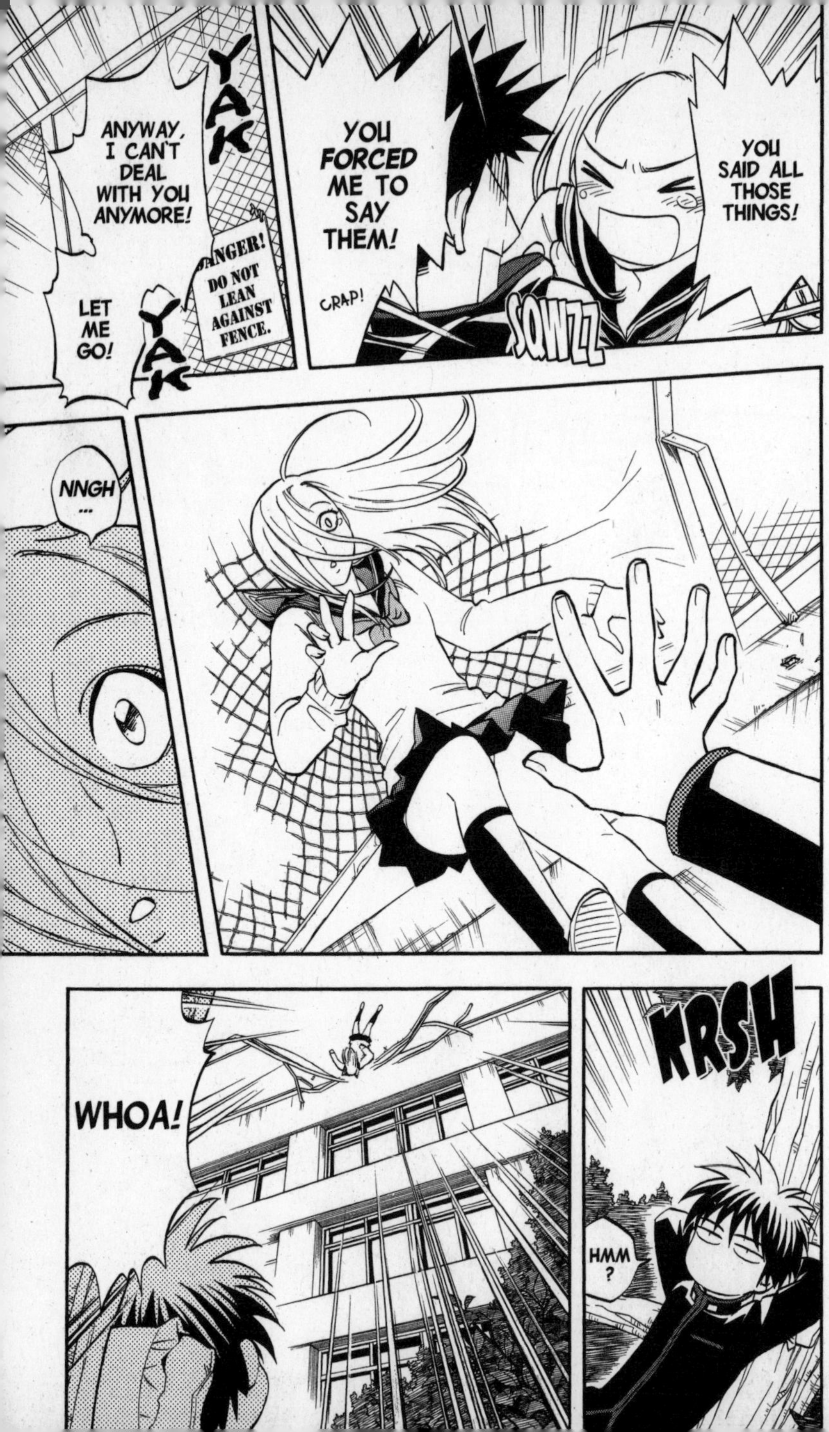
YOU SAID ALL THOSE THINGS!
YOU FORCED ME TO SAY THEM!
CRAP!
SQWZZ
YAK
ANYWAY, I CAN'T DEAL WITH YOU ANYMORE!
ANGER! DO NOT LEAN AGAINST FENCE.
LET ME GO!
YAK
NNGH ...
KRSH
HMM ?
WHOA!

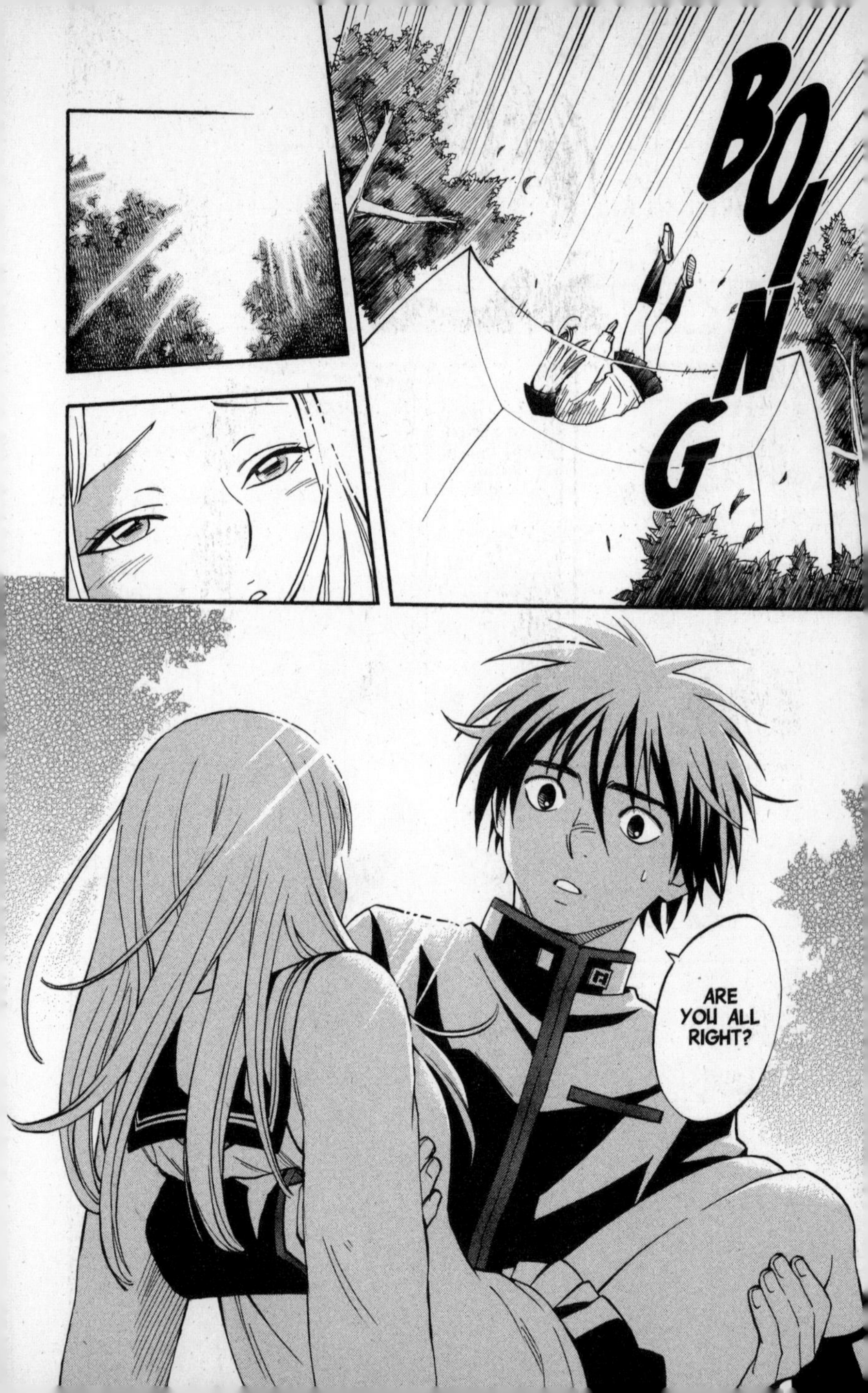
BOING
ARE YOU ALL RIGHT?

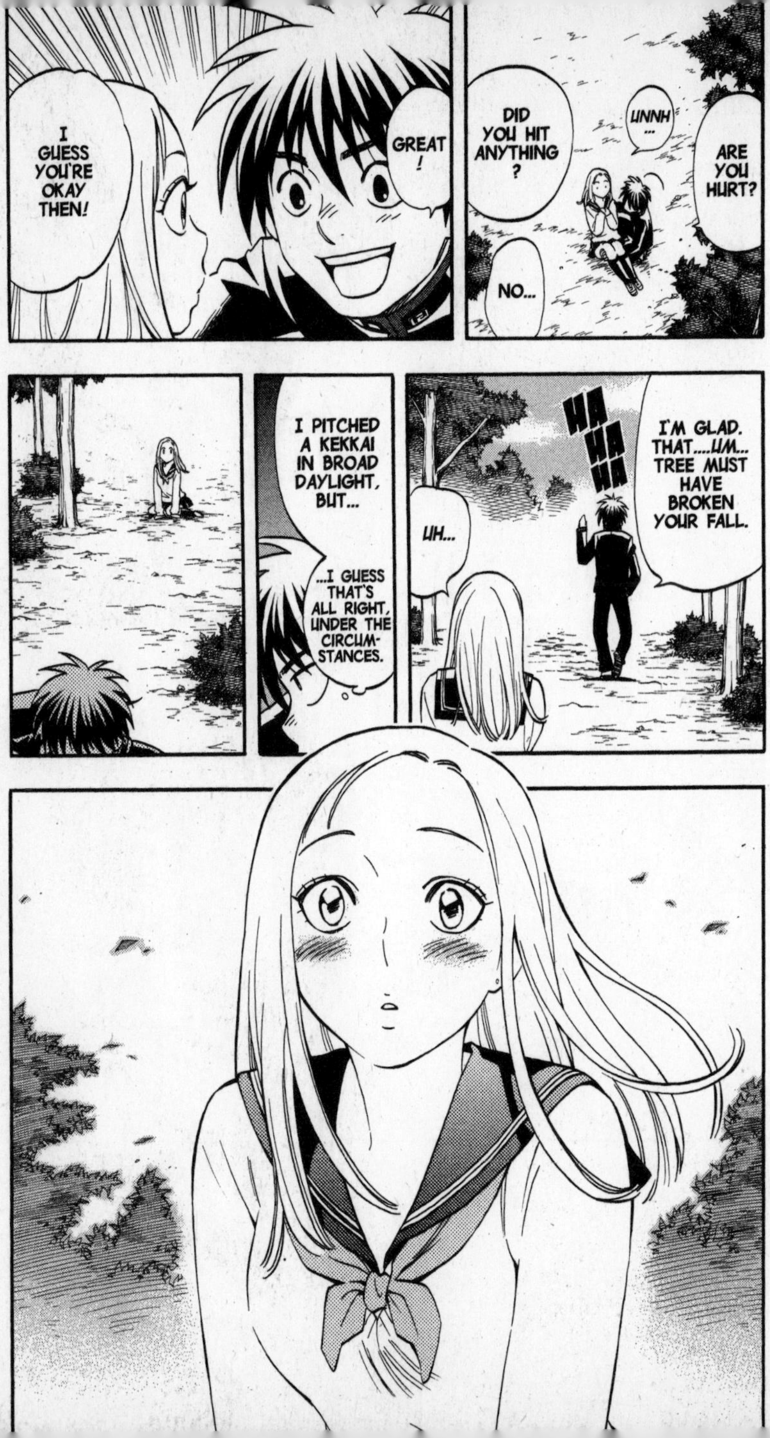
ARE YOU HURT?
UNNH...
DID YOU HIT ANYTHING?
NO...
GREAT!
I GUESS YOU'RE OKAY THEN!
I'M GLAD. THAT....UM... TREE MUST HAVE BROKEN YOUR FALL.
HA HA HA HA
UH...
I PITCHED A KEKKAI IN BROAD DAYLIGHT, BUT...
...I GUESS THAT'S ALL RIGHT, UNDER THE CIRCUMSTANCES.

CHAPTER 148: JULIA

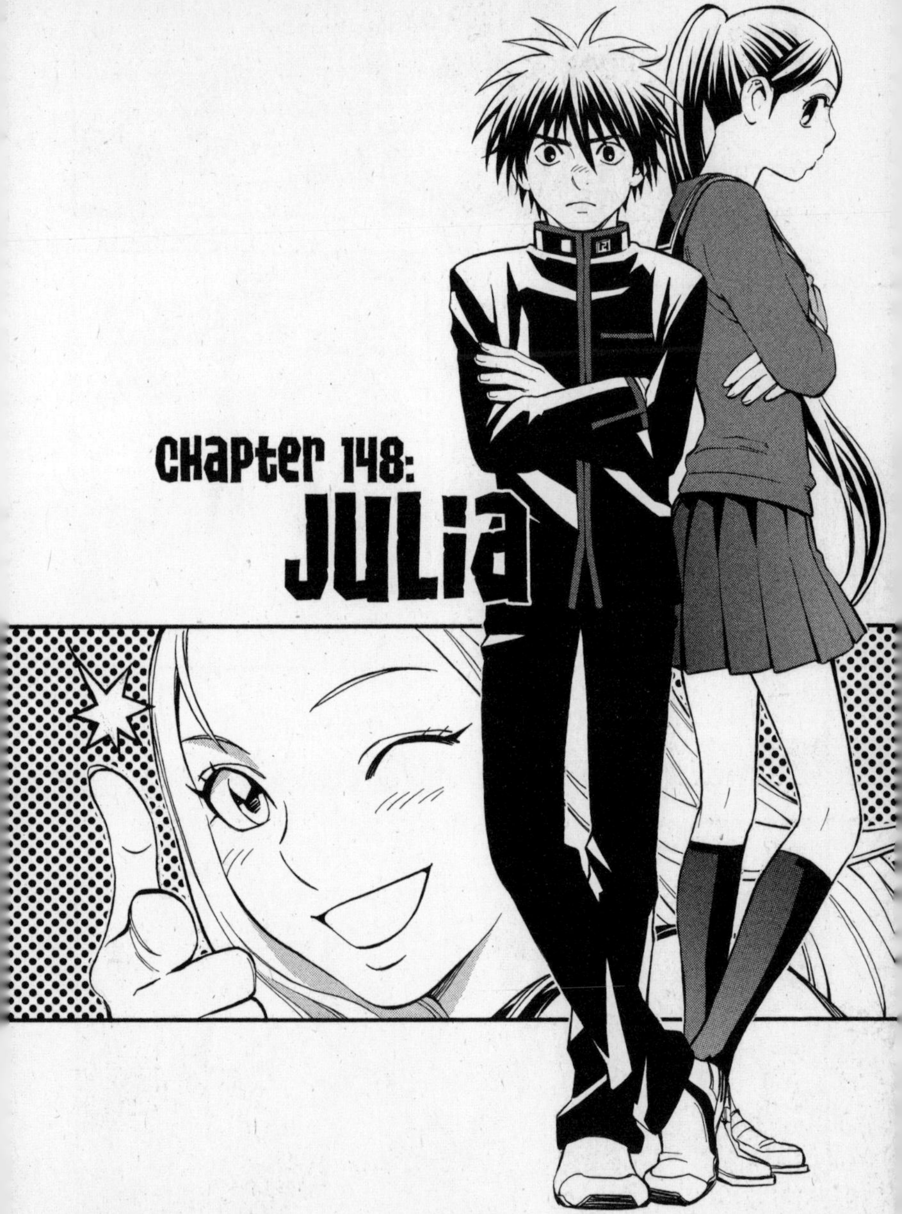

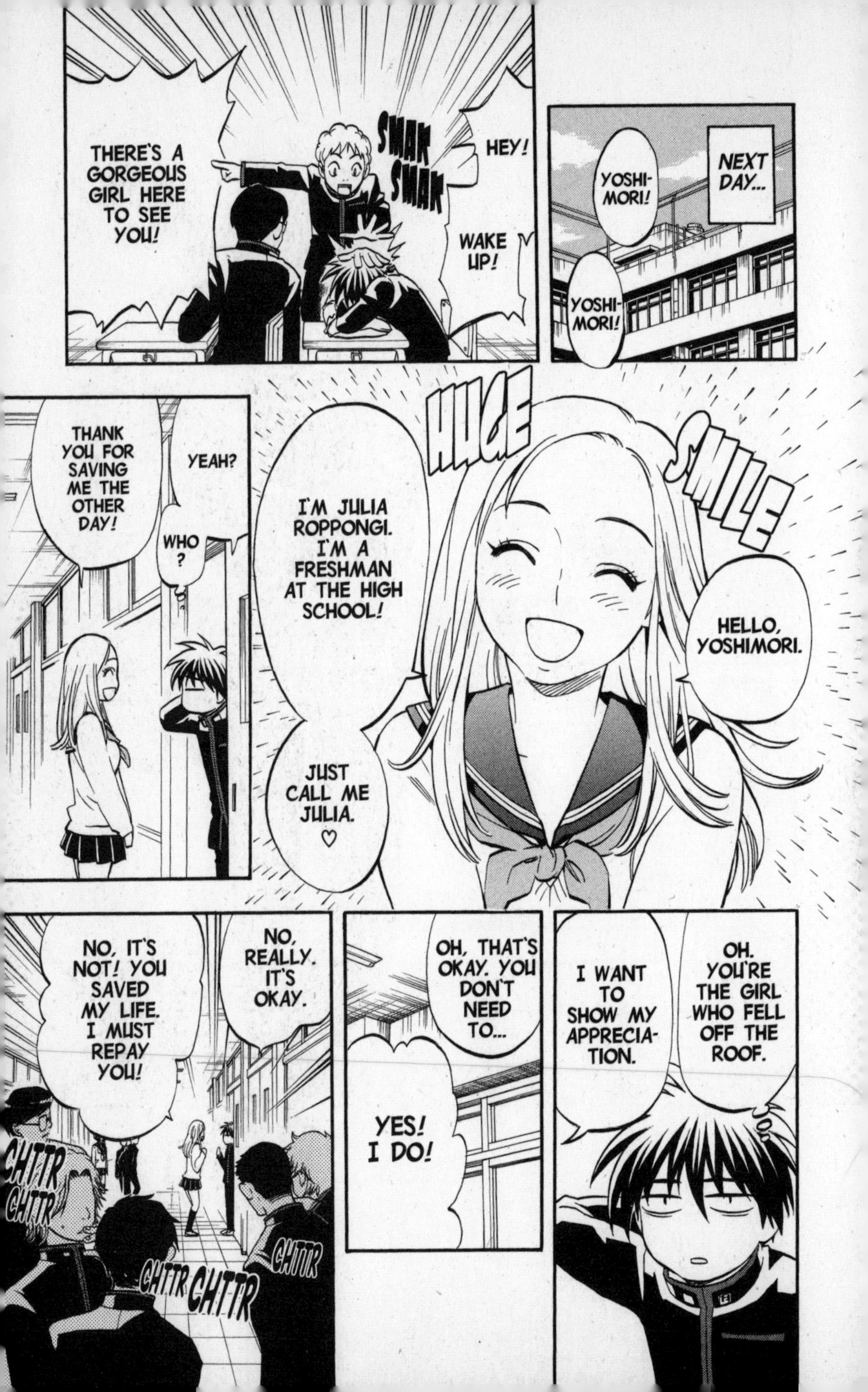
NEXT DAY...
YOSHIMORI!
YOSHIMORI!
HEY!
WAKE UP!
SMAK SMAK
THERE'S A GORGEOUS GIRL HERE TO SEE YOU!
HUGE SMILE
HELLO, YOSHIMORI.
I'M JULIA ROPPONGI. I'M A FRESHMAN AT THE HIGH SCHOOL!
JUST CALL ME JULIA. ♡
YEAH?
WHO?
THANK YOU FOR SAVING ME THE OTHER DAY!
OH. YOU'RE THE GIRL WHO FELL OFF THE ROOF.
I WANT TO SHOW MY APPRECIATION.
OH, THAT'S OKAY. YOU DON'T NEED TO...
YES! I DO!
NO, REALLY. IT'S OKAY.
NO, IT'S NOT! YOU SAVED MY LIFE. I MUST REPAY YOU!
CHTTR CHTTR
CHTTR
CHTTR CHTTR

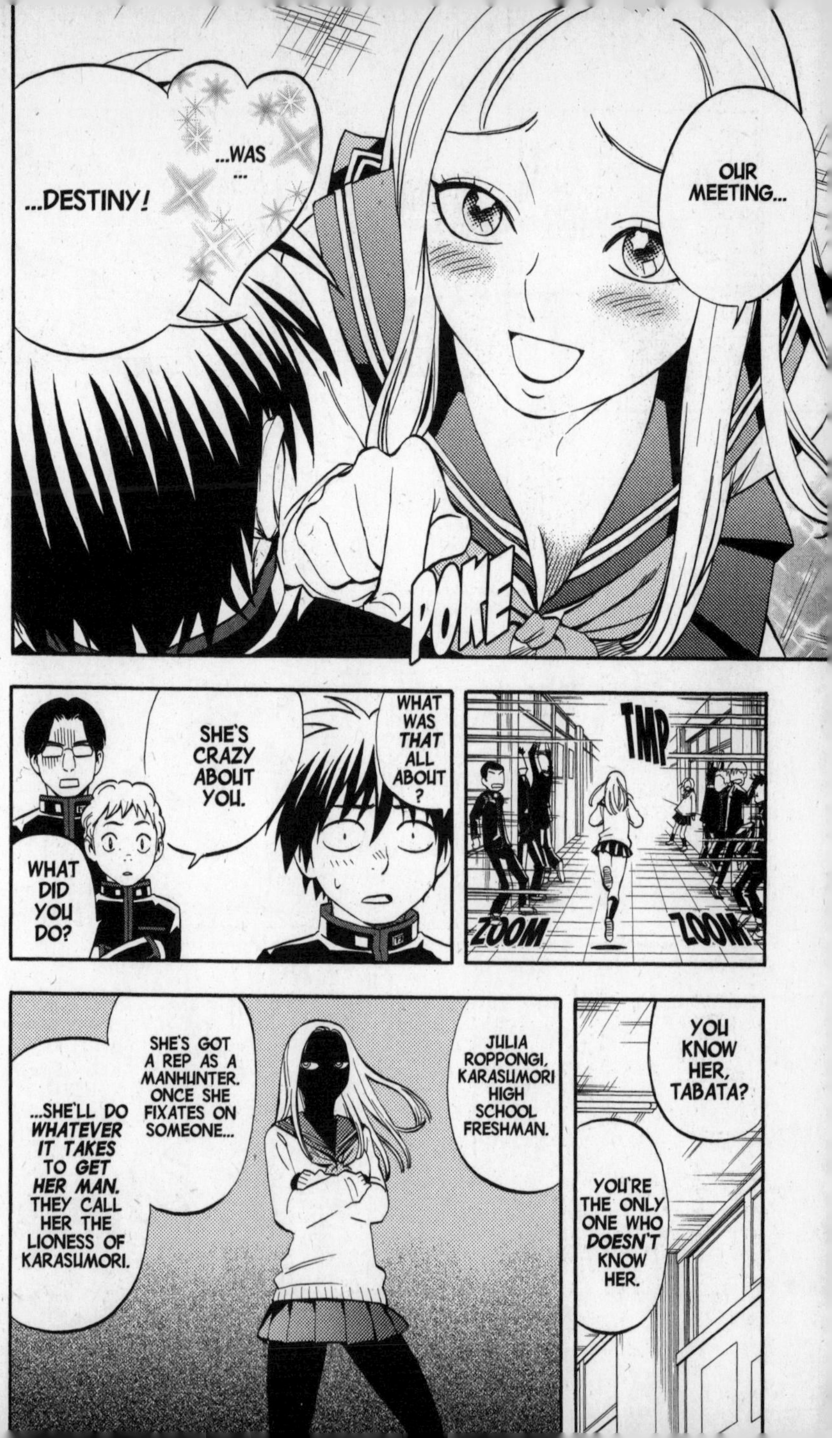
OUR MEETING...
...WAS ...
...DESTINY!
POKE
TMP
ZOOM
ZOOM
WHAT WAS *THAT* ALL ABOUT?
SHE'S CRAZY ABOUT YOU.
WHAT DID YOU DO?
YOU KNOW HER, TABATA?
YOU'RE THE ONLY ONE WHO *DOESN'T* KNOW HER.
JULIA ROPPONGI, KARASUMORI HIGH SCHOOL FRESHMAN.
SHE'S GOT A REP AS A MANHUNTER. ONCE SHE FIXATES ON SOMEONE...
...SHE'LL DO ***WHATEVER IT TAKES*** TO ***GET HER MAN.*** THEY CALL HER THE LIONESS OF KARASUMORI.

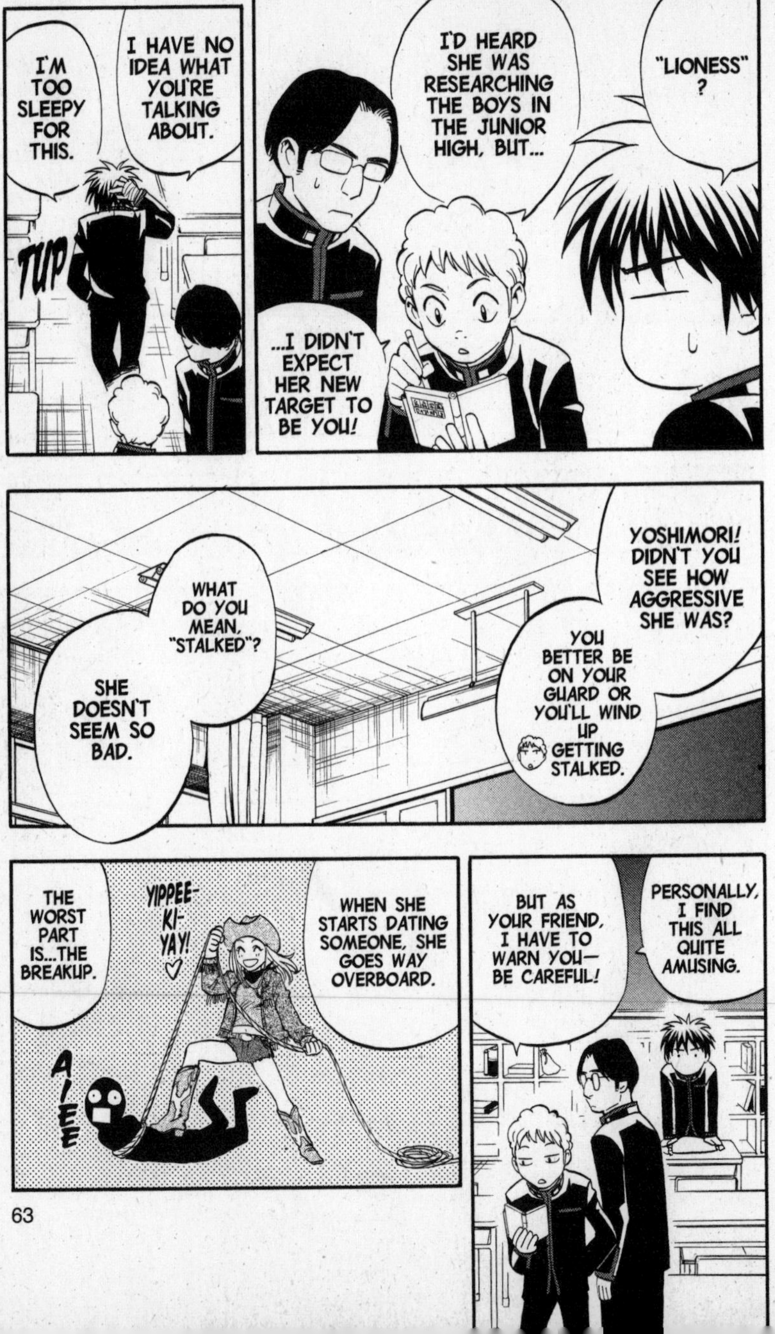
"LIONESS"?
I'D HEARD SHE WAS RESEARCHING THE BOYS IN THE JUNIOR HIGH, BUT...
...I DIDN'T EXPECT HER NEW TARGET TO BE YOU!
I HAVE NO IDEA WHAT YOU'RE TALKING ABOUT.
I'M TOO SLEEPY FOR THIS.
TUP
YOSHIMORI! DIDN'T YOU SEE HOW AGGRESSIVE SHE WAS?
YOU BETTER BE ON YOUR GUARD OR YOU'LL WIND UP GETTING STALKED.
WHAT DO YOU MEAN, "STALKED"?
SHE DOESN'T SEEM SO BAD.
PERSONALLY, I FIND THIS ALL QUITE AMUSING.
BUT AS YOUR FRIEND, I HAVE TO WARN YOU—BE CAREFUL!
WHEN SHE STARTS DATING SOMEONE, SHE GOES WAY OVERBOARD.
YIPPEE-KI-YAY! ♡
THE WORST PART IS...THE BREAKUP.
AIEE

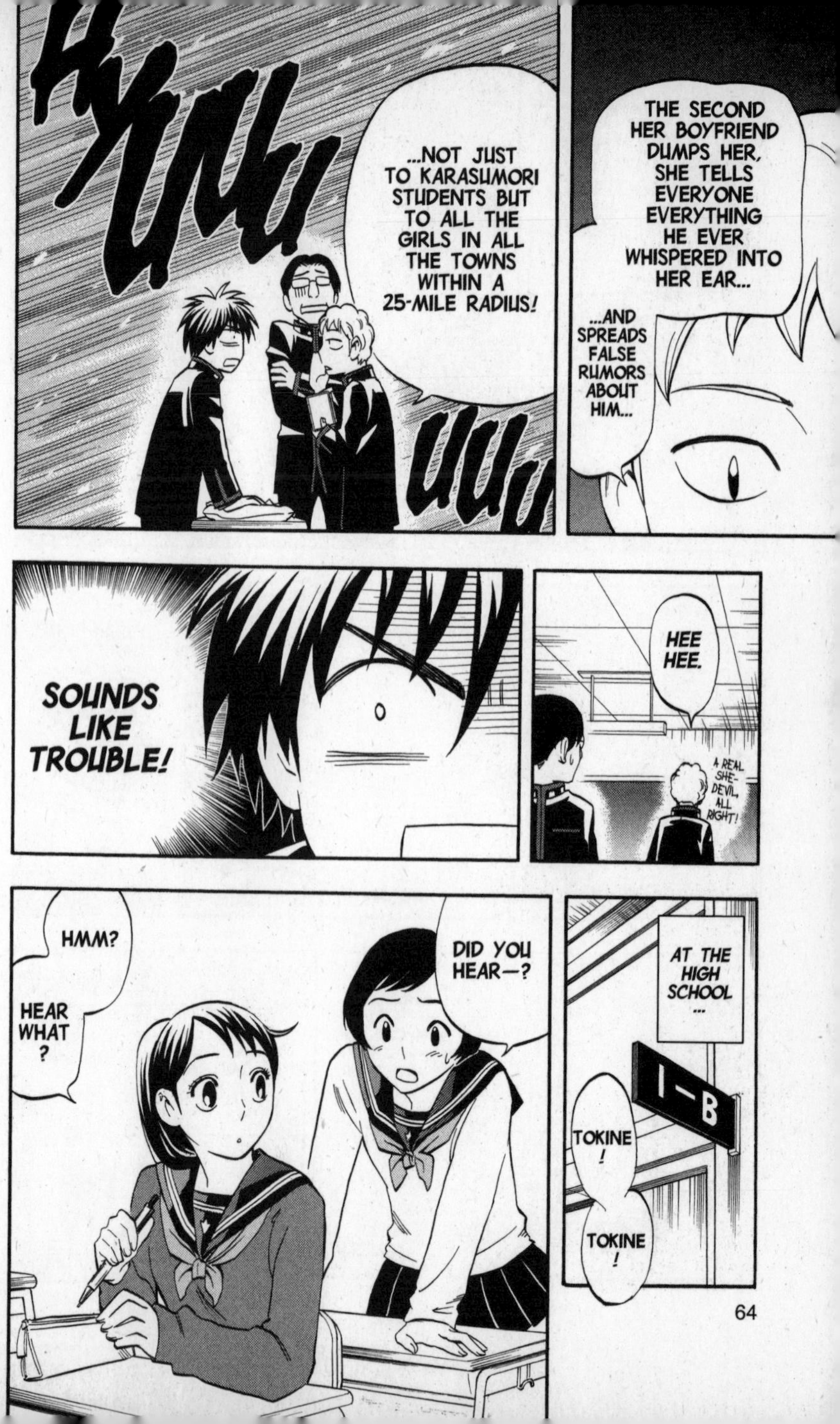
THE SECOND HER BOYFRIEND DUMPS HER, SHE TELLS EVERYONE EVERYTHING HE EVER WHISPERED INTO HER EAR...
...AND SPREADS FALSE RUMORS ABOUT HIM...
...NOT JUST TO KARASUMORI STUDENTS BUT TO ALL THE GIRLS IN ALL THE TOWNS WITHIN A 25-MILE RADIUS!
HEE HEE.
A REAL SHE-DEVIL, ALL RIGHT!
SOUNDS LIKE TROUBLE!
AT THE HIGH SCHOOL...
1-B
TOKINE!
TOKINE!
DID YOU HEAR—?
HMM?
HEAR WHAT?

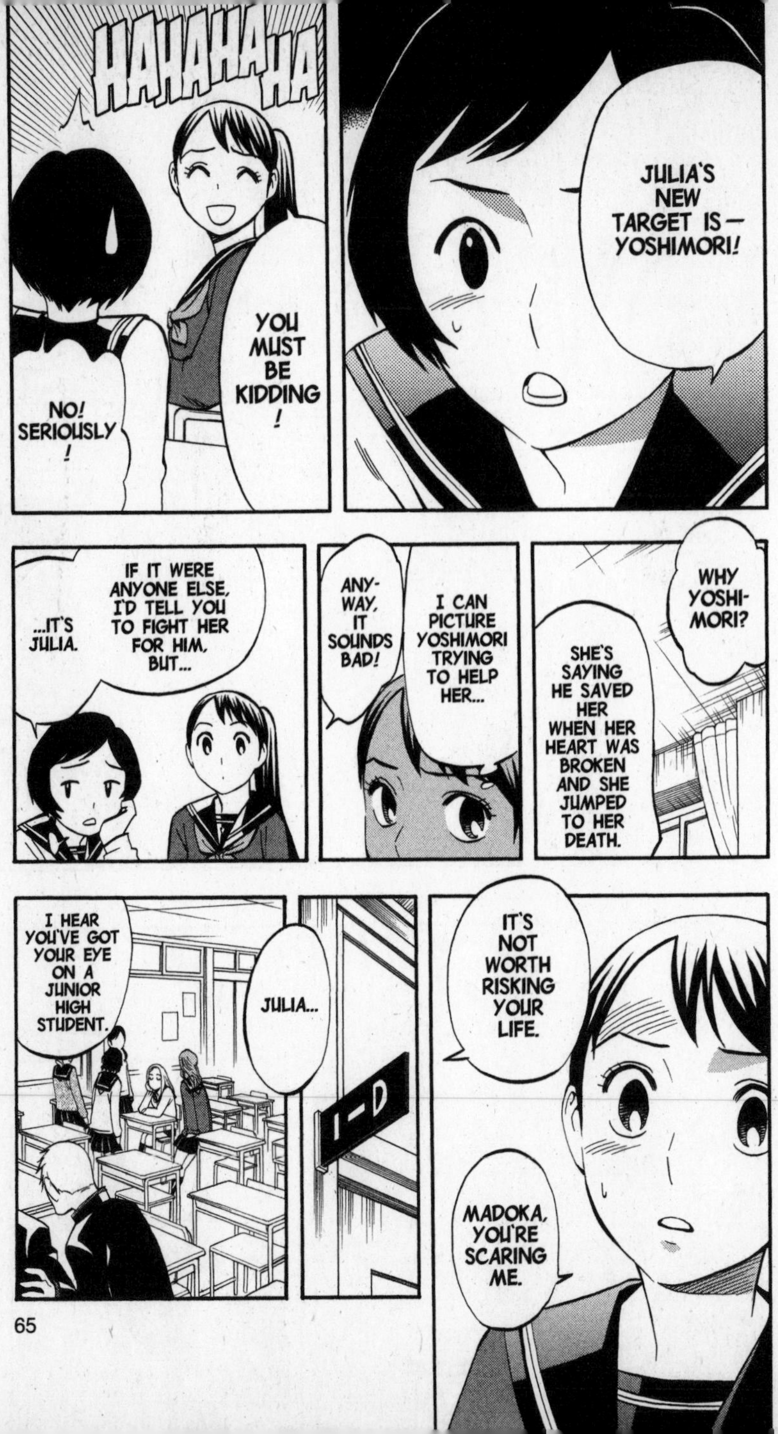
JULIA'S NEW TARGET IS— YOSHIMORI!
HAHAHAHAHA
YOU MUST BE KIDDING!
NO! SERIOUSLY!
WHY YOSHIMORI?
SHE'S SAYING HE SAVED HER WHEN HER HEART WAS BROKEN AND SHE JUMPED TO HER DEATH.
I CAN PICTURE YOSHIMORI TRYING TO HELP HER...
ANYWAY, IT SOUNDS BAD!
IF IT WERE ANYONE ELSE, I'D TELL YOU TO FIGHT HER FOR HIM, BUT...
...IT'S JULIA.
IT'S NOT WORTH RISKING YOUR LIFE.
MADOKA, YOU'RE SCARING ME.
JULIA...
1-D
I HEAR YOU'VE GOT YOUR EYE ON A JUNIOR HIGH STUDENT.

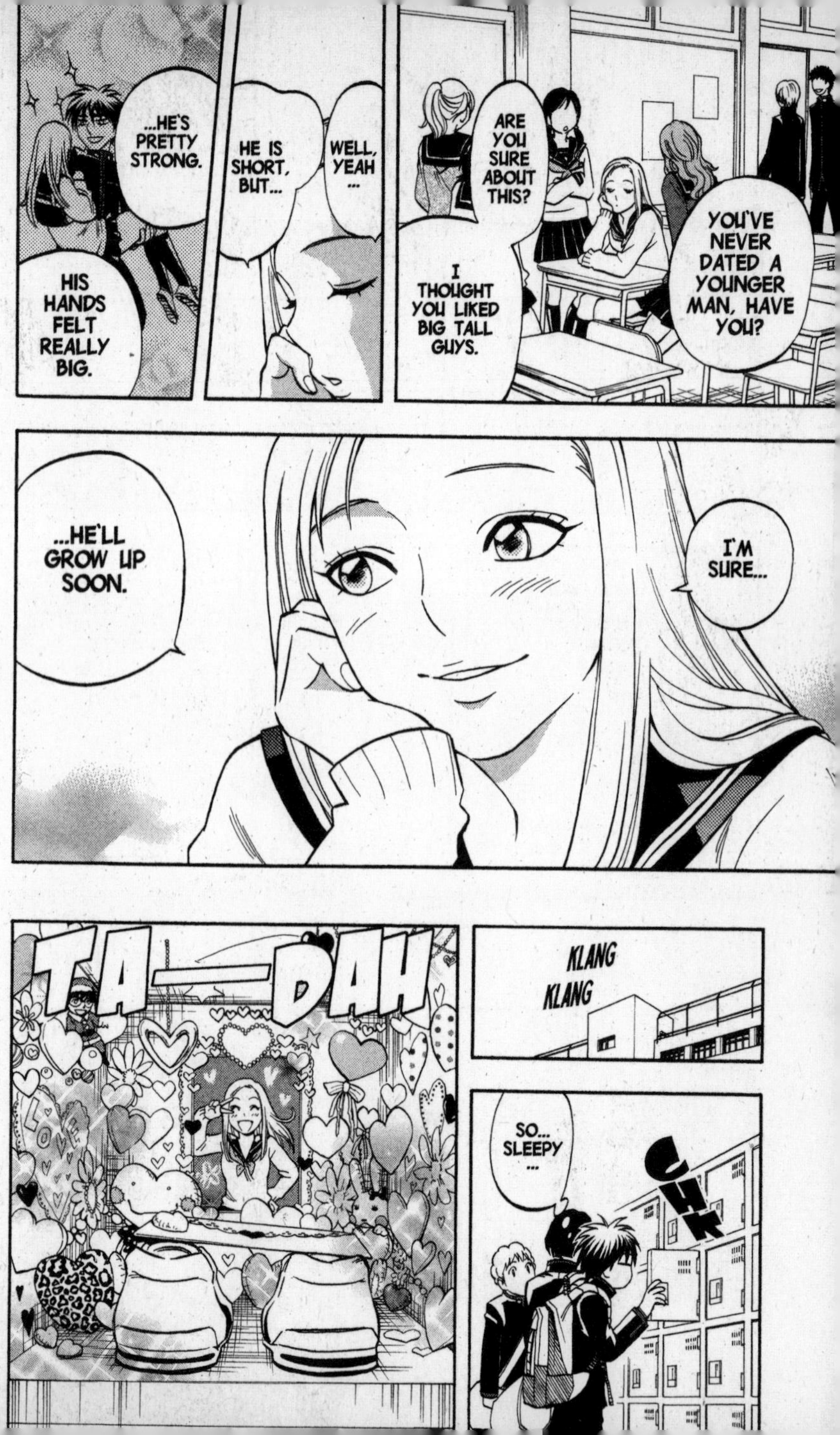
YOU'VE NEVER DATED A YOUNGER MAN, HAVE YOU?
ARE YOU SURE ABOUT THIS?
I THOUGHT YOU LIKED BIG TALL GUYS.
WELL, YEAH ...
HE IS SHORT, BUT...
...HE'S PRETTY STRONG.
HIS HANDS FELT REALLY BIG.
I'M SURE...
...HE'LL GROW UP SOON.
KLANG
KLANG
SO... SLEEPY ...
CHK
TA-DAH

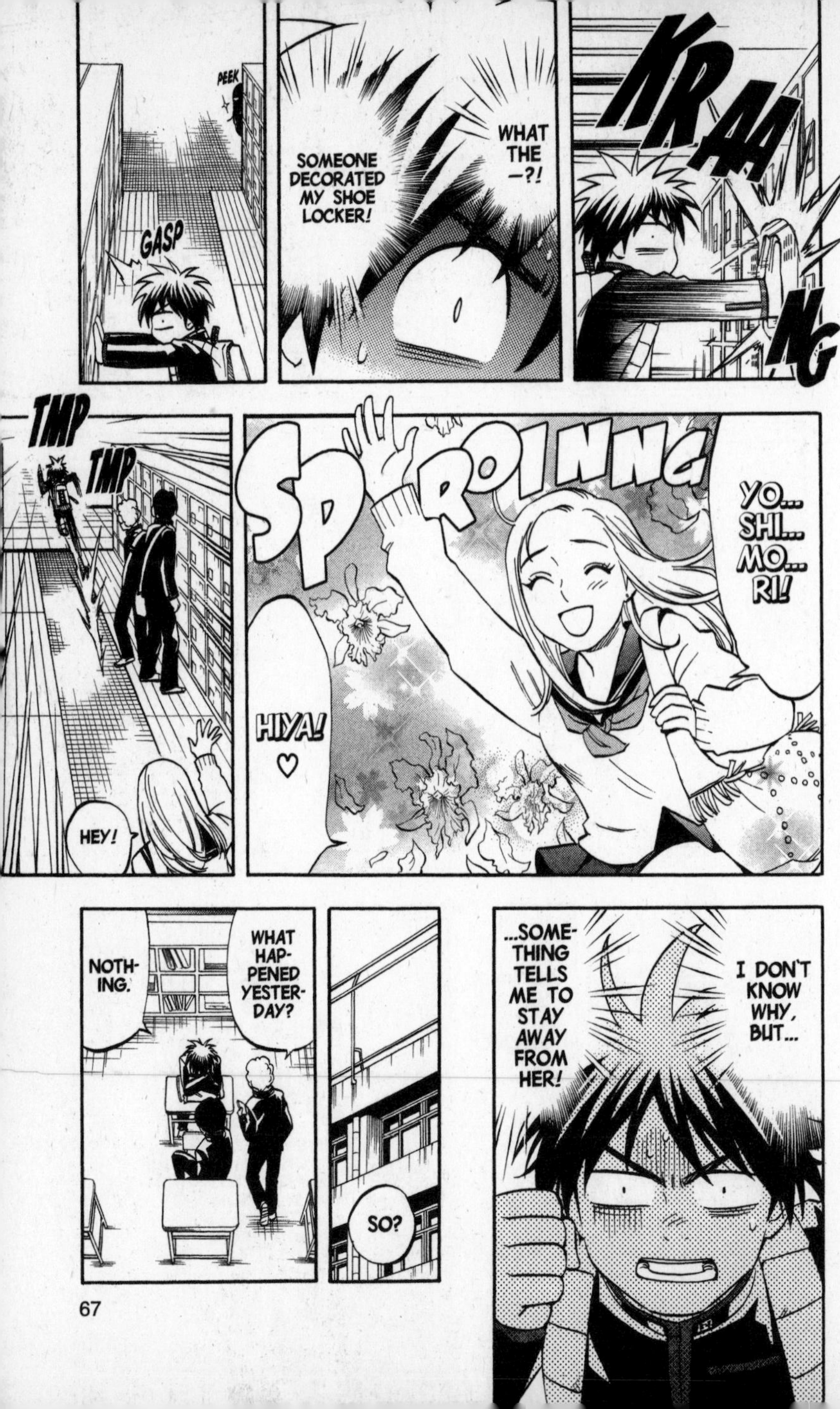
KRAA
NG
WHAT THE—?!
SOMEONE DECORATED MY SHOE LOCKER!
PEEK
GASP
YO... SHI... MO... RI!
SPROINNG
HIYA! ♡
TMP
TMP
HEY!
I DON'T KNOW WHY, BUT...
...SOMETHING TELLS ME TO STAY AWAY FROM HER!
SO?
WHAT HAPPENED YESTERDAY?
NOTHING.

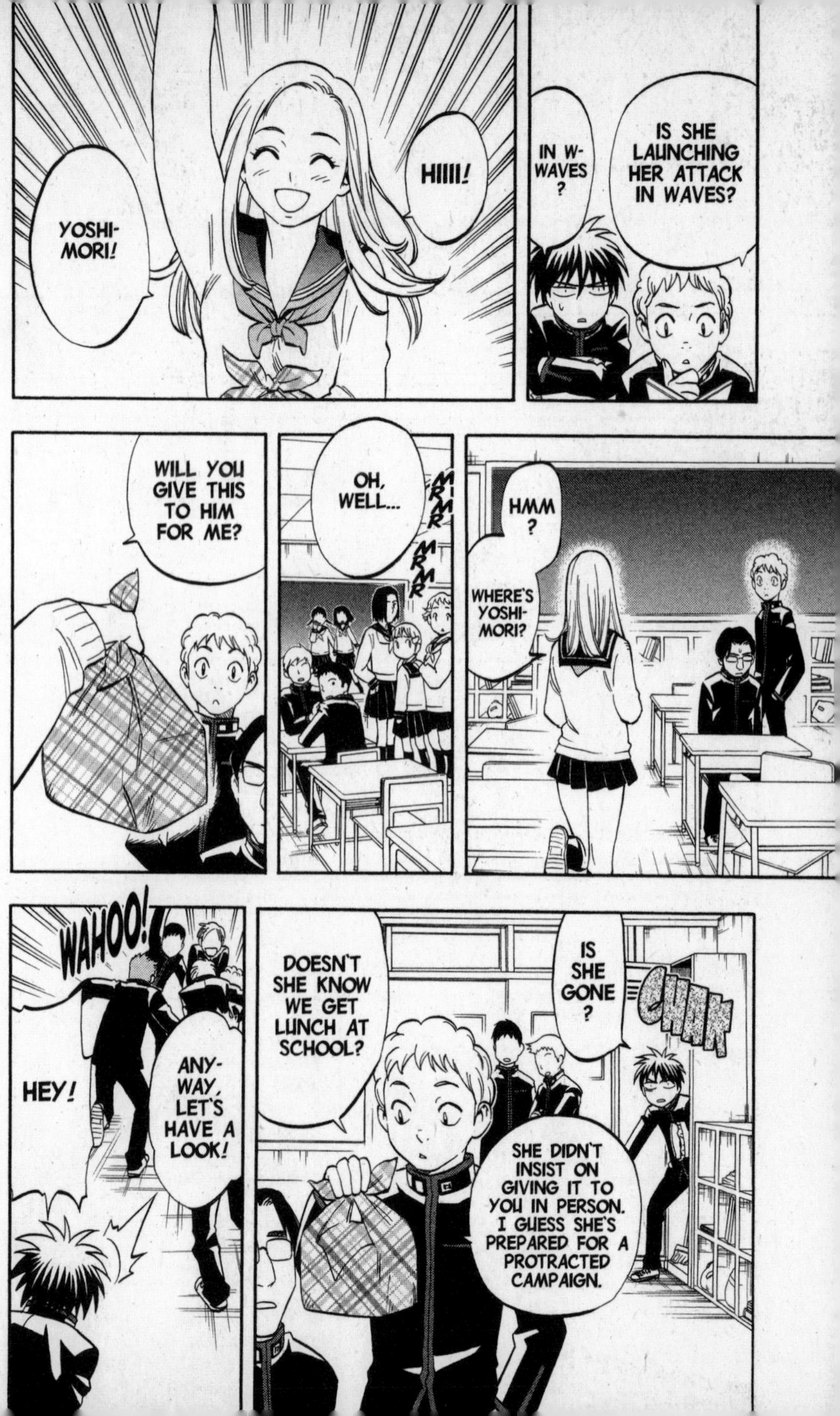
IS SHE LAUNCHING HER ATTACK IN WAVES?
IN W-WAVES?
HIIII!
YOSHI-MORI!
HMM?
WHERE'S YOSHI-MORI?
OH, WELL...
MRMR MRMR
WILL YOU GIVE THIS TO HIM FOR ME?
IS SHE GONE?
DOESN'T SHE KNOW WE GET LUNCH AT SCHOOL?
SHE DIDN'T INSIST ON GIVING IT TO YOU IN PERSON. I GUESS SHE'S PREPARED FOR A PROTRACTED CAMPAIGN.
WAHOO!
ANYWAY, LET'S HAVE A LOOK!
HEY!

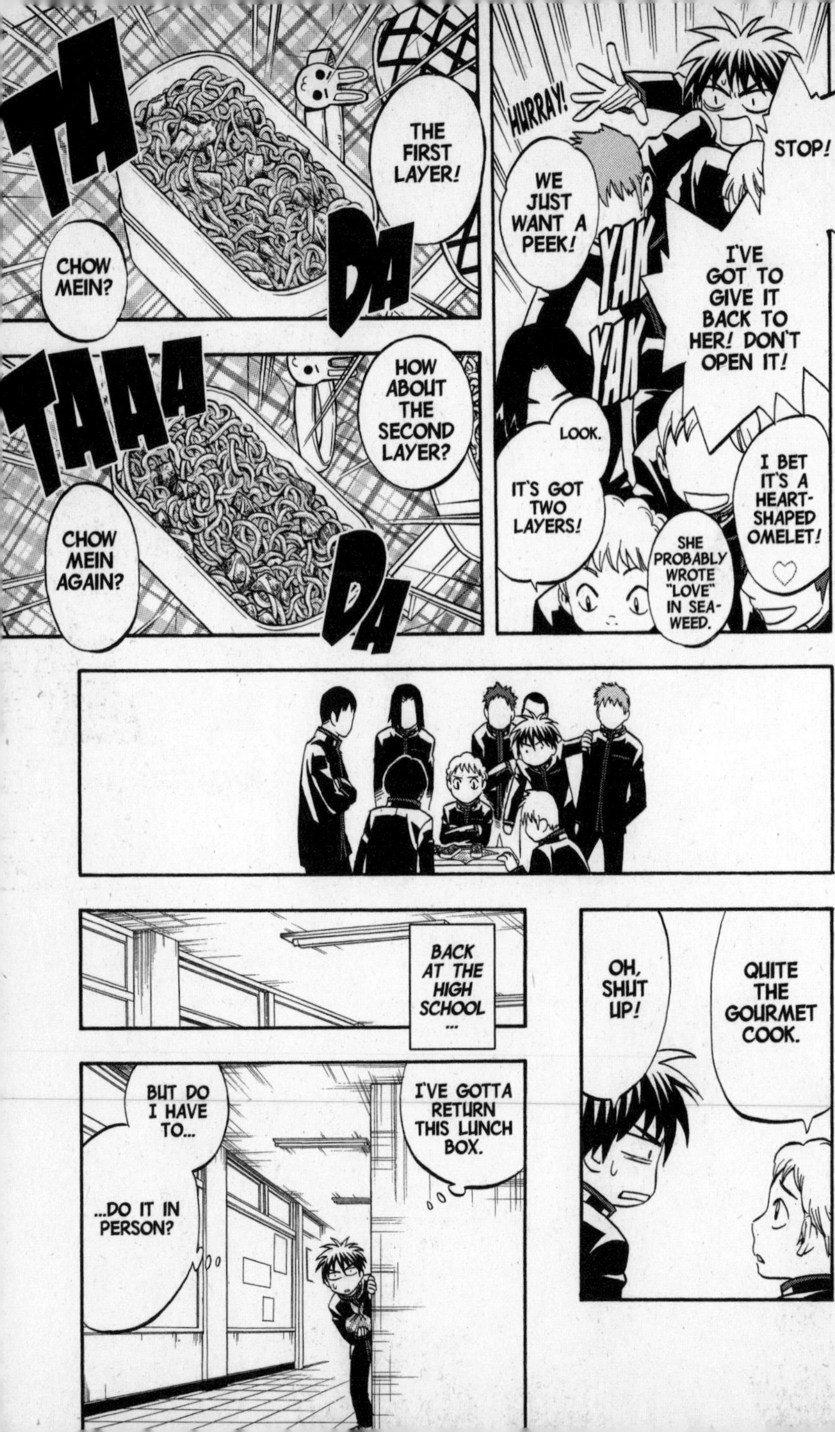
STOP!
HURRAY!
WE JUST WANT A PEEK!
YAK YAK
I'VE GOT TO GIVE IT BACK TO HER! DON'T OPEN IT!
I BET IT'S A HEART-SHAPED OMELET!
SHE PROBABLY WROTE "LOVE" IN SEA-WEED.
LOOK.
IT'S GOT TWO LAYERS!
THE FIRST LAYER!
TA DA
CHOW MEIN?
HOW ABOUT THE SECOND LAYER?
TAAA DA
CHOW MEIN AGAIN?
QUITE THE GOURMET COOK.
OH, SHUT UP!
BACK AT THE HIGH SCHOOL ...
I'VE GOTTA RETURN THIS LUNCH BOX.
BUT DO I HAVE TO...
...DO IT IN PERSON?

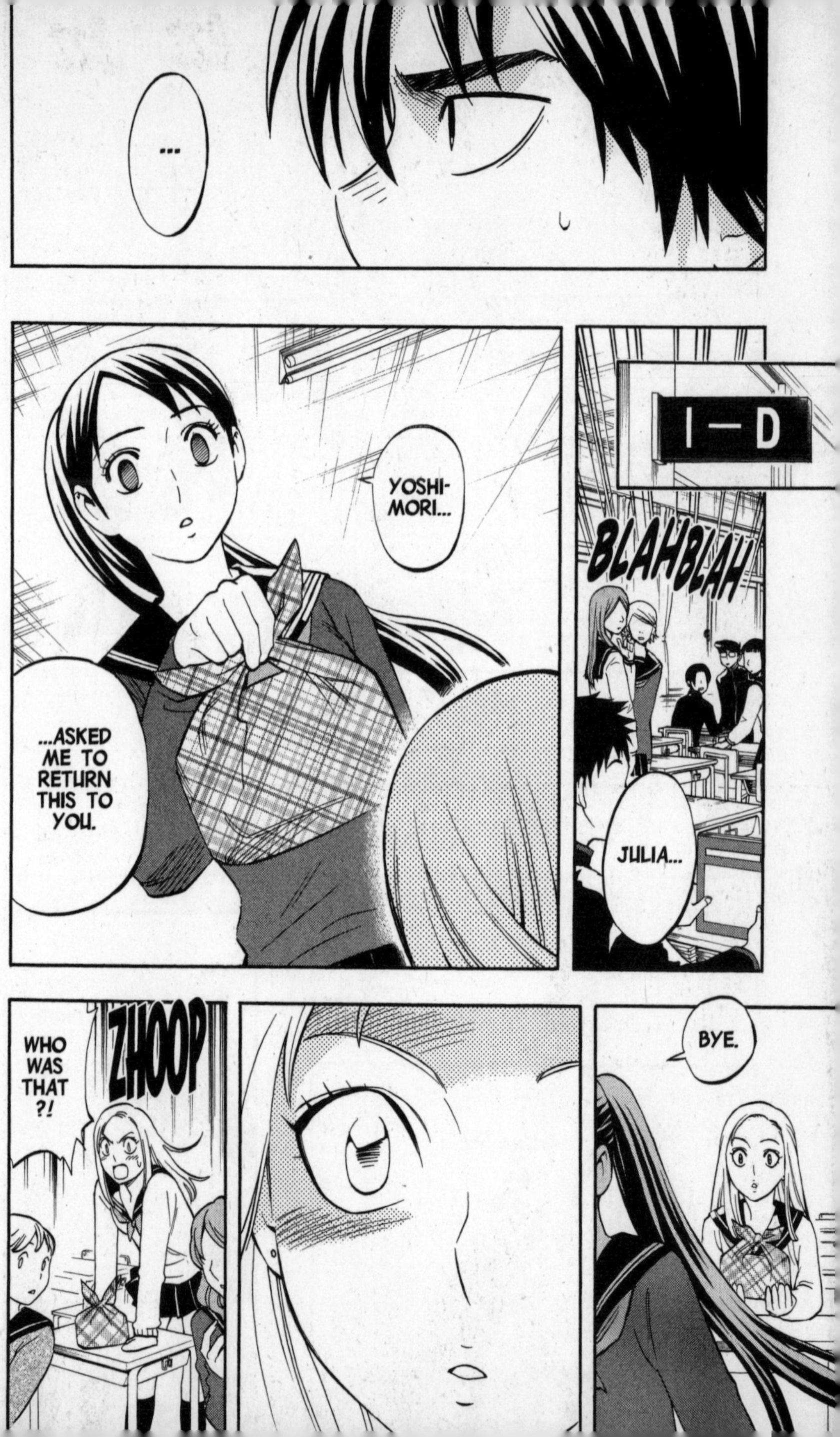
...
I-D
BLAHBLAH
JULIA...
YOSHI-MORI...
...ASKED ME TO RETURN THIS TO YOU.
BYE.
ZHOOP
WHO WAS THAT ?!

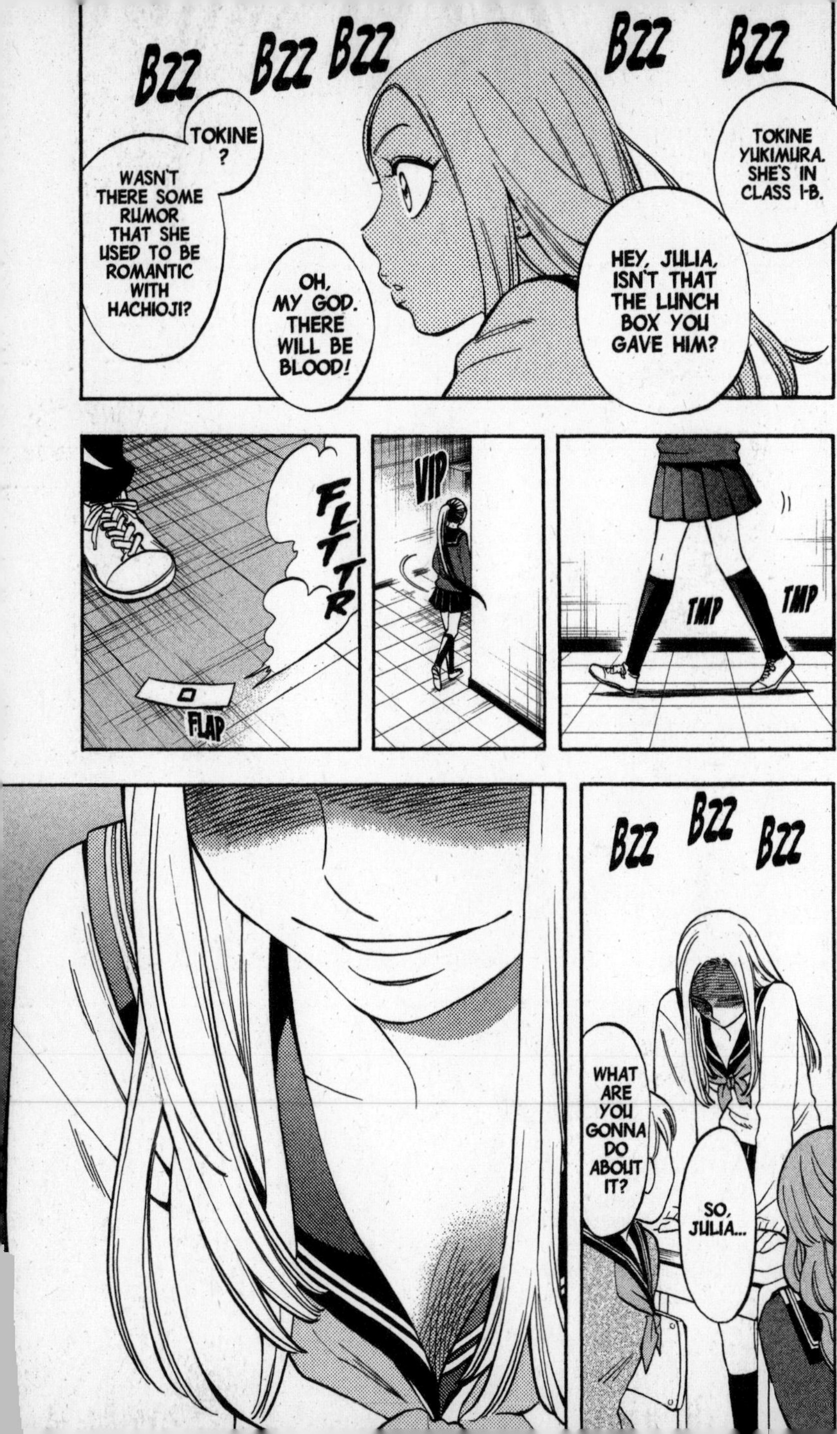
BZZ
BZZ
TOKINE YUKIMURA. SHE'S IN CLASS 1-B.
HEY, JULIA, ISN'T THAT THE LUNCH BOX YOU GAVE HIM?
BZZ
BZZ
BZZ
OH, MY GOD. THERE WILL BE BLOOD!
TOKINE?
WASN'T THERE SOME RUMOR THAT SHE USED TO BE ROMANTIC WITH HACHIOJI?
TMP
TMP
VIP
FLTTR
FLAP
BZZ
BZZ
BZZ
SO, JULIA...
WHAT ARE YOU GONNA DO ABOUT IT?

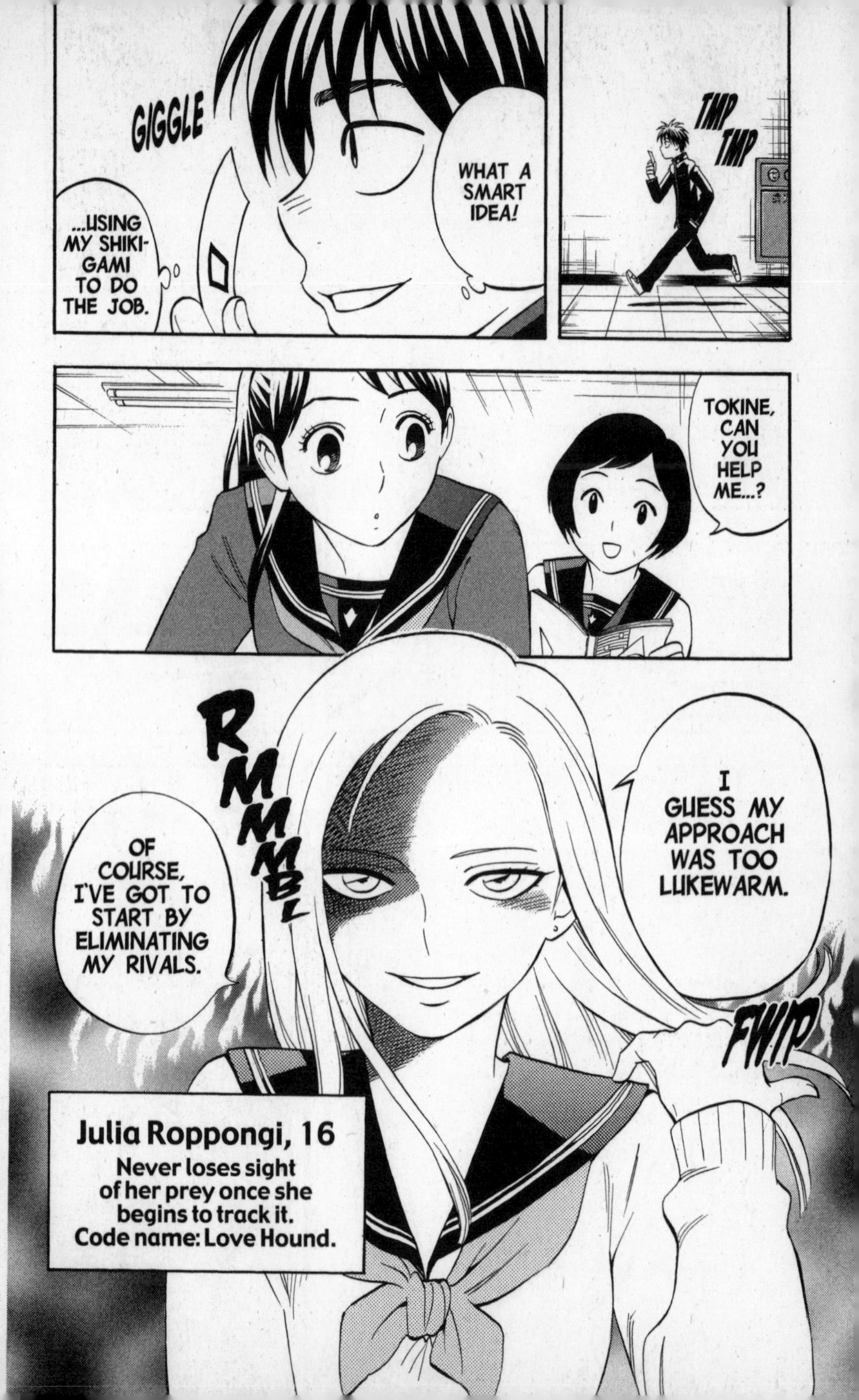
TMP TMP
WHAT A SMART IDEA!
GIGGLE
...USING MY SHIKI-GAMI TO DO THE JOB.
TOKINE, CAN YOU HELP ME...?
I GUESS MY APPROACH WAS TOO LUKEWARM.
RMMMBL
OF COURSE, I'VE GOT TO START BY ELIMINATING MY RIVALS.
FWIP
Julia Roppongi, 16
Never loses sight of her prey once she begins to track it. Code name: Love Hound.

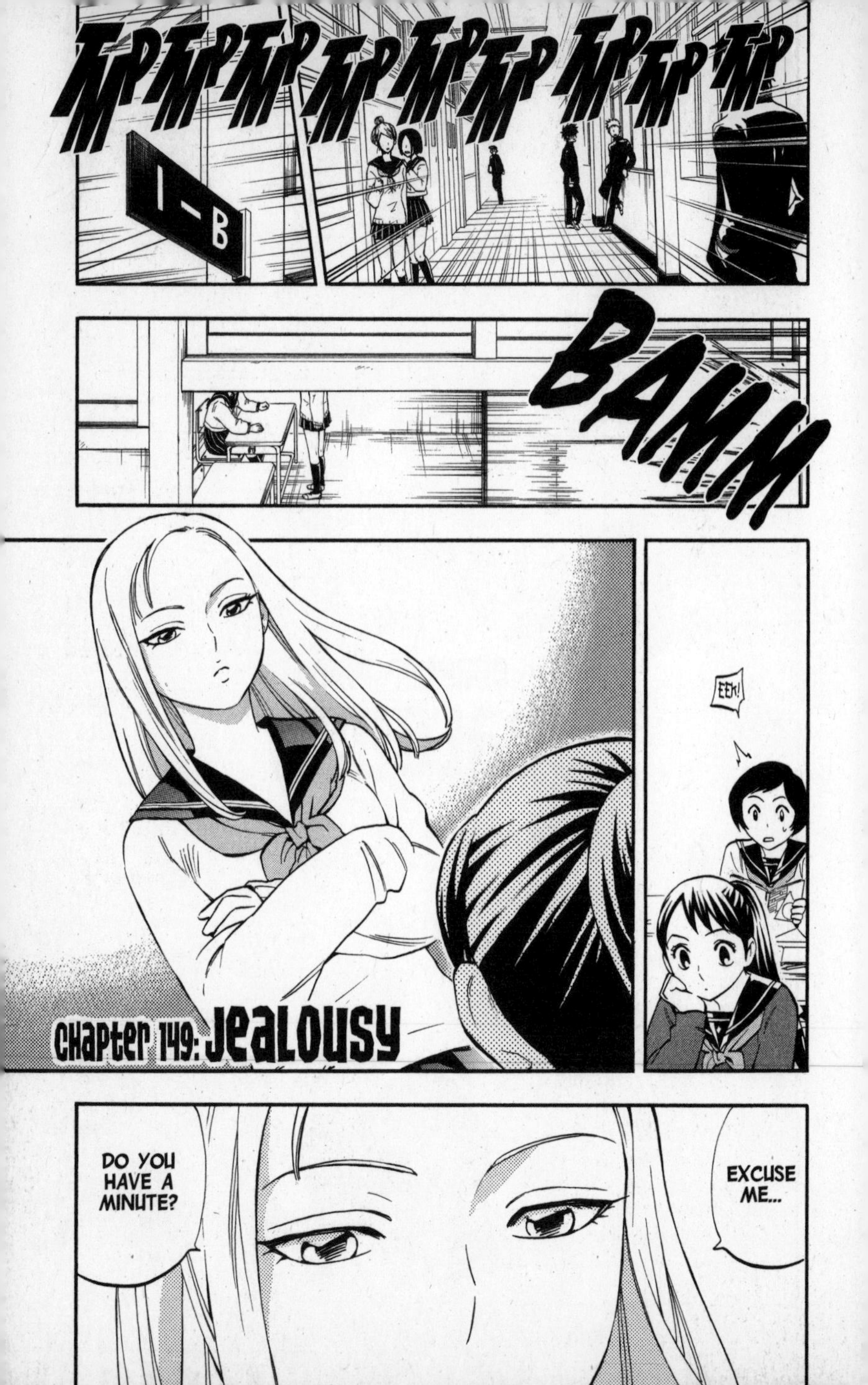

TMP TMP TMP TMP TMP TMP TMP TMP TMP TMP
1-B
BAMM
EEK!
Chapter 149: Jealousy
EXCUSE ME...
DO YOU HAVE A MINUTE?

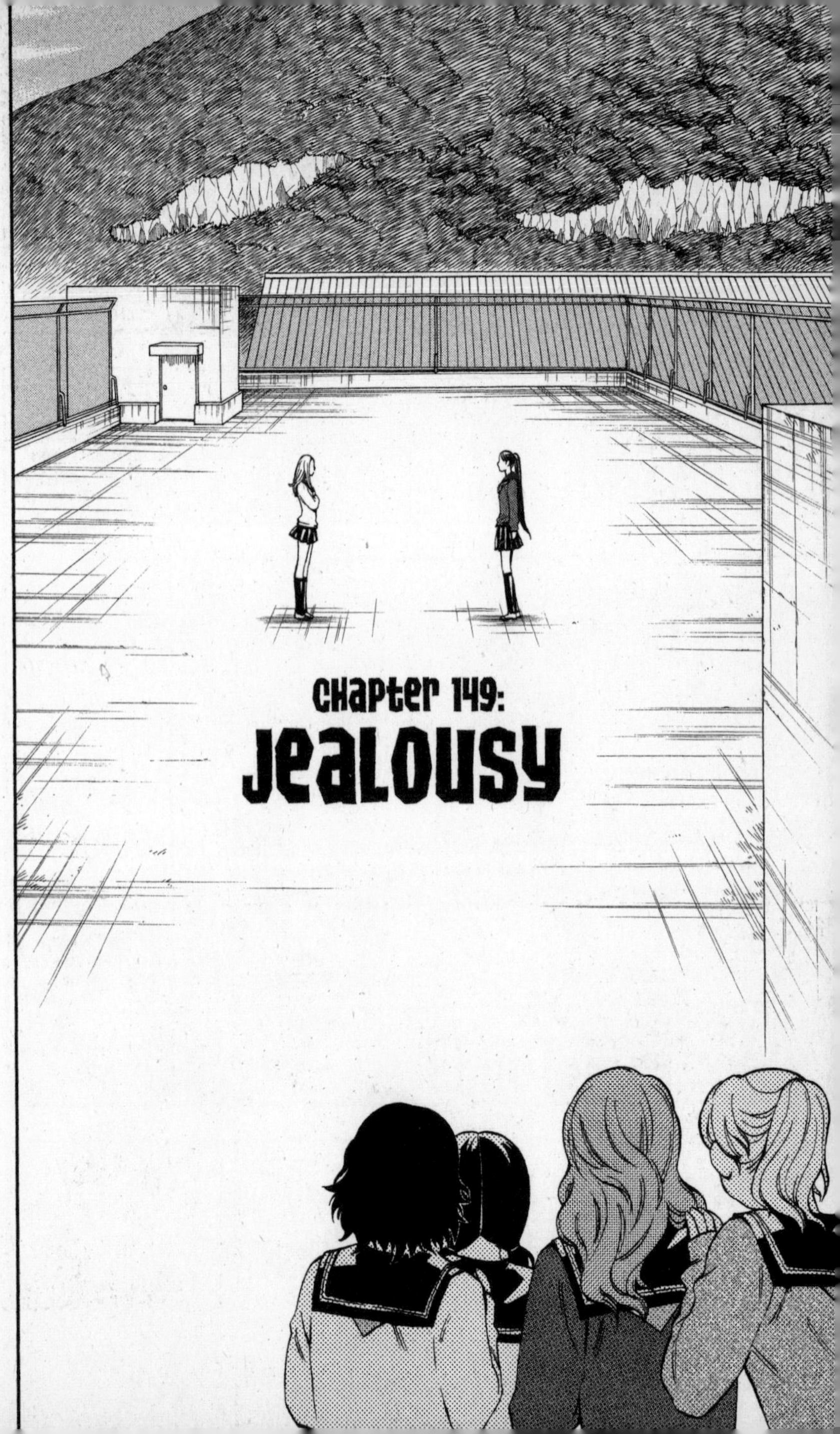
Chapter 149:
Jealousy

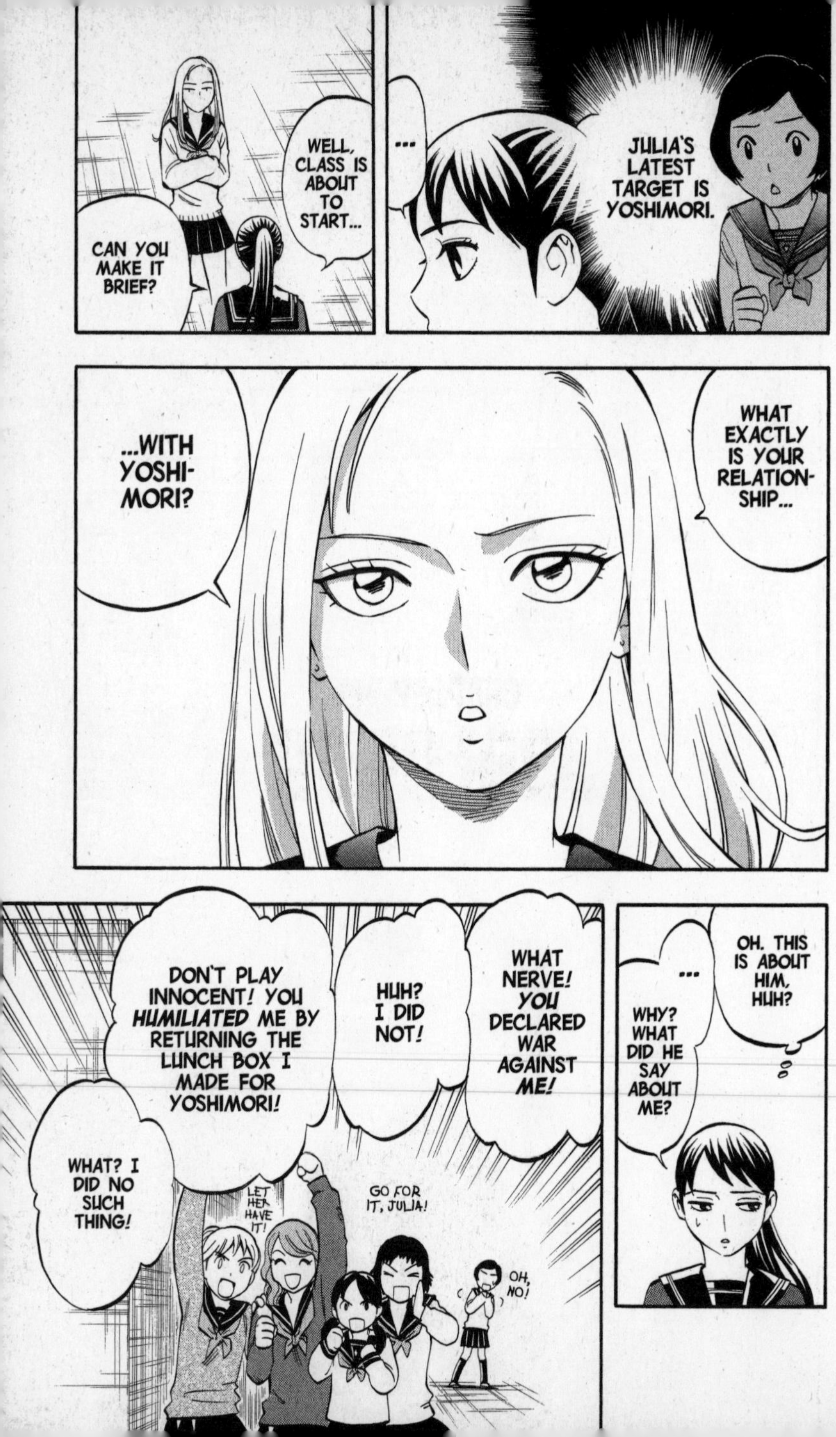
JULIA'S LATEST TARGET IS YOSHIMORI.
...
WELL, CLASS IS ABOUT TO START...
CAN YOU MAKE IT BRIEF?
WHAT EXACTLY IS YOUR RELATIONSHIP...
...WITH YOSHIMORI?
OH. THIS IS ABOUT HIM, HUH?
...
WHY? WHAT DID HE SAY ABOUT ME?
WHAT NERVE! YOU DECLARED WAR AGAINST ME!
HUH? I DID NOT!
DON'T PLAY INNOCENT! YOU HUMILIATED ME BY RETURNING THE LUNCH BOX I MADE FOR YOSHIMORI!
WHAT? I DID NO SUCH THING!
OH, NO!
GO FOR IT, JULIA!
LET HER HAVE IT!

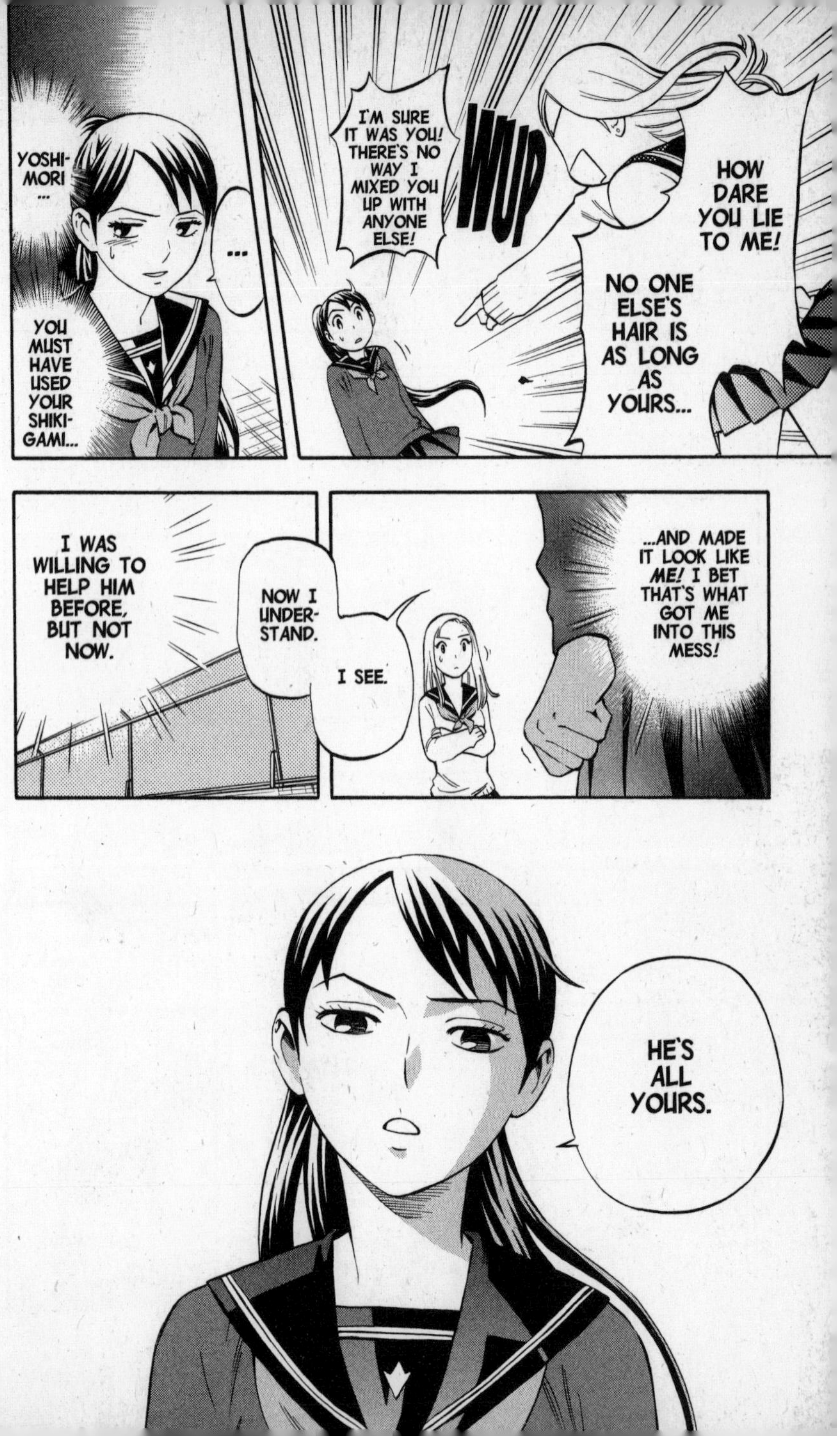
HOW DARE YOU LIE TO ME!
NO ONE ELSE'S HAIR IS AS LONG AS YOURS...
WUP
I'M SURE IT WAS YOU! THERE'S NO WAY I MIXED YOU UP WITH ANYONE ELSE!
...
YOSHIMORI ...
YOU MUST HAVE USED YOUR SHIKIGAMI...
...AND MADE IT LOOK LIKE ME! I BET THAT'S WHAT GOT ME INTO THIS MESS!
NOW I UNDERSTAND.
I SEE.
I WAS WILLING TO HELP HIM BEFORE, BUT NOT NOW.
HE'S ALL YOURS.

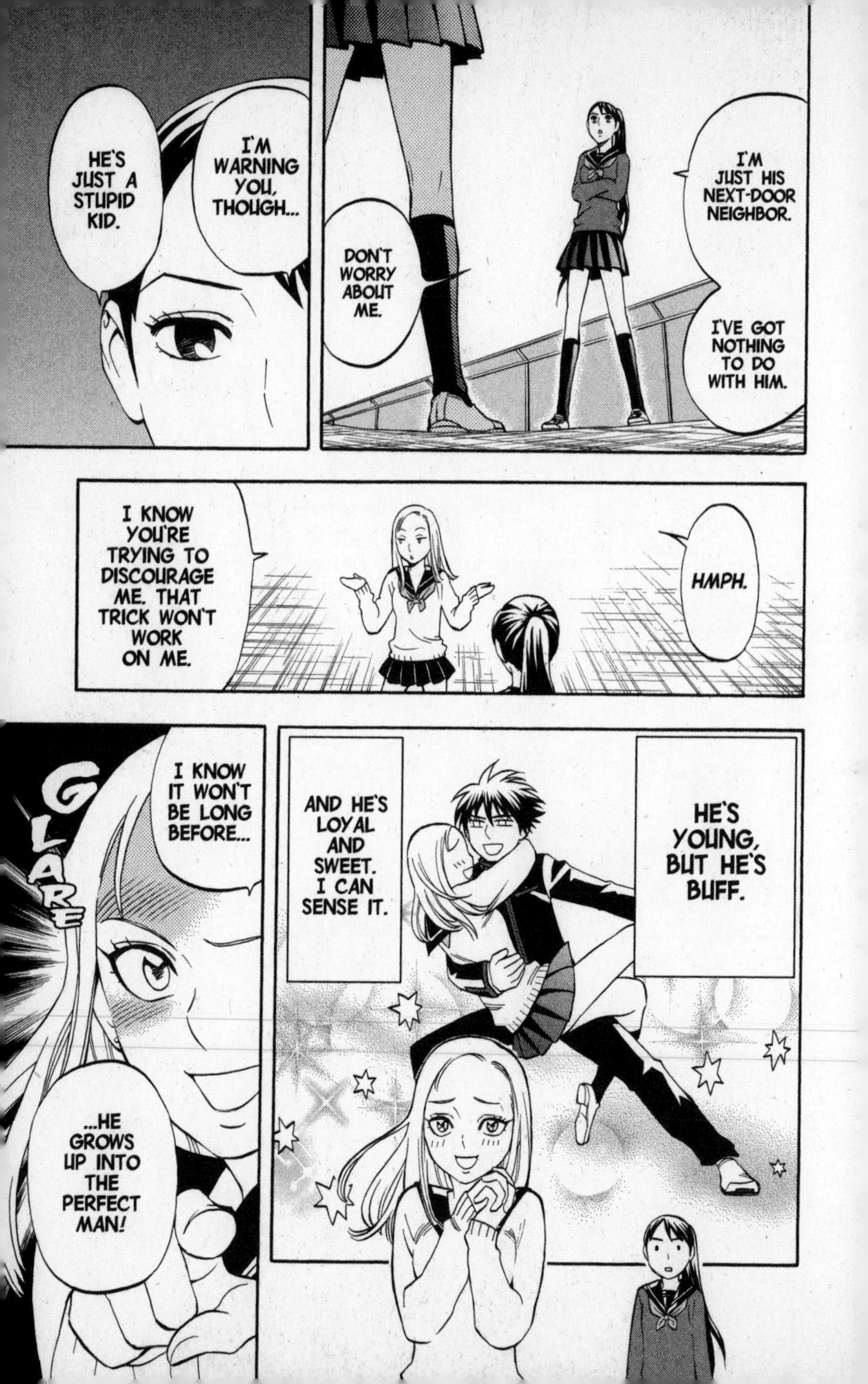
I'M JUST HIS NEXT-DOOR NEIGHBOR.
I'VE GOT NOTHING TO DO WITH HIM.
DON'T WORRY ABOUT ME.
I'M WARNING YOU, THOUGH...
HE'S JUST A STUPID KID.
HMPH.
I KNOW YOU'RE TRYING TO DISCOURAGE ME. THAT TRICK WON'T WORK ON ME.
HE'S YOUNG, BUT HE'S BUFF.
AND HE'S LOYAL AND SWEET. I CAN SENSE IT.
I KNOW IT WON'T BE LONG BEFORE...
GLARE
...HE GROWS UP INTO THE PERFECT MAN!

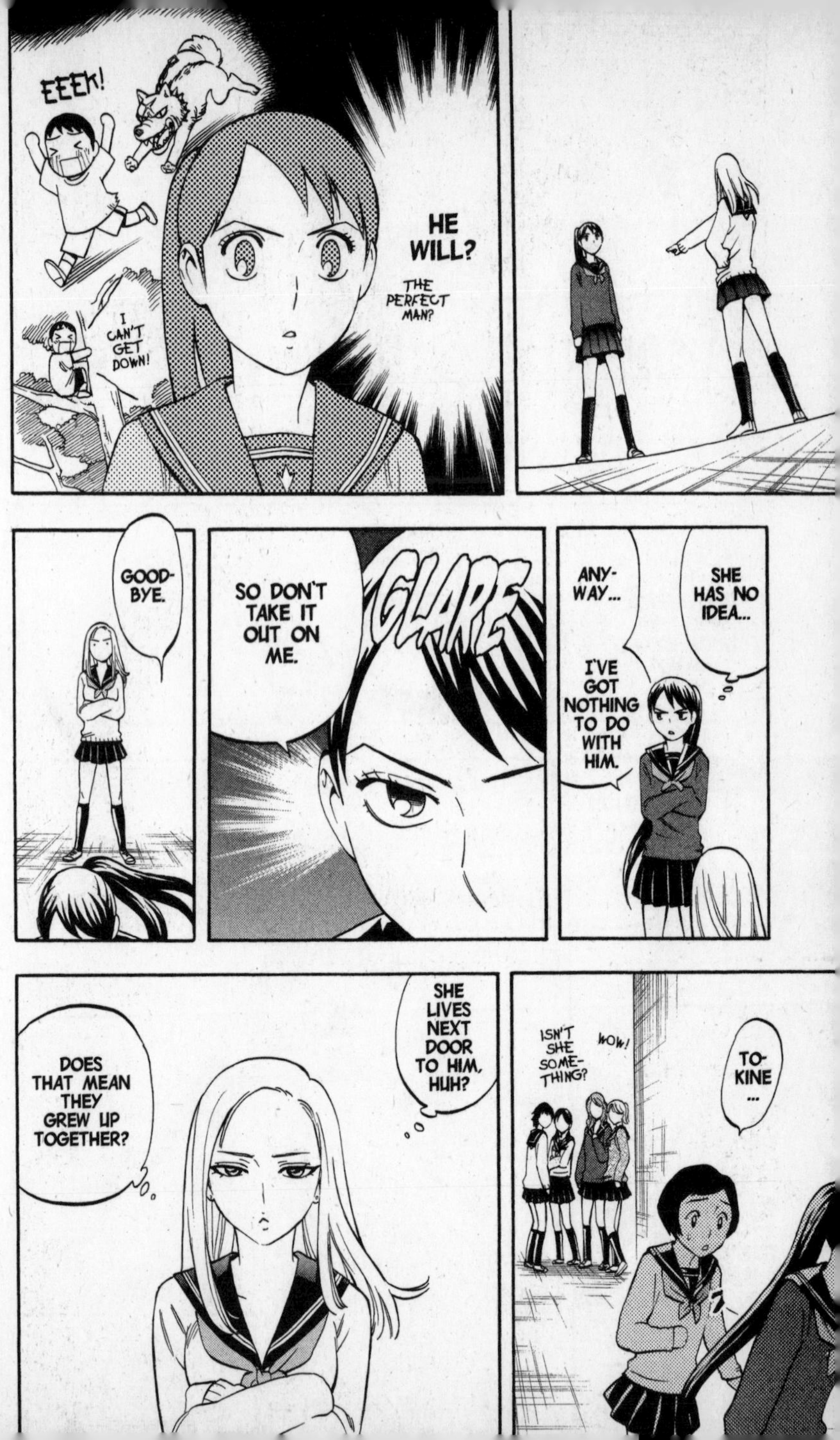
HE WILL?
THE PERFECT MAN?
EEEK!
I CAN'T GET DOWN!
SHE HAS NO IDEA...
ANY-WAY...
I'VE GOT NOTHING TO DO WITH HIM.
GLARE
SO DON'T TAKE IT OUT ON ME.
GOOD-BYE.
TO-KINE ...
WOW!
ISN'T SHE SOME-THING?
SHE LIVES NEXT DOOR TO HIM, HUH?
DOES THAT MEAN THEY GREW UP TOGETHER?

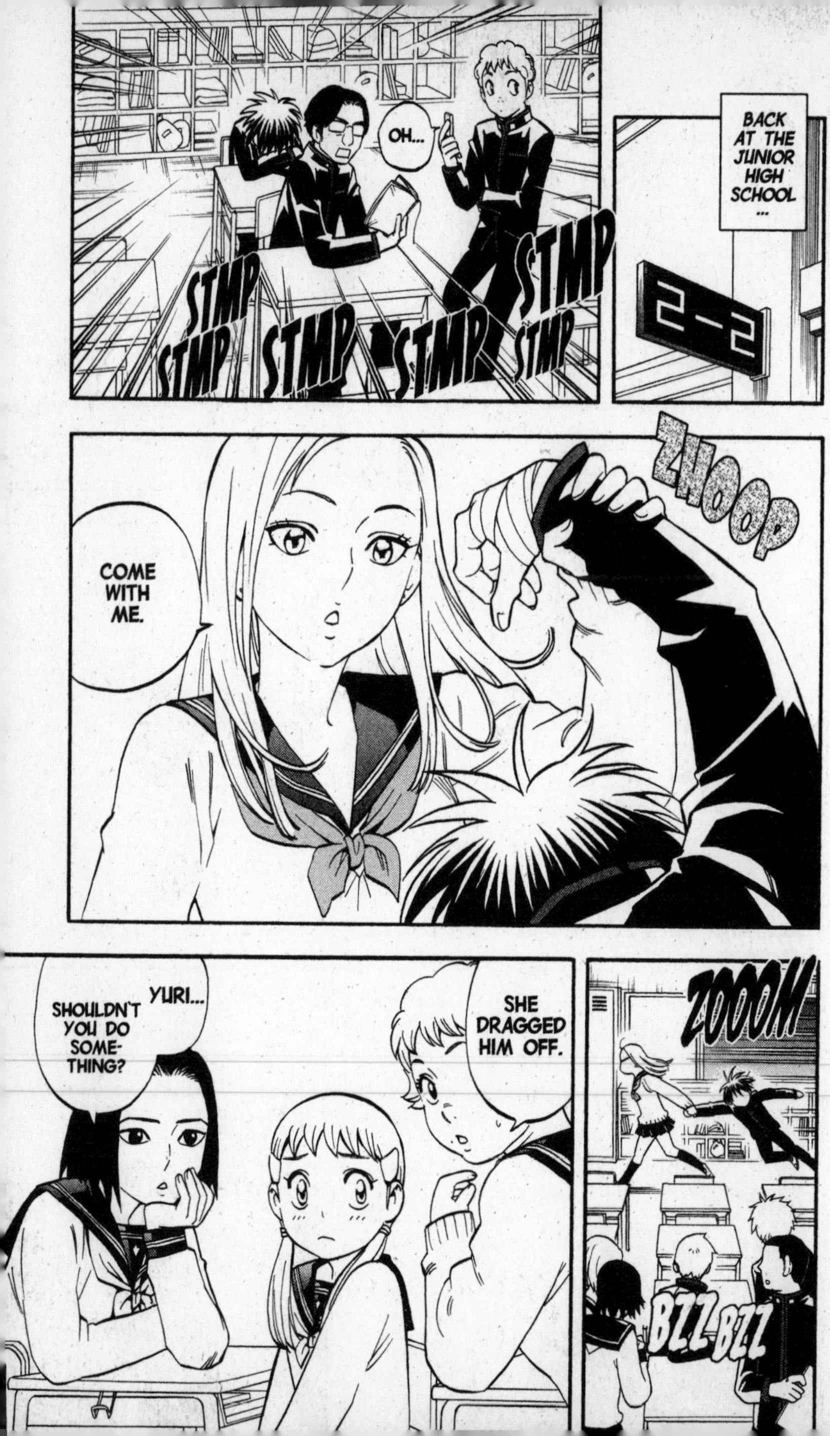
BACK AT THE JUNIOR HIGH SCHOOL ...
2-2
OH...
STMP STMP STMP STMP STMP STMP STMP
ZHOOP
COME WITH ME.
ZOOOM
BZZ BZZ
SHE DRAGGED HIM OFF.
YURI... SHOULDN'T YOU DO SOME-THING?

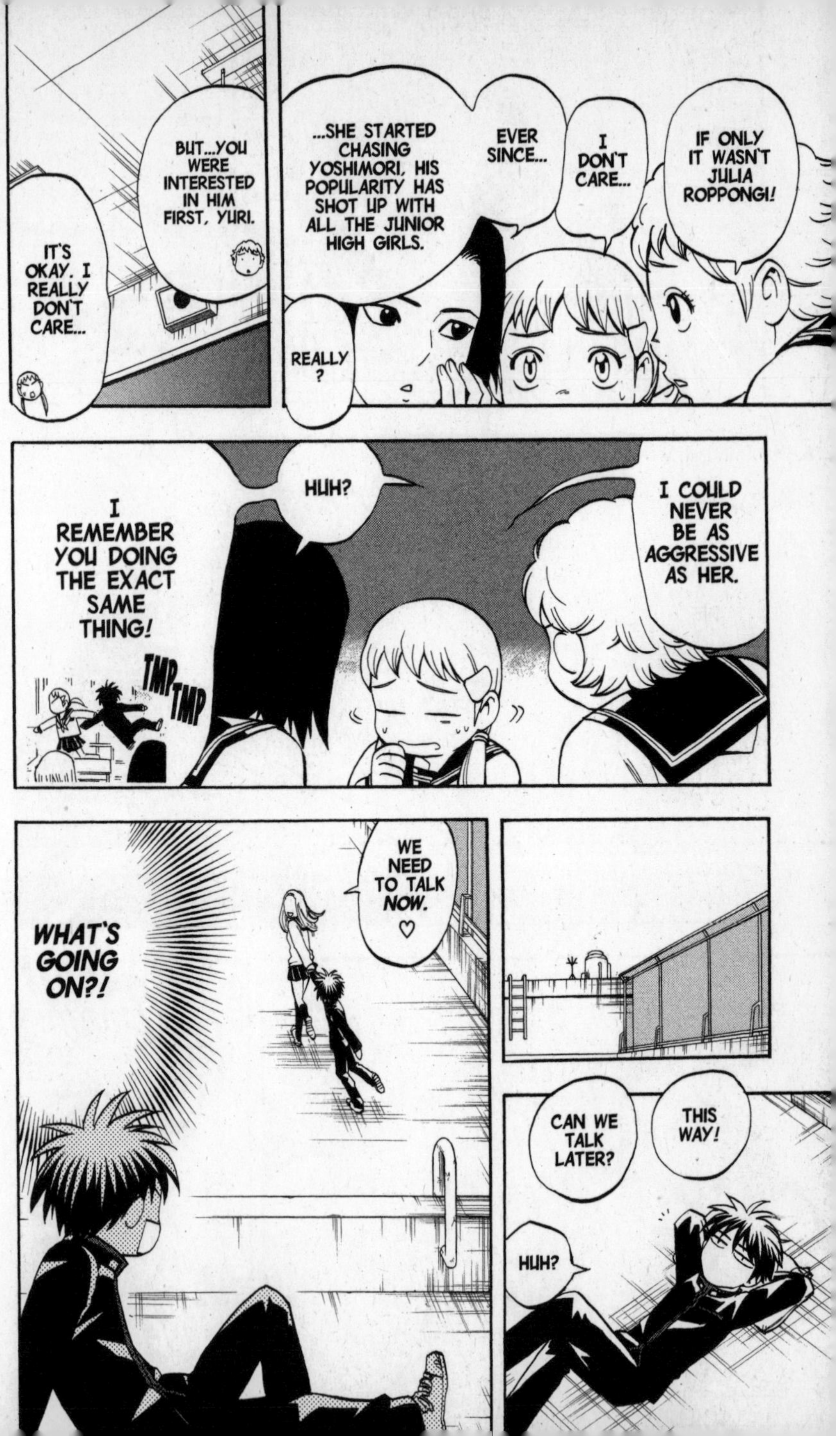
IF ONLY IT WASN'T JULIA ROPPONGI!
I DON'T CARE...
EVER SINCE...
...SHE STARTED CHASING YOSHIMORI, HIS POPULARITY HAS SHOT UP WITH ALL THE JUNIOR HIGH GIRLS.
REALLY?
BUT...YOU WERE INTERESTED IN HIM FIRST, YURI.
IT'S OKAY. I REALLY DON'T CARE...
I COULD NEVER BE AS AGGRESSIVE AS HER.
HUH?
I REMEMBER YOU DOING THE EXACT SAME THING!
TMP TMP
THIS WAY!
CAN WE TALK LATER?
HUH?
WE NEED TO TALK NOW. ♡
WHAT'S GOING ON?!

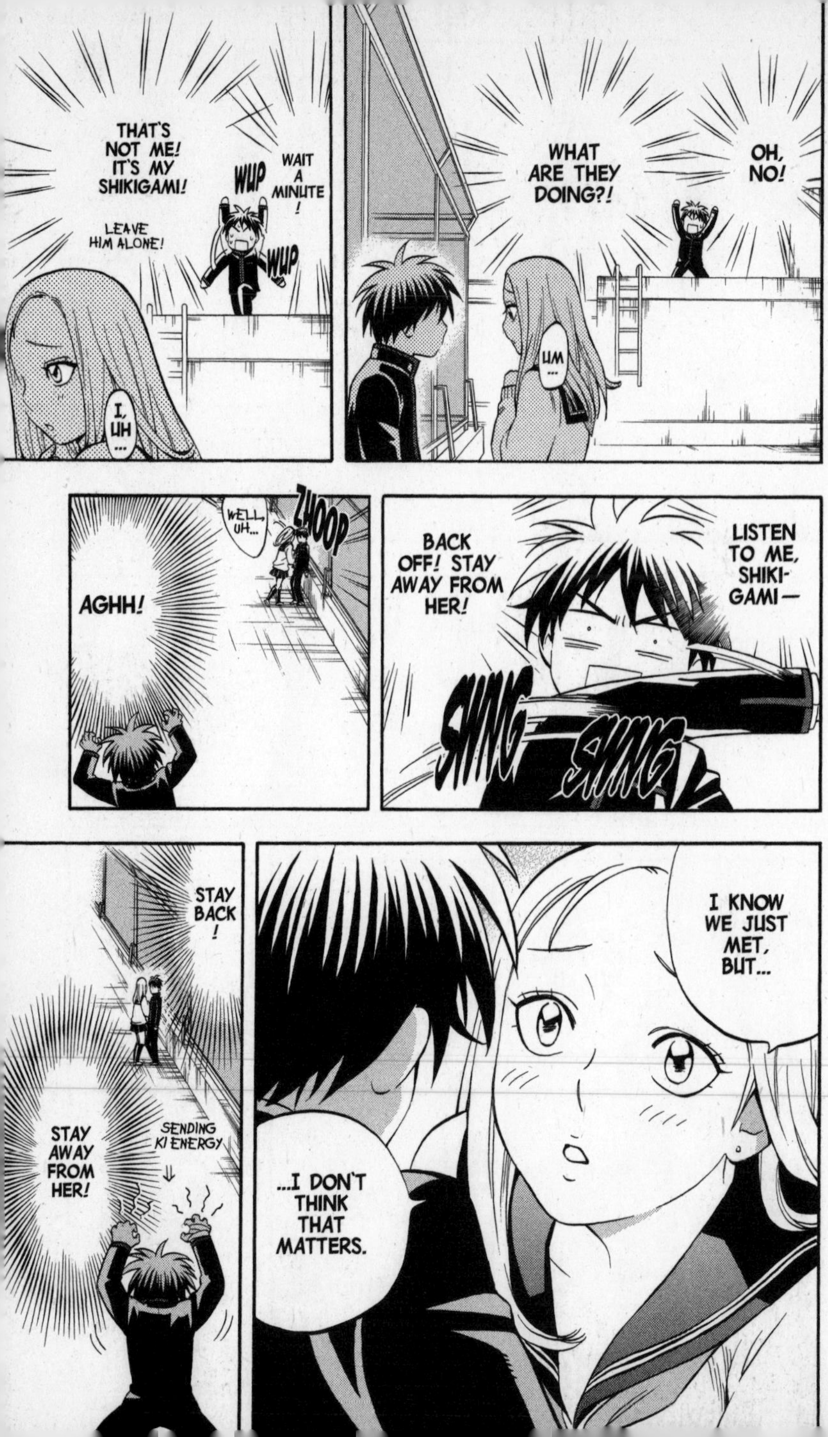
OH, NO!
WHAT ARE THEY DOING?!
UM...
WAIT A MINUTE!
WUP
THAT'S NOT ME! IT'S MY SHIKIGAMI!
LEAVE HIM ALONE!
WUP
I, UH...
LISTEN TO ME, SHIKI-GAMI—
BACK OFF! STAY AWAY FROM HER!
SHING
SHING
ZHOOP
WELL, UH...
AGHH!
I KNOW WE JUST MET, BUT...
...I DON'T THINK THAT MATTERS.
STAY BACK!
SENDING KI ENERGY
STAY AWAY FROM HER!

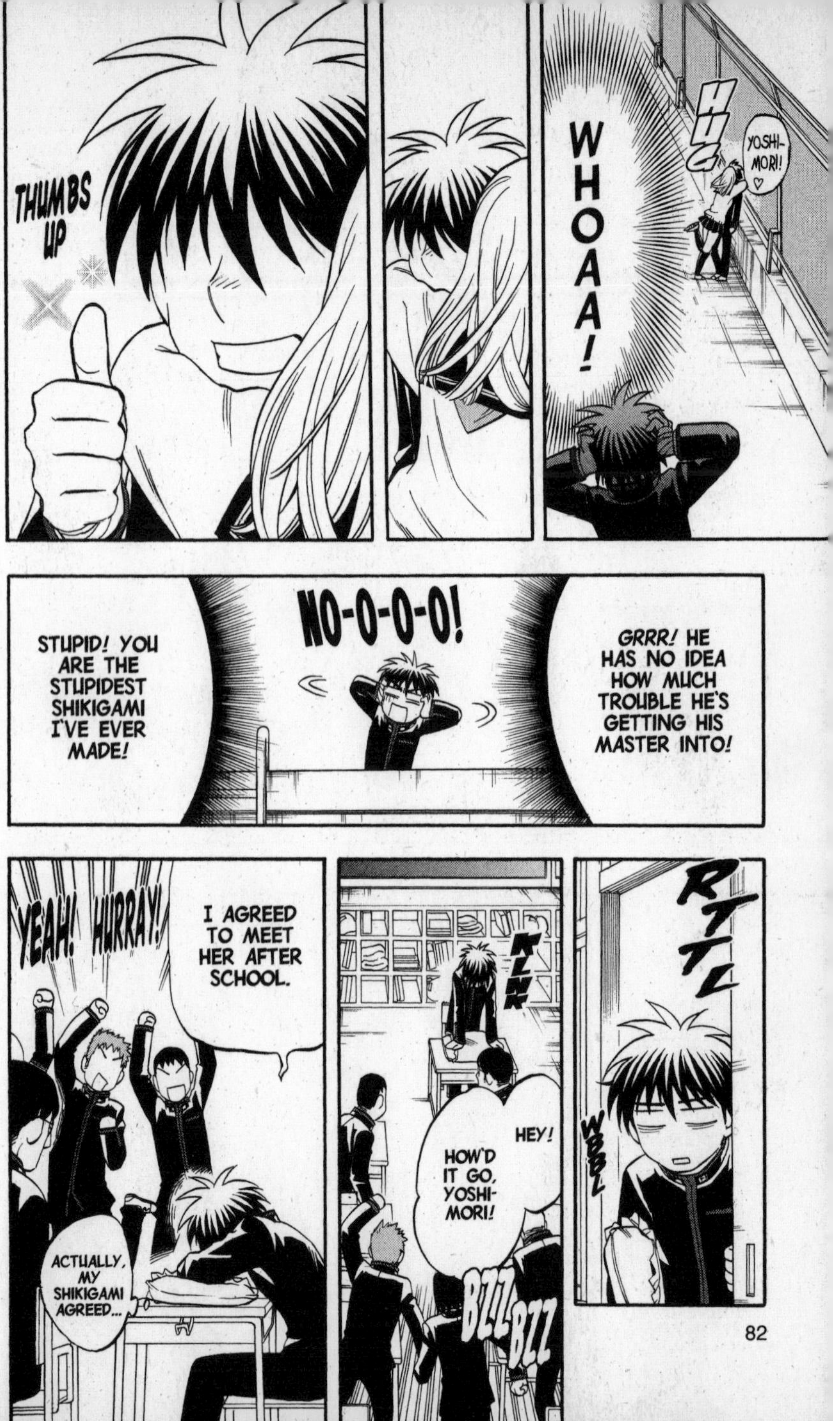
HUG
YOSHI-MORI! ♡
WHOAAA!
THUMBS UP
GRRR! HE HAS NO IDEA HOW MUCH TROUBLE HE'S GETTING HIS MASTER INTO!
NO-O-O-O!
STUPID! YOU ARE THE STUPIDEST SHIKIGAMI I'VE EVER MADE!
RTTL
WBBL
KLNK
HEY!
HOW'D IT GO, YOSHI-MORI!
BZZ BZZ
I AGREED TO MEET HER AFTER SCHOOL.
YEAH! HURRAY!
ACTUALLY, MY SHIKIGAMI AGREED...

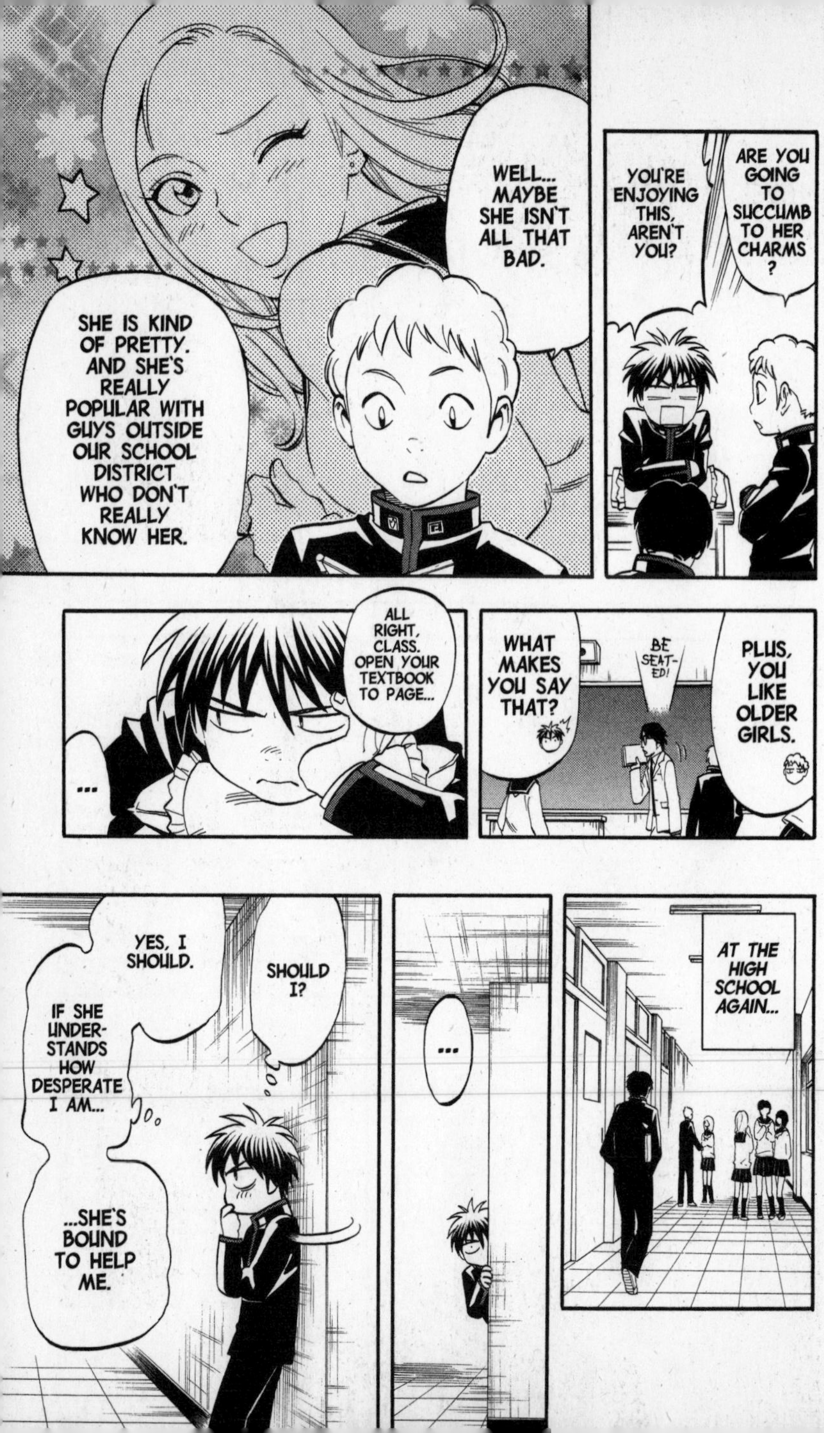
ARE YOU GOING TO SUCCUMB TO HER CHARMS?
YOU'RE ENJOYING THIS, AREN'T YOU?
WELL... MAYBE SHE ISN'T ALL THAT BAD.
SHE IS KIND OF PRETTY. AND SHE'S REALLY POPULAR WITH GUYS OUTSIDE OUR SCHOOL DISTRICT WHO DON'T REALLY KNOW HER.
PLUS, YOU LIKE OLDER GIRLS.
BE SEAT-ED!
WHAT MAKES YOU SAY THAT?
ALL RIGHT, CLASS. OPEN YOUR TEXTBOOK TO PAGE...
...
AT THE HIGH SCHOOL AGAIN...
...
SHOULD I?
YES, I SHOULD.
IF SHE UNDER-STANDS HOW DESPERATE I AM...
...SHE'S BOUND TO HELP ME.

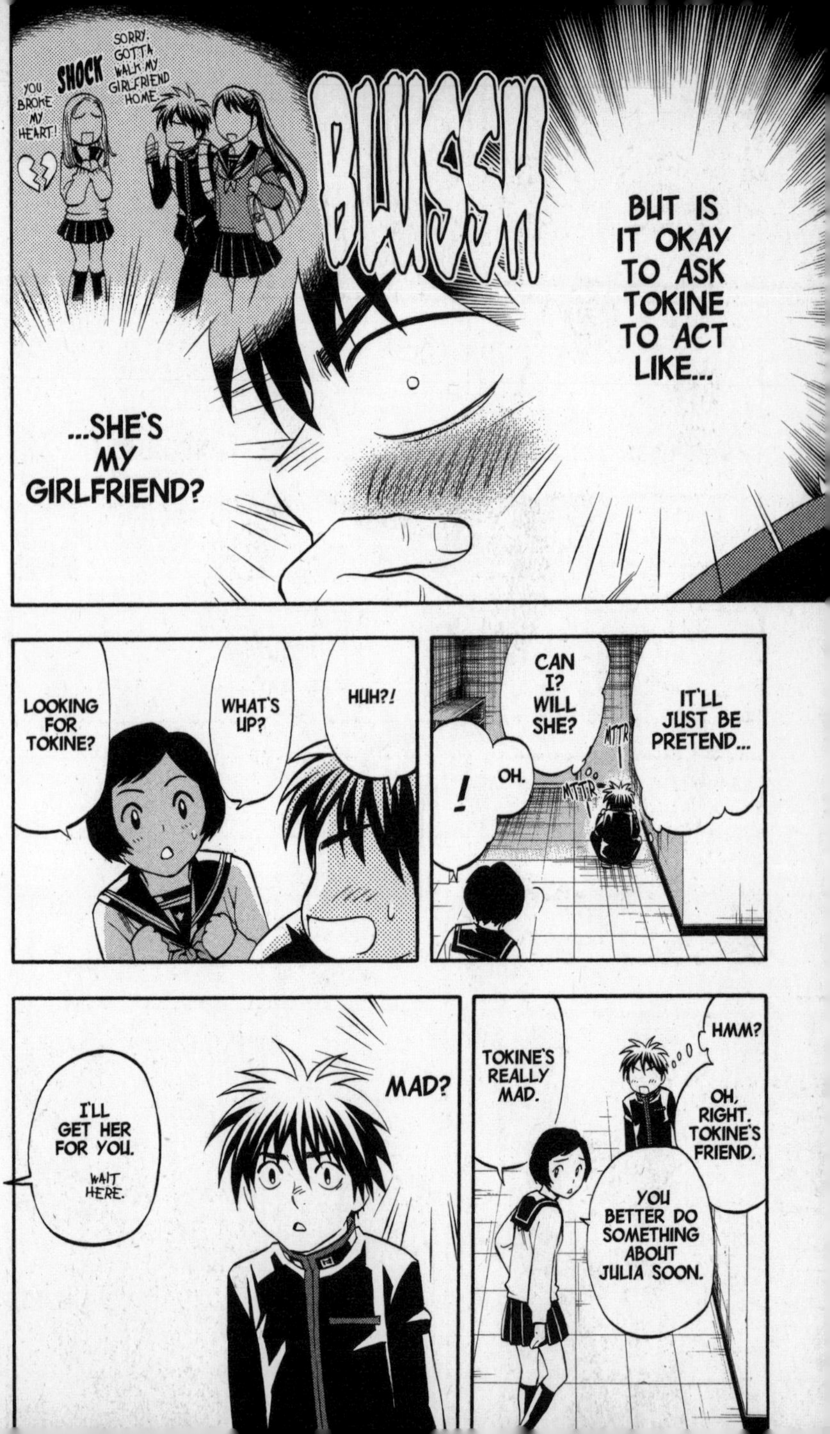
BUT IS IT OKAY TO ASK TOKINE TO ACT LIKE...
BWSCH
SORRY. GOTTA WALK MY GIRLFRIEND HOME.
SHOCK
YOU BROKE MY HEART!
...SHE'S MY GIRLFRIEND?
IT'LL JUST BE PRETEND...
CAN I? WILL SHE?
MTTR
MTTR
OH.
!
HUH?!
WHAT'S UP?
LOOKING FOR TOKINE?
HMM?
OH, RIGHT. TOKINE'S FRIEND.
TOKINE'S REALLY MAD.
YOU BETTER DO SOMETHING ABOUT JULIA SOON.
MAD?
I'LL GET HER FOR YOU.
WAIT HERE.

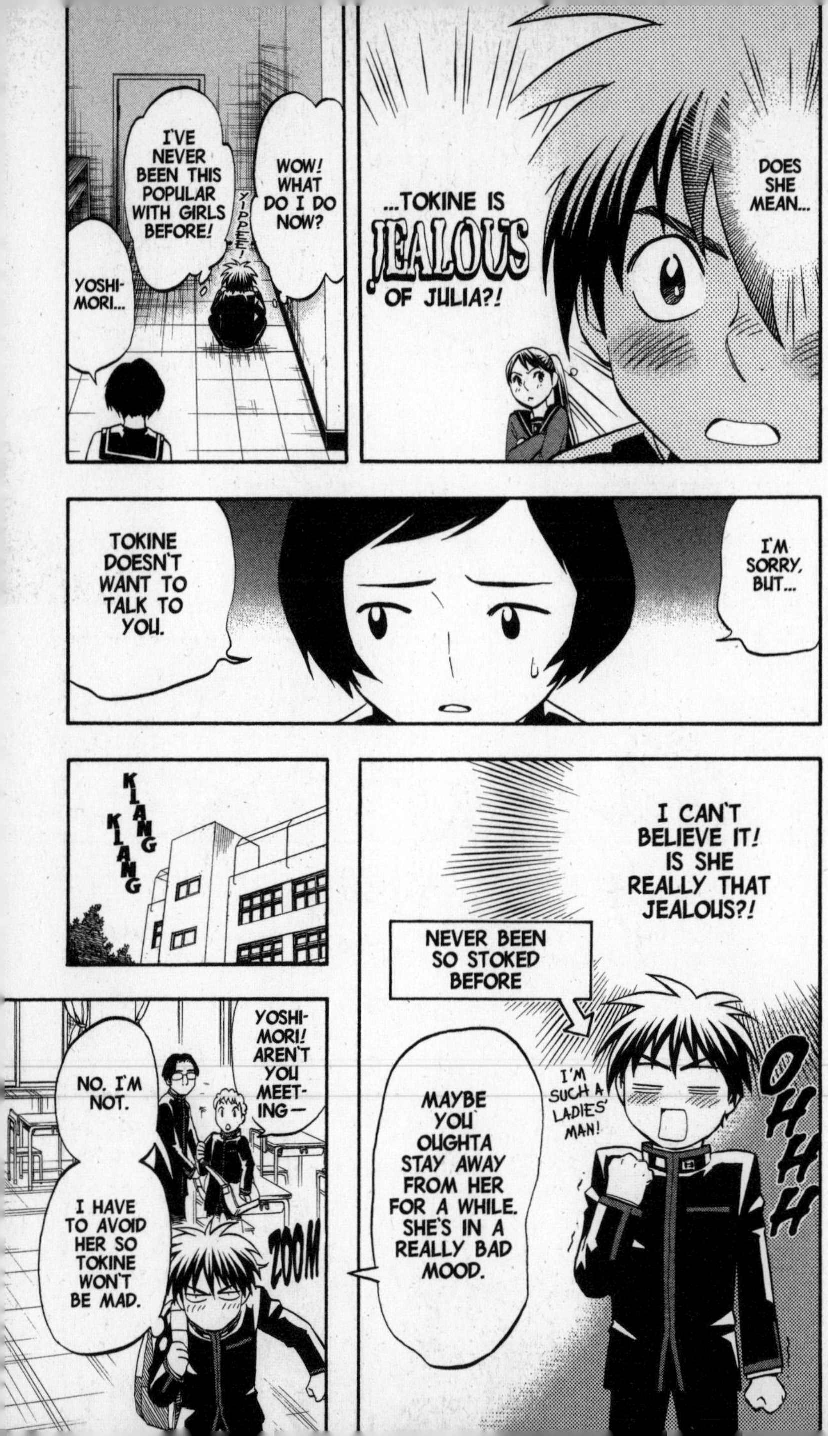
DOES SHE MEAN...
...TOKINE IS JEALOUS OF JULIA?!
WOW! WHAT DO I DO NOW?
I'VE NEVER BEEN THIS POPULAR WITH GIRLS BEFORE!
YIPPEE!
YOSHI-MORI...
I'M SORRY, BUT...
TOKINE DOESN'T WANT TO TALK TO YOU.
I CAN'T BELIEVE IT! IS SHE REALLY THAT JEALOUS?!
NEVER BEEN SO STOKED BEFORE
OHHHH
I'M SUCH A LADIES' MAN!
MAYBE YOU OUGHTA STAY AWAY FROM HER FOR A WHILE. SHE'S IN A REALLY BAD MOOD.
KLANG KLANG
YOSHI-MORI! AREN'T YOU MEET-ING—
NO. I'M NOT.
I HAVE TO AVOID HER SO TOKINE WON'T BE MAD.
ZOOM

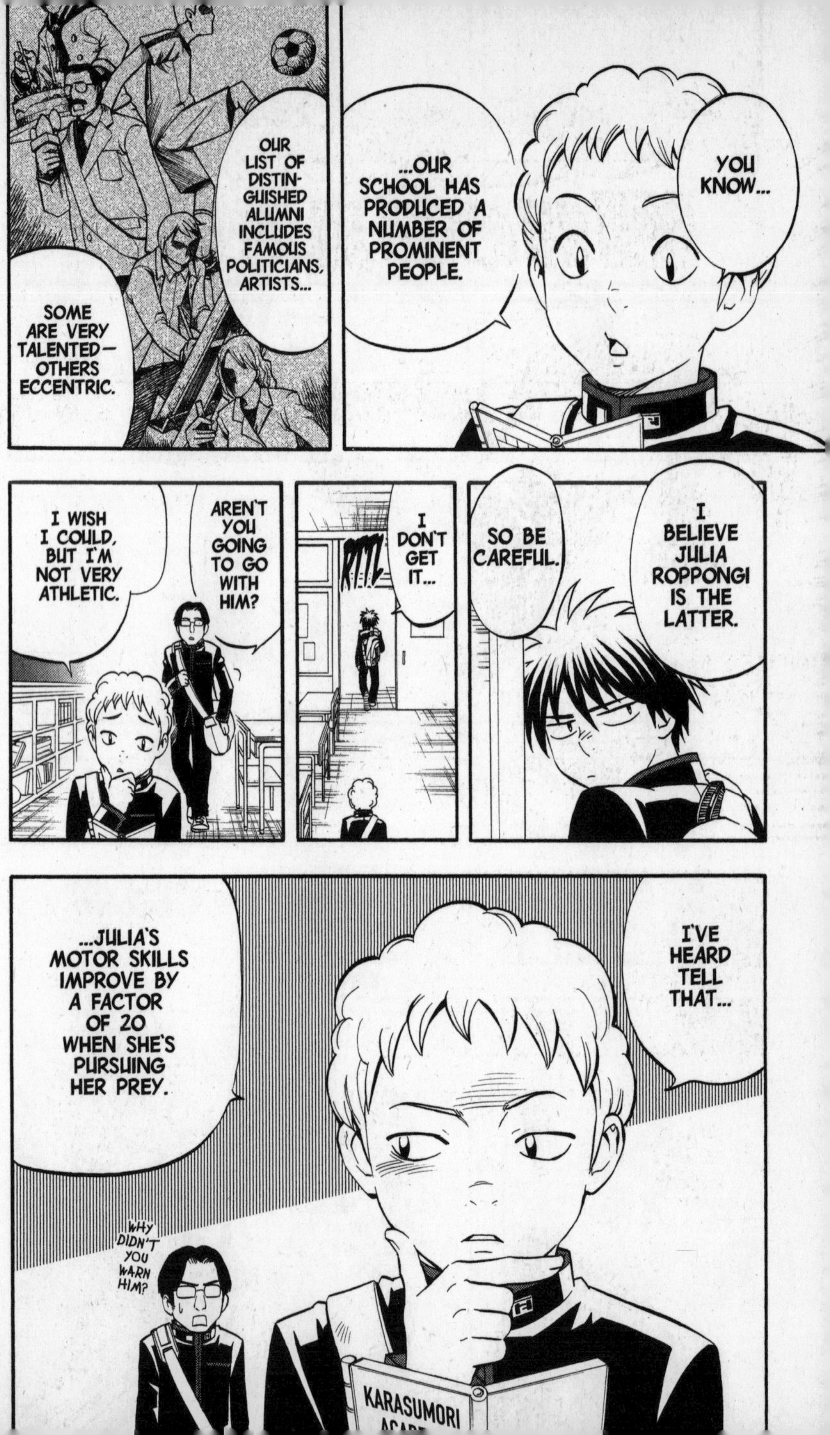
YOU KNOW...
...OUR SCHOOL HAS PRODUCED A NUMBER OF PROMINENT PEOPLE.
OUR LIST OF DISTIN-GUISHED ALUMNI INCLUDES FAMOUS POLITICIANS, ARTISTS...
SOME ARE VERY TALENTED—OTHERS ECCENTRIC.
I BELIEVE JULIA ROPPONGI IS THE LATTER.
SO BE CAREFUL.
I DON'T GET IT...
RTTL
AREN'T YOU GOING TO GO WITH HIM?
I WISH I COULD, BUT I'M NOT VERY ATHLETIC.
I'VE HEARD TELL THAT...
...JULIA'S MOTOR SKILLS IMPROVE BY A FACTOR OF 20 WHEN SHE'S PURSUING HER PREY.
WHY DIDN'T YOU WARN HIM?
KARASUMORI

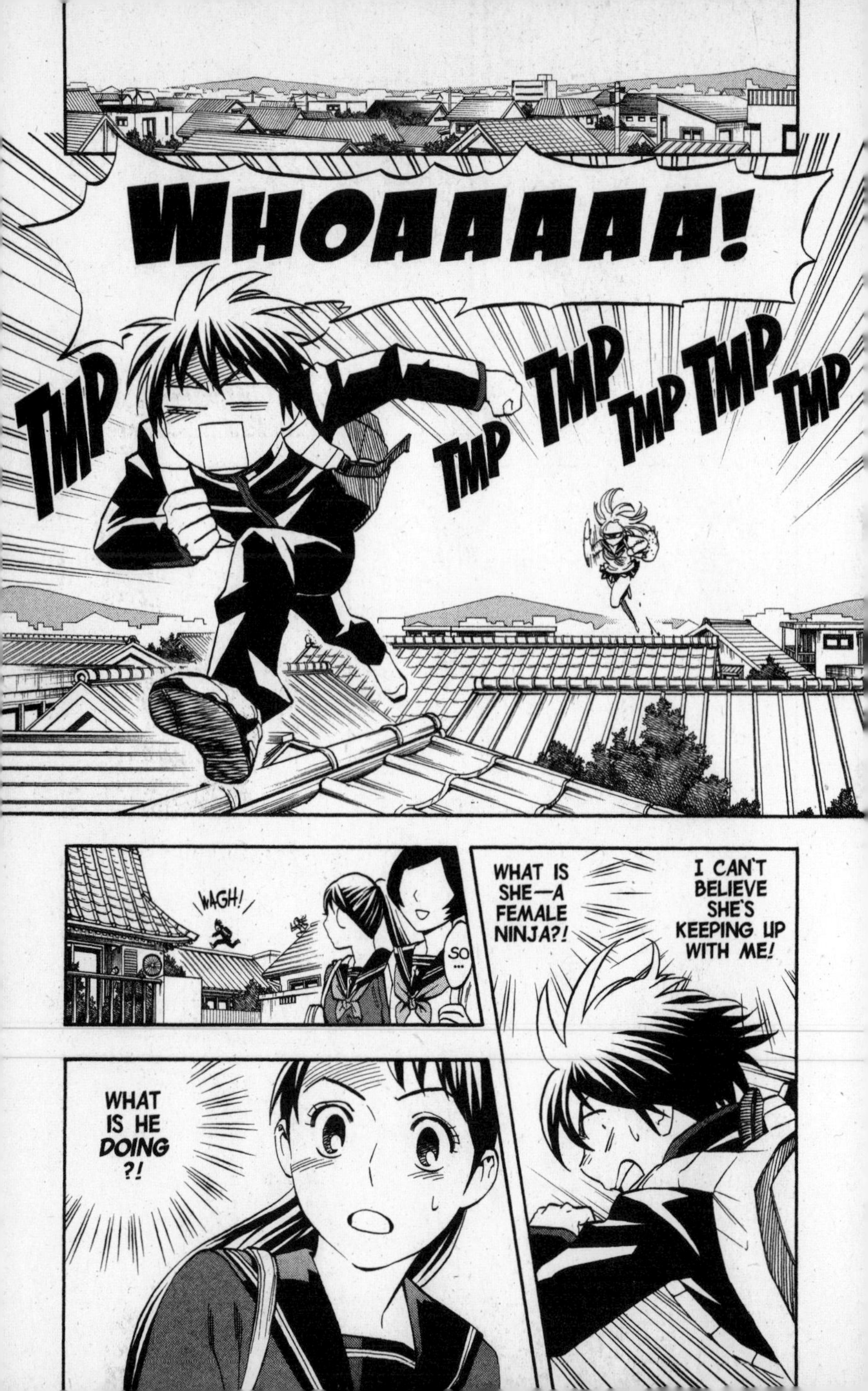
WHOAAAAAA!
TMP
TMP
TMP
TMP
TMP
TMP
I CAN'T BELIEVE SHE'S KEEPING UP WITH ME!
WHAT IS SHE—A FEMALE NINJA?!
WAGH!
SO...
WHAT IS HE DOING?!

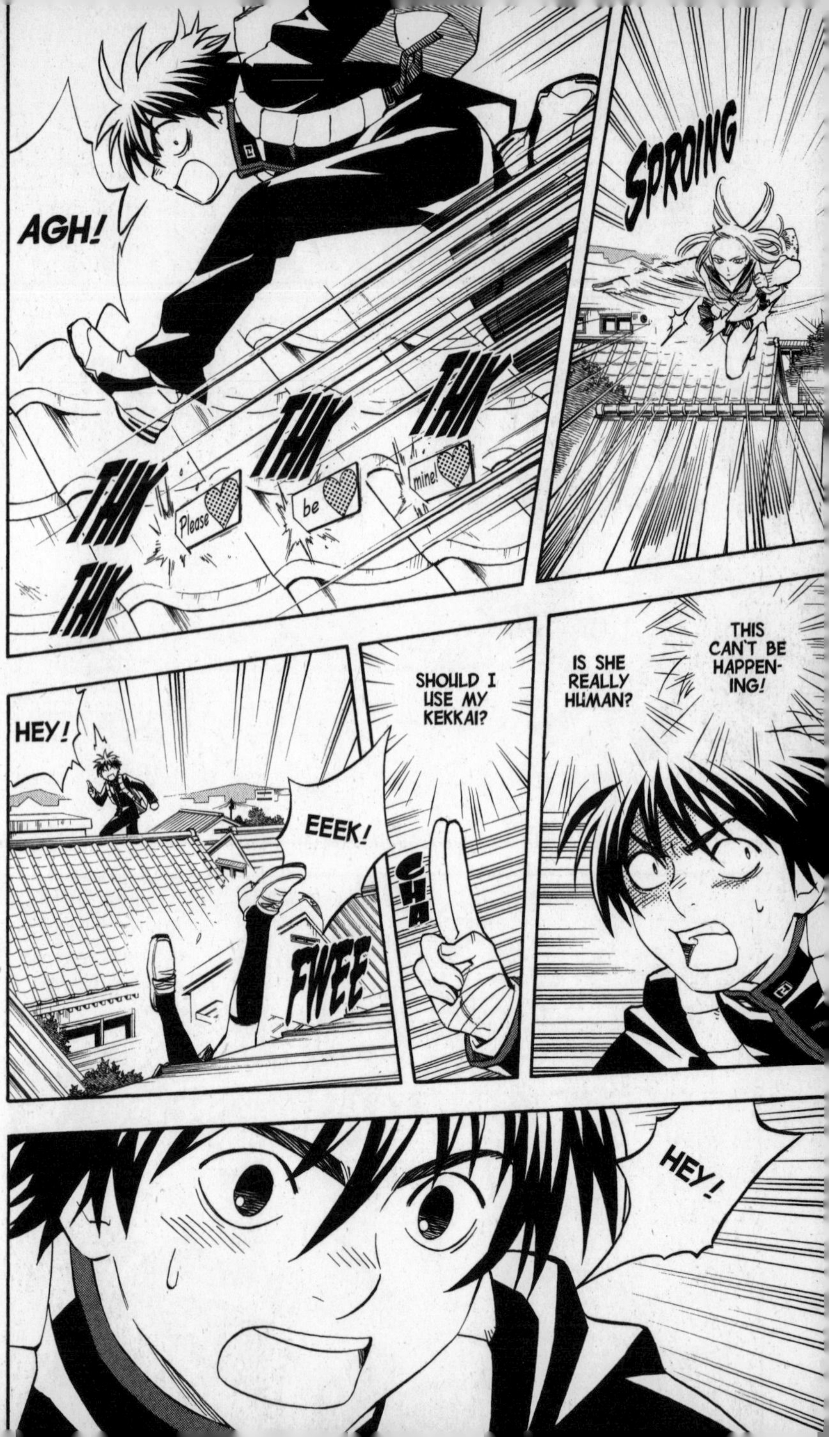
SPROING
AGH!
THK
THK
THK
THK
Please
be
mine!
THIS CAN'T BE HAPPEN-ING!
IS SHE REALLY HUMAN?
SHOULD I USE MY KEKKAI?
CHA
EEEK!
FWEE
HEY!
HEY!

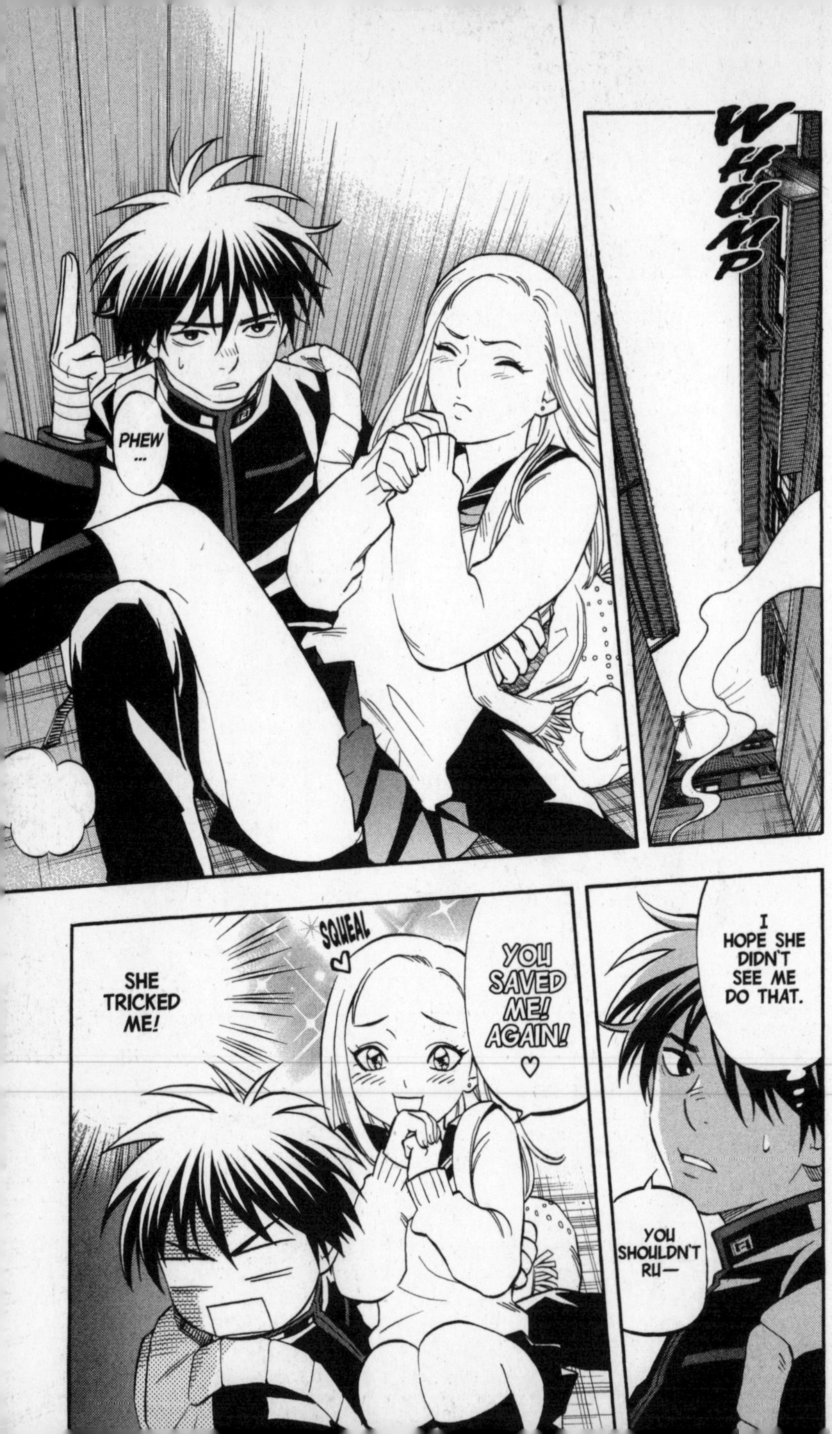
WHUMP
PHEW ...
I HOPE SHE DIDN'T SEE ME DO THAT.
YOU SHOULDN'T RU—
YOU SAVED ME! AGAIN! ♥
SQUEAL ♥
SHE TRICKED ME!

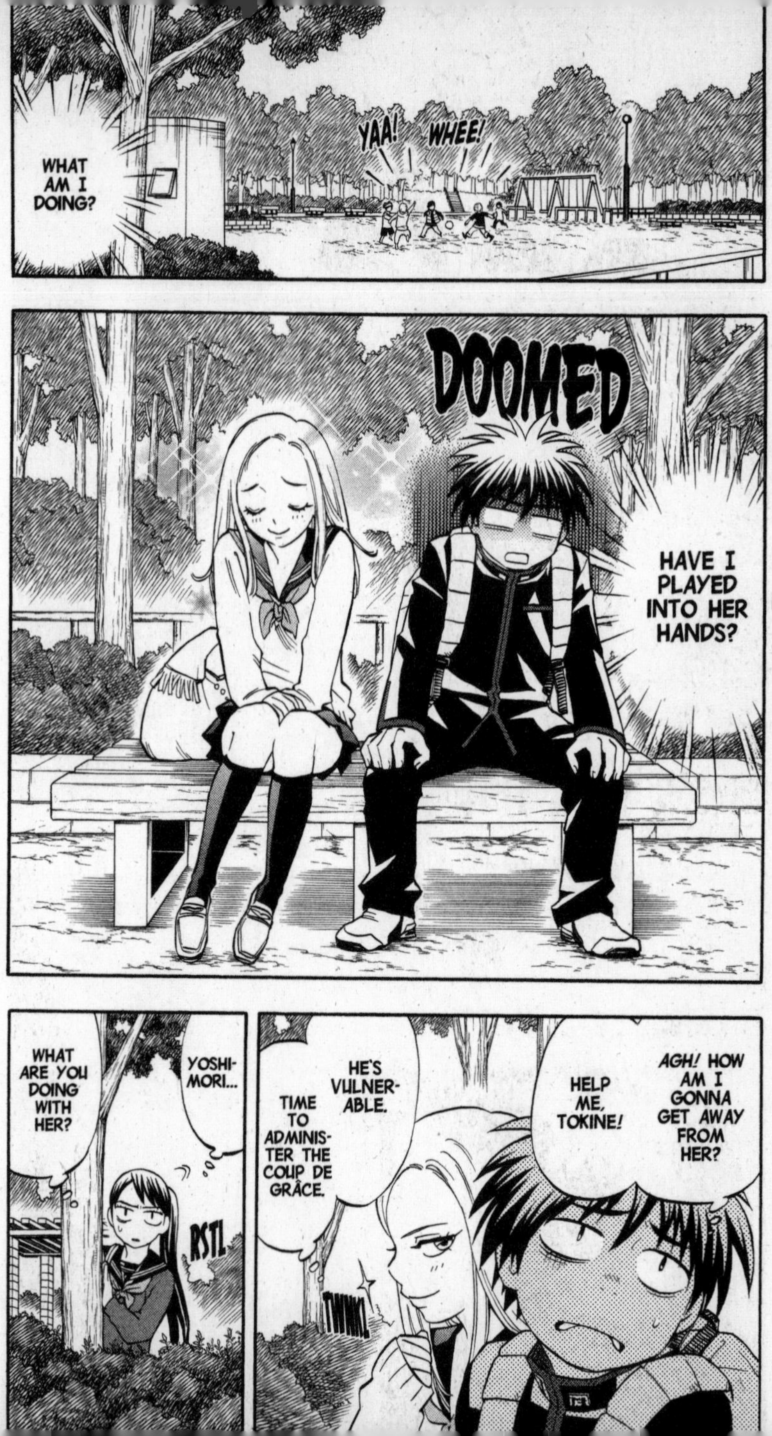
WHEE!
YAA!
WHAT AM I DOING?
DOOMED
HAVE I PLAYED INTO HER HANDS?
AGH! HOW AM I GONNA GET AWAY FROM HER?
HELP ME, TOKINE!
HE'S VULNERABLE.
TIME TO ADMINISTER THE COUP DE GRÂCE.
TWNK!
YOSHIMORI...
WHAT ARE YOU DOING WITH HER?
RSTL

YOU KNOW, EVER SINCE...

NUDGE

YOSHI-MORI...

...WE MET JUST A FEW DAYS AGO...

SSS'

CHAPTER 150: LOVE TRIANGLE

SHE'S SO PUSHY!

WHOA!

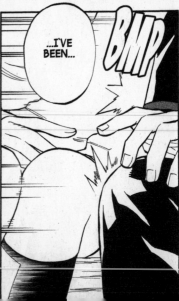

...I'VE BEEN...

BMP

SHE'S CROWDING ME OFF THE BENCH!

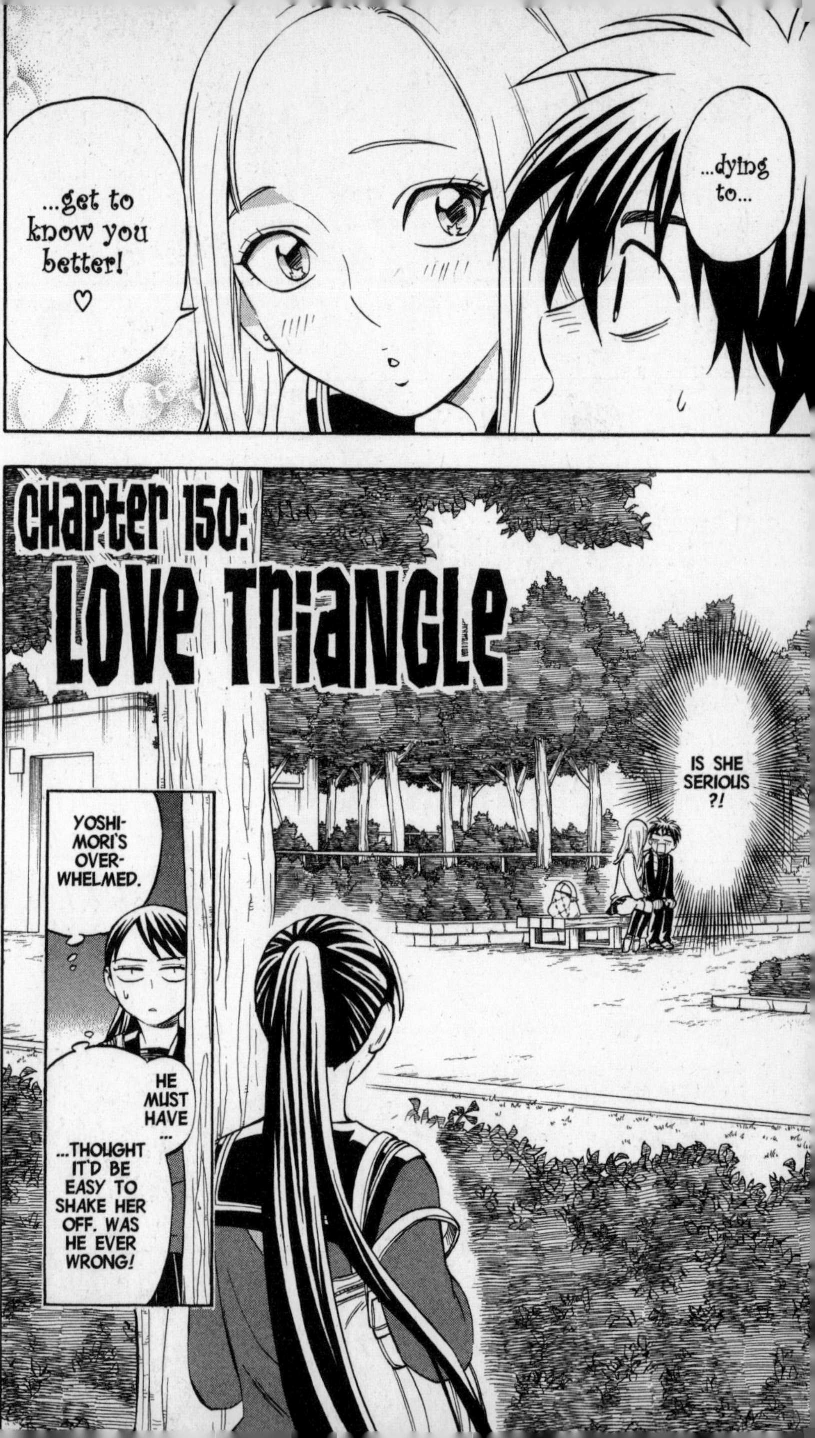

...dying to...
...get to know you better! ♡
Chapter 150: Love Triangle
IS SHE SERIOUS ?!
YOSHI-MORI'S OVER-WHELMED.
HE MUST HAVE ...
...THOUGHT IT'D BE EASY TO SHAKE HER OFF. WAS HE EVER WRONG!

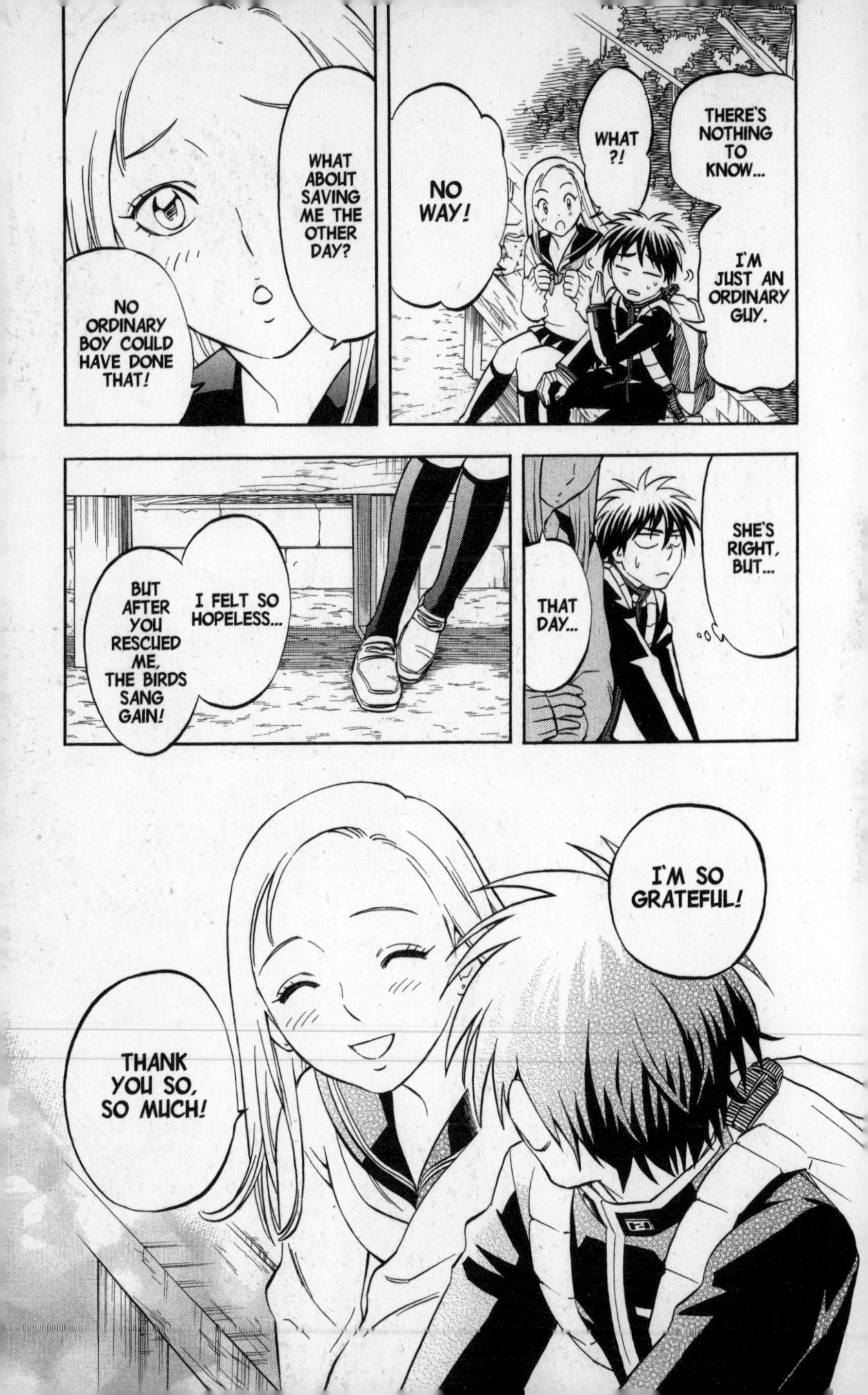
THERE'S NOTHING TO KNOW...
I'M JUST AN ORDINARY GUY.
WHAT ?!
NO WAY!
WHAT ABOUT SAVING ME THE OTHER DAY?
NO ORDINARY BOY COULD HAVE DONE THAT!
SHE'S RIGHT, BUT...
THAT DAY...
I FELT SO HOPELESS...
BUT AFTER YOU RESCUED ME, THE BIRDS SANG GAIN!
I'M SO GRATEFUL!
THANK YOU SO, SO MUCH!

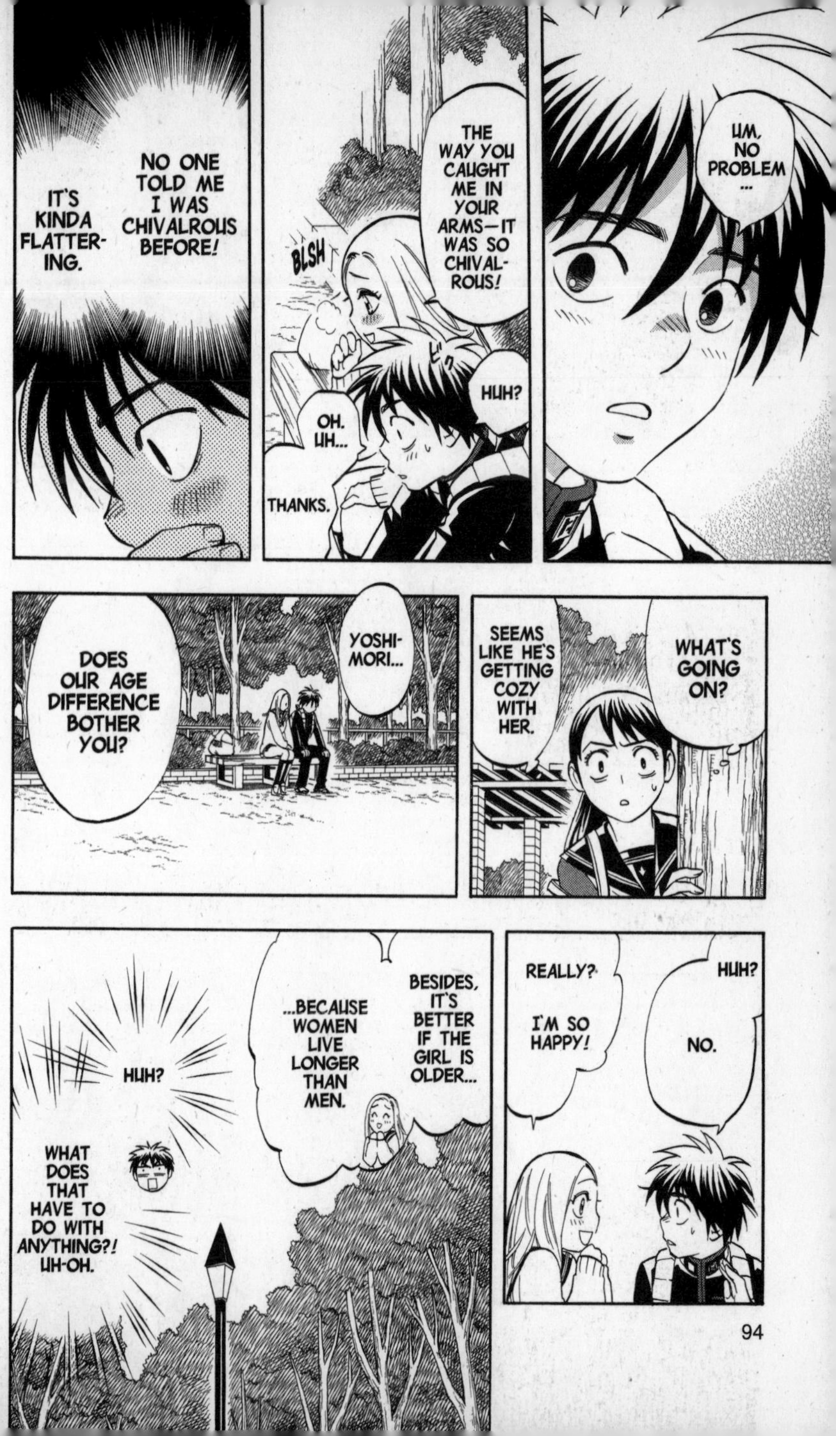
UM, NO PROBLEM...
THE WAY YOU CAUGHT ME IN YOUR ARMS—IT WAS SO CHIVALROUS!
BLSH
HUH?
OH. UH...
THANKS.
NO ONE TOLD ME I WAS CHIVALROUS BEFORE!
IT'S KINDA FLATTERING.
WHAT'S GOING ON?
SEEMS LIKE HE'S GETTING COZY WITH HER.
YOSHIMORI...
DOES OUR AGE DIFFERENCE BOTHER YOU?
HUH?
NO.
REALLY?
I'M SO HAPPY!
BESIDES, IT'S BETTER IF THE GIRL IS OLDER...
...BECAUSE WOMEN LIVE LONGER THAN MEN.
HUH?
WHAT DOES THAT HAVE TO DO WITH ANYTHING?! UH-OH.

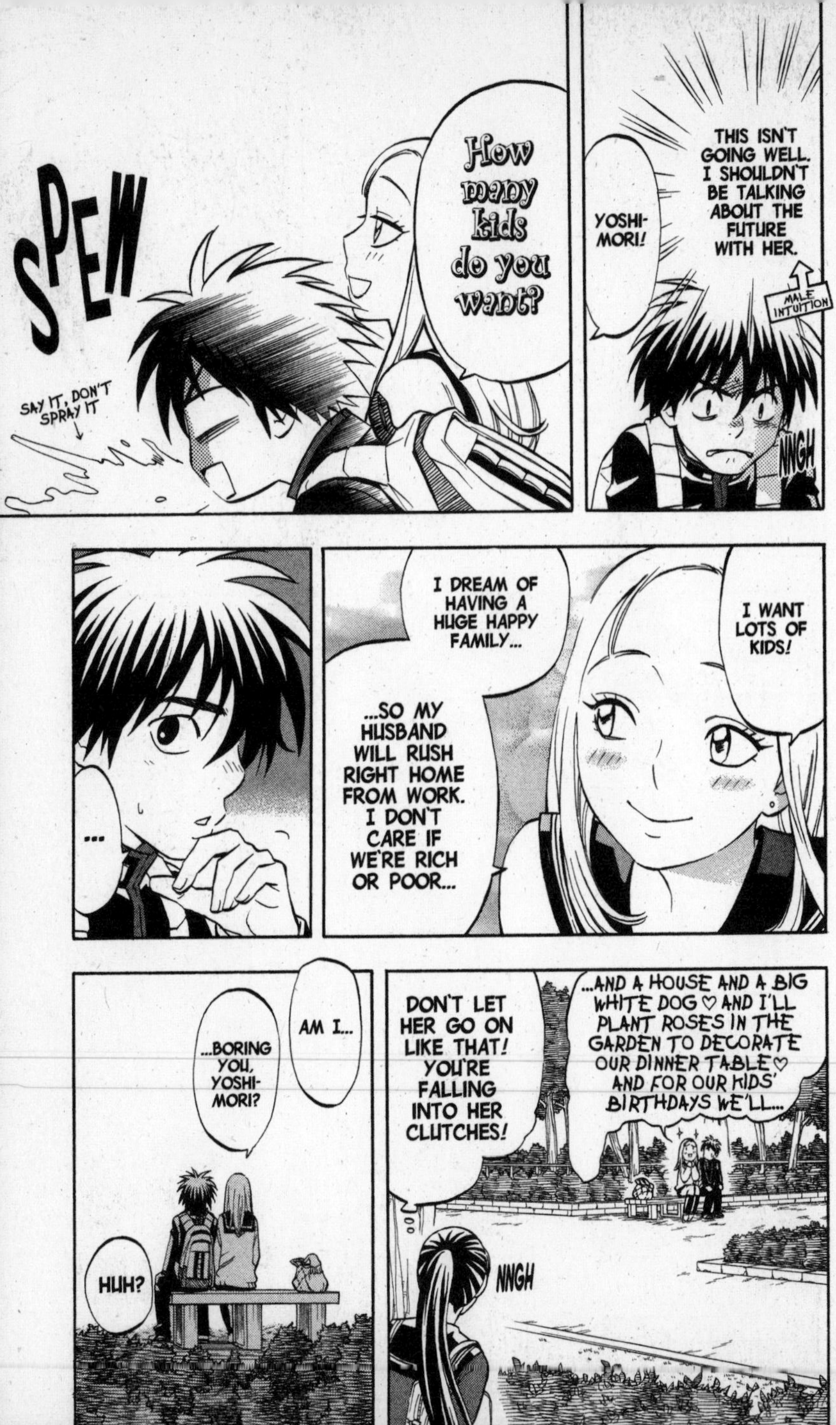
YOSHI-MORI!
THIS ISN'T GOING WELL. I SHOULDN'T BE TALKING ABOUT THE FUTURE WITH HER.
MALE INTUITION
NNGH
How many kids do you want?
SPEW
SAY IT, DON'T SPRAY IT
I WANT LOTS OF KIDS!
I DREAM OF HAVING A HUGE HAPPY FAMILY...
...SO MY HUSBAND WILL RUSH RIGHT HOME FROM WORK. I DON'T CARE IF WE'RE RICH OR POOR...
...
...AND A HOUSE AND A BIG WHITE DOG ♡ AND I'LL PLANT ROSES IN THE GARDEN TO DECORATE OUR DINNER TABLE ♡ AND FOR OUR KIDS' BIRTHDAYS WE'LL...
DON'T LET HER GO ON LIKE THAT! YOU'RE FALLING INTO HER CLUTCHES!
NNGH
AM I...
...BORING YOU, YOSHI-MORI?
HUH?

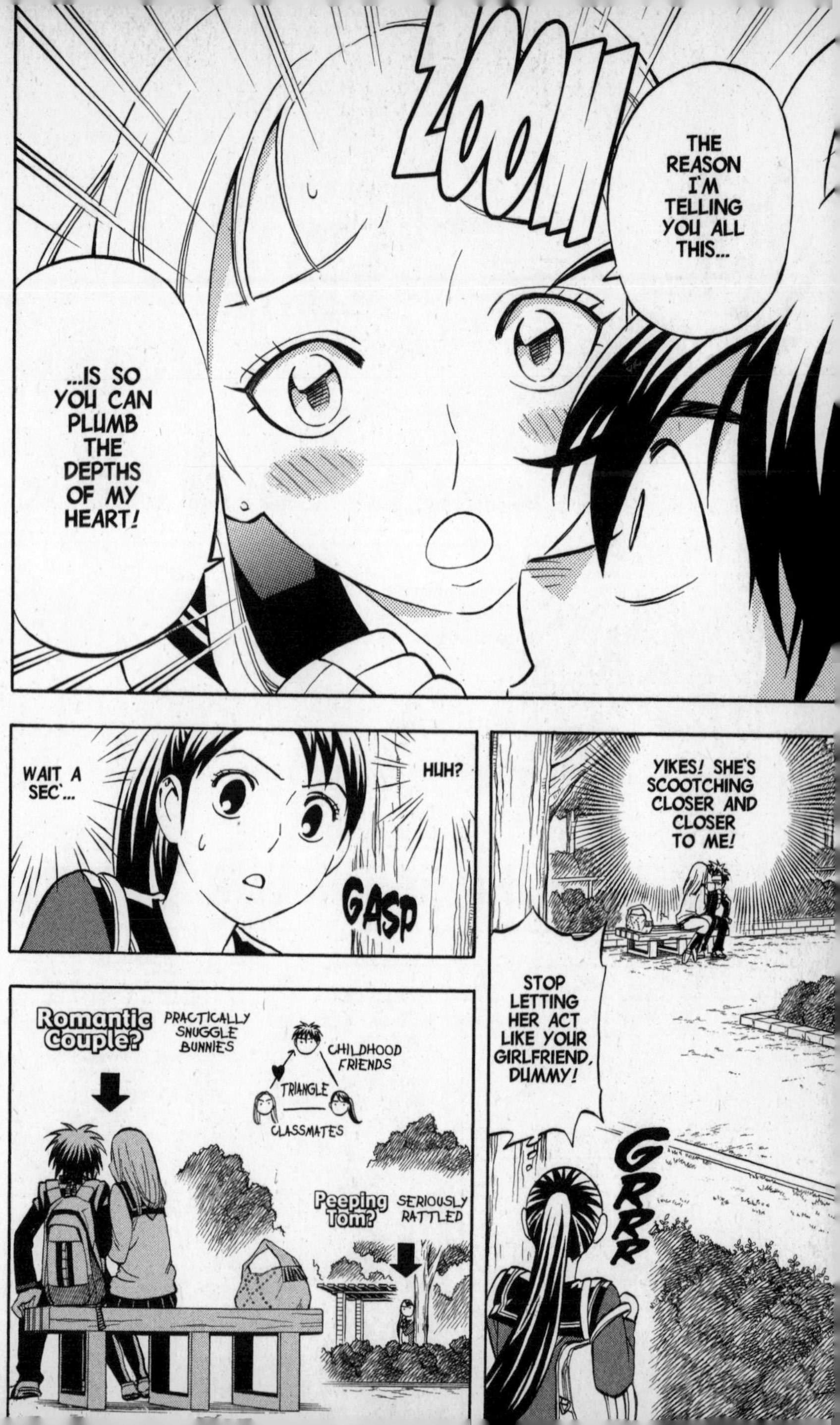
ZOOM
THE REASON I'M TELLING YOU ALL THIS...
...IS SO YOU CAN PLUMB THE DEPTHS OF MY HEART!
YIKES! SHE'S SCOOTCHING CLOSER AND CLOSER TO ME!
STOP LETTING HER ACT LIKE YOUR GIRLFRIEND, DUMMY!
GRRR
HUH?
WAIT A SEC'...
GASP
Romantic Couple?
PRACTICALLY SNUGGLE BUNNIES
CHILDHOOD FRIENDS
TRIANGLE
CLASSMATES
Peeping Tom?
SERIOUSLY RATTLED

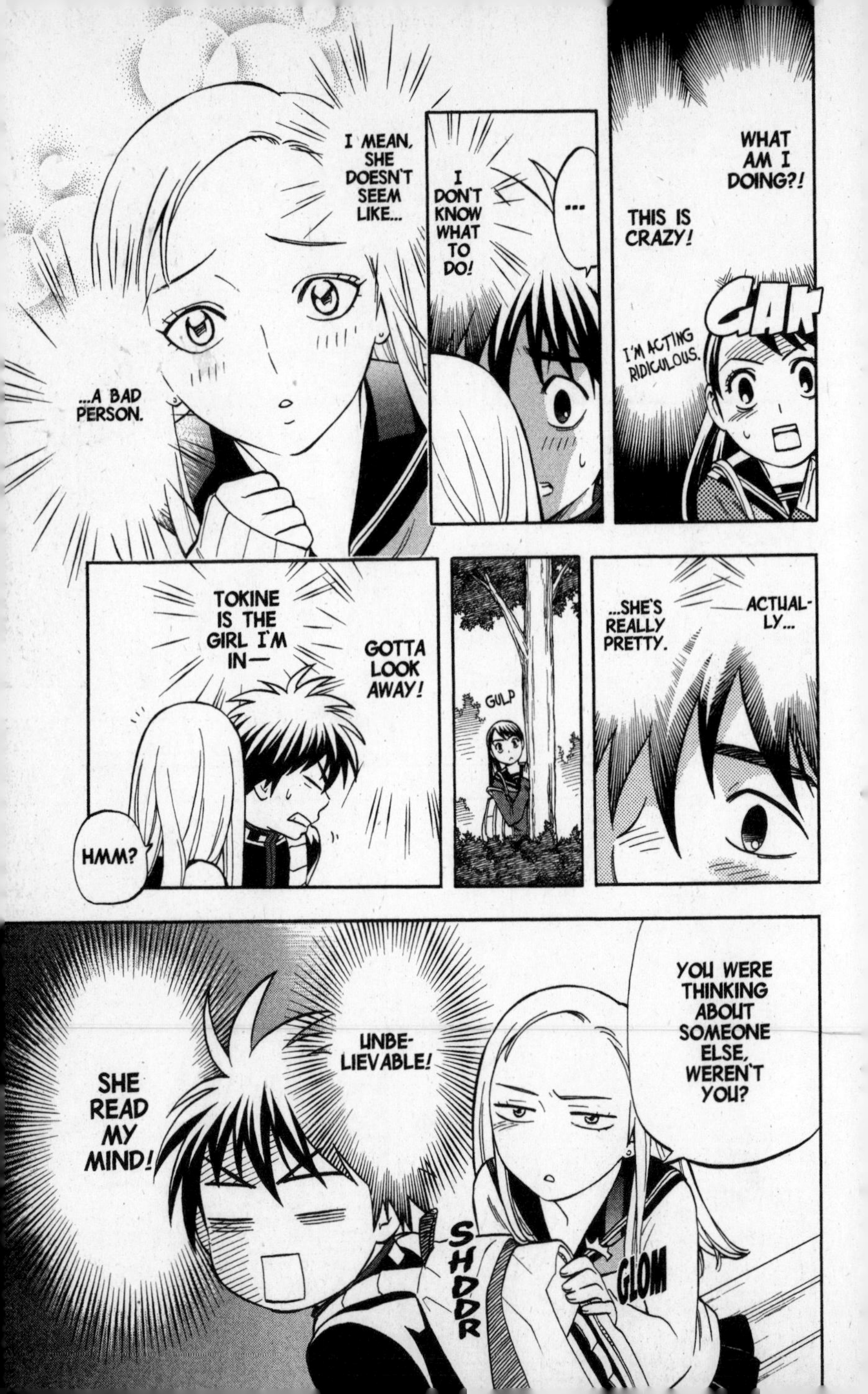

WHAT AM I DOING?!
THIS IS CRAZY!
GAK
I'M ACTING RIDICULOUS.
...
I DON'T KNOW WHAT TO DO!
I MEAN, SHE DOESN'T SEEM LIKE...
...A BAD PERSON.
ACTUAL-LY...
...SHE'S REALLY PRETTY.
GULP
GOTTA LOOK AWAY!
TOKINE IS THE GIRL I'M IN—
HMM?
YOU WERE THINKING ABOUT SOMEONE ELSE, WEREN'T YOU?
GLOM
SHDDR
UNBE-LIEVABLE!
SHE READ MY MIND!

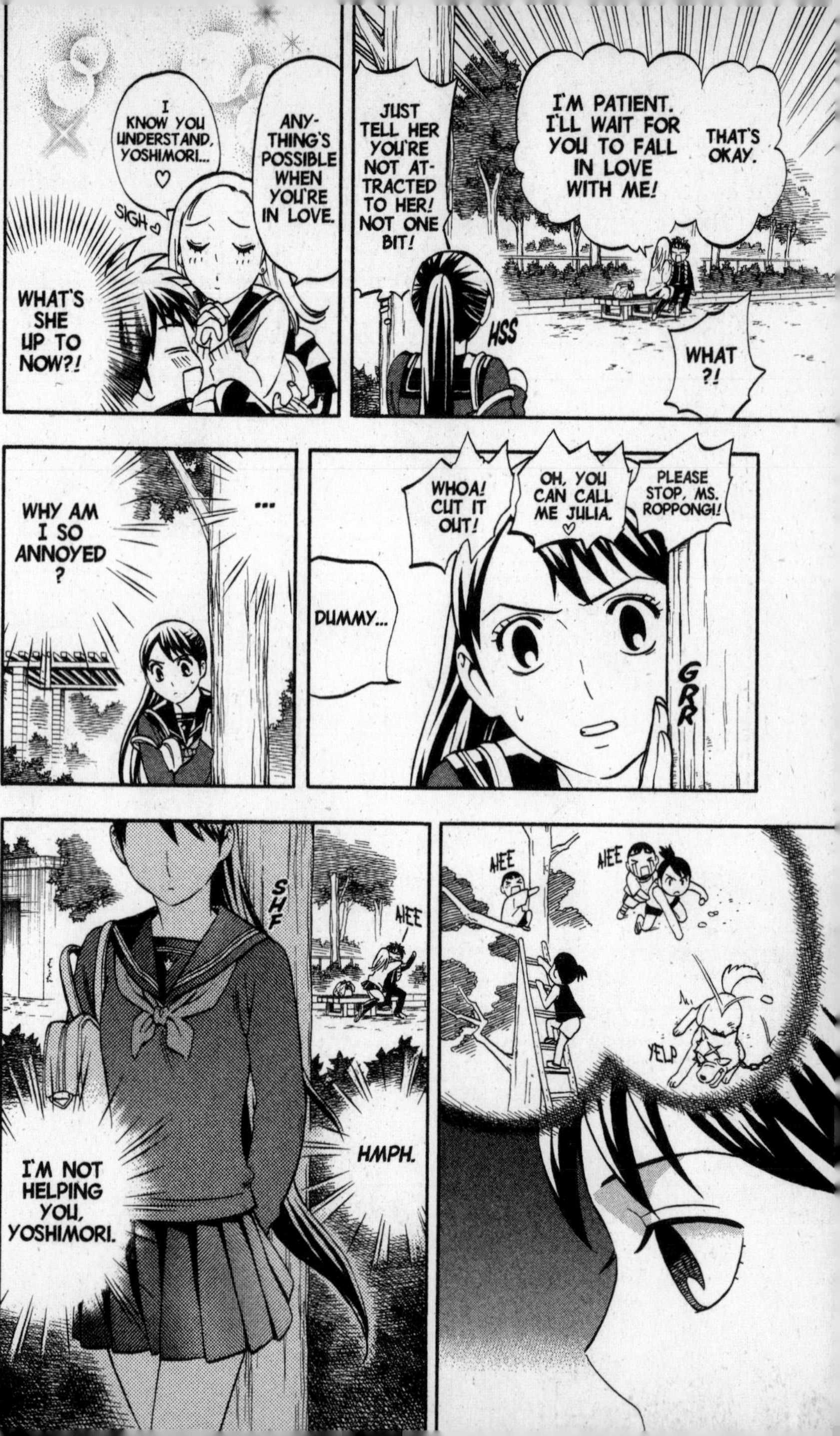
THAT'S OKAY.
I'M PATIENT. I'LL WAIT FOR YOU TO FALL IN LOVE WITH ME!
WHAT?!
JUST TELL HER YOU'RE NOT AT-TRACTED TO HER! NOT ONE BIT!
HSS
ANY-THING'S POSSIBLE WHEN YOU'RE IN LOVE.
I KNOW YOU UNDERSTAND, YOSHIMORI... ♡
SIGH ♡
WHAT'S SHE UP TO NOW?!
PLEASE STOP, MS. ROPPONGI!
OH, YOU CAN CALL ME JULIA. ♡
WHOA! CUT IT OUT!
DUMMY...
GRR
...
WHY AM I SO ANNOYED?
AHEE
AHEE
YELP
SHF
AHEE
HMPH.
I'M NOT HELPING YOU, YOSHIMORI.

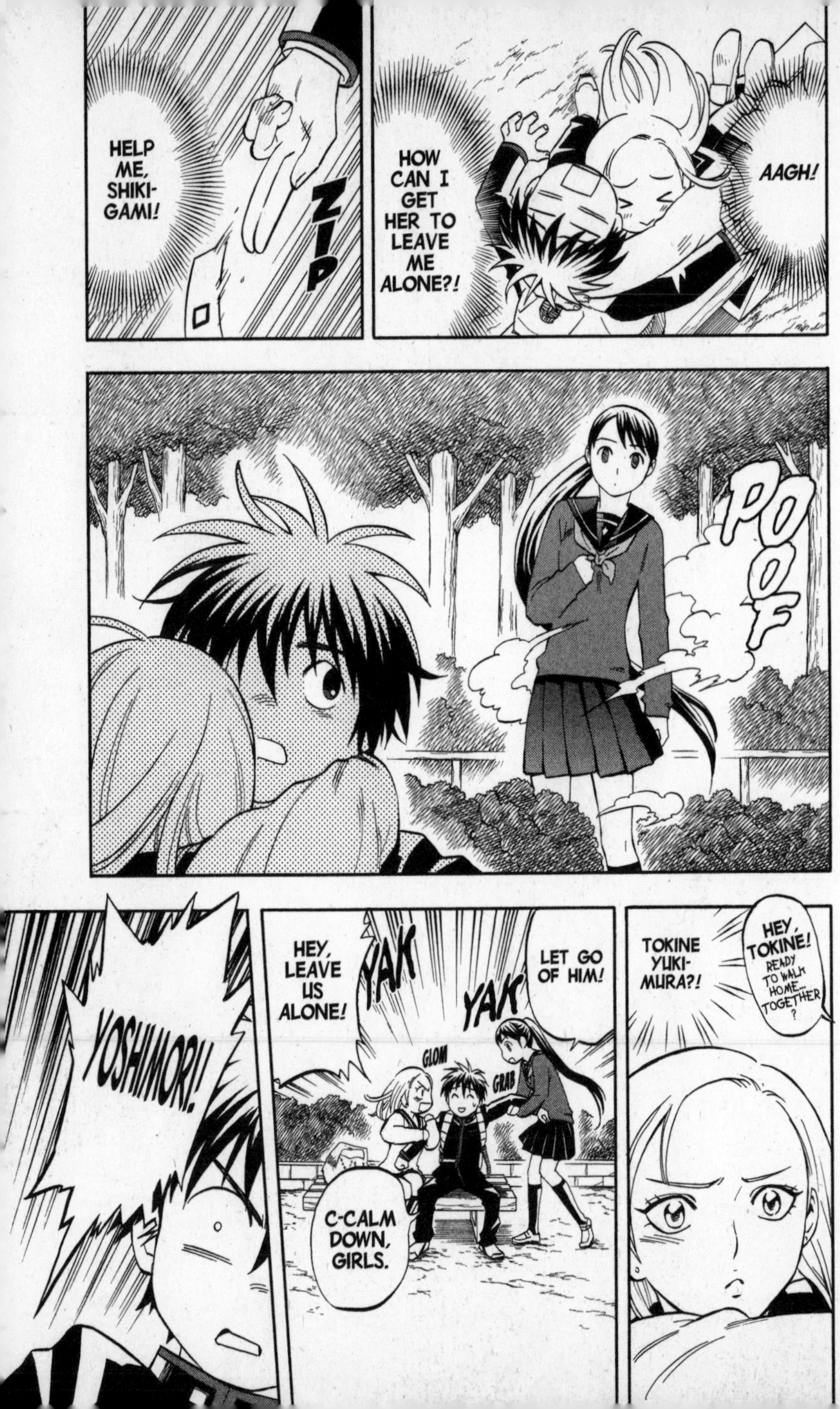
AAGH!
HOW CAN I GET HER TO LEAVE ME ALONE?!
ZIP
HELP ME, SHIKI-GAMI!
POOF
HEY, TOKINE! READY TO WALK HOME... TOGETHER?
TOKINE YUKI-MURA?!
LET GO OF HIM!
YAK
YAK
HEY, LEAVE US ALONE!
GRAB
GLOM
C-CALM DOWN, GIRLS.
YOSHIMORI!

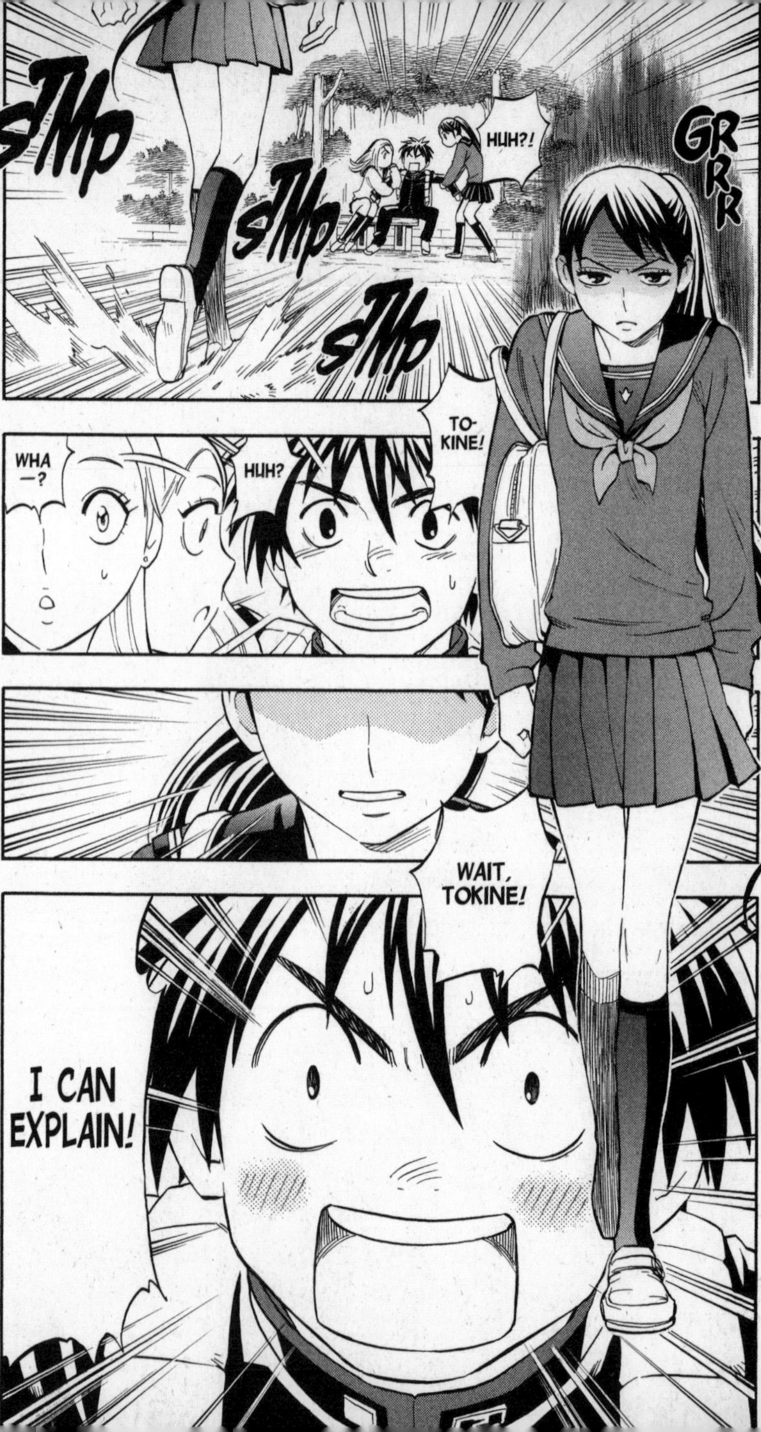
GRRR
HUH?!
STMP STMP STMP STMP
TO-KINE!
HUH?
WHA—?
WAIT, TOKINE!
I CAN EXPLAIN!

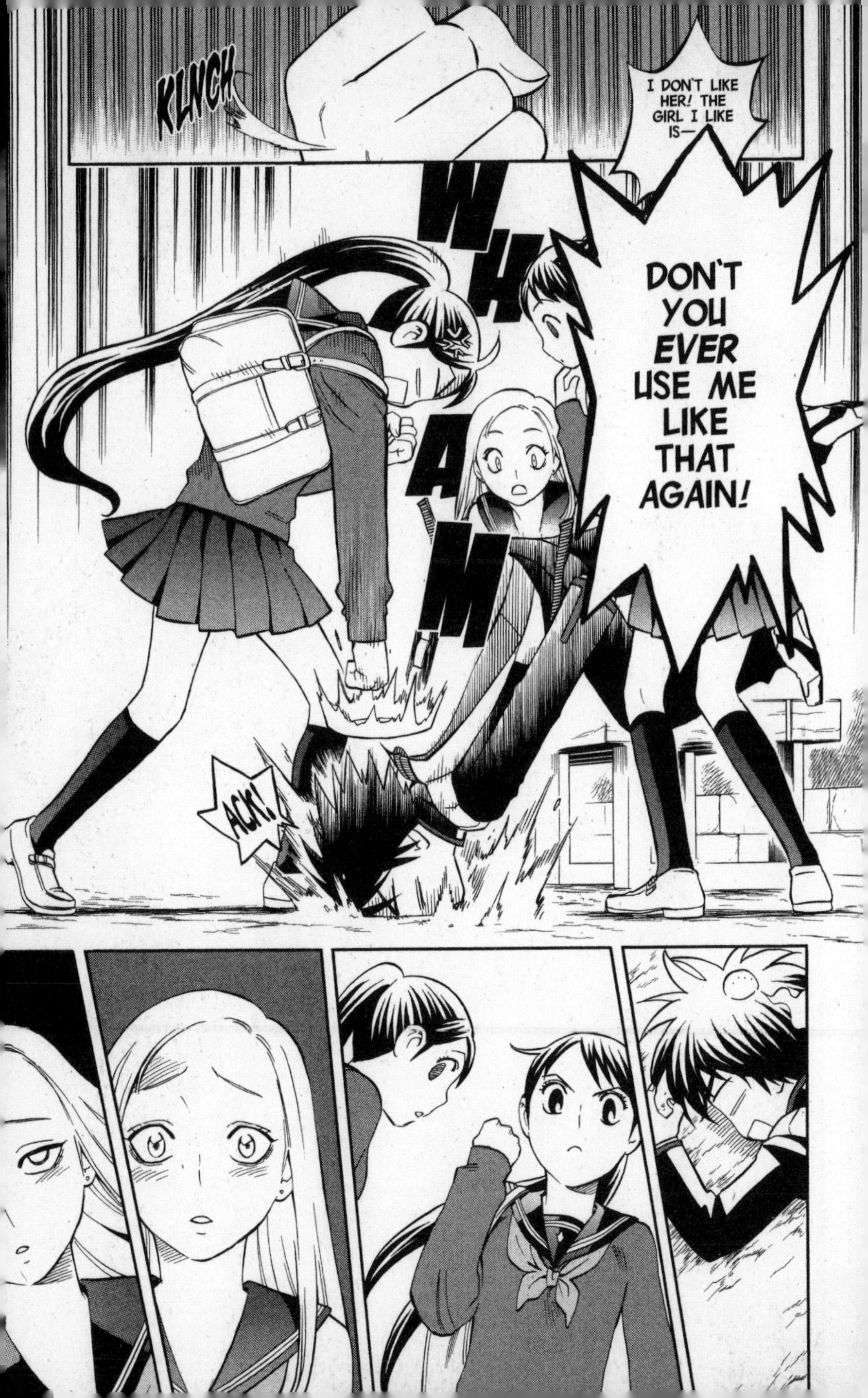
I DON'T LIKE HER! THE GIRL I LIKE IS—
KLNCH
DON'T YOU *EVER* USE ME LIKE THAT AGAIN!
WHAM
ACK!

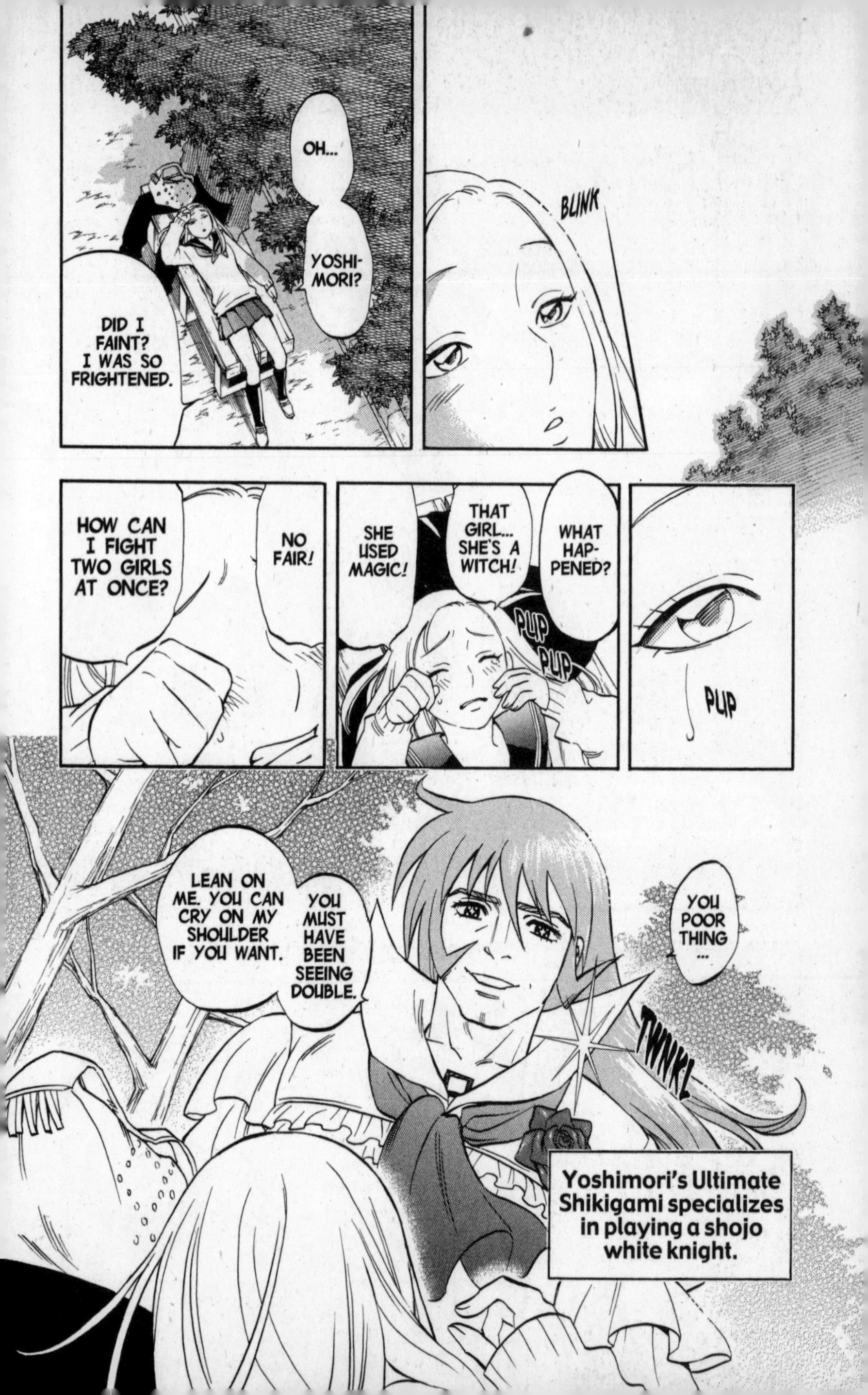
BLINK
OH...
YOSHI-MORI?
DID I FAINT? I WAS SO FRIGHTENED.
PUP
WHAT HAP-PENED?
THAT GIRL... SHE'S A WITCH!
SHE USED MAGIC!
PUP PUP
NO FAIR!
HOW CAN I FIGHT TWO GIRLS AT ONCE?
YOU POOR THING ...
TWNKL
YOU MUST HAVE BEEN SEEING DOUBLE.
LEAN ON ME. YOU CAN CRY ON MY SHOULDER IF YOU WANT.
Yoshimori's Ultimate Shikigami specializes in playing a shojo white knight.

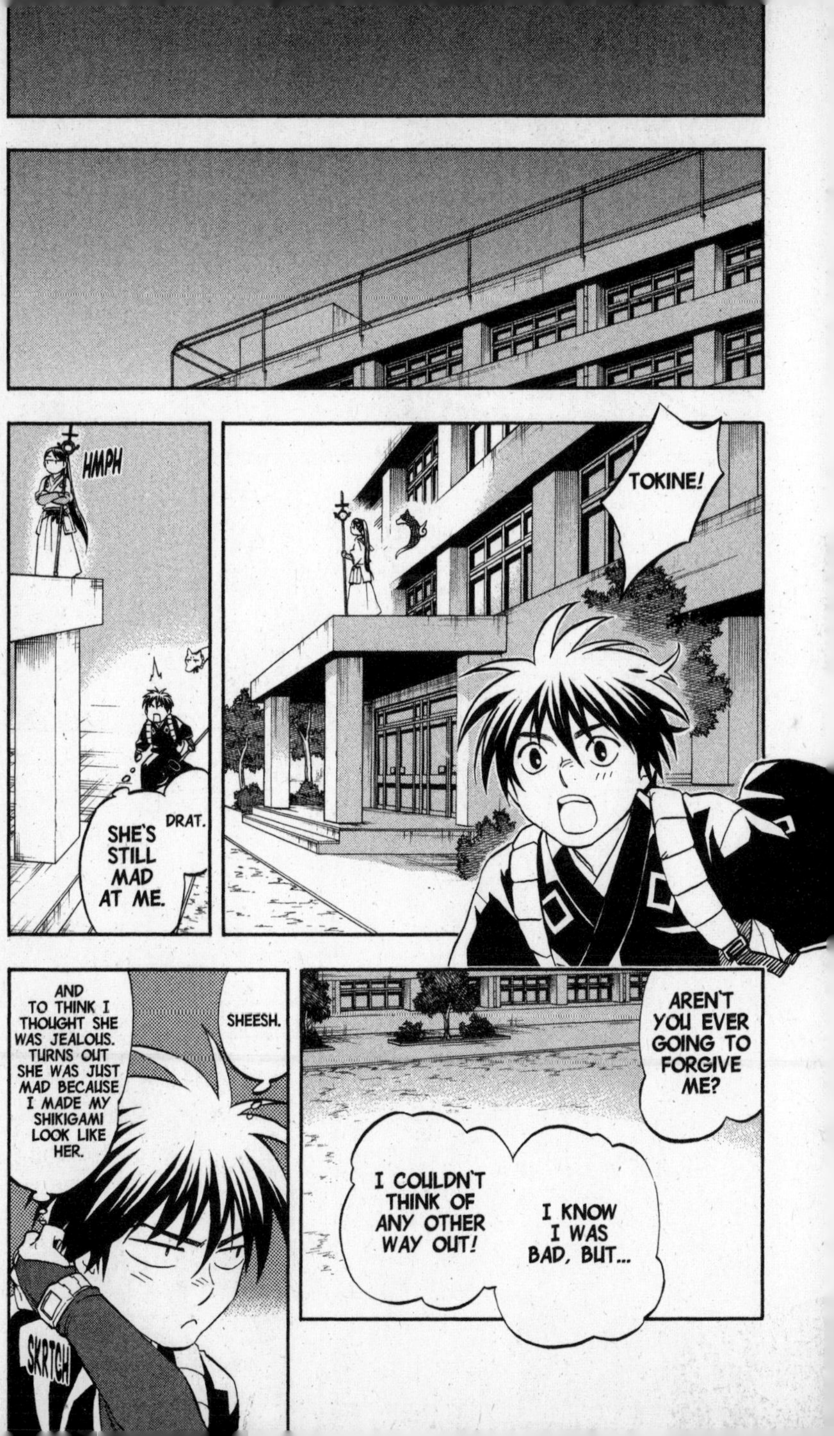
TOKINE!
HMPH
DRAT.
SHE'S STILL MAD AT ME.
AREN'T YOU EVER GOING TO FORGIVE ME?
I KNOW I WAS BAD, BUT...
I COULDN'T THINK OF ANY OTHER WAY OUT!
SHEESH.
AND TO THINK I THOUGHT SHE WAS JEALOUS. TURNS OUT SHE WAS JUST MAD BECAUSE I MADE MY SHIKIGAMI LOOK LIKE HER.
SKRTCH

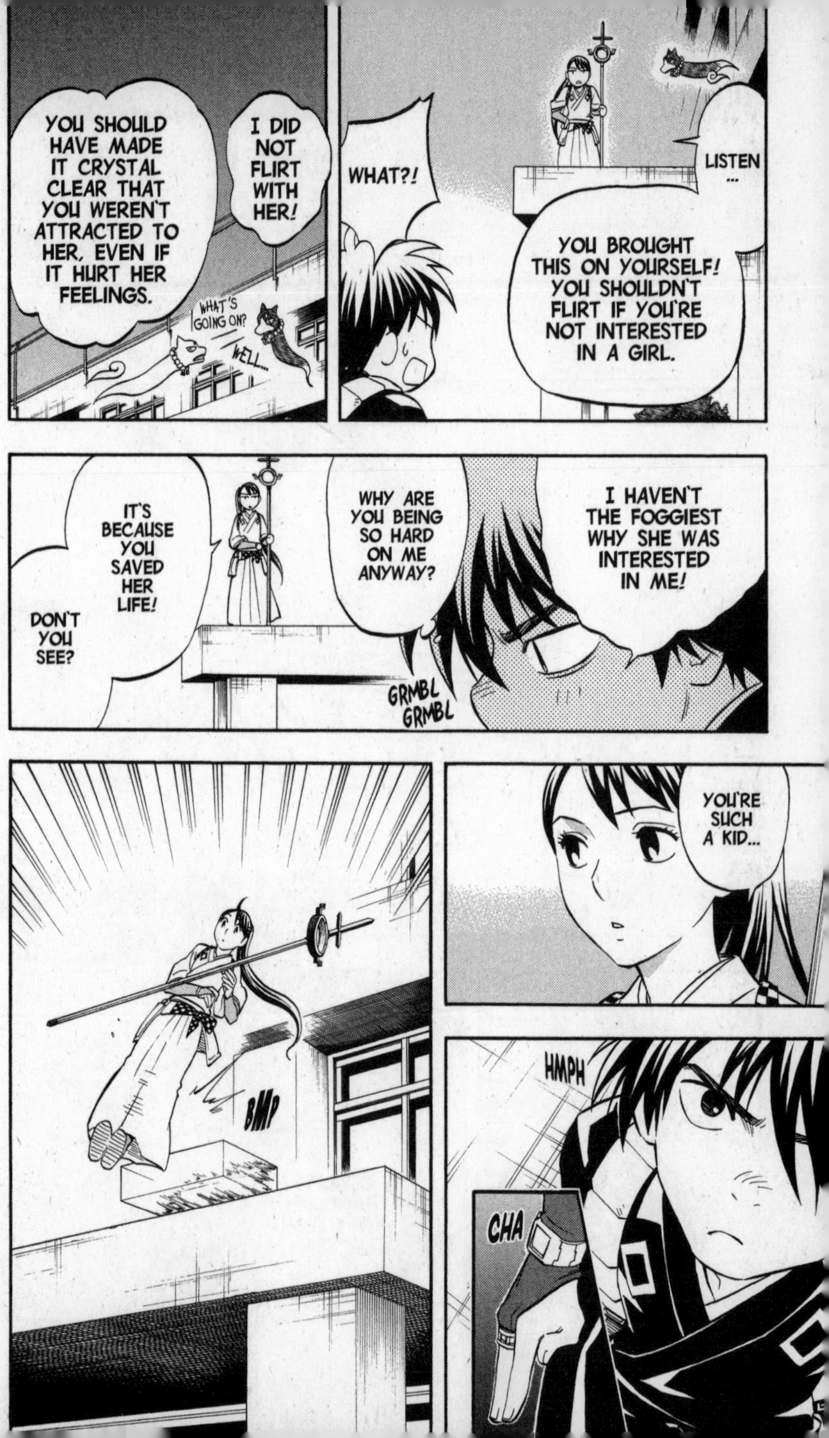
LISTEN ...
YOU BROUGHT THIS ON YOURSELF! YOU SHOULDN'T FLIRT IF YOU'RE NOT INTERESTED IN A GIRL.
WHAT?!
I DID NOT FLIRT WITH HER!
YOU SHOULD HAVE MADE IT CRYSTAL CLEAR THAT YOU WEREN'T ATTRACTED TO HER, EVEN IF IT HURT HER FEELINGS.
WHAT'S GOING ON?
WELL...
I HAVEN'T THE FOGGIEST WHY SHE WAS INTERESTED IN ME!
WHY ARE YOU BEING SO HARD ON ME ANYWAY?
GRMBL GRMBL
IT'S BECAUSE YOU SAVED HER LIFE!
DON'T YOU SEE?
YOU'RE SUCH A KID...
HMPH
CHA
BMP

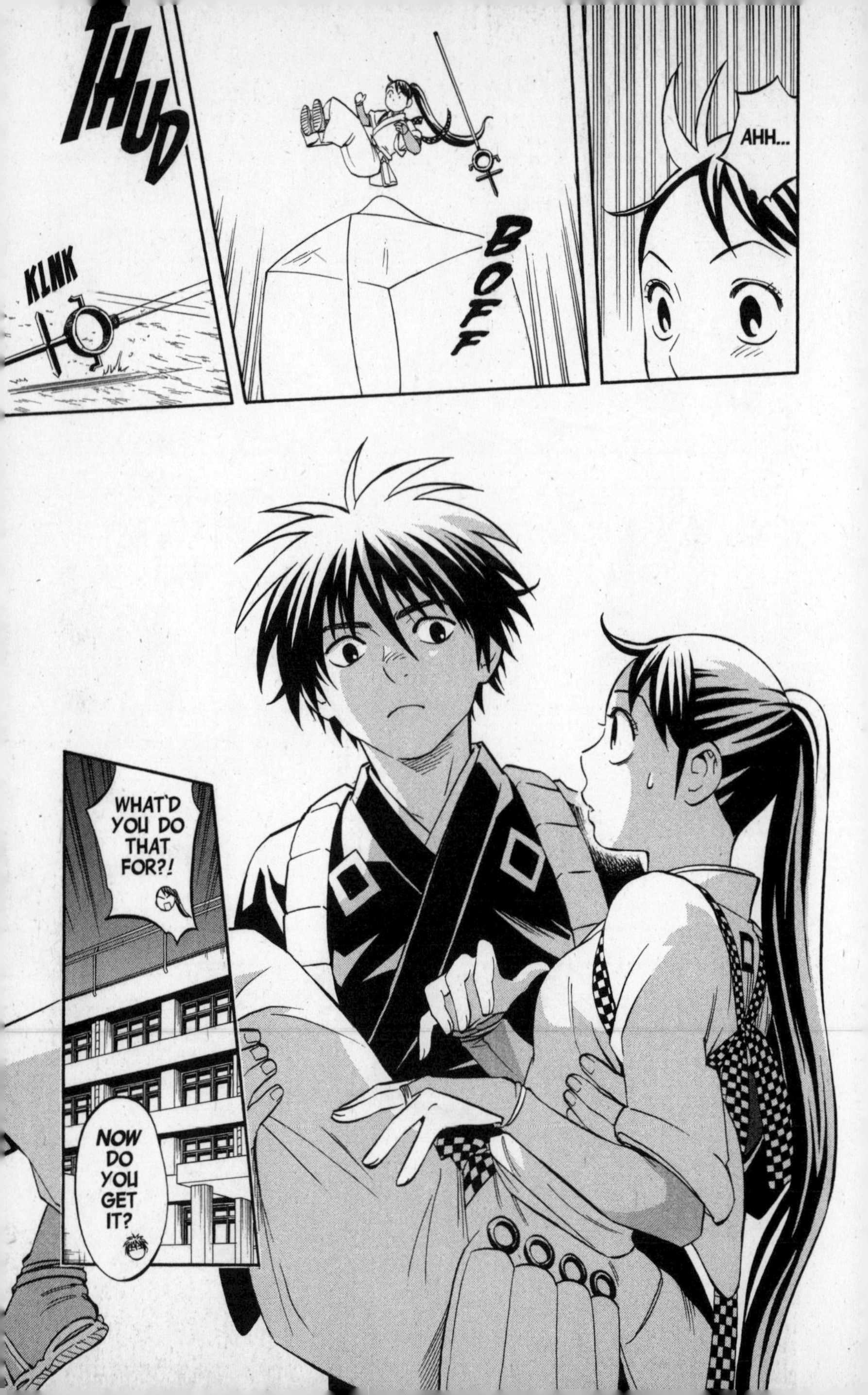
AHH...
BOFF
THUD
KLNK
WHAT'D YOU DO THAT FOR?!
NOW DO YOU GET IT?

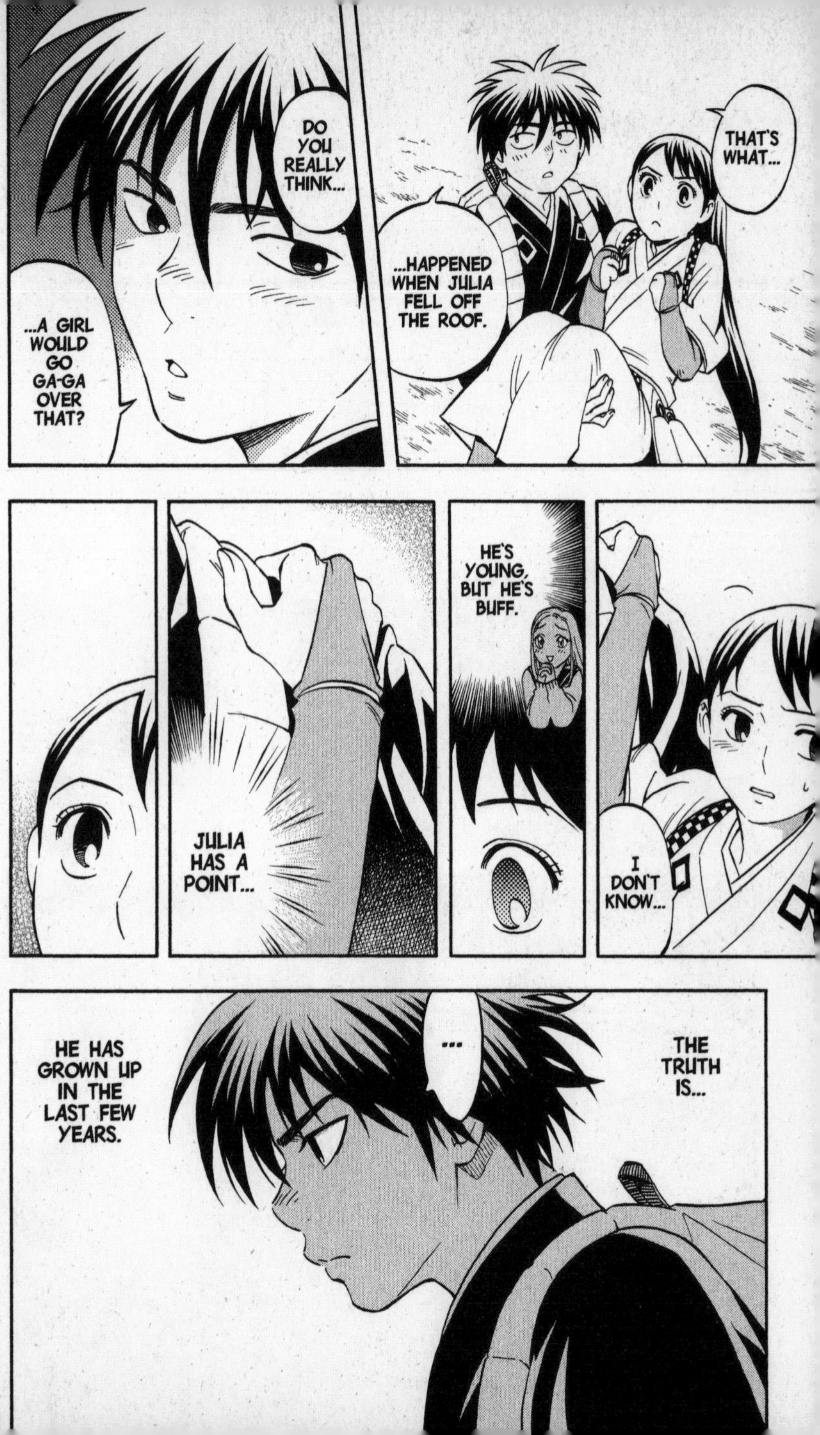
THAT'S WHAT...
...HAPPENED WHEN JULIA FELL OFF THE ROOF.
DO YOU REALLY THINK...
...A GIRL WOULD GO GA-GA OVER THAT?
I DON'T KNOW...
HE'S YOUNG, BUT HE'S BUFF.
JULIA HAS A POINT...
THE TRUTH IS...
...
HE HAS GROWN UP IN THE LAST FEW YEARS.

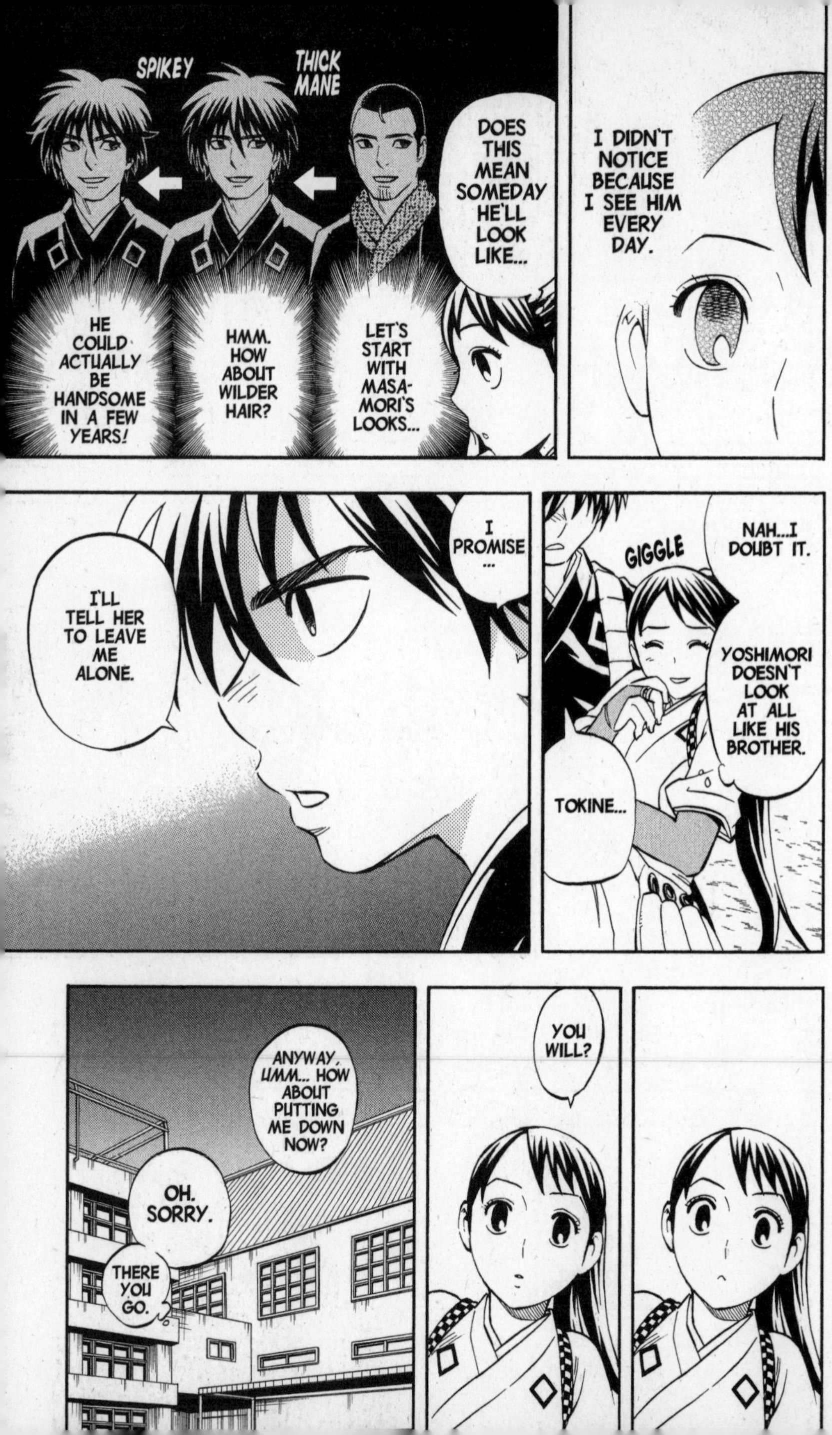
I DIDN'T NOTICE BECAUSE I SEE HIM EVERY DAY.
DOES THIS MEAN SOMEDAY HE'LL LOOK LIKE...
LET'S START WITH MASA-MORI'S LOOKS...
THICK MANE
HMM. HOW ABOUT WILDER HAIR?
SPIKEY
HE COULD ACTUALLY BE HANDSOME IN A FEW YEARS!
NAH...I DOUBT IT.
GIGGLE
YOSHIMORI DOESN'T LOOK AT ALL LIKE HIS BROTHER.
TOKINE...
I PROMISE ...
I'LL TELL HER TO LEAVE ME ALONE.
YOU WILL?
ANYWAY, UMM... HOW ABOUT PUTTING ME DOWN NOW?
OH. SORRY.
THERE YOU GO.

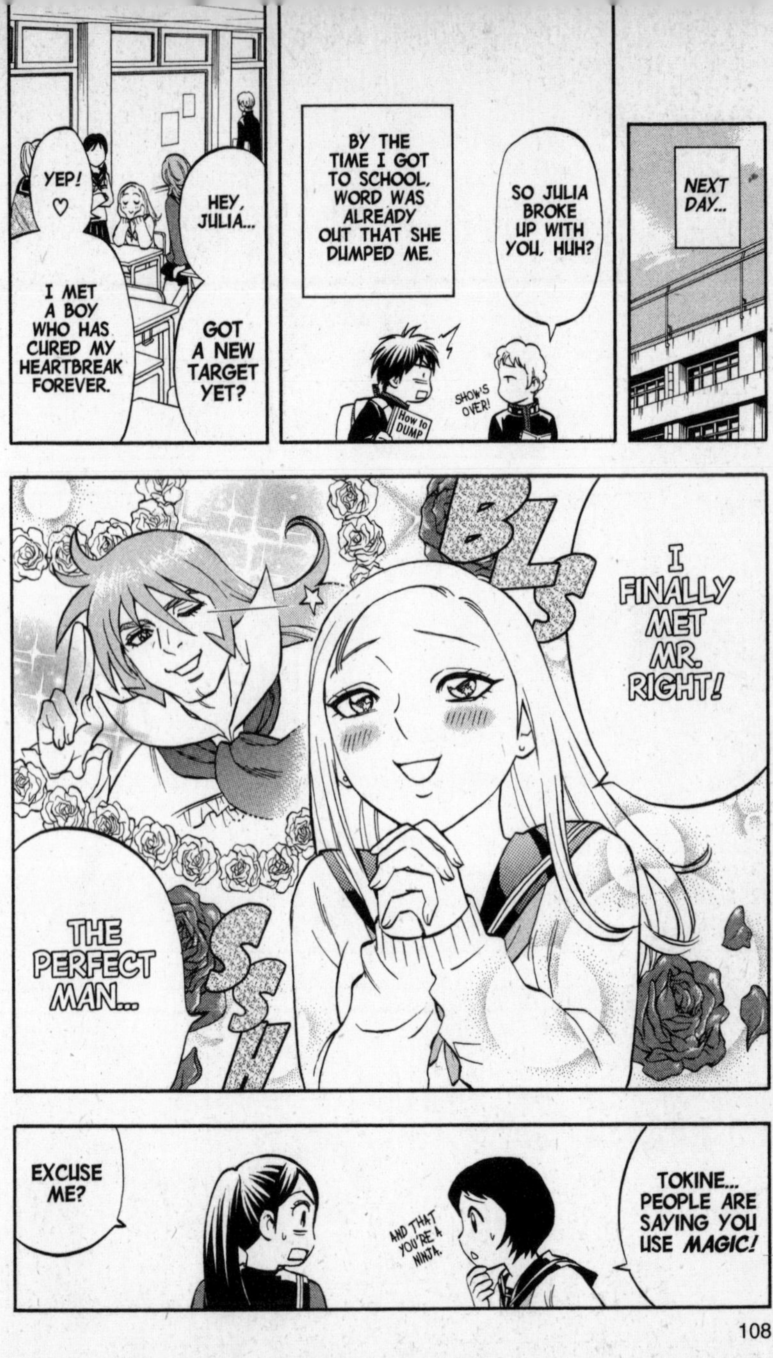
NEXT DAY...
SO JULIA BROKE UP WITH YOU, HUH?
BY THE TIME I GOT TO SCHOOL, WORD WAS ALREADY OUT THAT SHE DUMPED ME.
SHOW'S OVER!
How to DUMP
HEY, JULIA...
GOT A NEW TARGET YET?
YEP! ♡
I MET A BOY WHO HAS CURED MY HEARTBREAK FOREVER.
I FINALLY MET MR. RIGHT!
THE PERFECT MAN...
TOKINE... PEOPLE ARE SAYING YOU USE *MAGIC!*
AND THAT YOU'RE A NINJA.
EXCUSE ME?

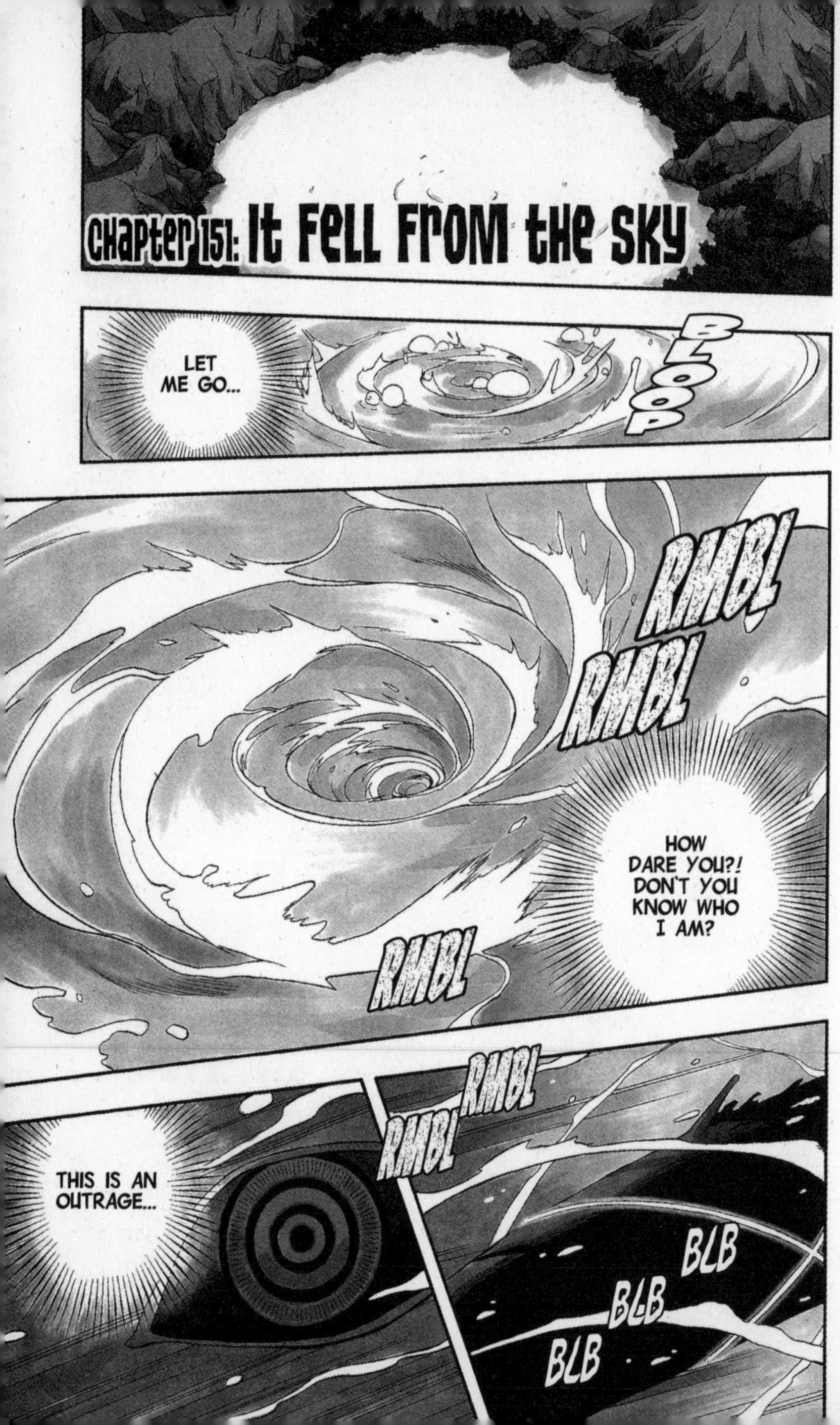
Chapter 151: It Fell From the Sky
BLOOP
LET ME GO...
RMBL
RMBL
HOW DARE YOU?! DON'T YOU KNOW WHO I AM?
RMBL
RMBL
RMBL
BLB
BLB
BLB
THIS IS AN OUTRAGE...

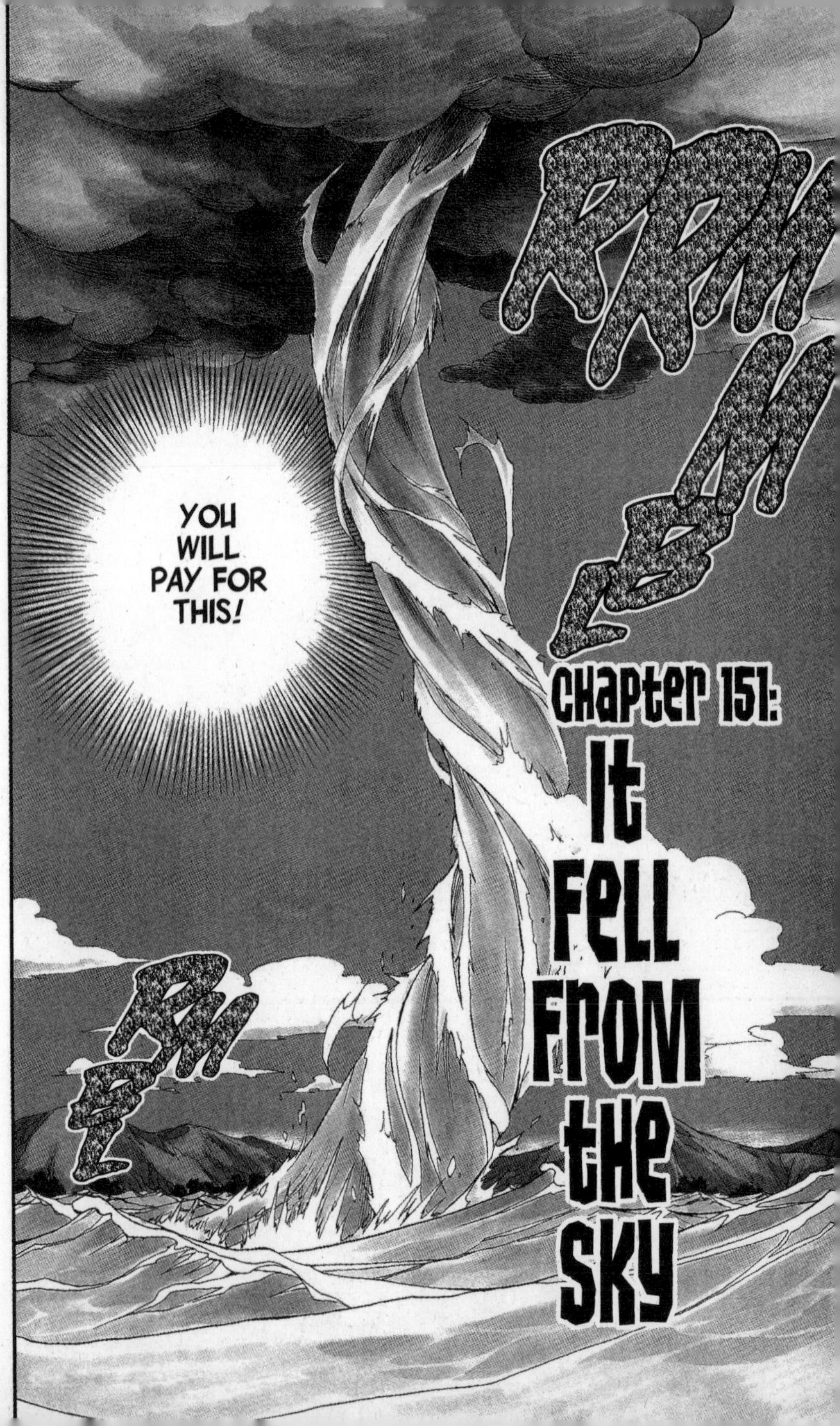
RRMMBL
Chapter 151:
It Fell From the Sky
YOU WILL PAY FOR THIS!
RMBL

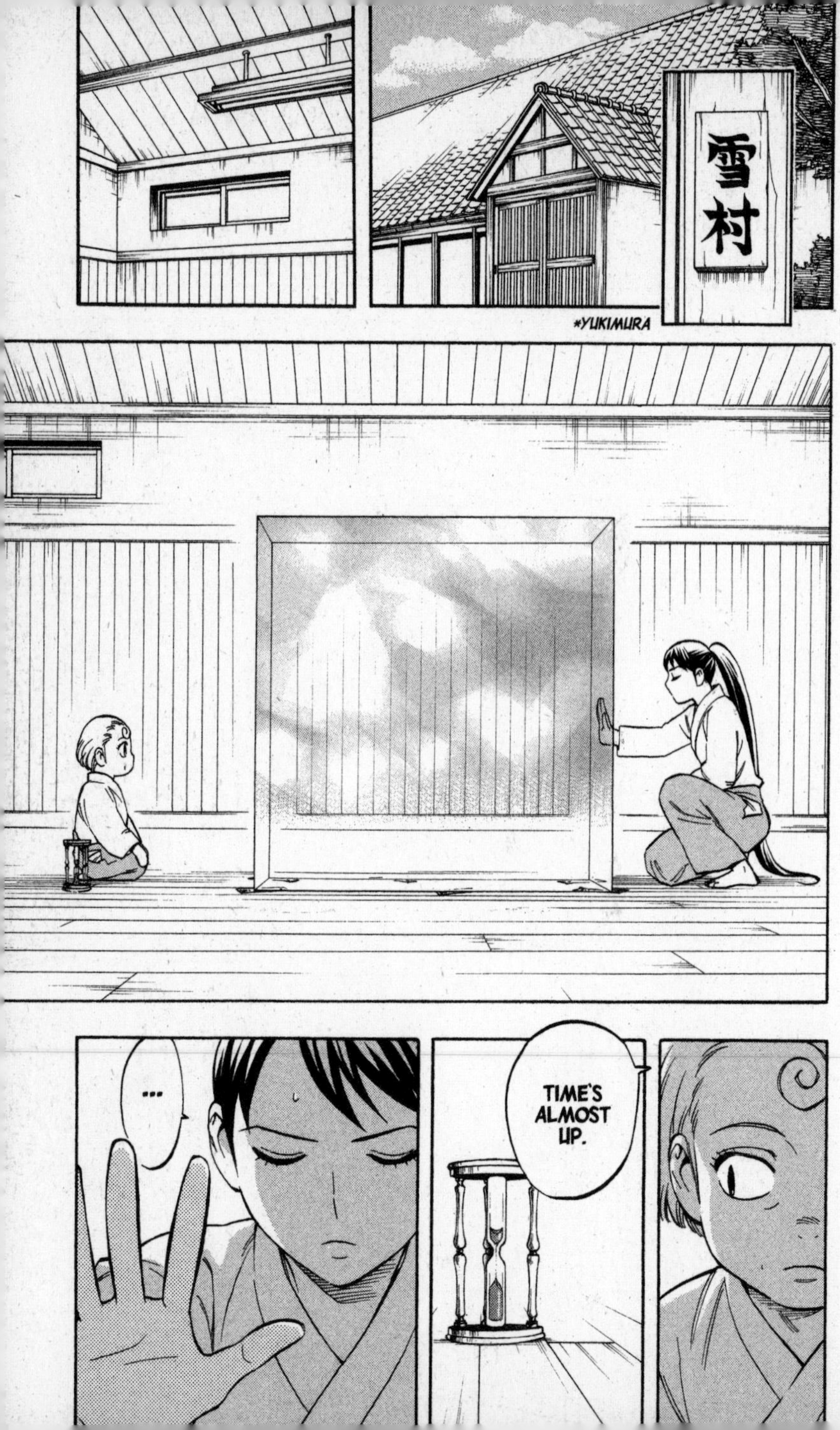

雪村
*YUKIMURA
TIME'S ALMOST UP.
...

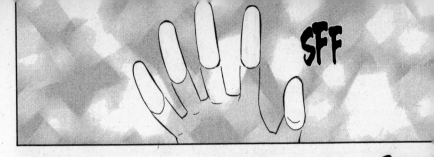

SFF

POOF

YES. GOOD WORK.

SSS

DID IT!

TMP

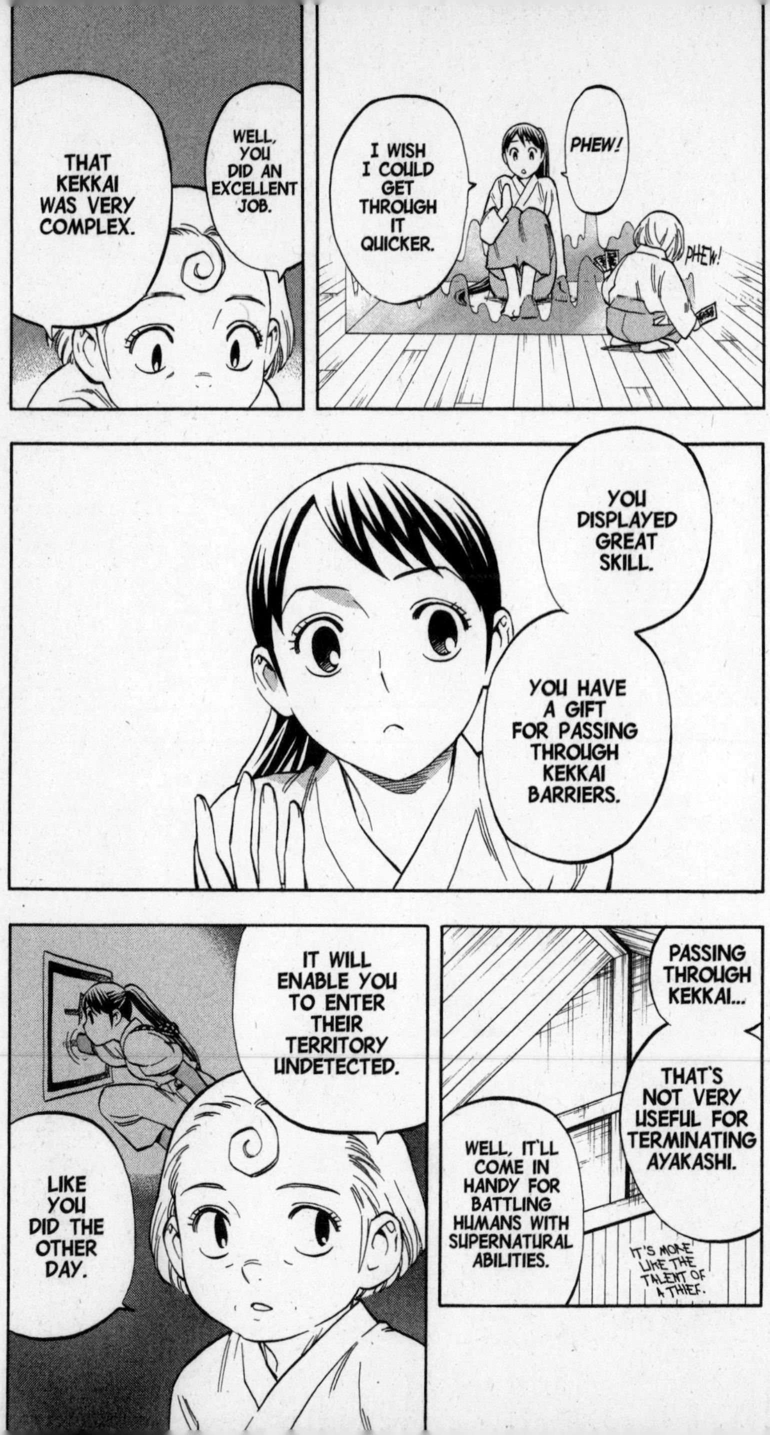
PHEW!
I WISH I COULD GET THROUGH IT QUICKER.
PHEW!
WELL, YOU DID AN EXCELLENT JOB.
THAT KEKKAI WAS VERY COMPLEX.
YOU DISPLAYED GREAT SKILL.
YOU HAVE A GIFT FOR PASSING THROUGH KEKKAI BARRIERS.
PASSING THROUGH KEKKAI...
THAT'S NOT VERY USEFUL FOR TERMINATING AYAKASHI.
WELL, IT'LL COME IN HANDY FOR BATTLING HUMANS WITH SUPERNATURAL ABILITIES.
IT'S MORE LIKE THE TALENT OF A THIEF.
IT WILL ENABLE YOU TO ENTER THEIR TERRITORY UNDETECTED.
LIKE YOU DID THE OTHER DAY.

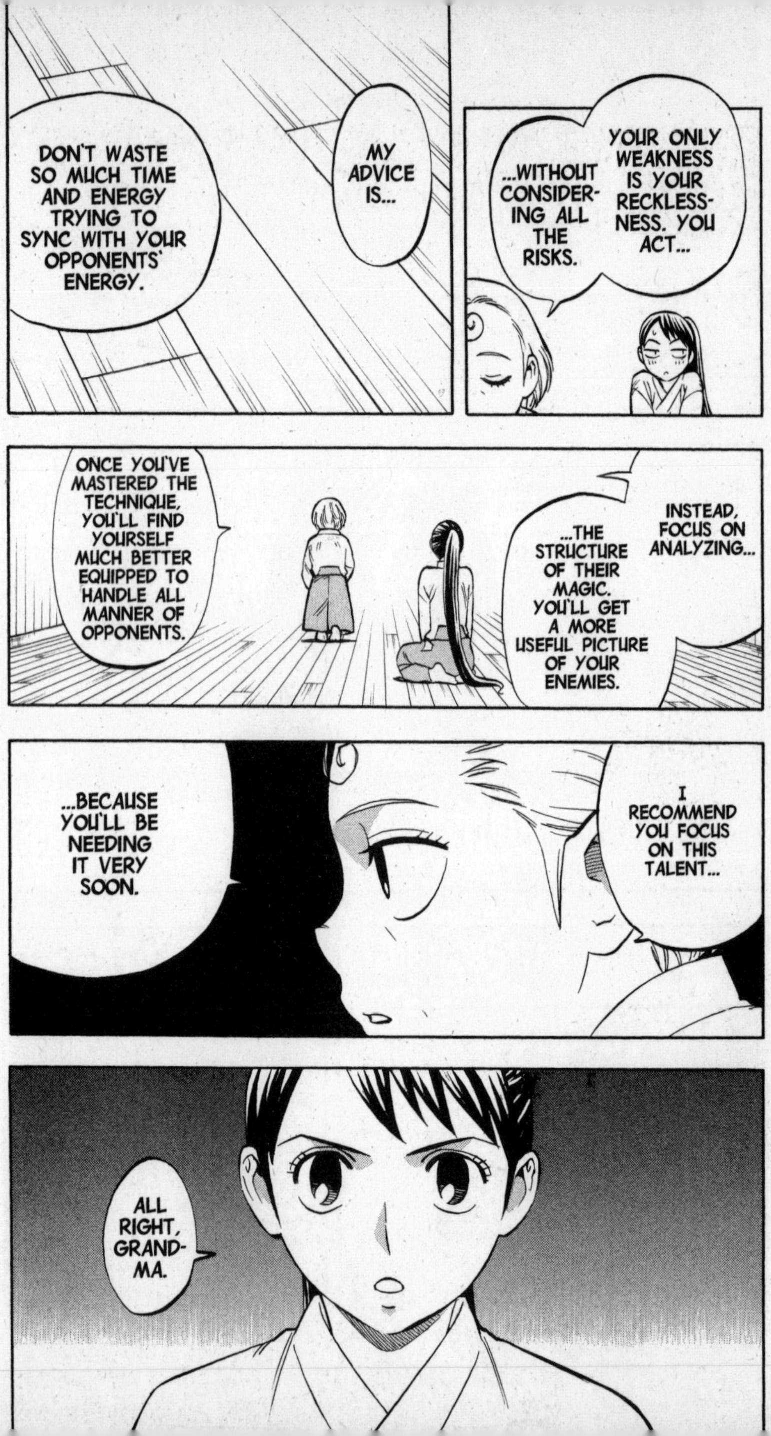
YOUR ONLY WEAKNESS IS YOUR RECKLESS-NESS. YOU ACT...
...WITHOUT CONSIDER-ING ALL THE RISKS.
MY ADVICE IS...
DON'T WASTE SO MUCH TIME AND ENERGY TRYING TO SYNC WITH YOUR OPPONENTS' ENERGY.
INSTEAD, FOCUS ON ANALYZING...
...THE STRUCTURE OF THEIR MAGIC. YOU'LL GET A MORE USEFUL PICTURE OF YOUR ENEMIES.
ONCE YOU'VE MASTERED THE TECHNIQUE, YOU'LL FIND YOURSELF MUCH BETTER EQUIPPED TO HANDLE ALL MANNER OF OPPONENTS.
I RECOMMEND YOU FOCUS ON THIS TALENT...
...BECAUSE YOU'LL BE NEEDING IT VERY SOON.
ALL RIGHT, GRAND-MA.

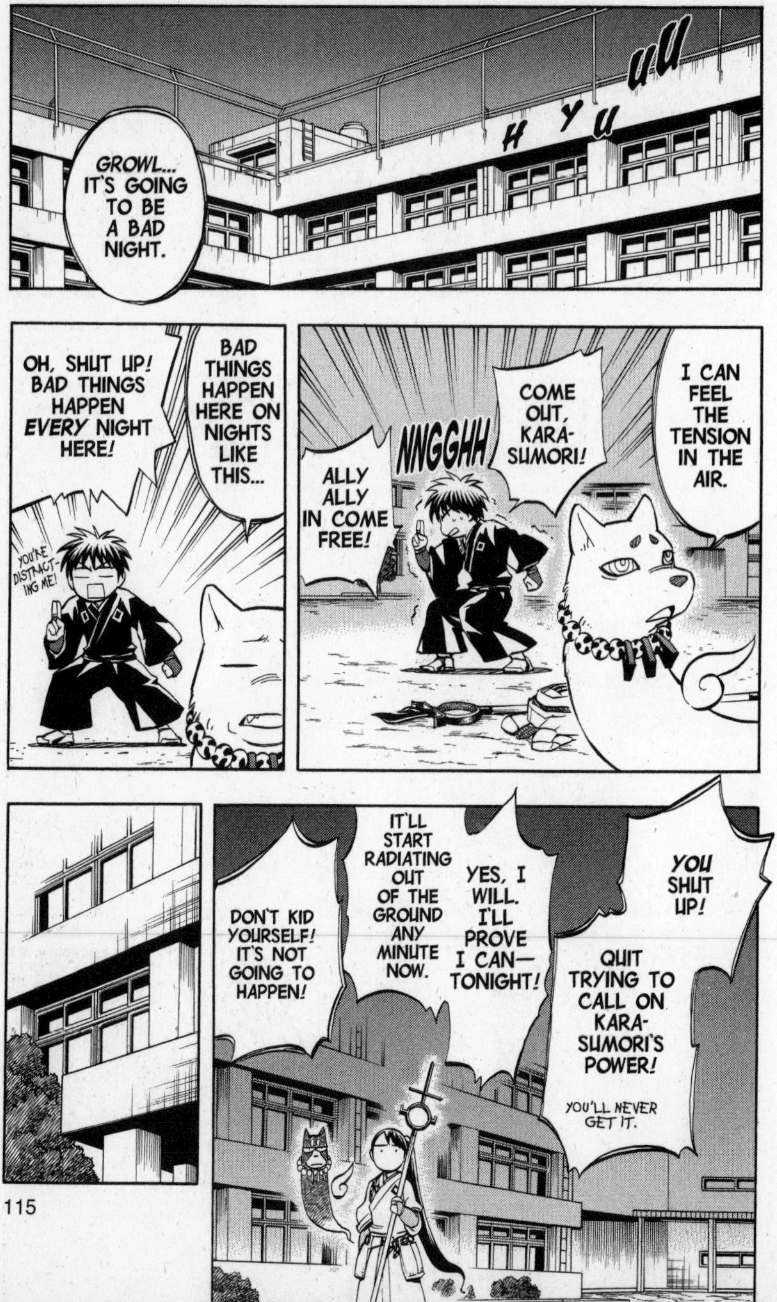
HYUUU
GROWL... IT'S GOING TO BE A BAD NIGHT.
I CAN FEEL THE TENSION IN THE AIR.
COME OUT, KARA-SUMORI!
NNGGHH
ALLY ALLY IN COME FREE!
BAD THINGS HAPPEN HERE ON NIGHTS LIKE THIS...
OH, SHUT UP! BAD THINGS HAPPEN *EVERY* NIGHT HERE!
YOU'RE DISTRACT-ING ME!
YOU SHUT UP!
QUIT TRYING TO CALL ON KARA-SUMORI'S POWER!
YOU'LL NEVER GET IT.
YES, I WILL. I'LL PROVE I CAN—TONIGHT!
IT'LL START RADIATING OUT OF THE GROUND ANY MINUTE NOW.
DON'T KID YOURSELF! IT'S NOT GOING TO HAPPEN!

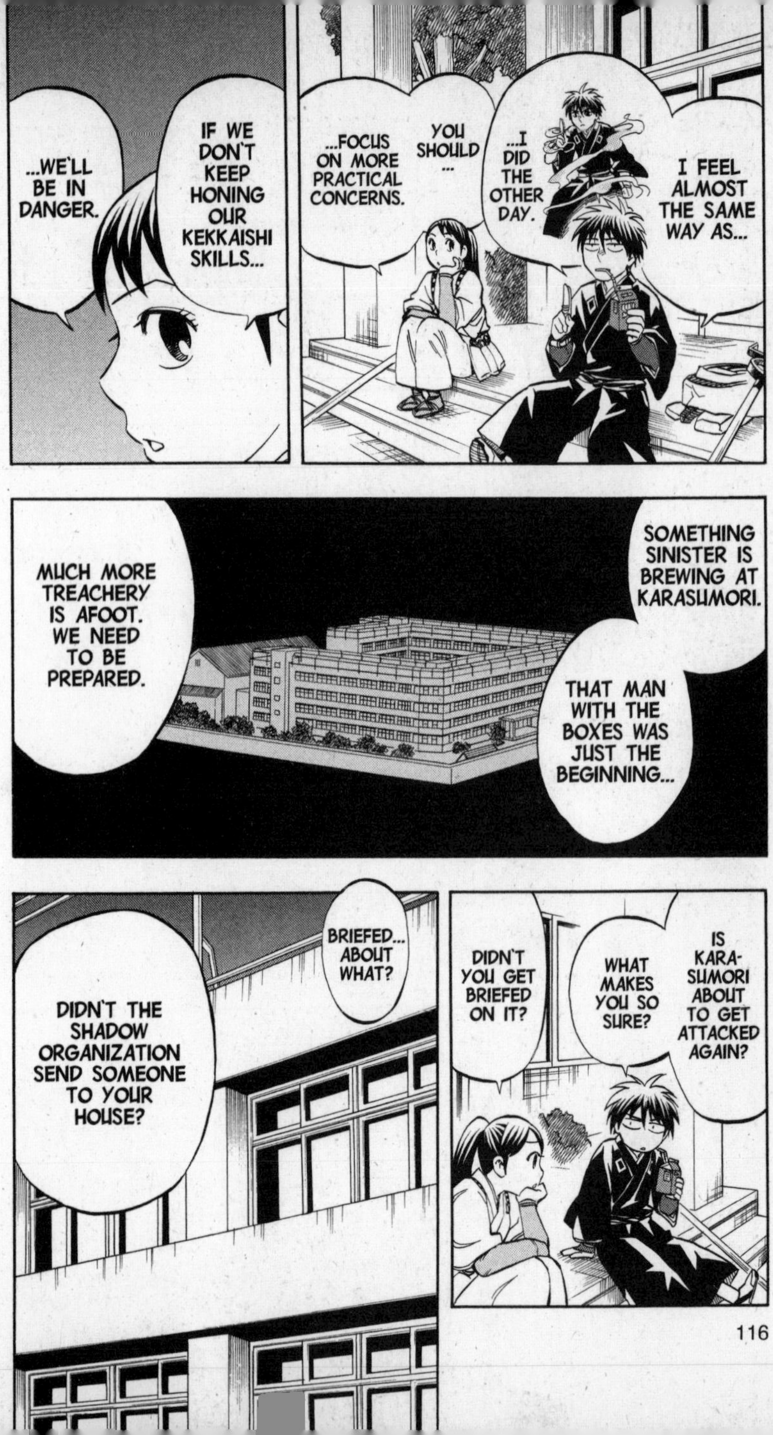
I FEEL ALMOST THE SAME WAY AS...
...I DID THE OTHER DAY.
YOU SHOULD...
...FOCUS ON MORE PRACTICAL CONCERNS.
IF WE DON'T KEEP HONING OUR KEKKAISHI SKILLS...
...WE'LL BE IN DANGER.
SOMETHING SINISTER IS BREWING AT KARASUMORI.
THAT MAN WITH THE BOXES WAS JUST THE BEGINNING...
MUCH MORE TREACHERY IS AFOOT. WE NEED TO BE PREPARED.
IS KARA-SUMORI ABOUT TO GET ATTACKED AGAIN?
WHAT MAKES YOU SO SURE?
DIDN'T YOU GET BRIEFED ON IT?
BRIEFED... ABOUT WHAT?
DIDN'T THE SHADOW ORGANIZATION SEND SOMEONE TO YOUR HOUSE?

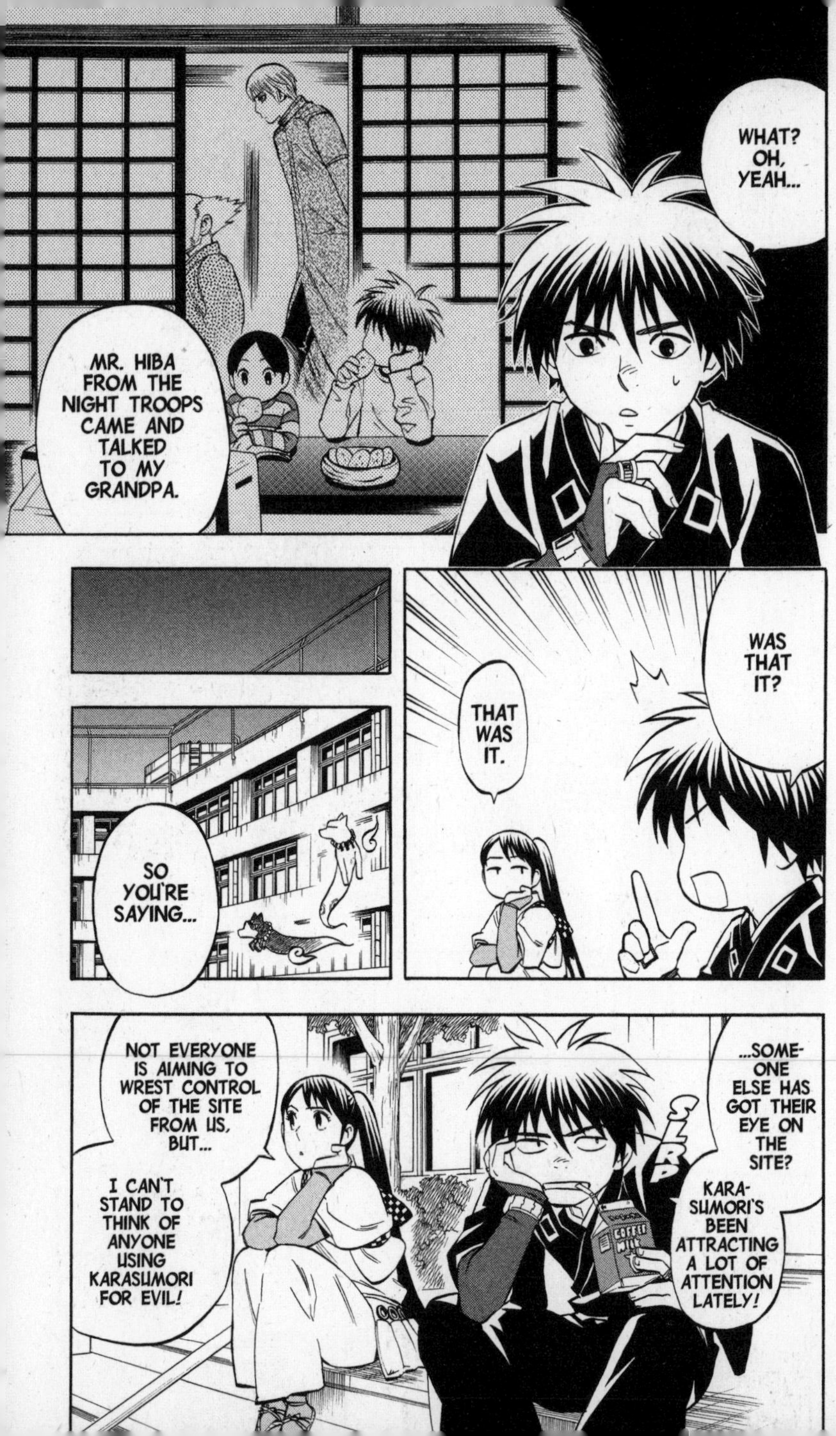
WHAT? OH, YEAH...
MR. HIBA FROM THE NIGHT TROOPS CAME AND TALKED TO MY GRANDPA.
WAS THAT IT?
THAT WAS IT.
SO YOU'RE SAYING...
...SOME-ONE ELSE HAS GOT THEIR EYE ON THE SITE?
SLRP
KARA-SUMORI'S BEEN ATTRACTING A LOT OF ATTENTION LATELY!
NOT EVERYONE IS AIMING TO WREST CONTROL OF THE SITE FROM US, BUT...
I CAN'T STAND TO THINK OF ANYONE USING KARASUMORI FOR EVIL!
COFFEE MILK

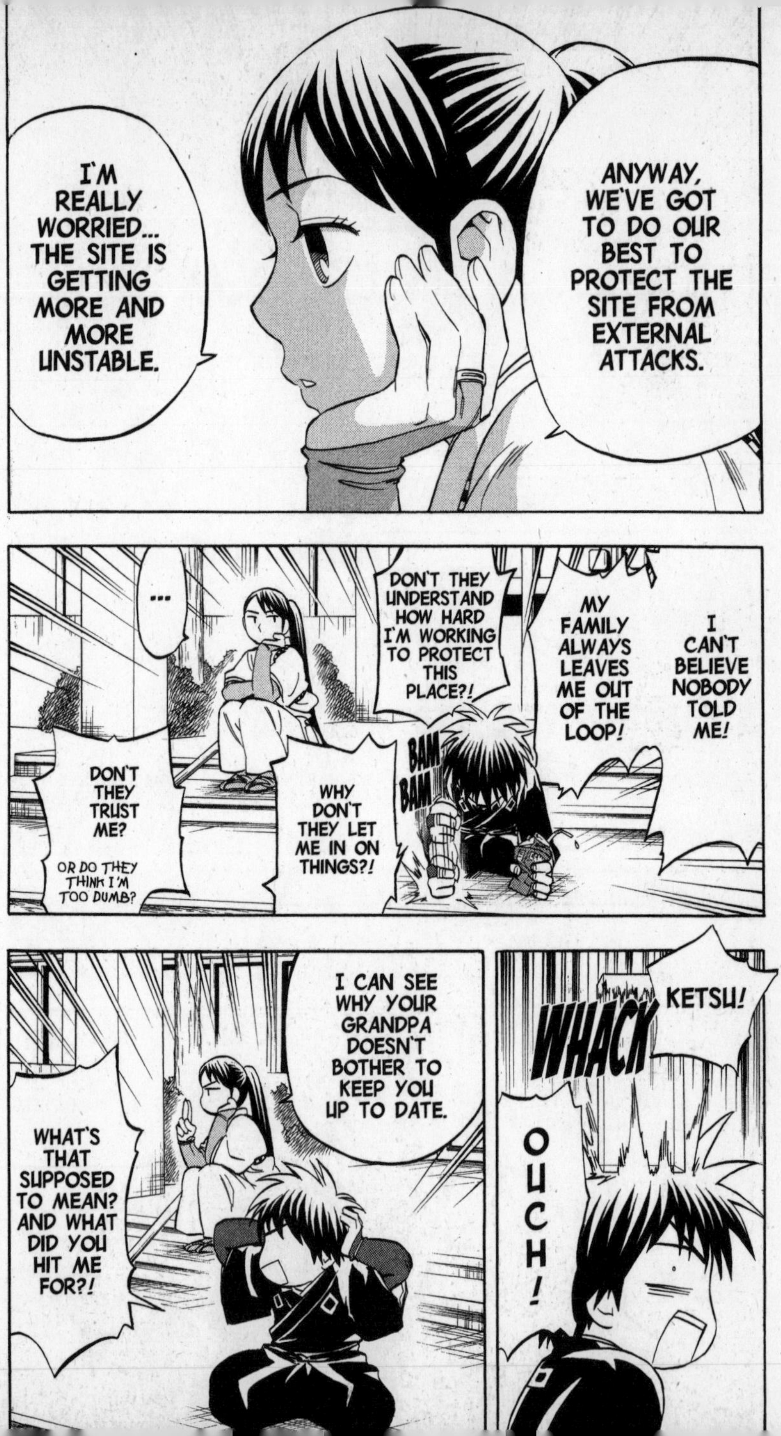
ANYWAY, WE'VE GOT TO DO OUR BEST TO PROTECT THE SITE FROM EXTERNAL ATTACKS.
I'M REALLY WORRIED... THE SITE IS GETTING MORE AND MORE UNSTABLE.
I CAN'T BELIEVE NOBODY TOLD ME!
MY FAMILY ALWAYS LEAVES ME OUT OF THE LOOP!
DON'T THEY UNDERSTAND HOW HARD I'M WORKING TO PROTECT THIS PLACE?!
BAM BAM
...
WHY DON'T THEY LET ME IN ON THINGS?!
DON'T THEY TRUST ME?
OR DO THEY THINK I'M TOO DUMB?
KETSU!
WHACK
OUCH!
I CAN SEE WHY YOUR GRANDPA DOESN'T BOTHER TO KEEP YOU UP TO DATE.
WHAT'S THAT SUPPOSED TO MEAN? AND WHAT DID YOU HIT ME FOR?!

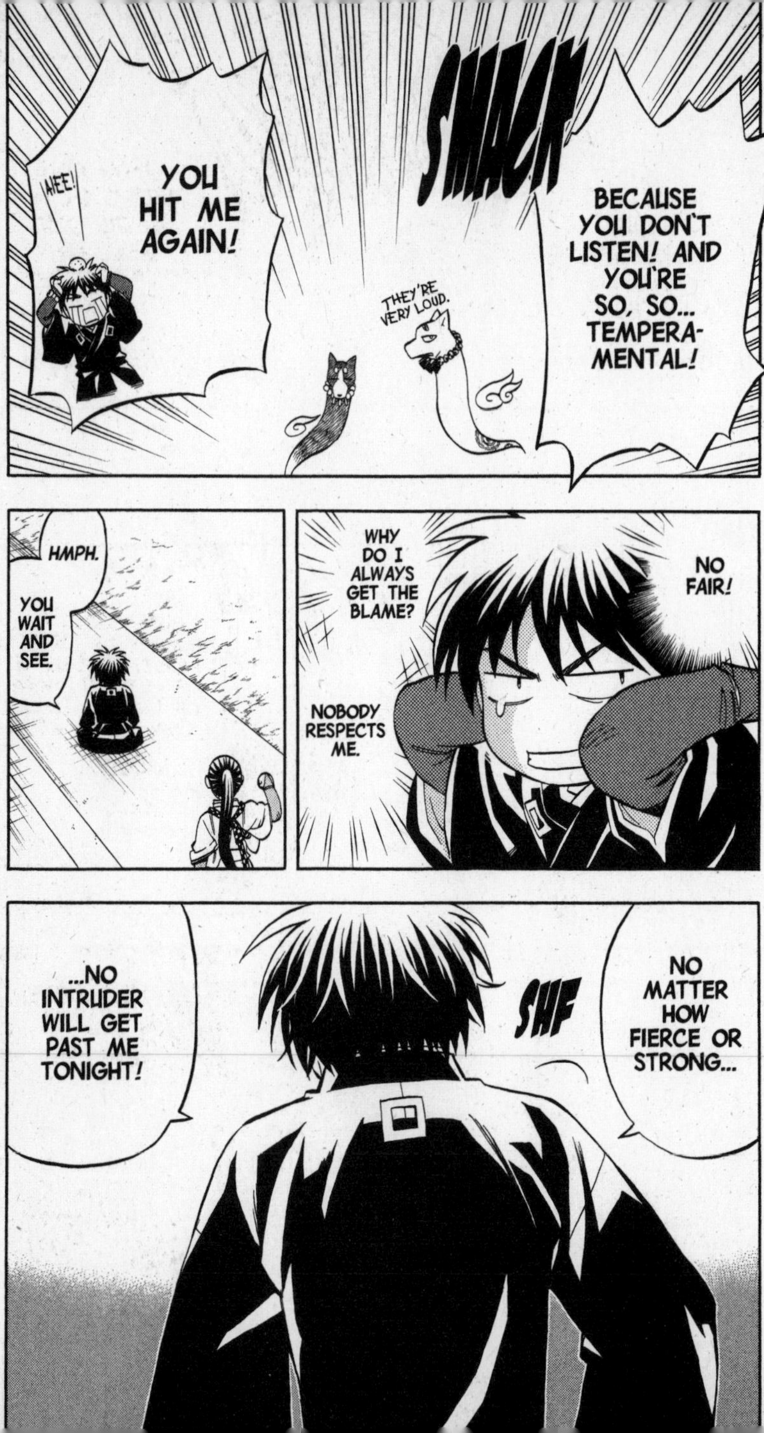
SMACK
BECAUSE YOU DON'T LISTEN! AND YOU'RE SO, SO... TEMPERA-MENTAL!
THEY'RE VERY LOUD.
YOU HIT ME AGAIN!
AIEE!
NO FAIR!
WHY DO I ALWAYS GET THE BLAME?
NOBODY RESPECTS ME.
HMPH.
YOU WAIT AND SEE.
NO MATTER HOW FIERCE OR STRONG...
SHF
...NO INTRUDER WILL GET PAST ME TONIGHT!

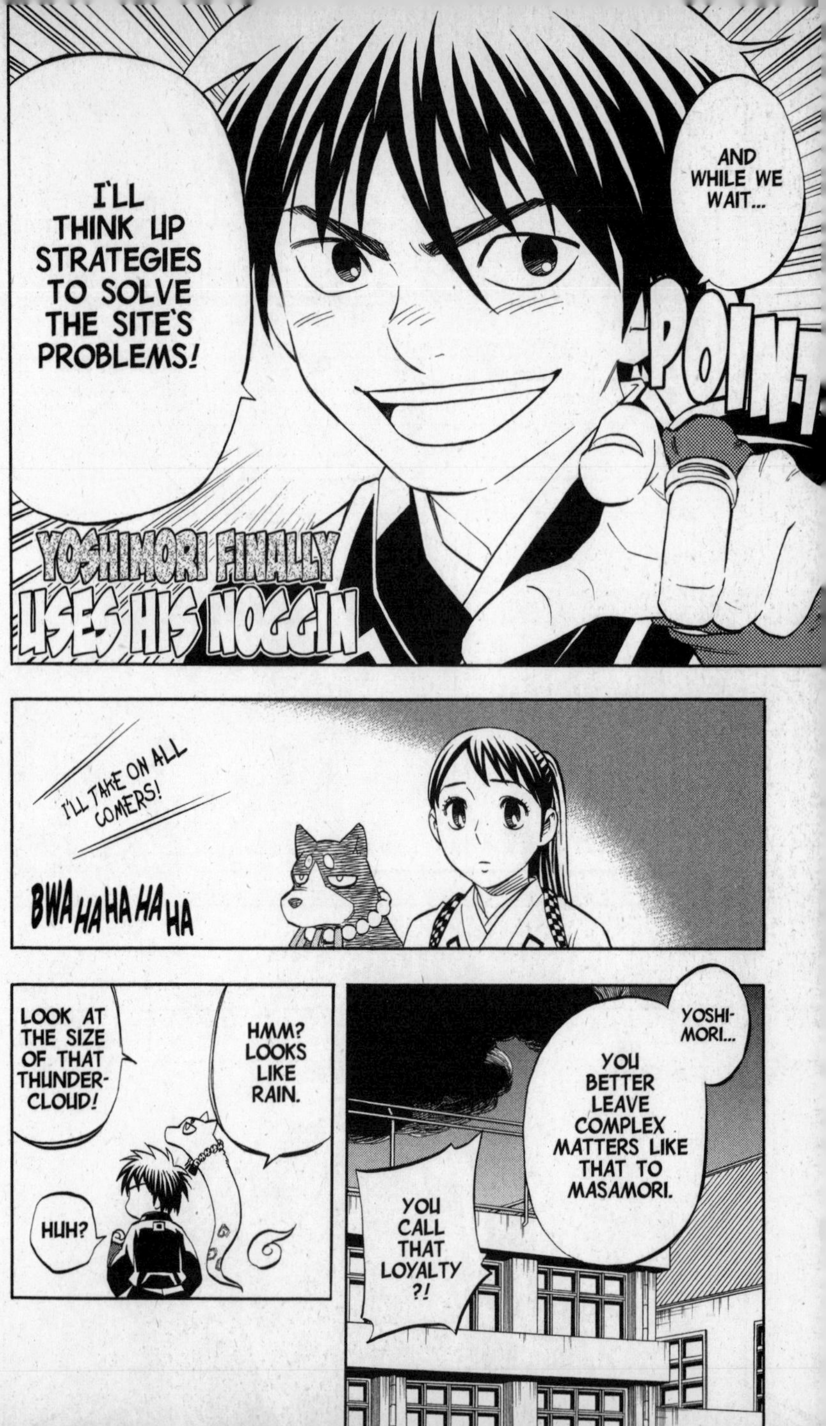
AND WHILE WE WAIT...
I'LL THINK UP STRATEGIES TO SOLVE THE SITE'S PROBLEMS!
POIN
YOSHIMORI FINALLY USES HIS NOGGIN
I'LL TAKE ON ALL COMERS!
BWAHAHAHAHA
YOSHI-MORI...
YOU BETTER LEAVE COMPLEX MATTERS LIKE THAT TO MASAMORI.
YOU CALL THAT LOYALTY?!
HMM? LOOKS LIKE RAIN.
LOOK AT THE SIZE OF THAT THUNDER-CLOUD!
HUH?

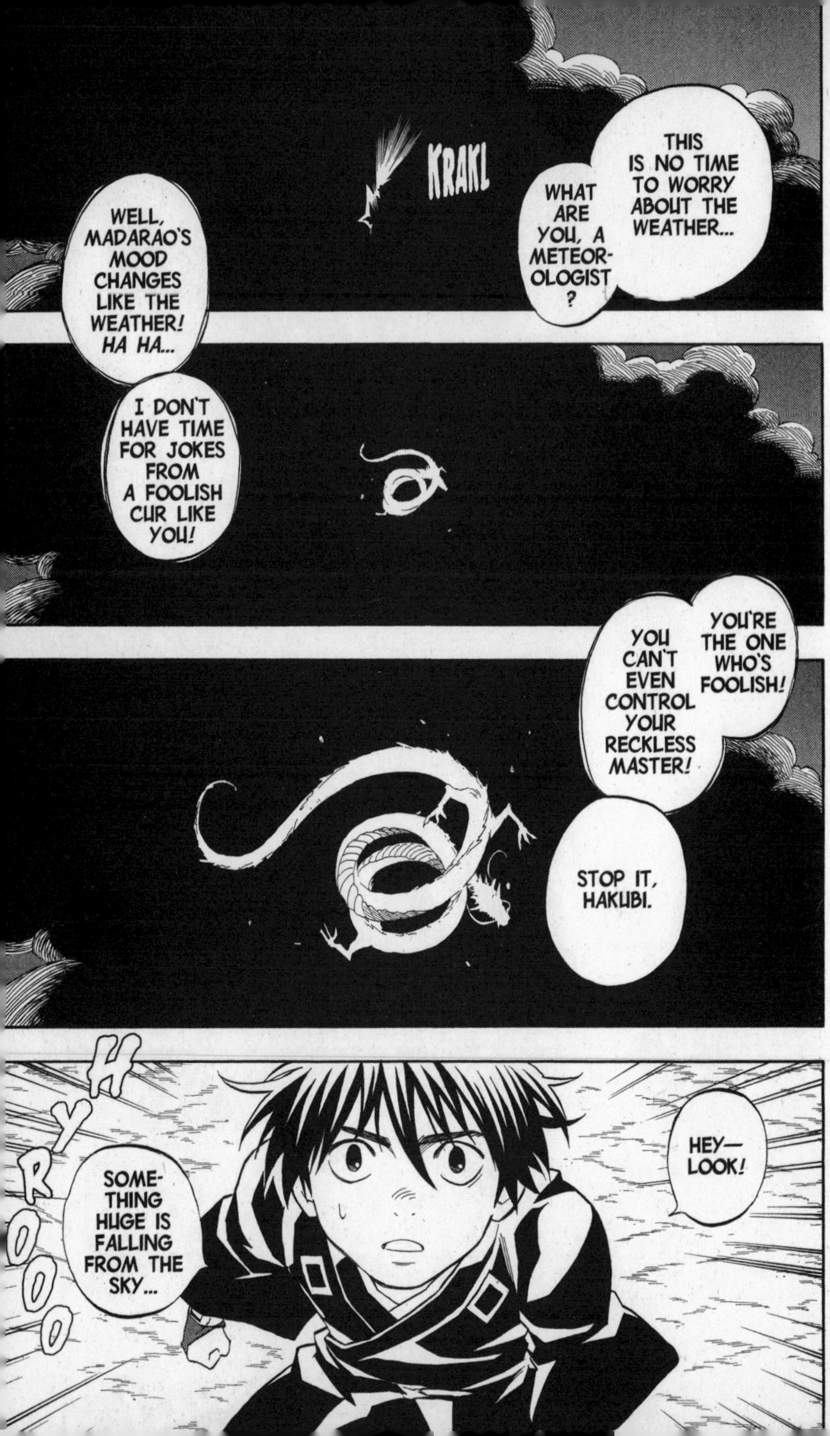
KRAKL
THIS IS NO TIME TO WORRY ABOUT THE WEATHER...
WHAT ARE YOU, A METEOR-OLOGIST?
WELL, MADARAO'S MOOD CHANGES LIKE THE WEATHER! HA HA...
I DON'T HAVE TIME FOR JOKES FROM A FOOLISH CUR LIKE YOU!
YOU'RE THE ONE WHO'S FOOLISH!
YOU CAN'T EVEN CONTROL YOUR RECKLESS MASTER!
STOP IT, HAKUBI.
HEY—LOOK!
SOME-THING HUGE IS FALLING FROM THE SKY...
HRYROOOO

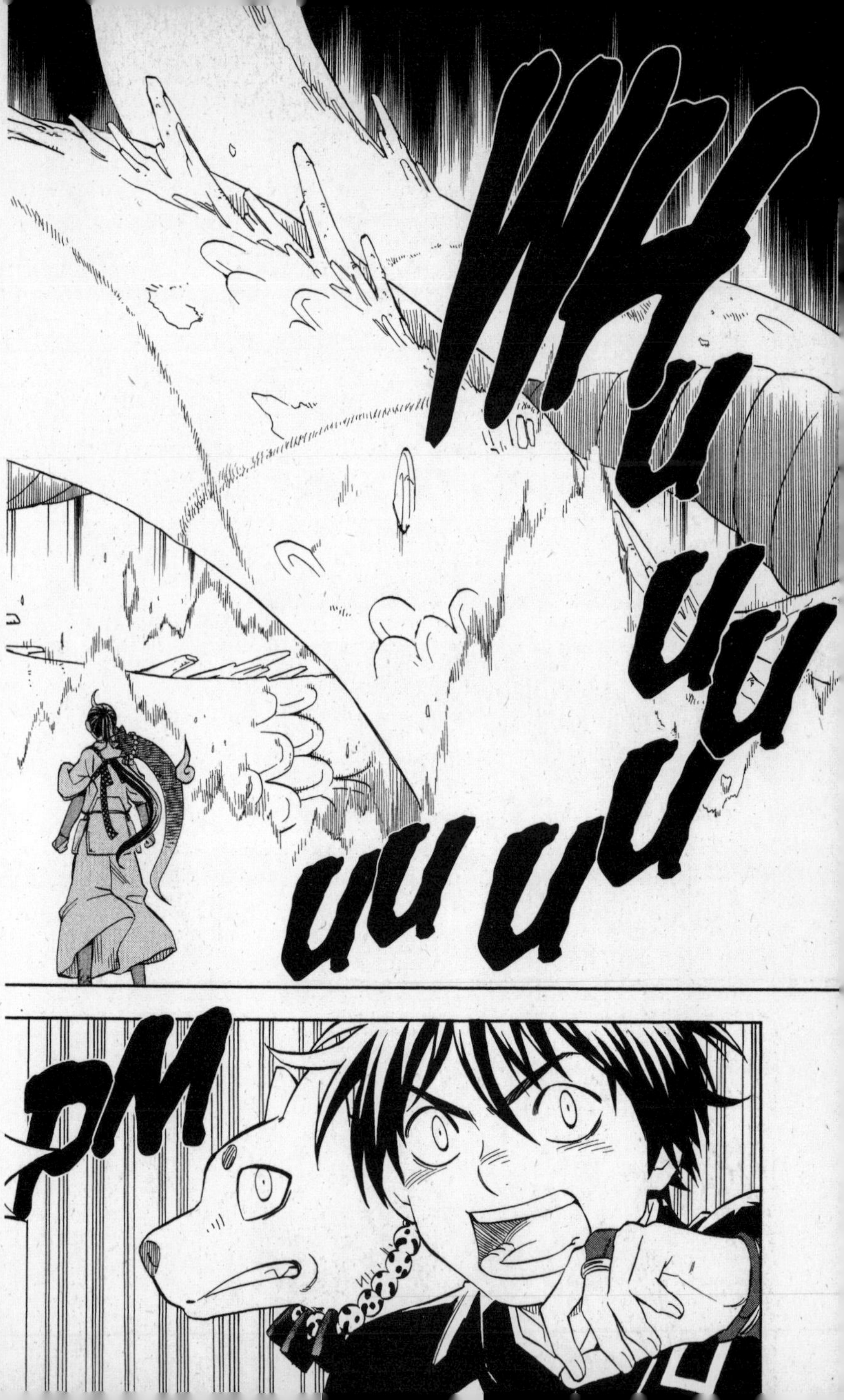
WHUUUUUUU
TM

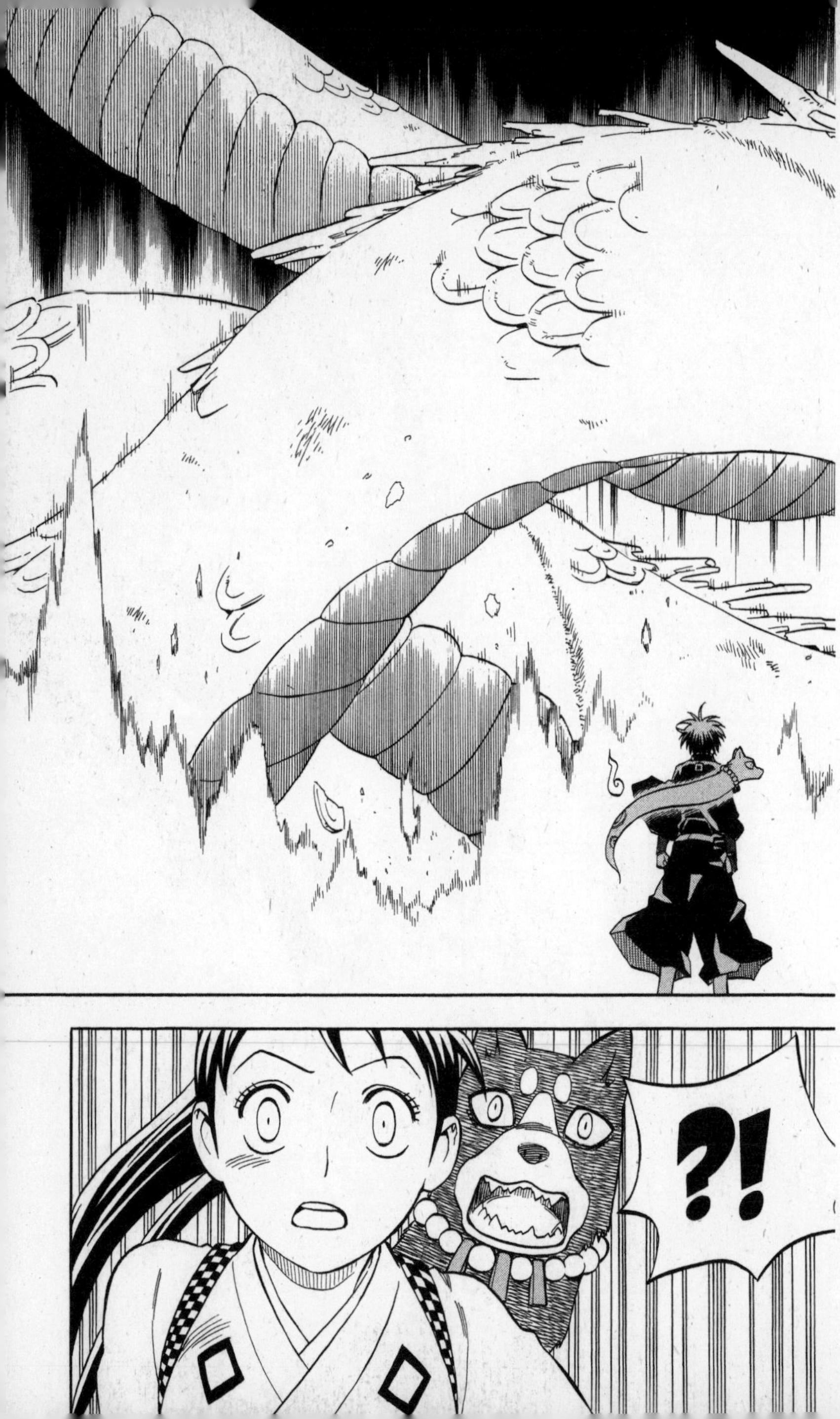
?!

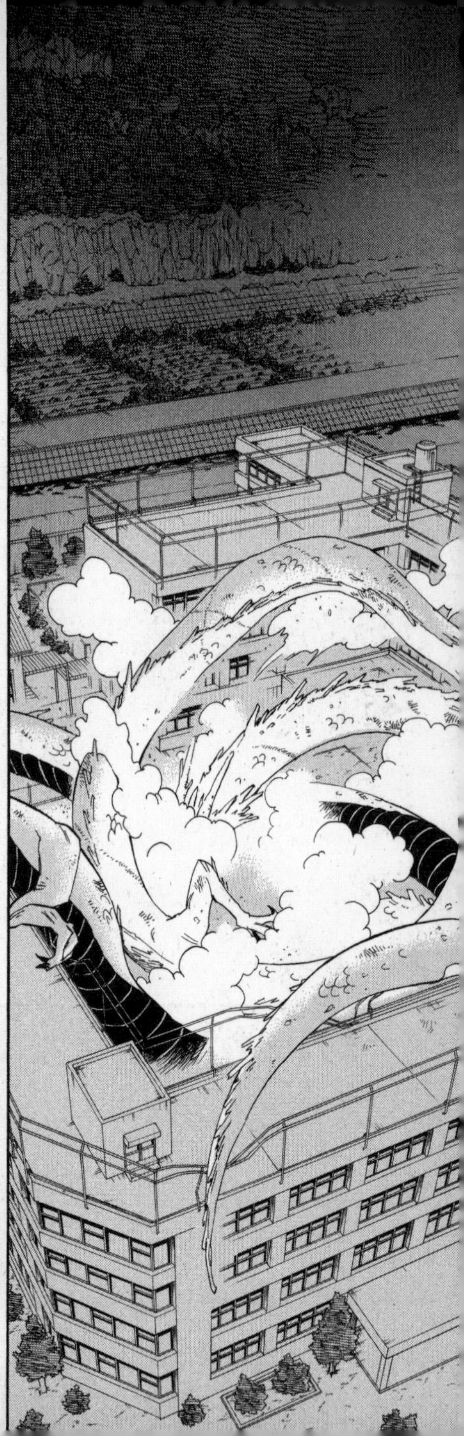
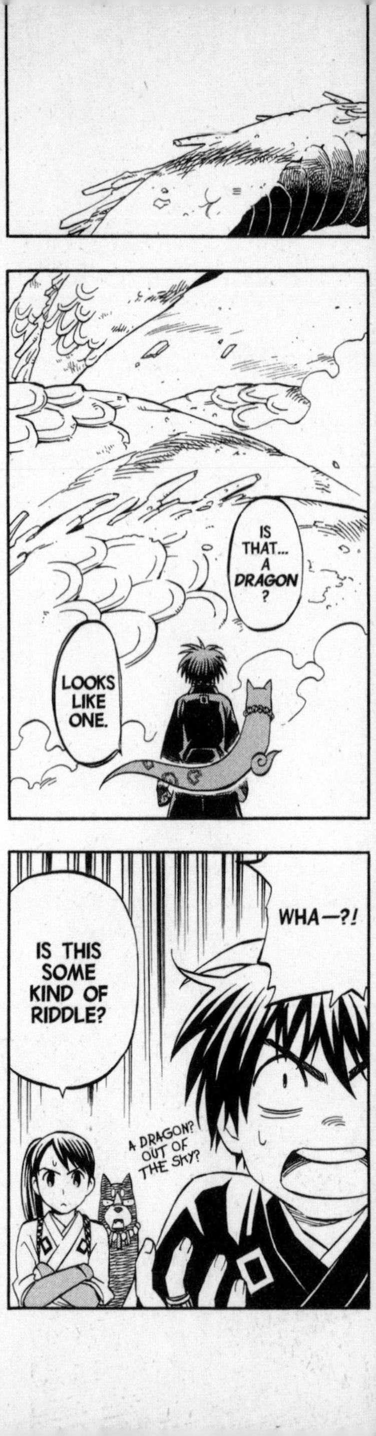
IS THAT... A DRAGON?
LOOKS LIKE ONE.
WHA—?!
IS THIS SOME KIND OF RIDDLE?
A DRAGON? OUT OF THE SKY?

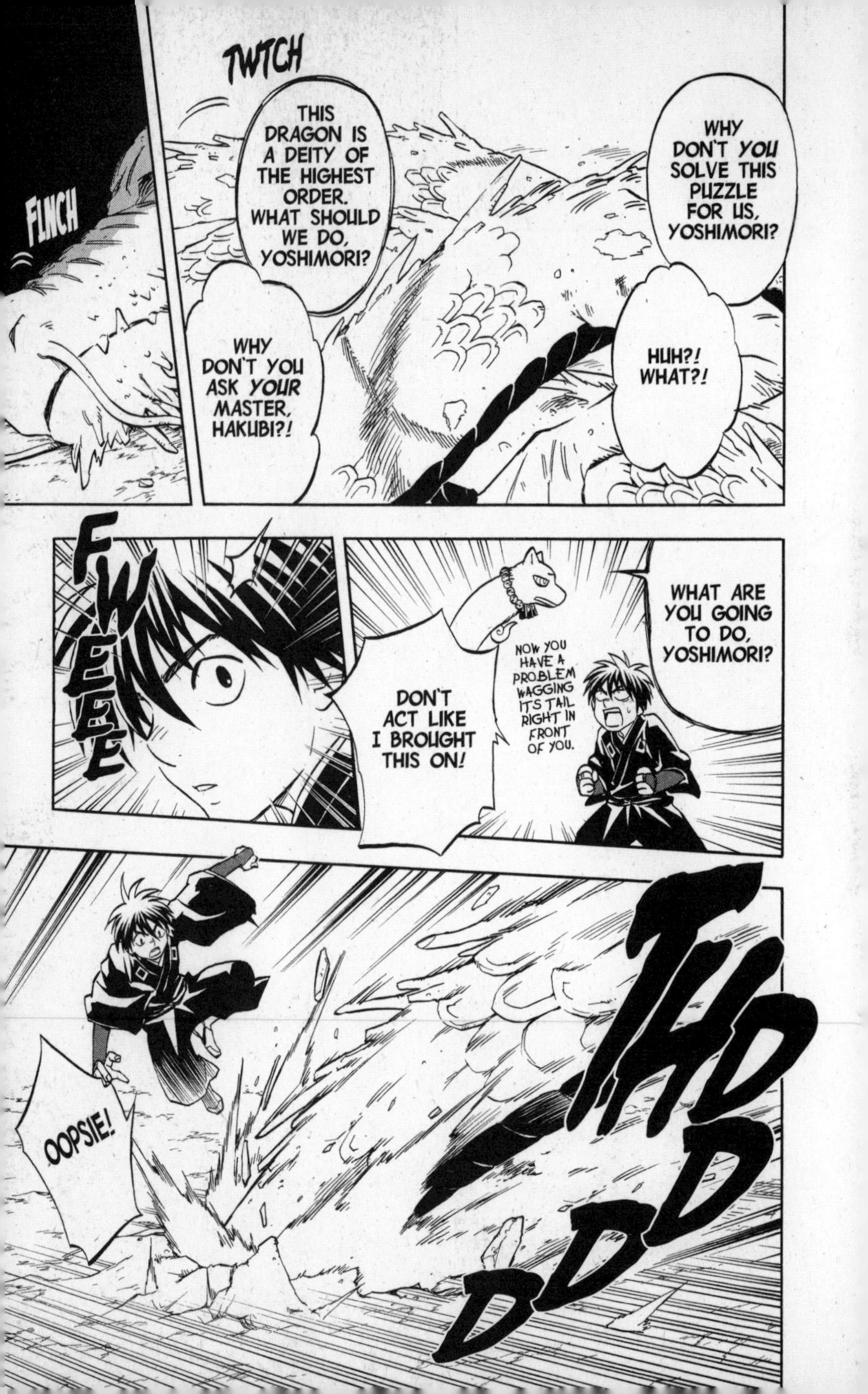
TWITCH
WHY DON'T YOU SOLVE THIS PUZZLE FOR US, YOSHIMORI?
THIS DRAGON IS A DEITY OF THE HIGHEST ORDER. WHAT SHOULD WE DO, YOSHIMORI?
HUH?! WHAT?!
WHY DON'T YOU ASK YOUR MASTER, HAKUBI?!
FLINCH
WHAT ARE YOU GOING TO DO, YOSHIMORI?
NOW YOU HAVE A PROBLEM WAGGING ITS TAIL RIGHT IN FRONT OF YOU.
DON'T ACT LIKE I BROUGHT THIS ON!
FWEEEE
THUDDDD
OOPSIE!

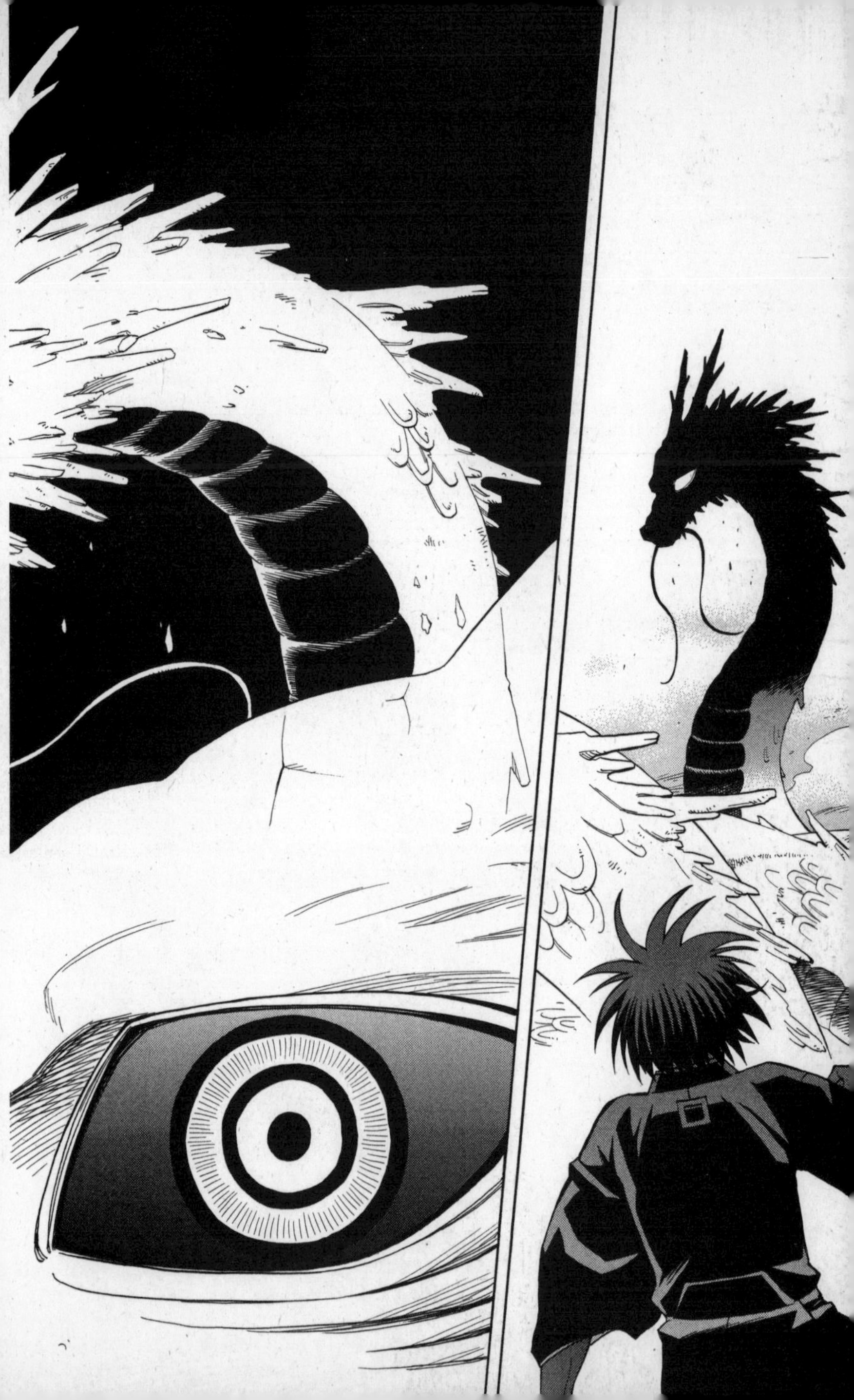

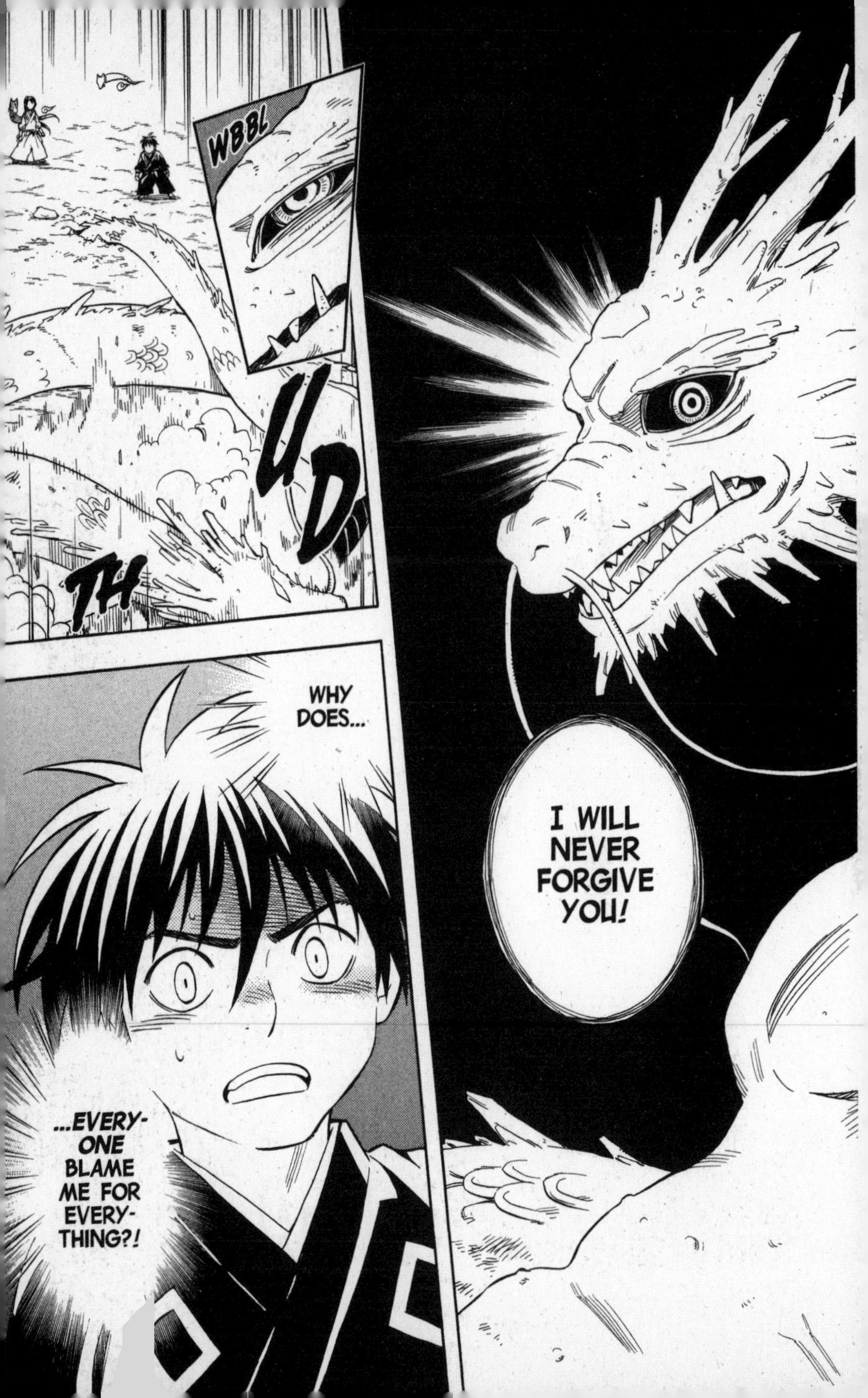
I WILL NEVER FORGIVE YOU!
WBBL
THUD
WHY DOES...
...EVERYONE BLAME ME FOR EVERYTHING?!

結界師

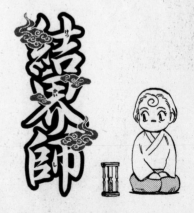

Chapter 152: Water Dragon

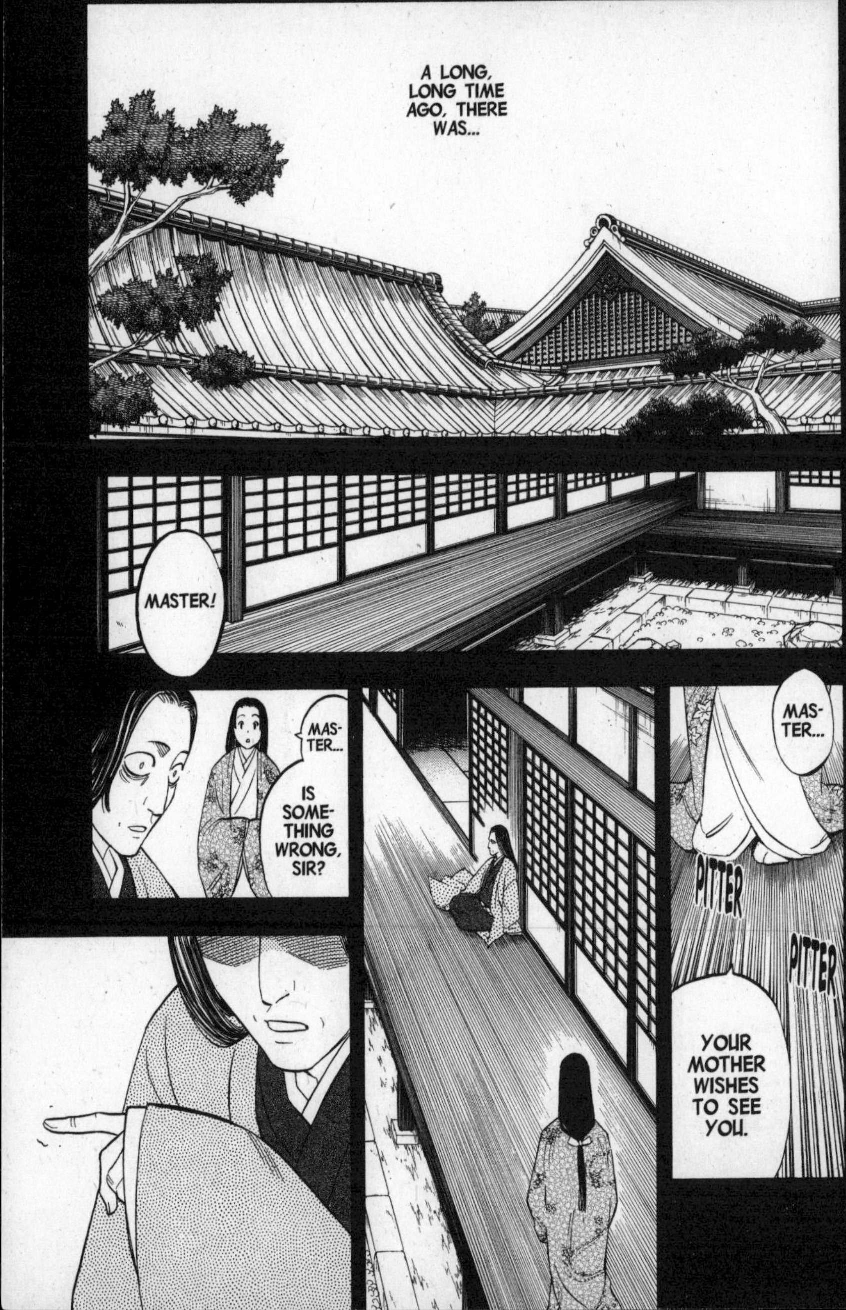
A LONG, LONG TIME AGO, THERE WAS...
MASTER!
MAS-TER...
PITTER
PITTER
YOUR MOTHER WISHES TO SEE YOU.
MAS-TER...
IS SOMETHING WRONG, SIR?

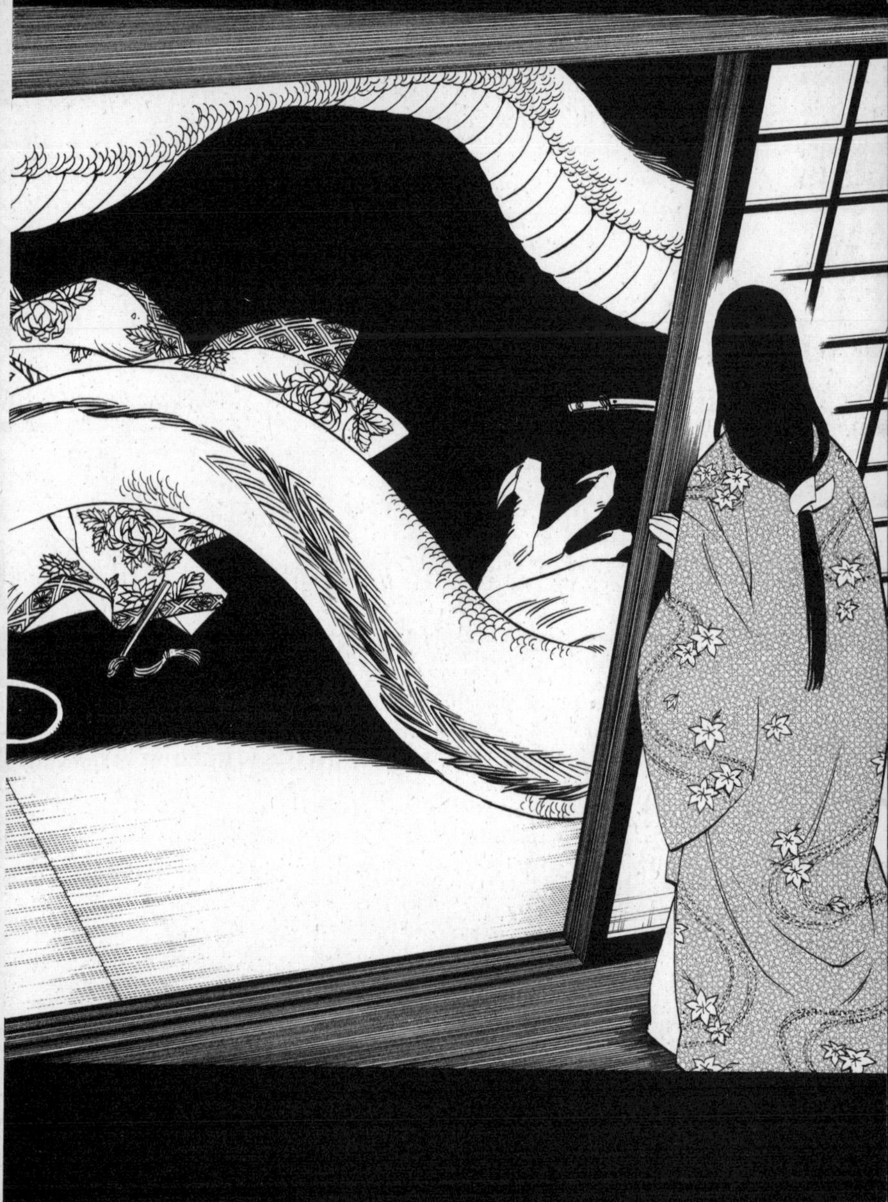

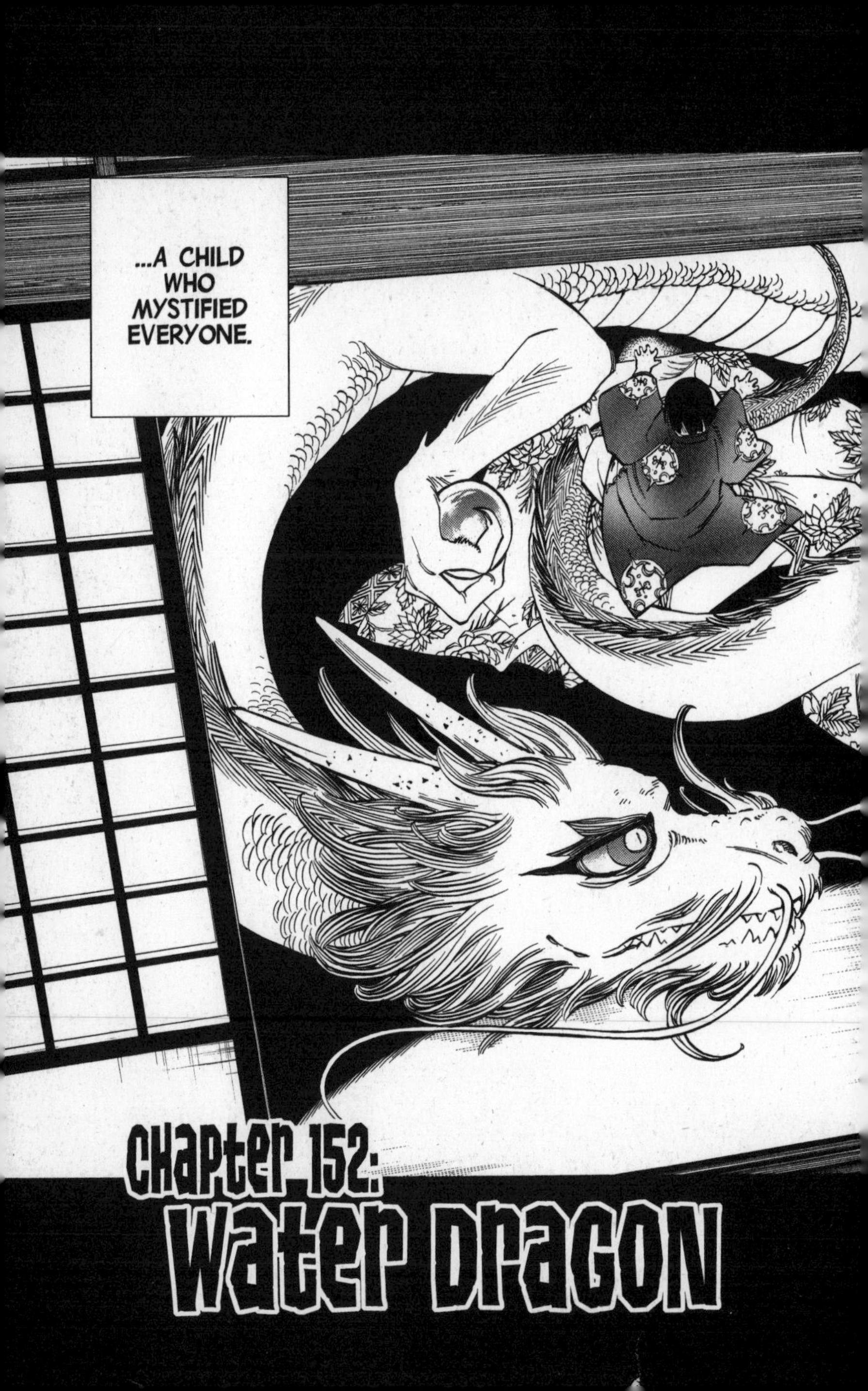
...A CHILD WHO MYSTIFIED EVERYONE.
CHAPTER 152:
WATER DRAGON

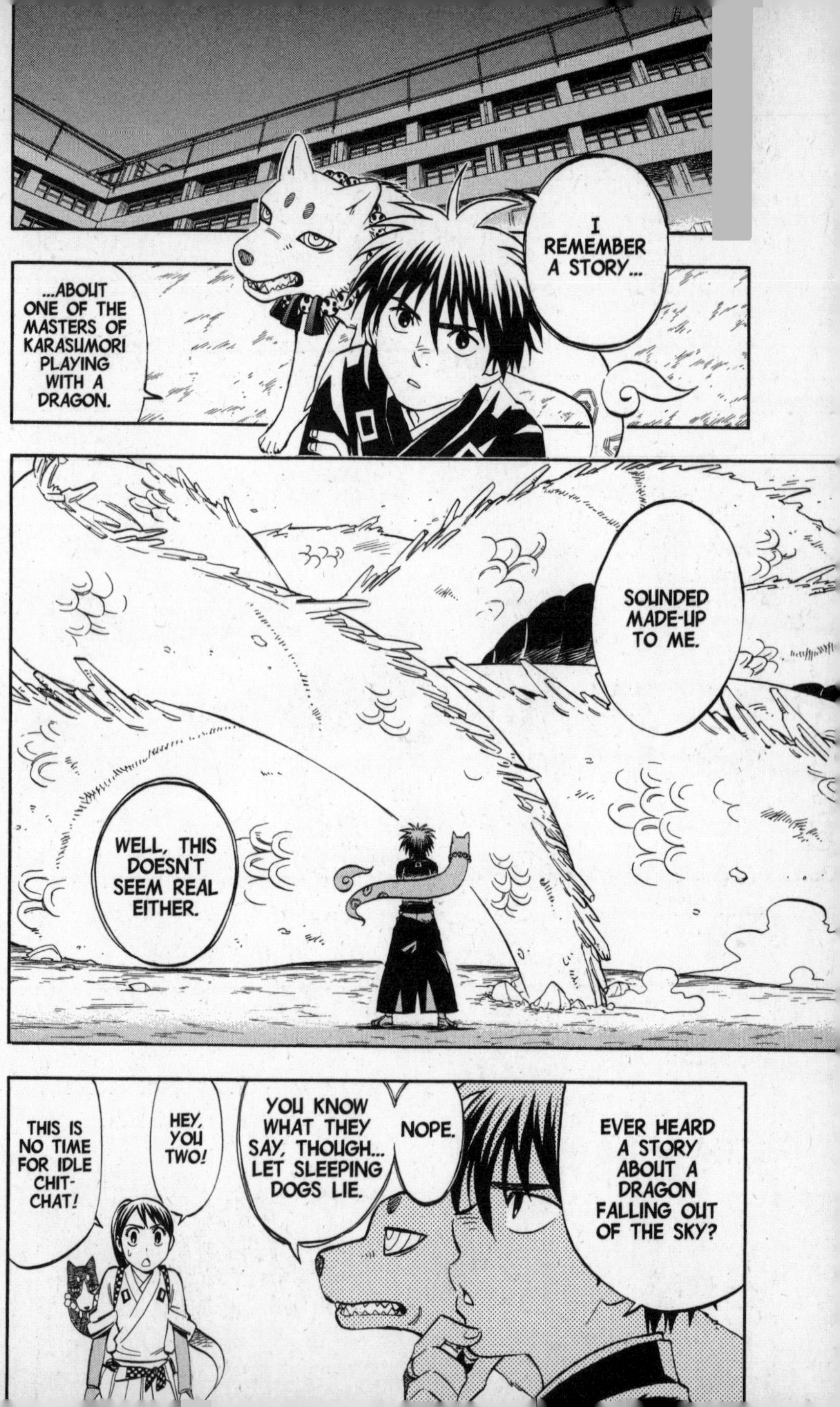
I REMEMBER A STORY...
...ABOUT ONE OF THE MASTERS OF KARASUMORI PLAYING WITH A DRAGON.
SOUNDED MADE-UP TO ME.
WELL, THIS DOESN'T SEEM REAL EITHER.
EVER HEARD A STORY ABOUT A DRAGON FALLING OUT OF THE SKY?
NOPE.
YOU KNOW WHAT THEY SAY, THOUGH... LET SLEEPING DOGS LIE.
HEY, YOU TWO!
THIS IS NO TIME FOR IDLE CHIT-CHAT!

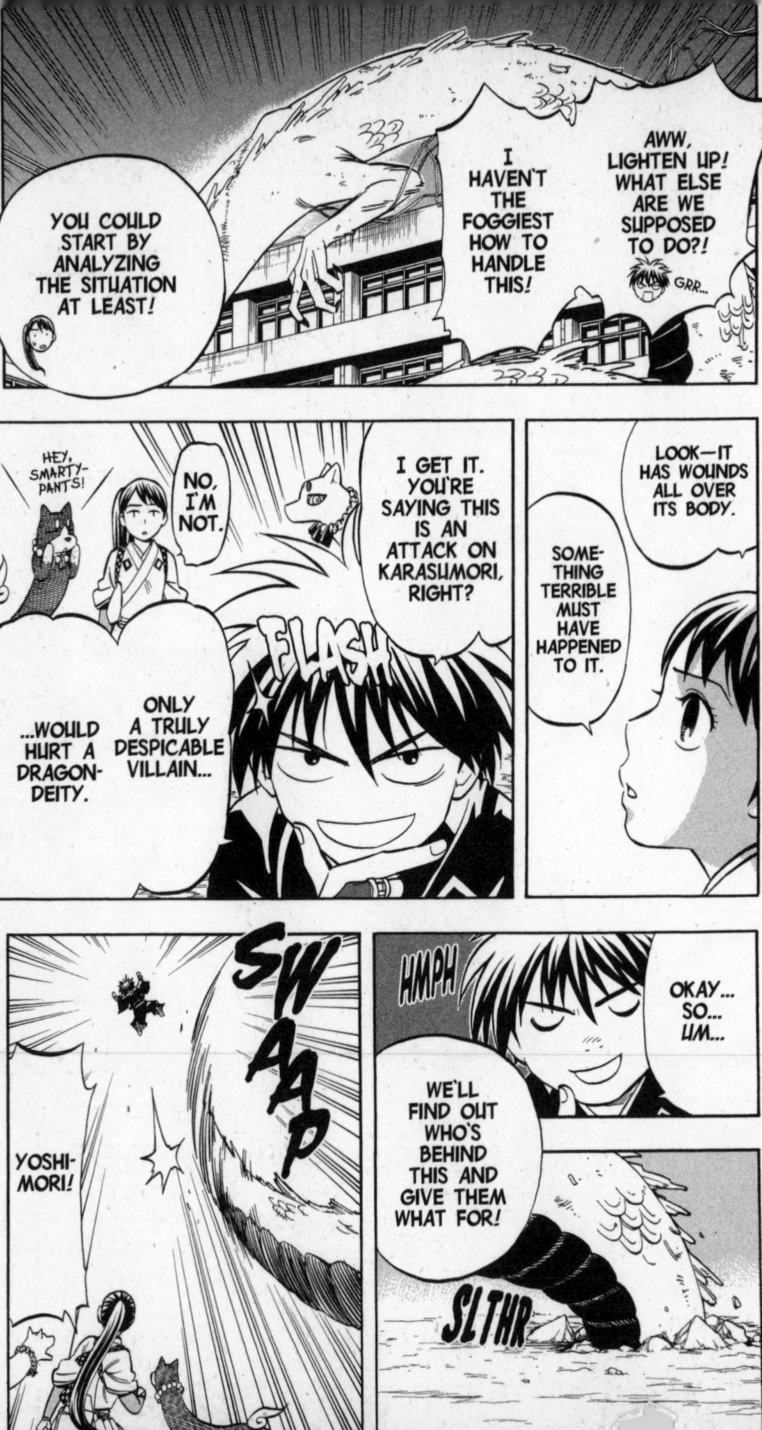
AWW, LIGHTEN UP! WHAT ELSE ARE WE SUPPOSED TO DO?!
GRR...
I HAVEN'T THE FOGGIEST HOW TO HANDLE THIS!
YOU COULD START BY ANALYZING THE SITUATION AT LEAST!
LOOK—IT HAS WOUNDS ALL OVER ITS BODY.
SOMETHING TERRIBLE MUST HAVE HAPPENED TO IT.
I GET IT. YOU'RE SAYING THIS IS AN ATTACK ON KARASUMORI, RIGHT?
FLASH
NO, I'M NOT.
HEY, SMARTY-PANTS!
ONLY A TRULY DESPICABLE VILLAIN...
...WOULD HURT A DRAGON-DEITY.
HMPH
OKAY... SO... UM...
WE'LL FIND OUT WHO'S BEHIND THIS AND GIVE THEM WHAT FOR!
SLTHR
SWAAAP
YOSHIMORI!

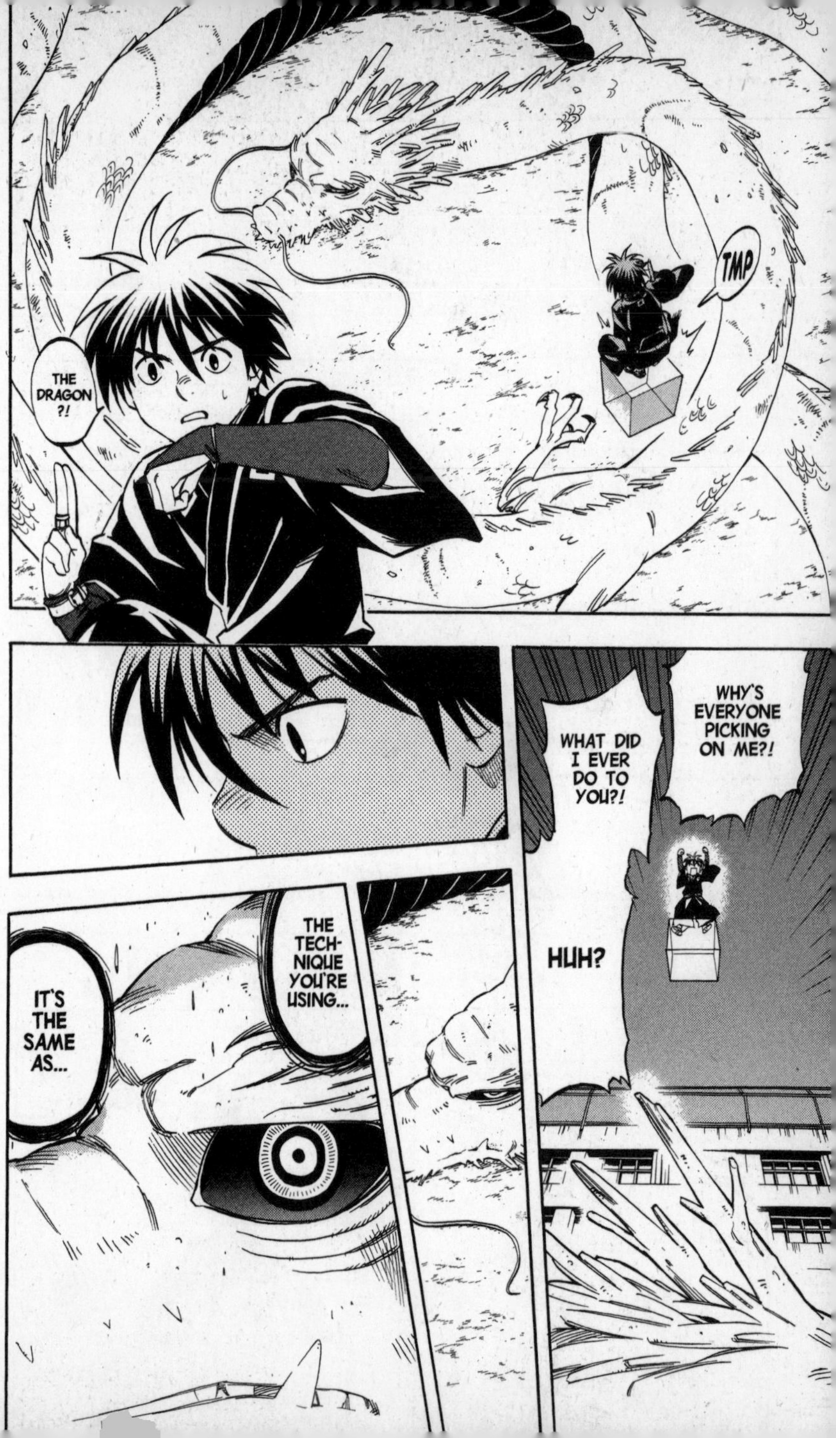
TMP
THE DRAGON?!
WHY'S EVERYONE PICKING ON ME?!
WHAT DID I EVER DO TO YOU?!
HUH?
THE TECHNIQUE YOU'RE USING...
IT'S THE SAME AS...

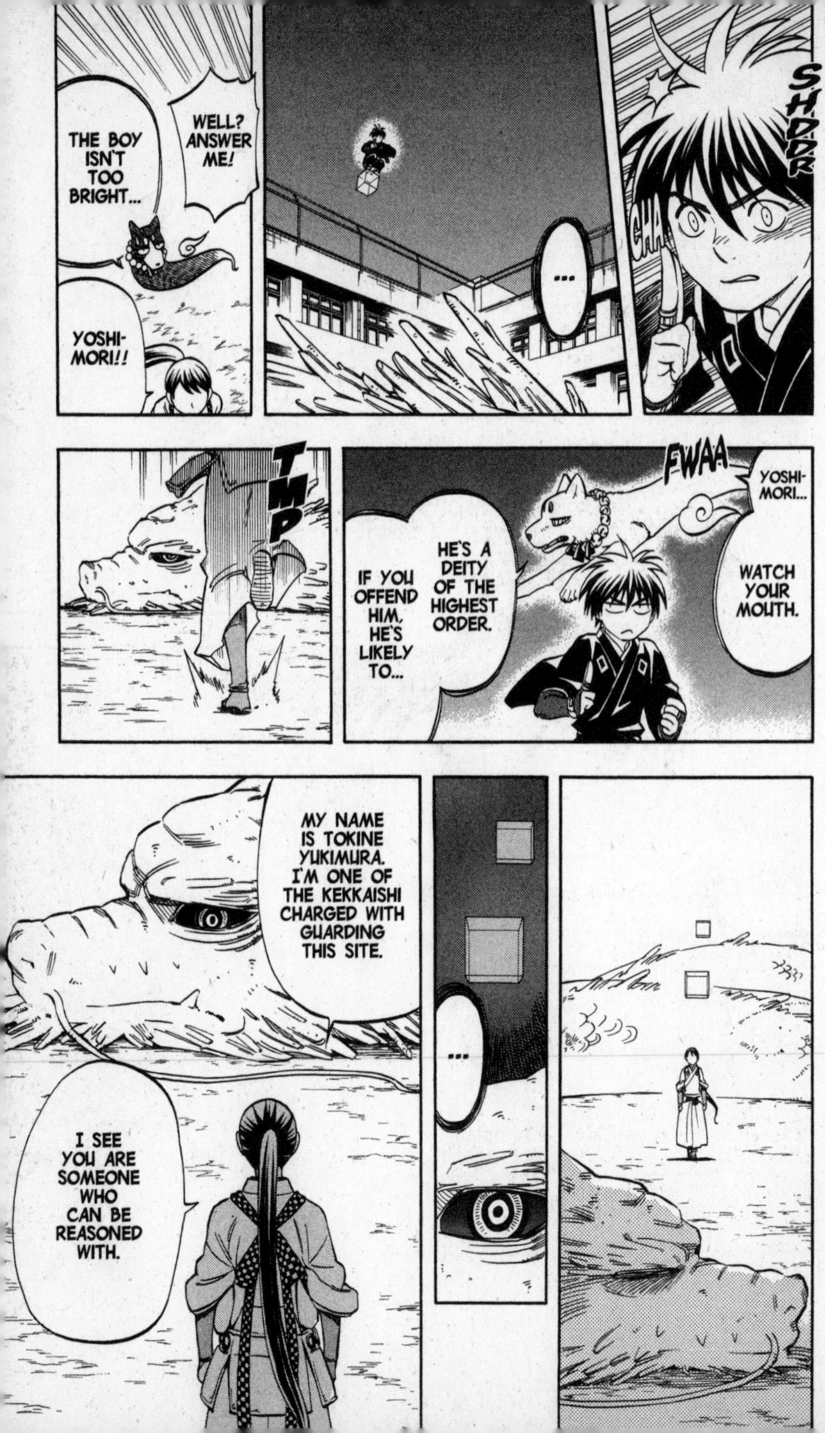
SHDDR
CHA
...
WELL? ANSWER ME!
THE BOY ISN'T TOO BRIGHT...
YOSHI-MORI!!
FWAA
YOSHI-MORI... WATCH YOUR MOUTH.
HE'S A DEITY OF THE HIGHEST ORDER.
IF YOU OFFEND HIM, HE'S LIKELY TO...
TMP
...
MY NAME IS TOKINE YUKIMURA. I'M ONE OF THE KEKKAISHI CHARGED WITH GUARDING THIS SITE.
I SEE YOU ARE SOMEONE WHO CAN BE REASONED WITH.

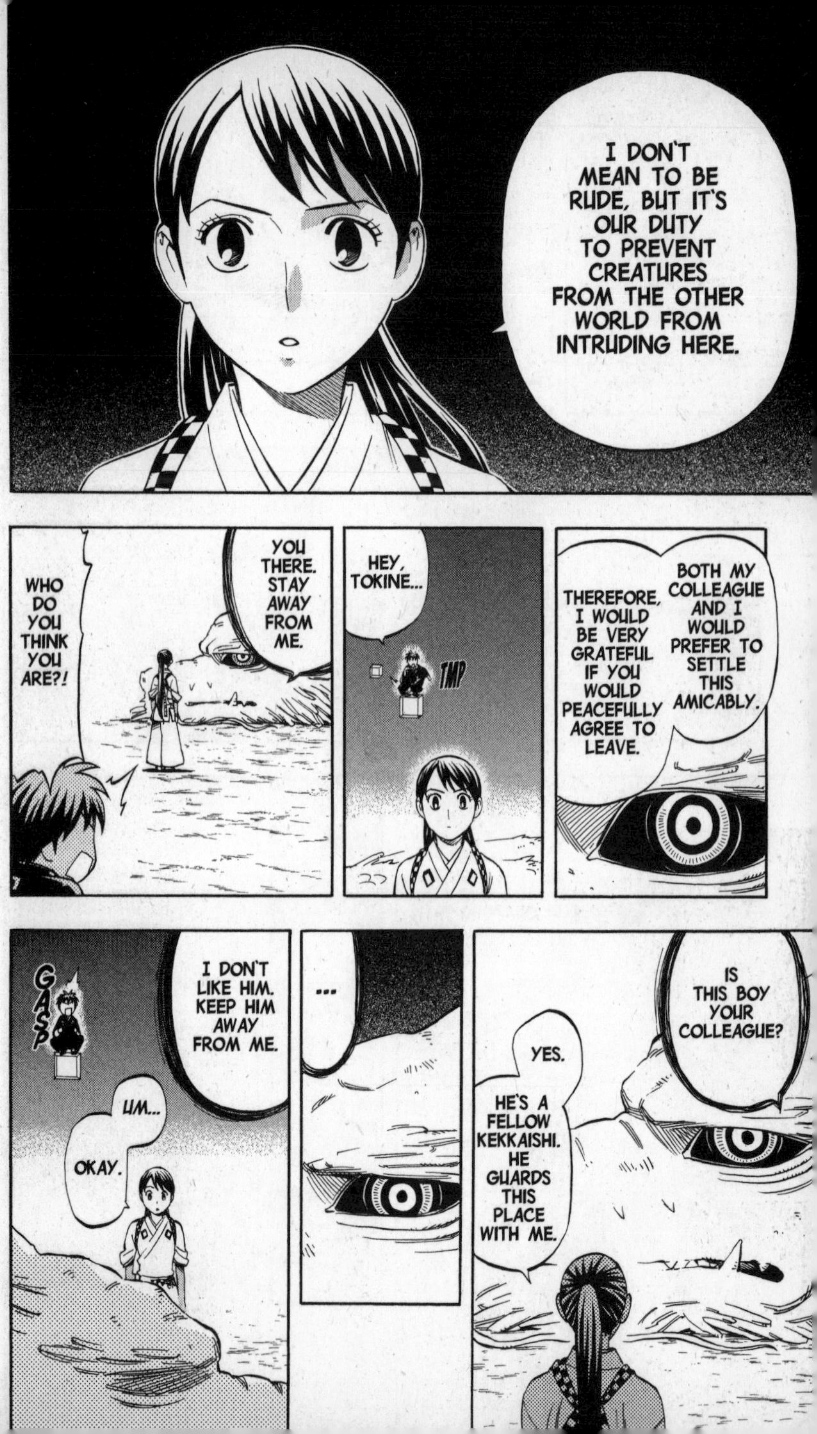
I DON'T MEAN TO BE RUDE, BUT IT'S OUR DUTY TO PREVENT CREATURES FROM THE OTHER WORLD FROM INTRUDING HERE.
BOTH MY COLLEAGUE AND I WOULD PREFER TO SETTLE THIS AMICABLY.
THEREFORE, I WOULD BE VERY GRATEFUL IF YOU WOULD PEACEFULLY AGREE TO LEAVE.
HEY, TOKINE...
TMP
YOU THERE. STAY AWAY FROM ME.
WHO DO YOU THINK YOU ARE?!
IS THIS BOY YOUR COLLEAGUE?
YES.
HE'S A FELLOW KEKKAISHI. HE GUARDS THIS PLACE WITH ME.
...
I DON'T LIKE HIM. KEEP HIM AWAY FROM ME.
GASP
UM...
OKAY.

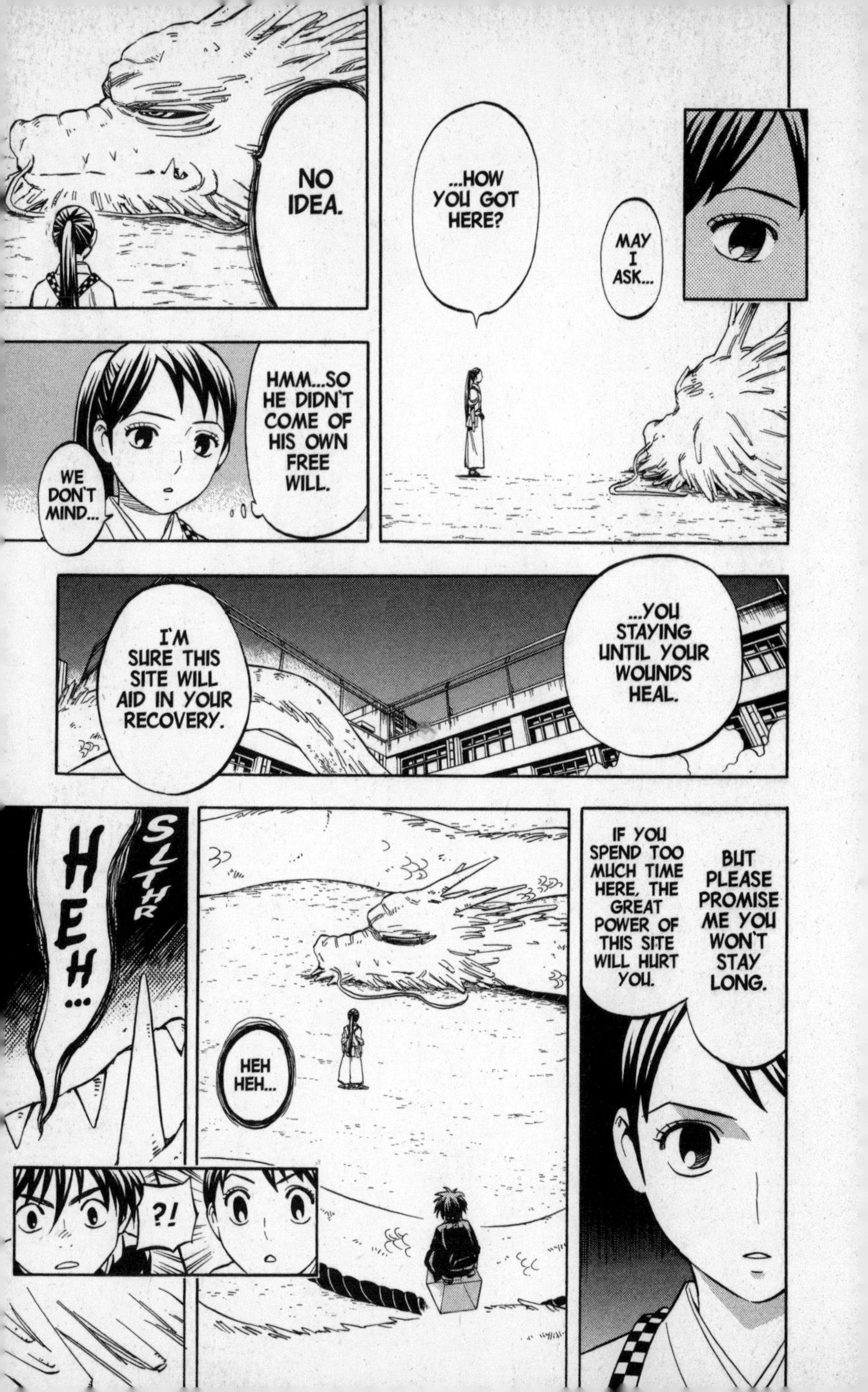
MAY I ASK...
...HOW YOU GOT HERE?
NO IDEA.
HMM...SO HE DIDN'T COME OF HIS OWN FREE WILL.
WE DON'T MIND...
...YOU STAYING UNTIL YOUR WOUNDS HEAL.
I'M SURE THIS SITE WILL AID IN YOUR RECOVERY.
BUT PLEASE PROMISE ME YOU WON'T STAY LONG.
IF YOU SPEND TOO MUCH TIME HERE, THE GREAT POWER OF THIS SITE WILL HURT YOU.
HEH HEH...
SLTHR
HEH...
?!

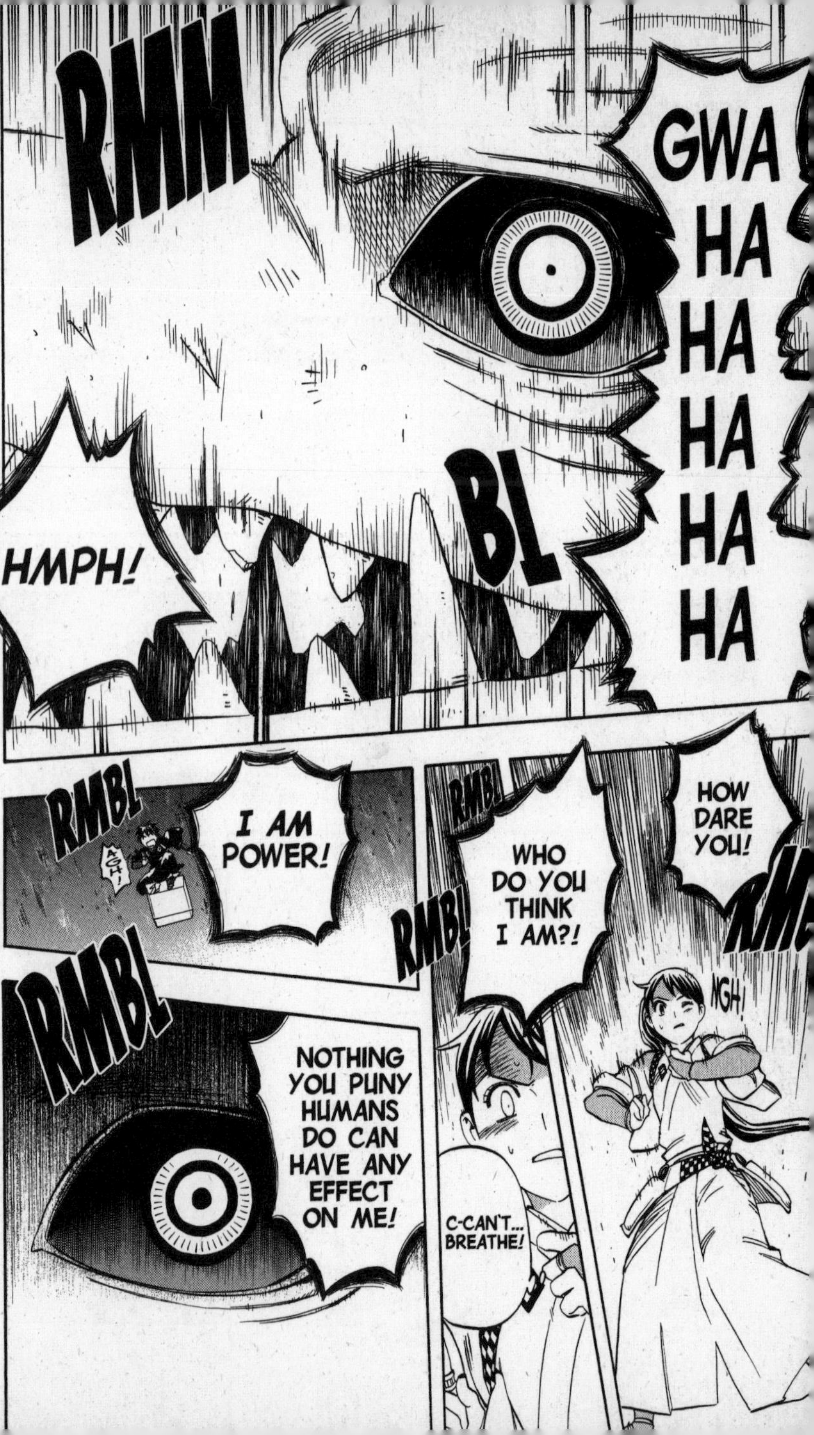
GWA HA HA HA HA HA HA HA
RMM
BL
HMPH!
HOW DARE YOU!
WHO DO YOU THINK I AM?!
RMBL
RMBL
I AM POWER!
RMBL
AGH!
NGH!
C-CAN'T... BREATHE!
NOTHING YOU PUNY HUMANS DO CAN HAVE ANY EFFECT ON ME!
RMBL

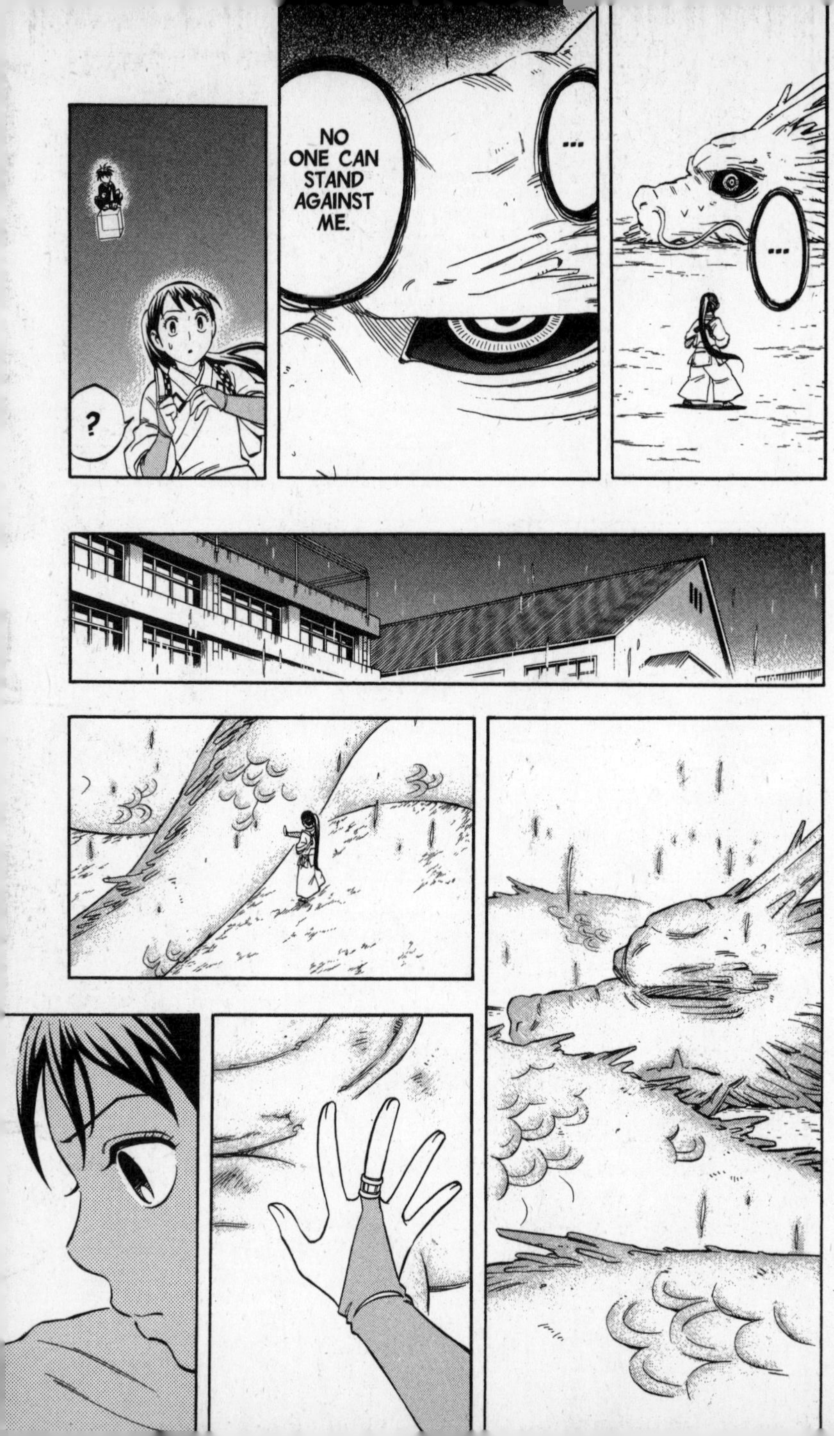
...
...
NO ONE CAN STAND AGAINST ME.
?

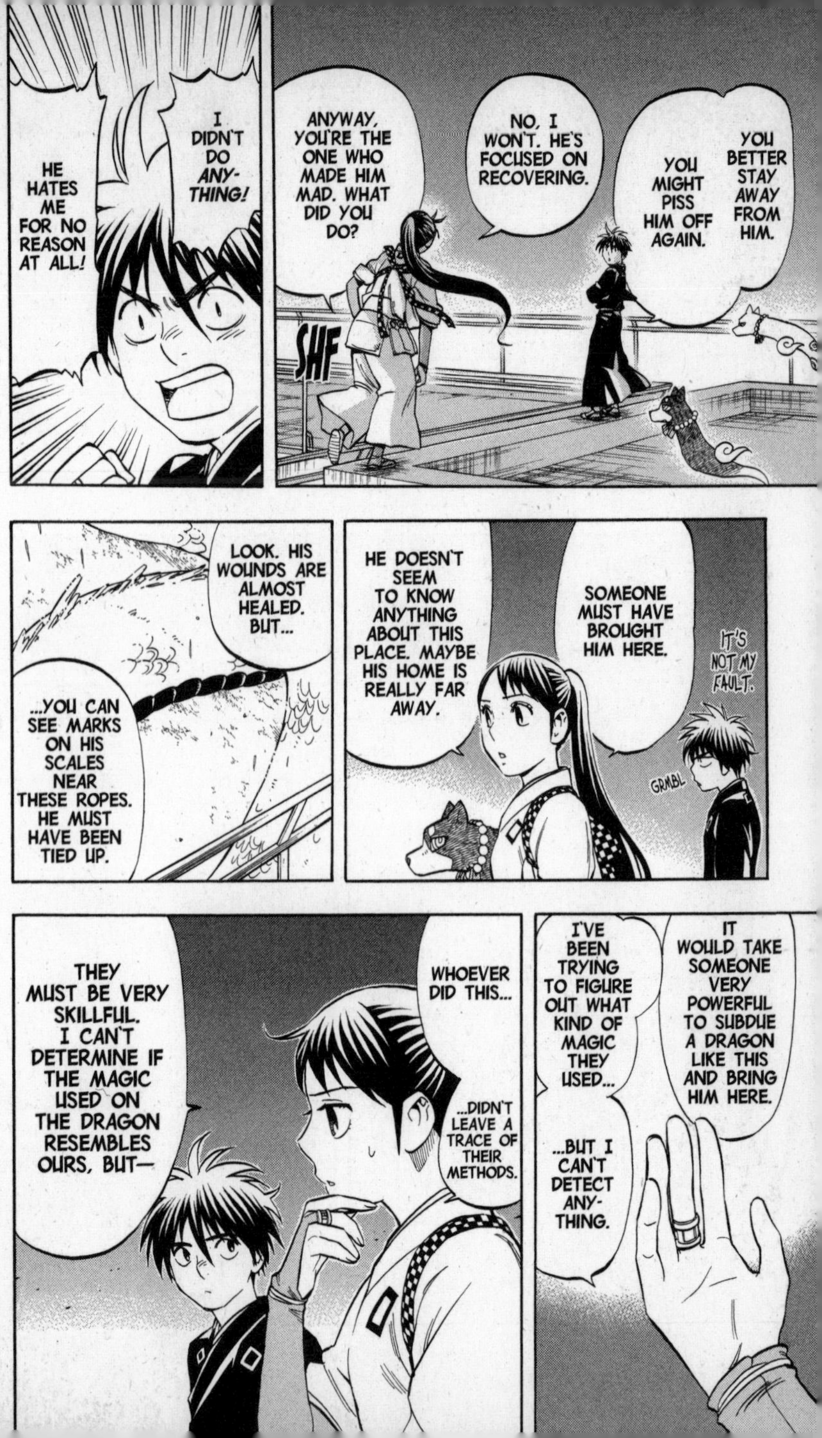
YOU BETTER STAY AWAY FROM HIM.
YOU MIGHT PISS HIM OFF AGAIN.
NO, I WON'T. HE'S FOCUSED ON RECOVERING.
ANYWAY, YOU'RE THE ONE WHO MADE HIM MAD. WHAT DID YOU DO?
SHF
I DIDN'T DO *ANYTHING!*
HE HATES ME FOR NO REASON AT ALL!
SOMEONE MUST HAVE BROUGHT HIM HERE.
HE DOESN'T SEEM TO KNOW ANYTHING ABOUT THIS PLACE. MAYBE HIS HOME IS REALLY FAR AWAY.
IT'S NOT MY FAULT.
GRMBL
LOOK. HIS WOUNDS ARE ALMOST HEALED. BUT...
...YOU CAN SEE MARKS ON HIS SCALES NEAR THESE ROPES. HE MUST HAVE BEEN TIED UP.
IT WOULD TAKE SOMEONE VERY POWERFUL TO SUBDUE A DRAGON LIKE THIS AND BRING HIM HERE.
I'VE BEEN TRYING TO FIGURE OUT WHAT KIND OF MAGIC THEY USED...
...BUT I CAN'T DETECT ANYTHING.
WHOEVER DID THIS...
...DIDN'T LEAVE A TRACE OF THEIR METHODS.
THEY MUST BE VERY SKILLFUL. I CAN'T DETERMINE IF THE MAGIC USED ON THE DRAGON RESEMBLES OURS, BUT—

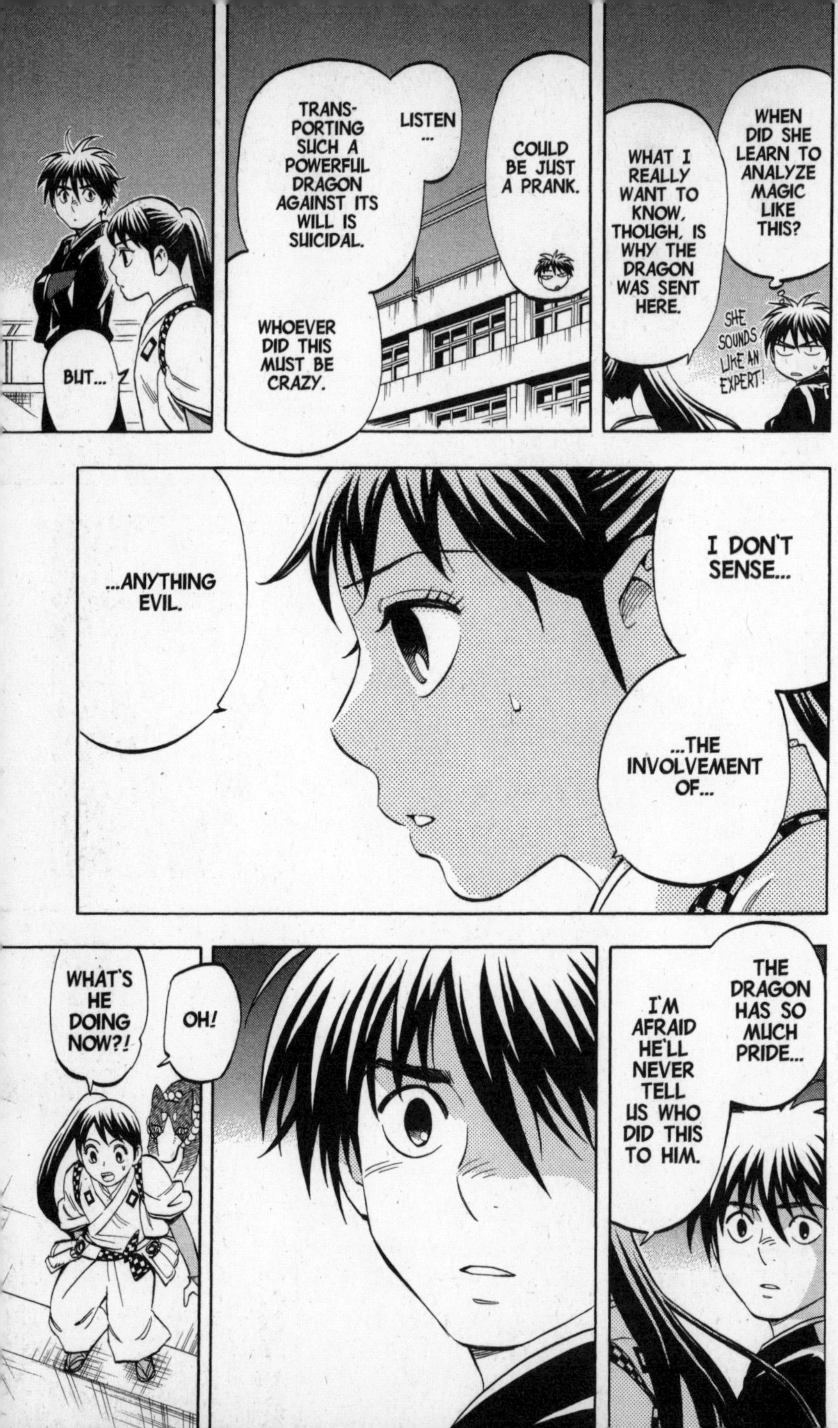
WHEN DID SHE LEARN TO ANALYZE MAGIC LIKE THIS?
WHAT I REALLY WANT TO KNOW, THOUGH, IS WHY THE DRAGON WAS SENT HERE.
SHE SOUNDS LIKE AN EXPERT!
COULD BE JUST A PRANK.
LISTEN ...
TRANS-PORTING SUCH A POWERFUL DRAGON AGAINST ITS WILL IS SUICIDAL.
WHOEVER DID THIS MUST BE CRAZY.
BUT...
I DON'T SENSE...
...THE INVOLVEMENT OF...
...ANYTHING EVIL.
THE DRAGON HAS SO MUCH PRIDE...
I'M AFRAID HE'LL NEVER TELL US WHO DID THIS TO HIM.
OH!
WHAT'S HE DOING NOW?!

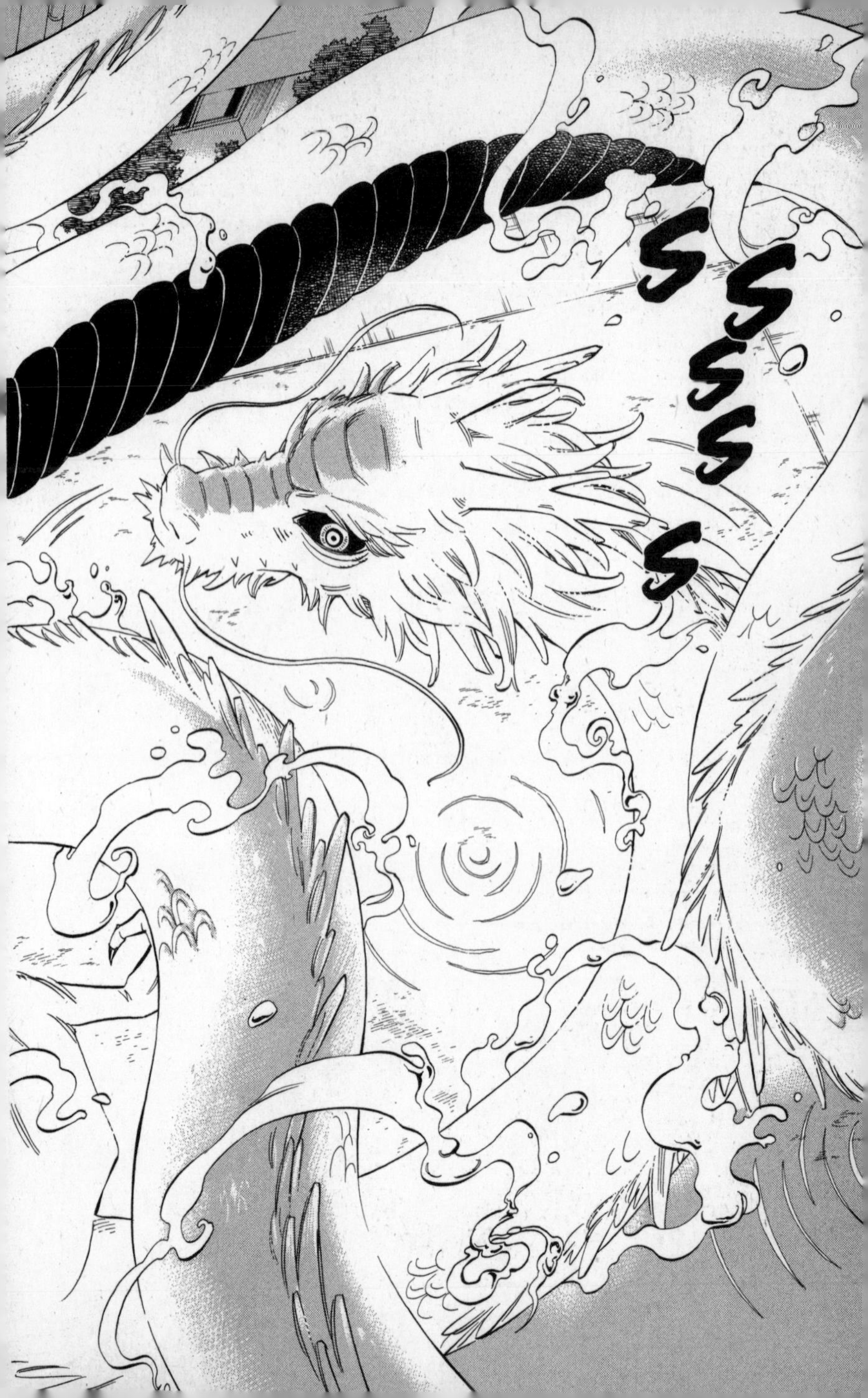
SSSSSS

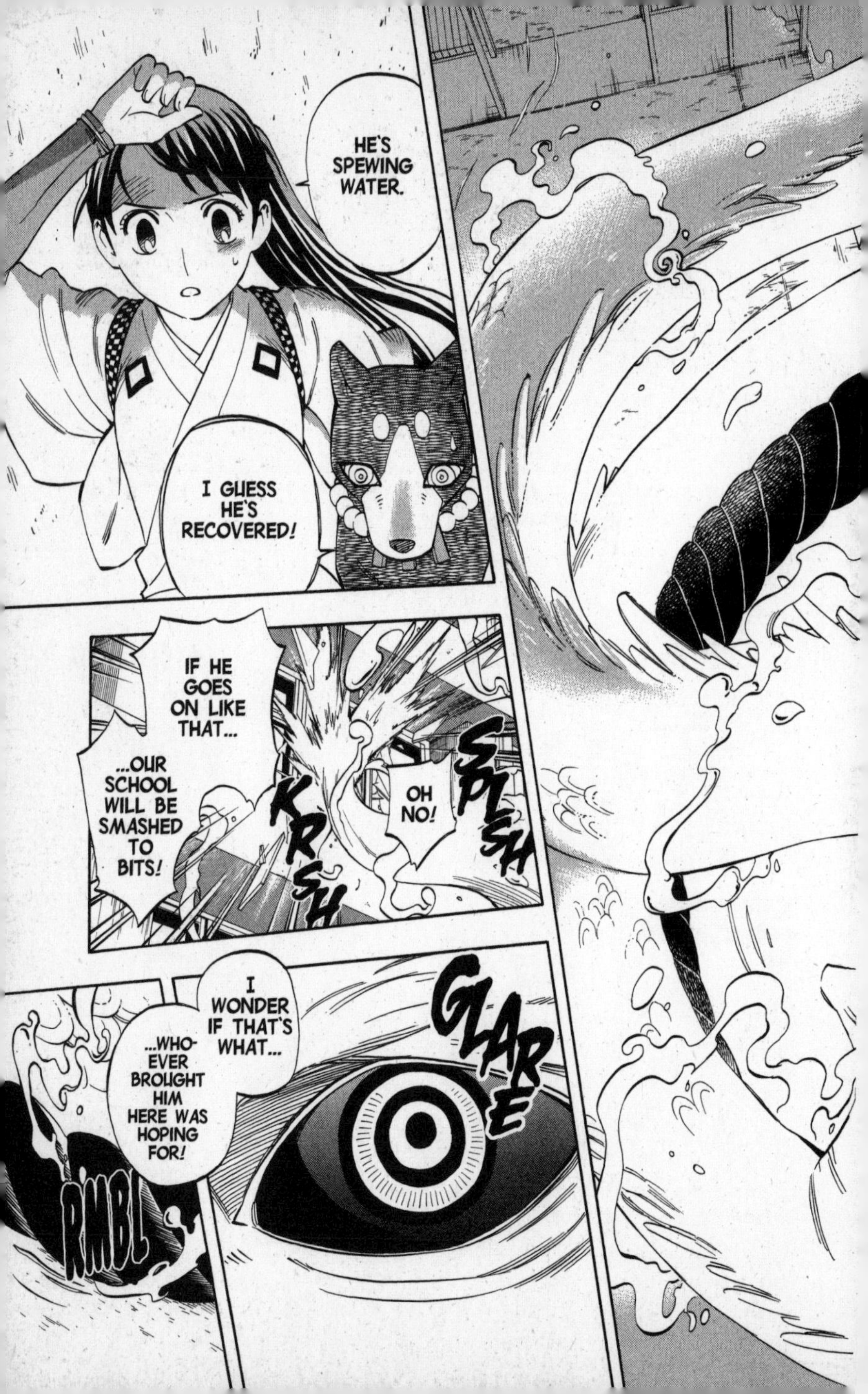
HE'S SPEWING WATER.
I GUESS HE'S RECOVERED!
SPLSH
OH NO!
IF HE GOES ON LIKE THAT...
...OUR SCHOOL WILL BE SMASHED TO BITS!
KRSH
GLARE
I WONDER IF THAT'S WHAT...
...WHOEVER BROUGHT HIM HERE WAS HOPING FOR!
RMBL

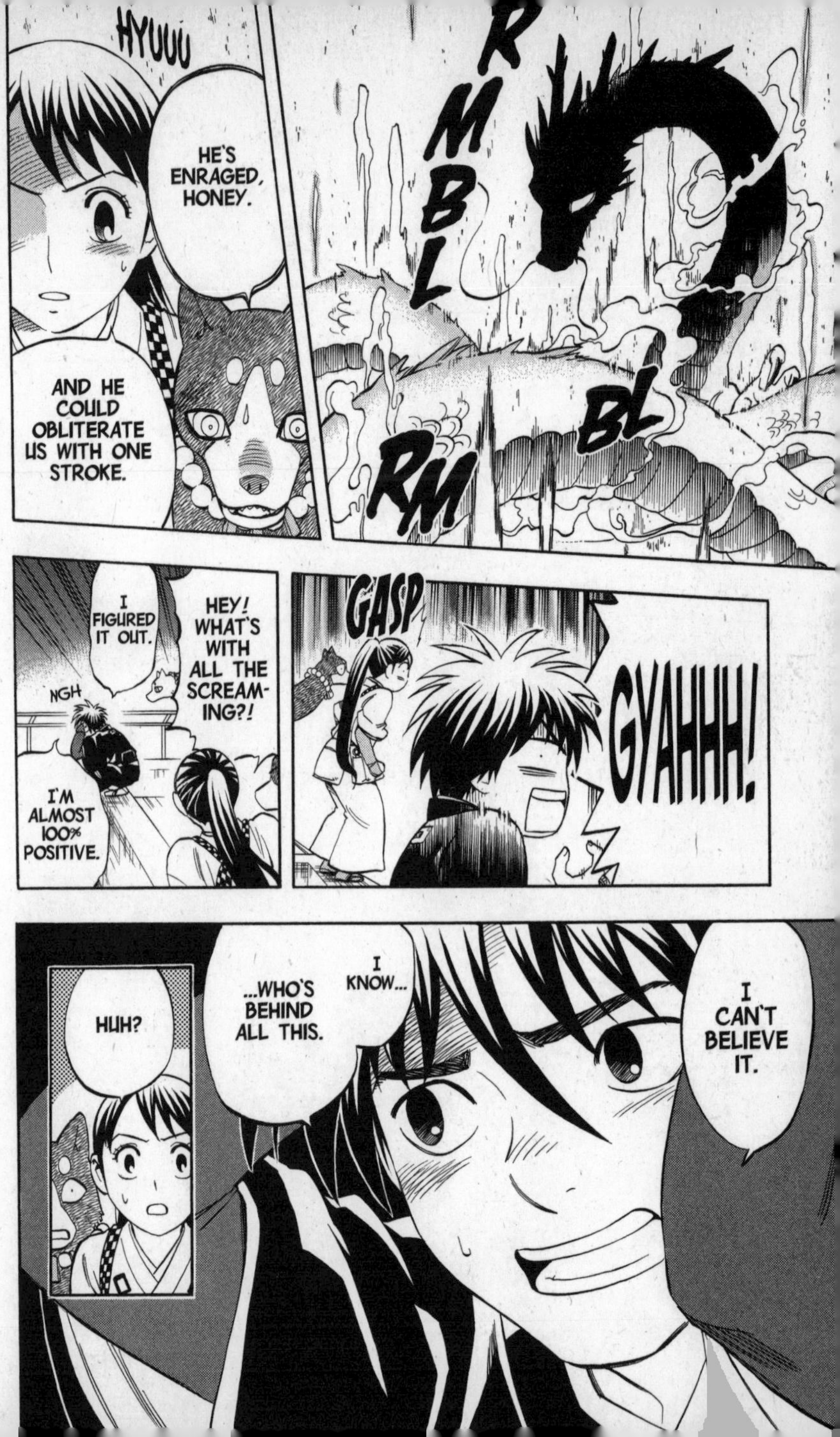
RMBL
RM
BL
HYUUU
HE'S ENRAGED, HONEY.
AND HE COULD OBLITERATE US WITH ONE STROKE.
GASP
GYAHHH!
HEY! WHAT'S WITH ALL THE SCREAMING?!
I FIGURED IT OUT.
NGH
I'M ALMOST 100% POSITIVE.
I CAN'T BELIEVE IT.
I KNOW...
...WHO'S BEHIND ALL THIS.
HUH?

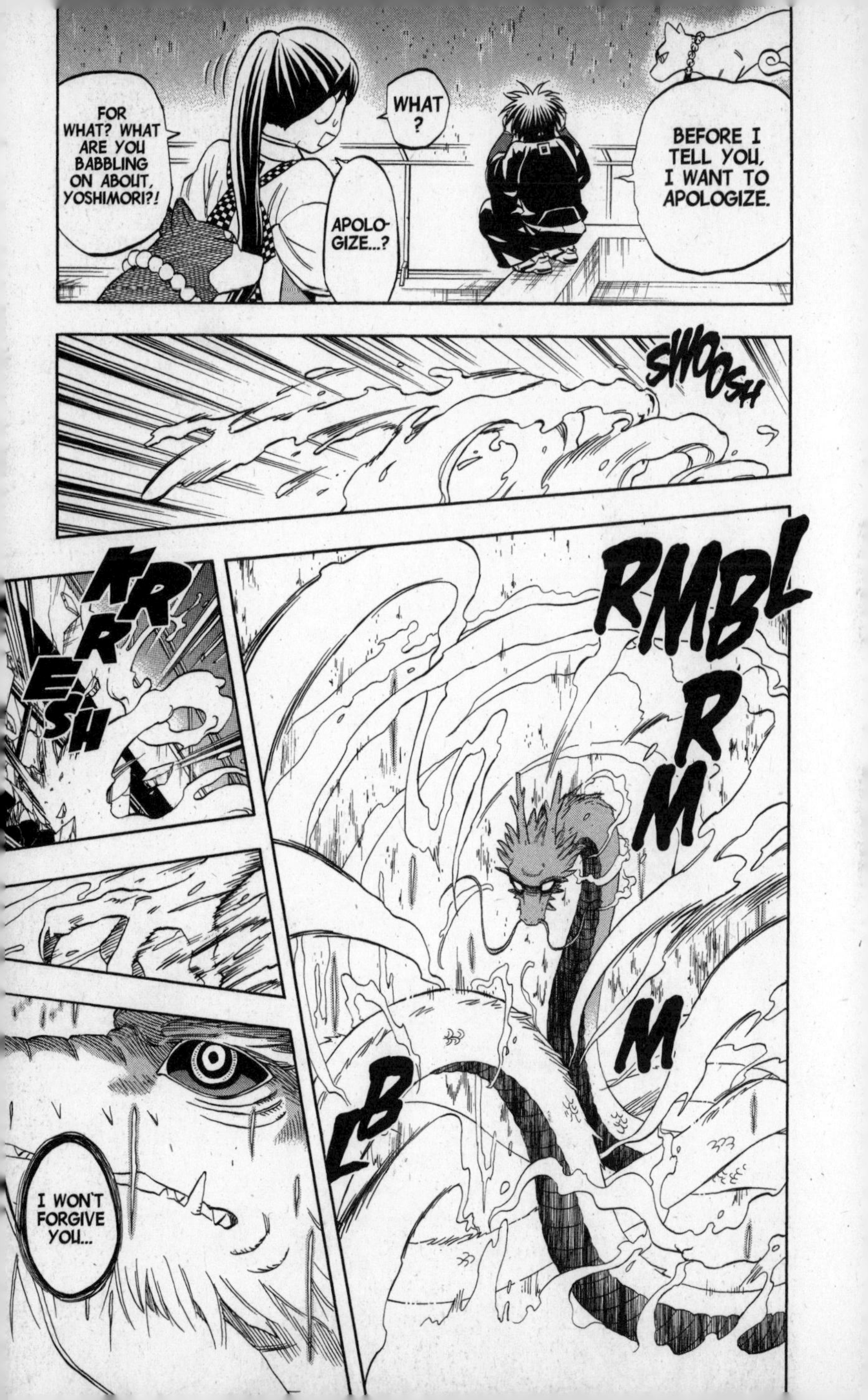
BEFORE I TELL YOU, I WANT TO APOLOGIZE.
WHAT?
APOLOGIZE...?
FOR WHAT? WHAT ARE YOU BABBLING ON ABOUT, YOSHIMORI?!
SHWOOSH
RMBL
KRRESH
I WON'T FORGIVE YOU...

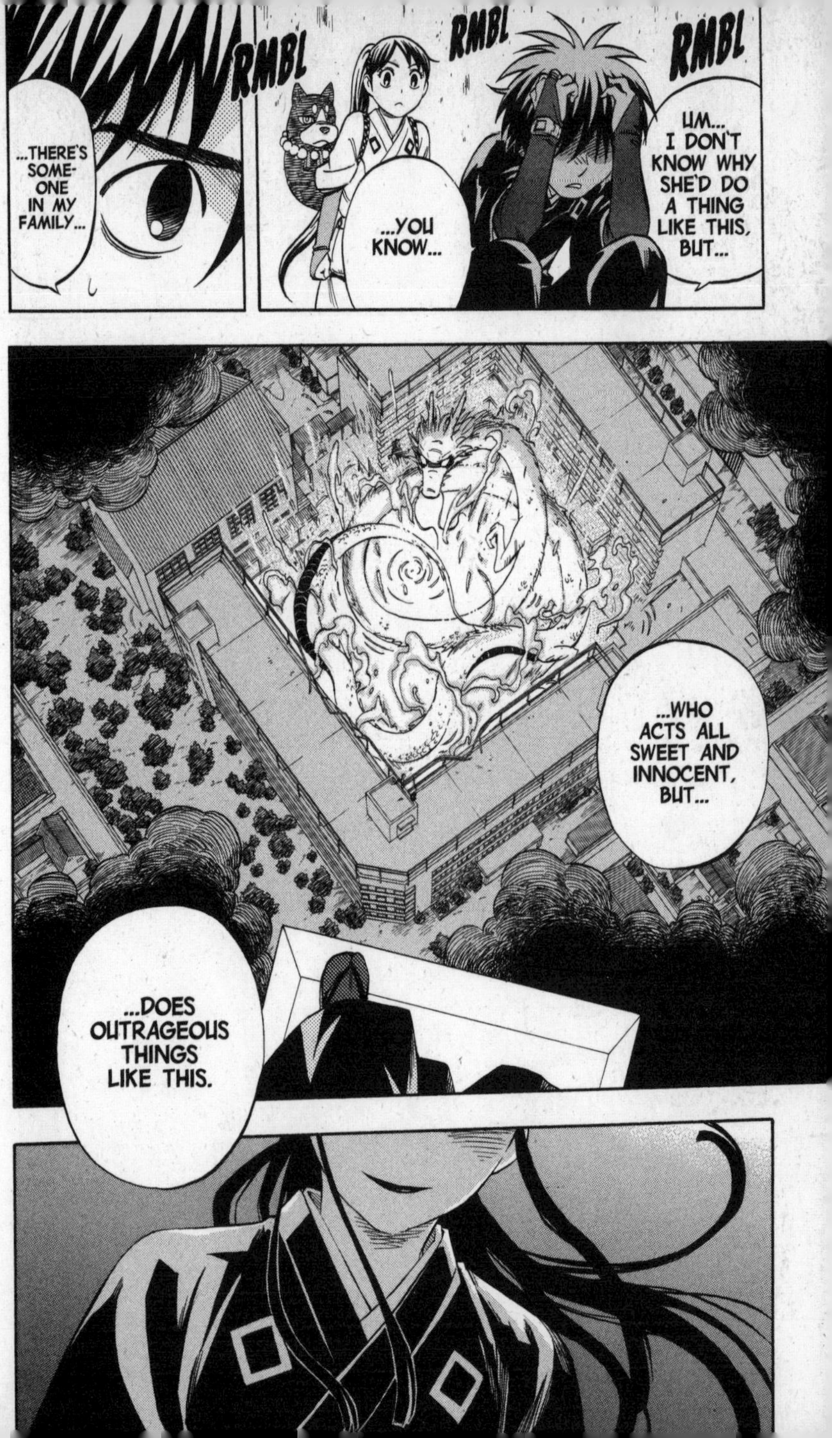
RMBL
RMBL
RMBL
UM... I DON'T KNOW WHY SHE'D DO A THING LIKE THIS, BUT...
...YOU KNOW...
...THERE'S SOME-ONE IN MY FAMILY...
...WHO ACTS ALL SWEET AND INNOCENT, BUT...
...DOES OUTRAGEOUS THINGS LIKE THIS.

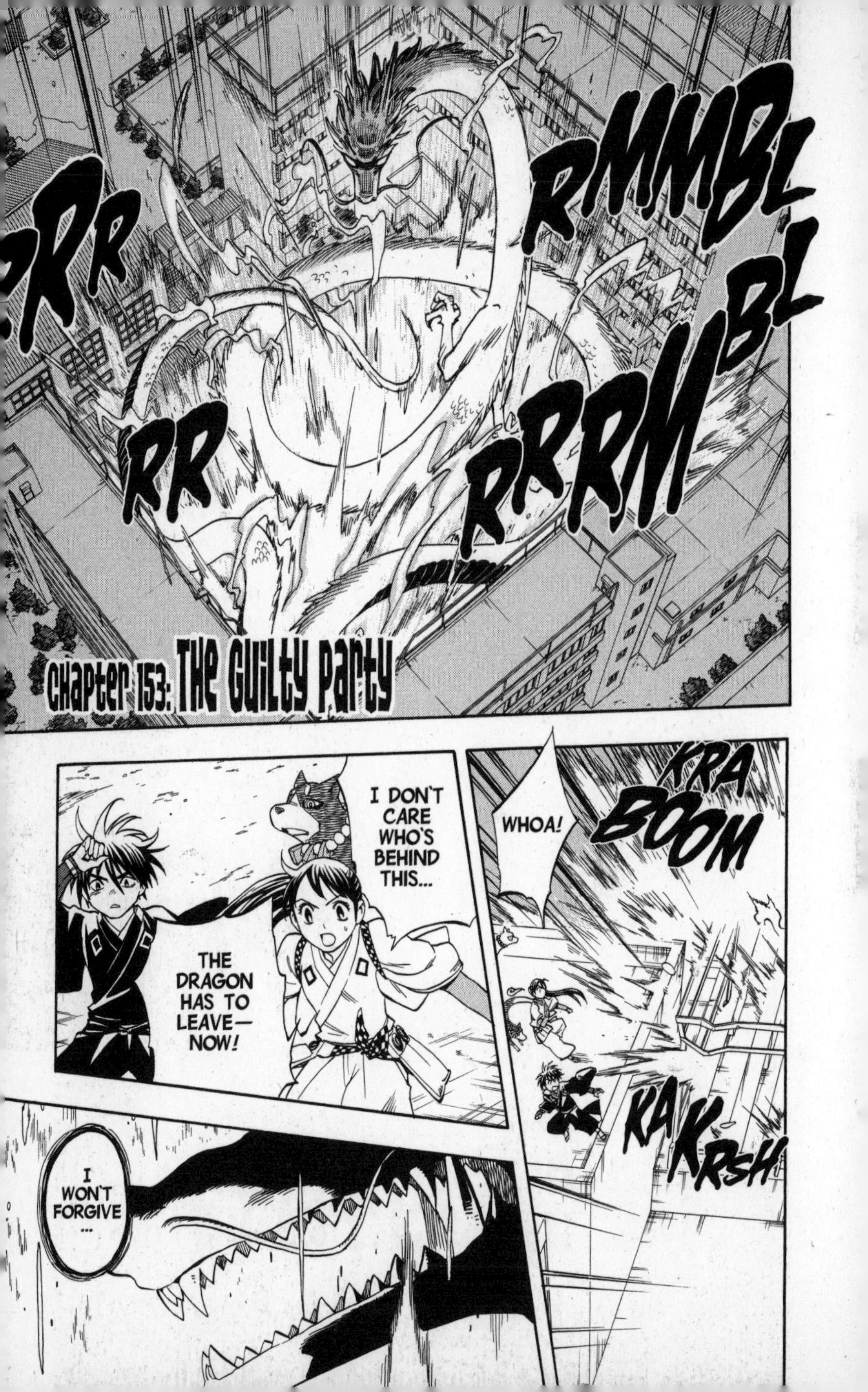
RRRR
RMMBL
BL
RRRM
Chapter 153: The Guilty Party
WHOA!
KRA BOOM
KA KRSH
I DON'T CARE WHO'S BEHIND THIS...
THE DRAGON HAS TO LEAVE— NOW!
I WON'T FORGIVE ...

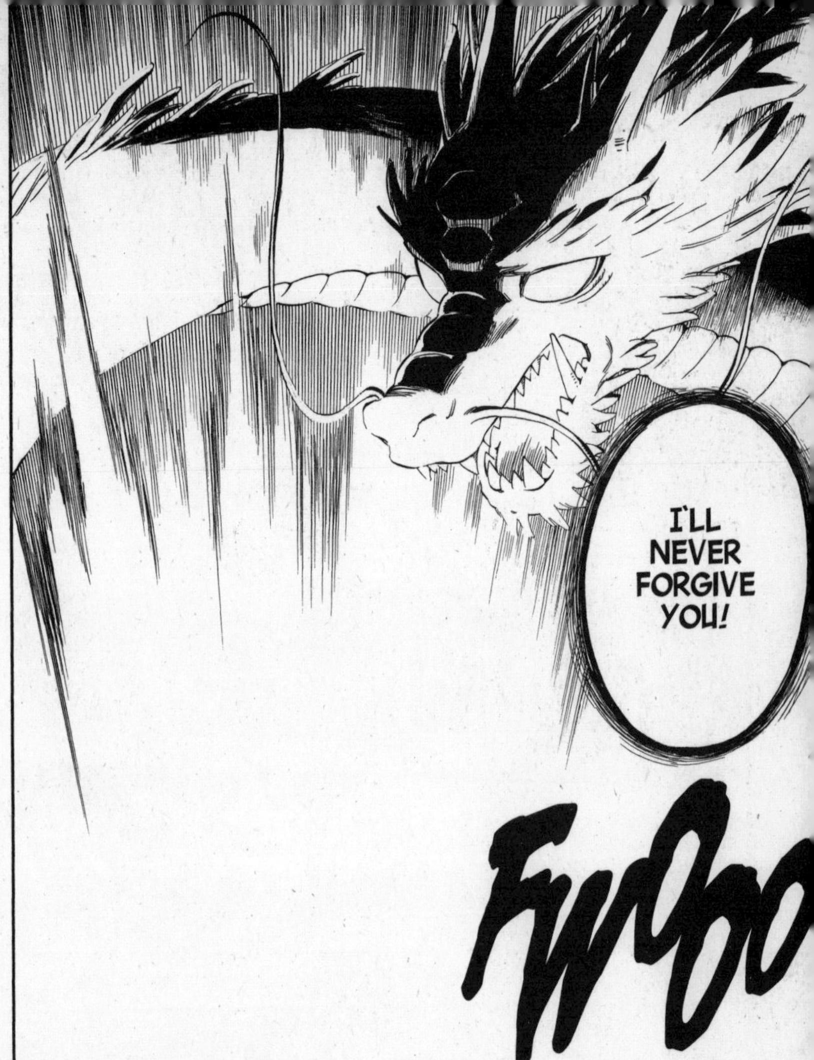
I'LL NEVER FORGIVE YOU!
FWOO

Chapter 153: The Guilty Party

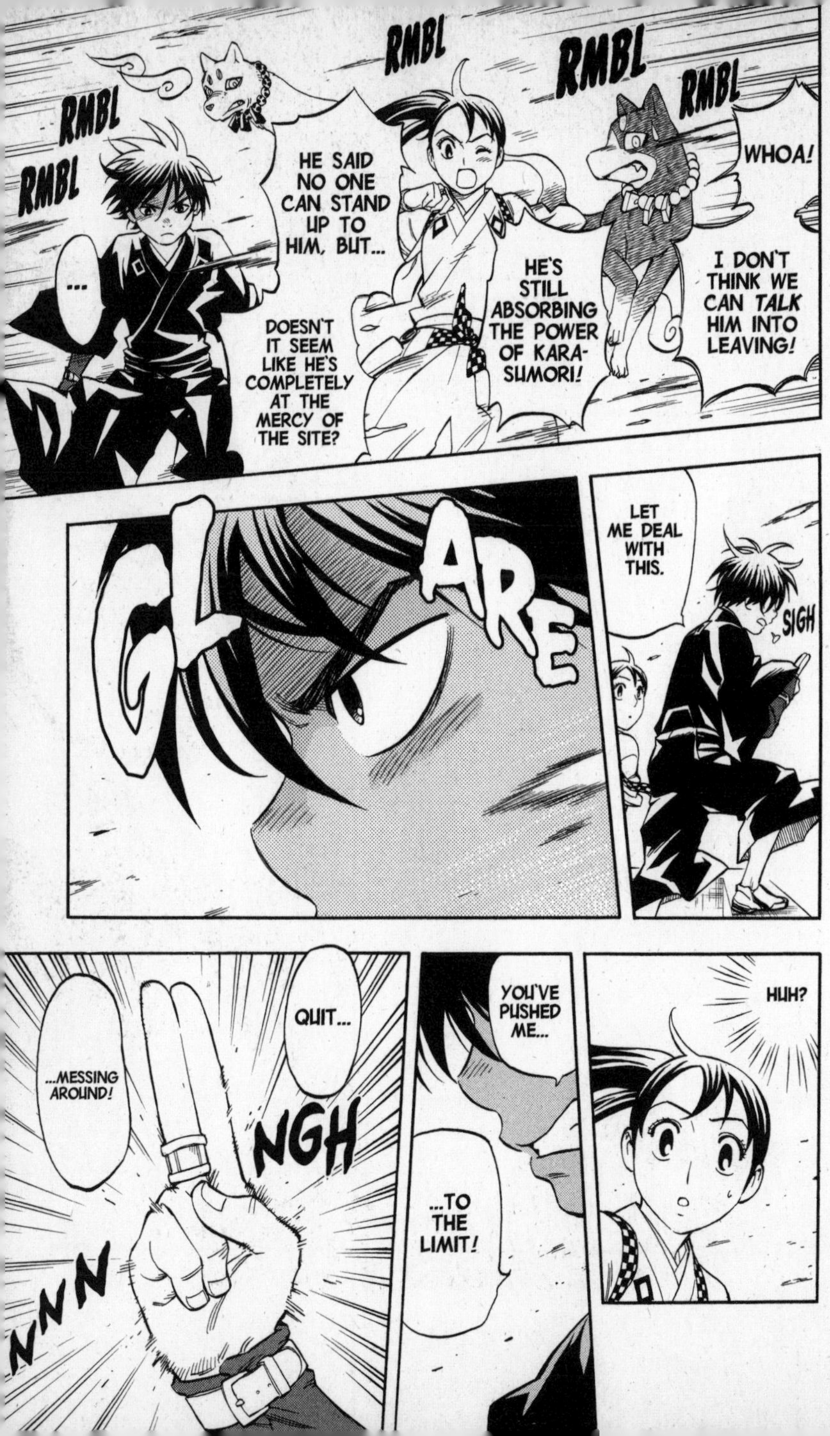
RMBL
WHOA!
I DON'T THINK WE CAN *TALK* HIM INTO LEAVING!
RMBL
RMBL
HE'S STILL ABSORBING THE POWER OF KARA-SUMORI!
HE SAID NO ONE CAN STAND UP TO HIM, BUT...
DOESN'T IT SEEM LIKE HE'S COMPLETELY AT THE MERCY OF THE SITE?
RMBL
RMBL
...
LET ME DEAL WITH THIS.
SIGH
GLARE
HUH?
YOU'VE PUSHED ME...
...TO THE LIMIT!
QUIT...
...MESSING AROUND!
NGH
NNN

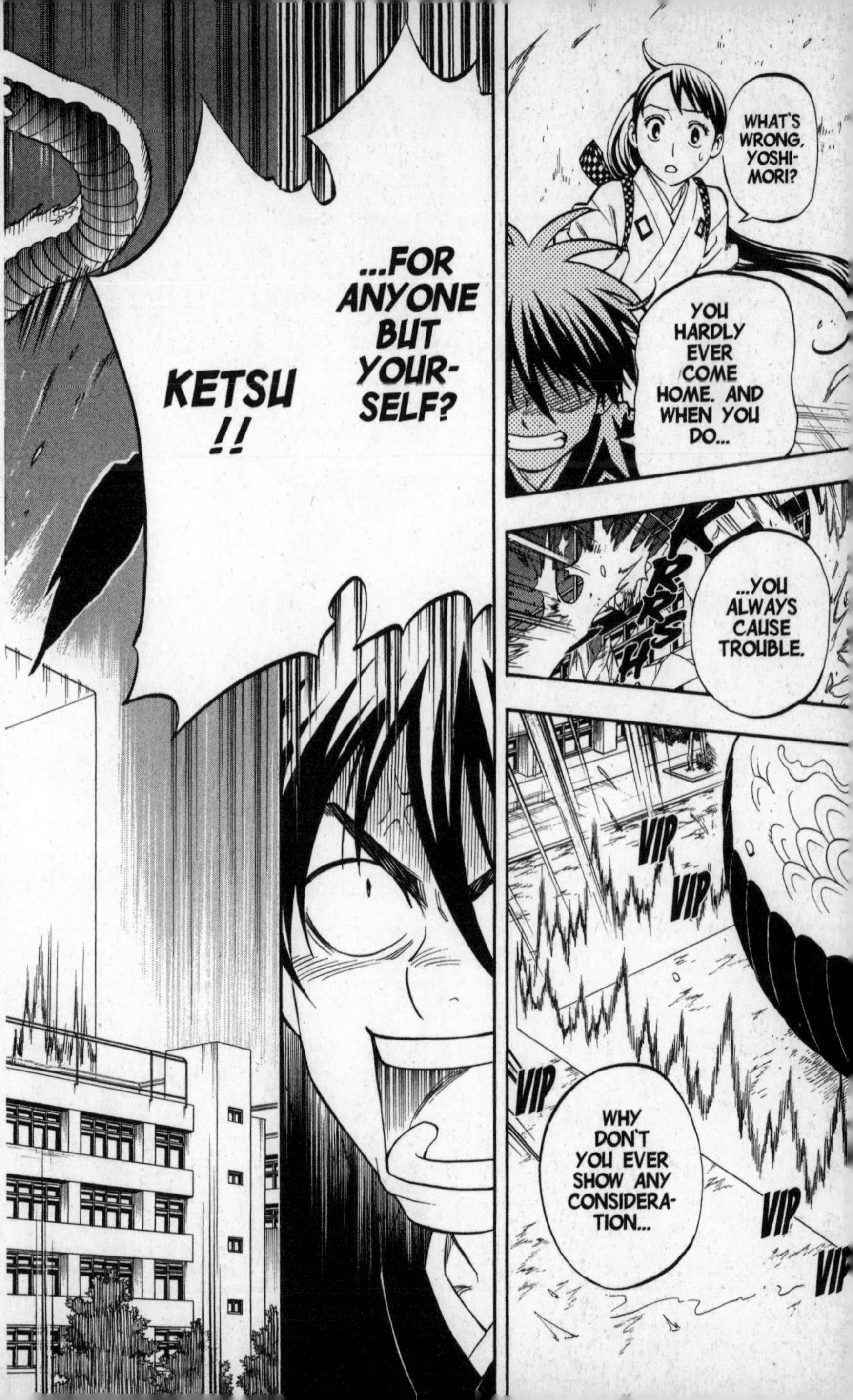
WHAT'S WRONG, YOSHIMORI?
YOU HARDLY EVER COME HOME. AND WHEN YOU DO...
KRRSH
...YOU ALWAYS CAUSE TROUBLE.
VIP
VIP
VIP
WHY DON'T YOU EVER SHOW ANY CONSIDERATION...
VIP
VIP
...FOR ANYONE BUT YOURSELF?
KETSU!!

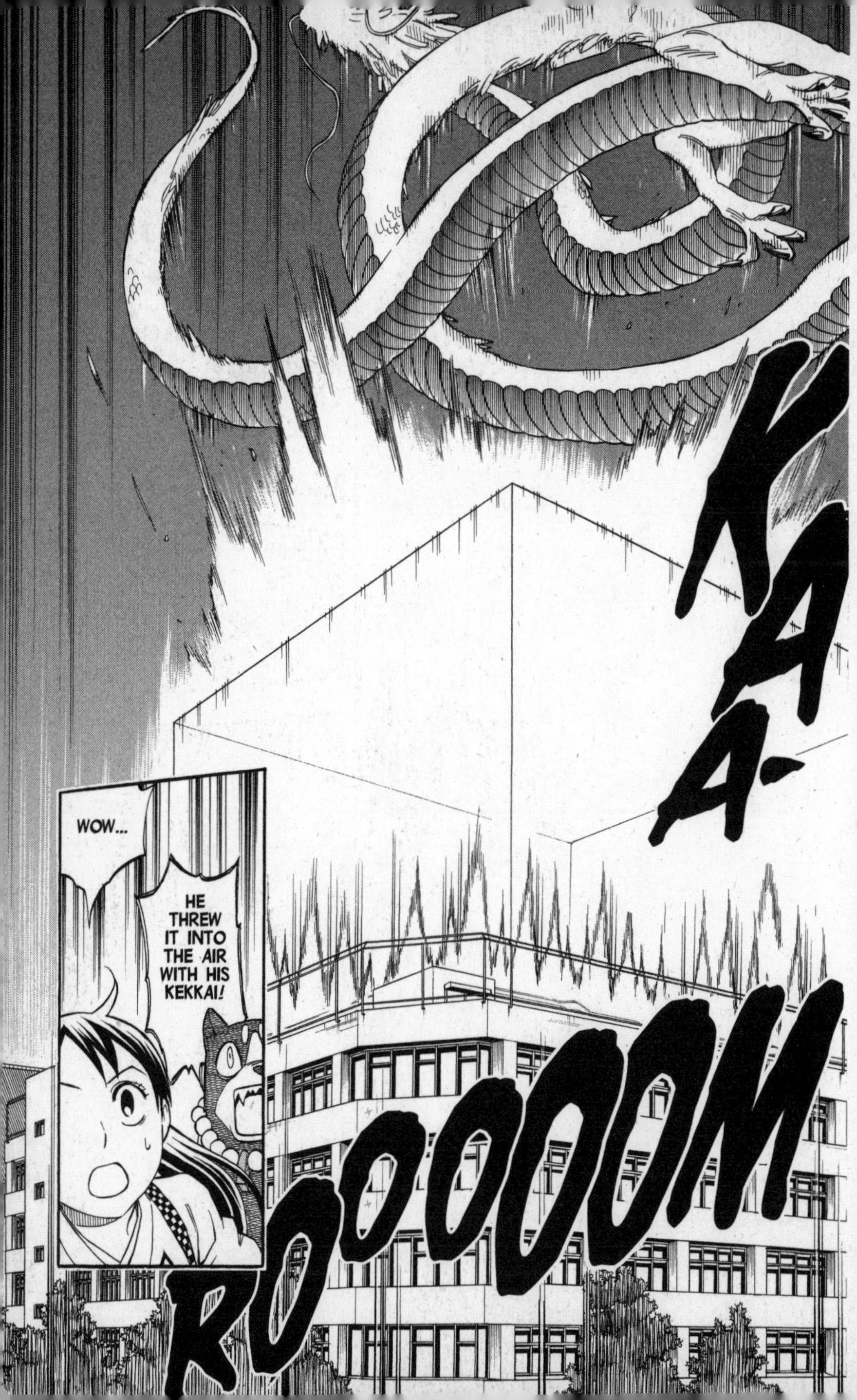
KAA-
ROOOOOM
WOW...
HE THREW IT INTO THE AIR WITH HIS KEKKAI!

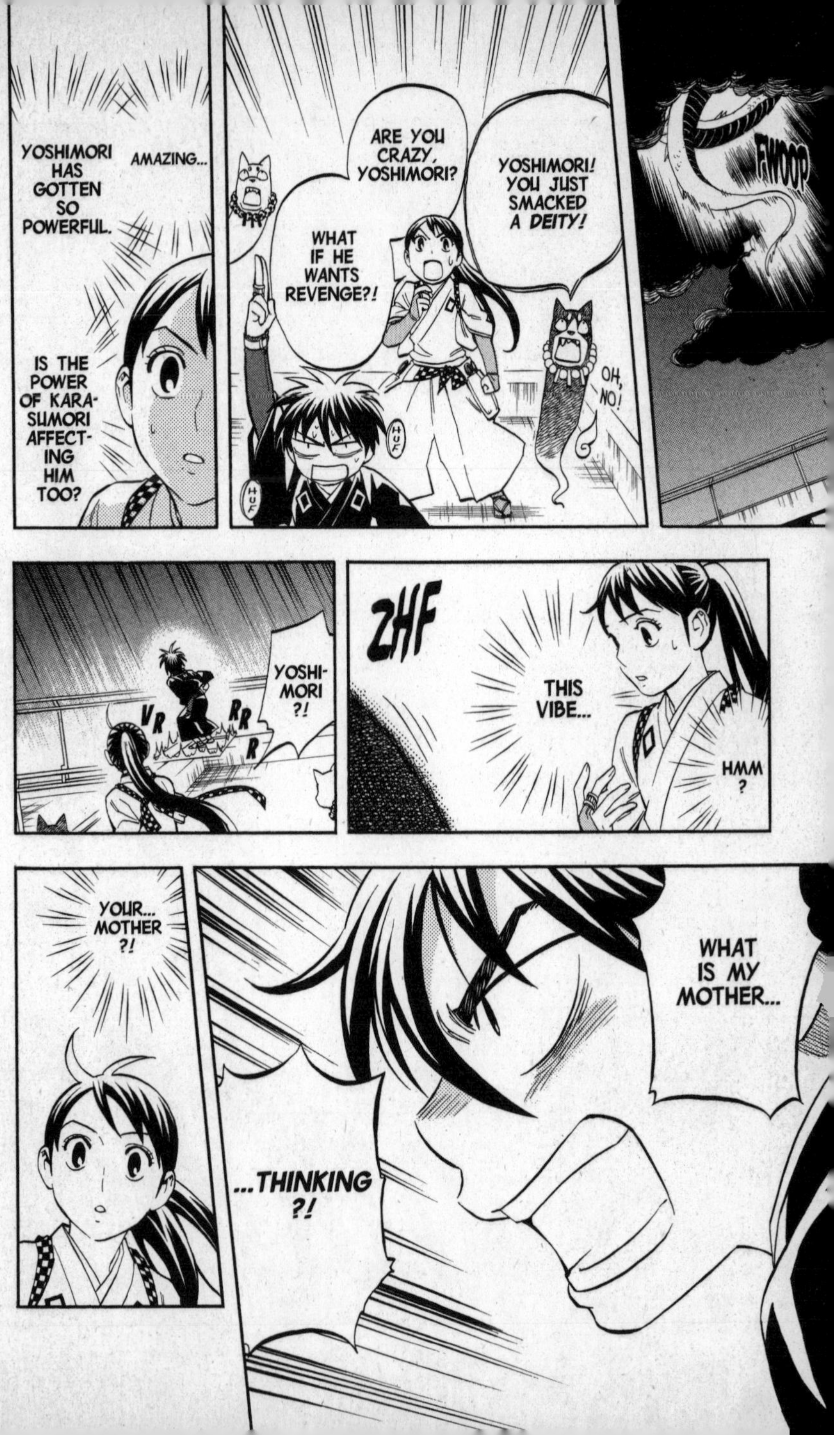
FWOOP
YOSHIMORI! YOU JUST SMACKED A DEITY!
OH, NO!
ARE YOU CRAZY, YOSHIMORI?
WHAT IF HE WANTS REVENGE?!
HUF
HUF
AMAZING...
YOSHIMORI HAS GOTTEN SO POWERFUL.
IS THE POWER OF KARA-SUMORI AFFECT-ING HIM TOO?
ZHF
HMM?
THIS VIBE...
YOSHI-MORI?!
VR
RRR
WHAT IS MY MOTHER...
...THINKING?!
YOUR... MOTHER?!

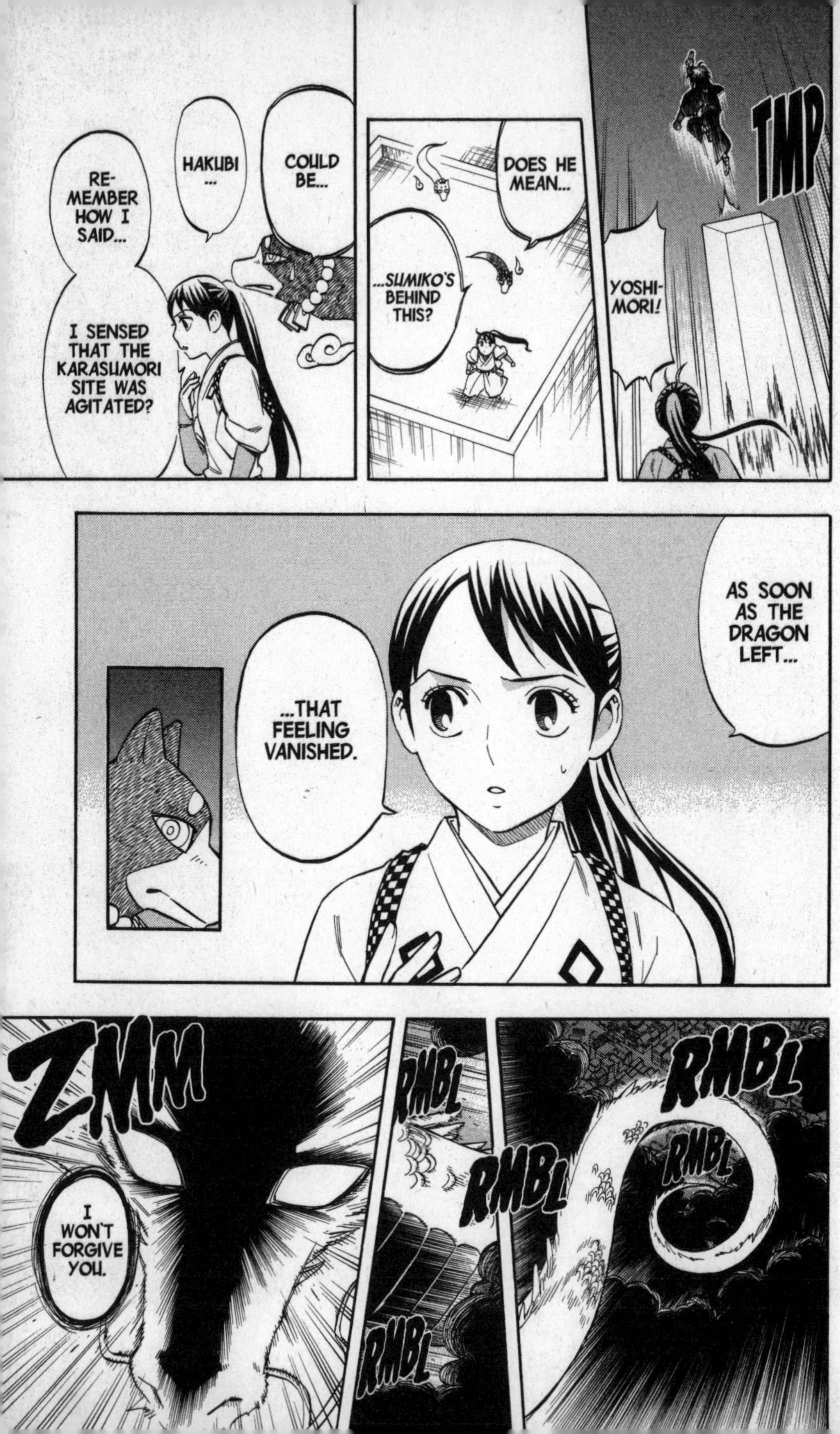
TMP
YOSHIMORI!
DOES HE MEAN...
...SUMIKO'S BEHIND THIS?
COULD BE...
HAKUBI...
REMEMBER HOW I SAID...
I SENSED THAT THE KARASUMORI SITE WAS AGITATED?
AS SOON AS THE DRAGON LEFT...
...THAT FEELING VANISHED.
RMBL
RMBL
RMBL
RMBL
RMBL
ZMM
I WON'T FORGIVE YOU.

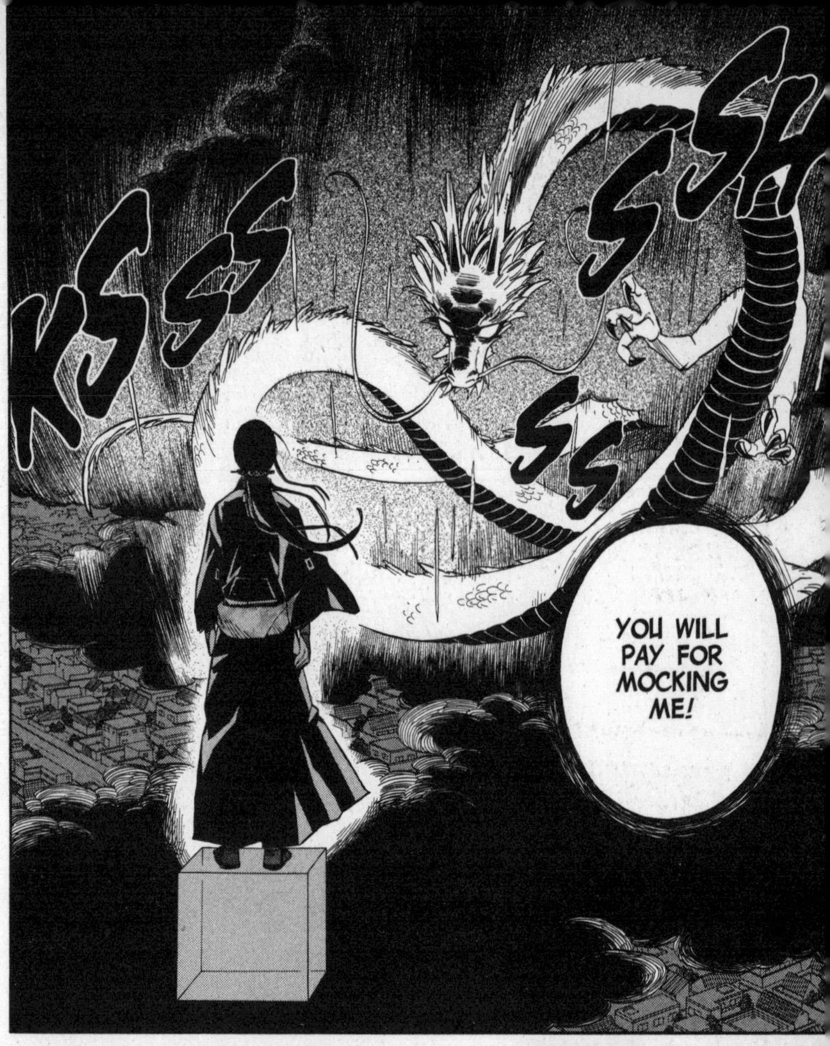
YOU WILL PAY FOR MOCKING ME!

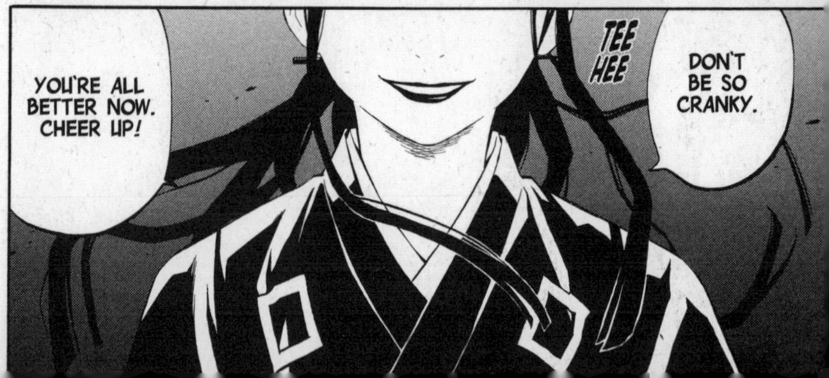
DON'T BE SO CRANKY.
TEE HEE
YOU'RE ALL BETTER NOW. CHEER UP!

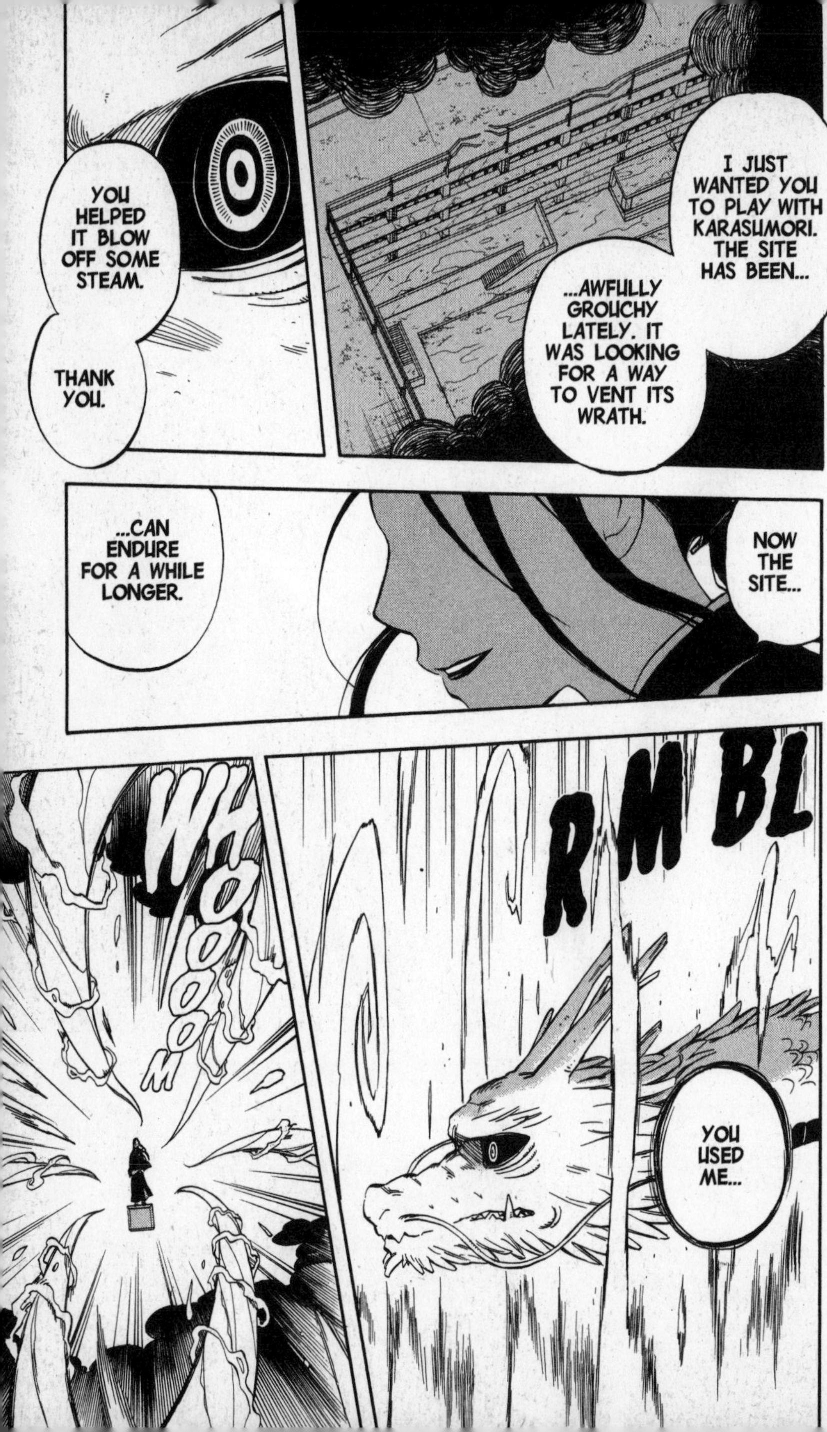
I JUST WANTED YOU TO PLAY WITH KARASUMORI. THE SITE HAS BEEN...
...AWFULLY GROUCHY LATELY. IT WAS LOOKING FOR A WAY TO VENT ITS WRATH.
YOU HELPED IT BLOW OFF SOME STEAM.
THANK YOU.
NOW THE SITE...
...CAN ENDURE FOR A WHILE LONGER.
RMBL
YOU USED ME...
WHOOOOOOM

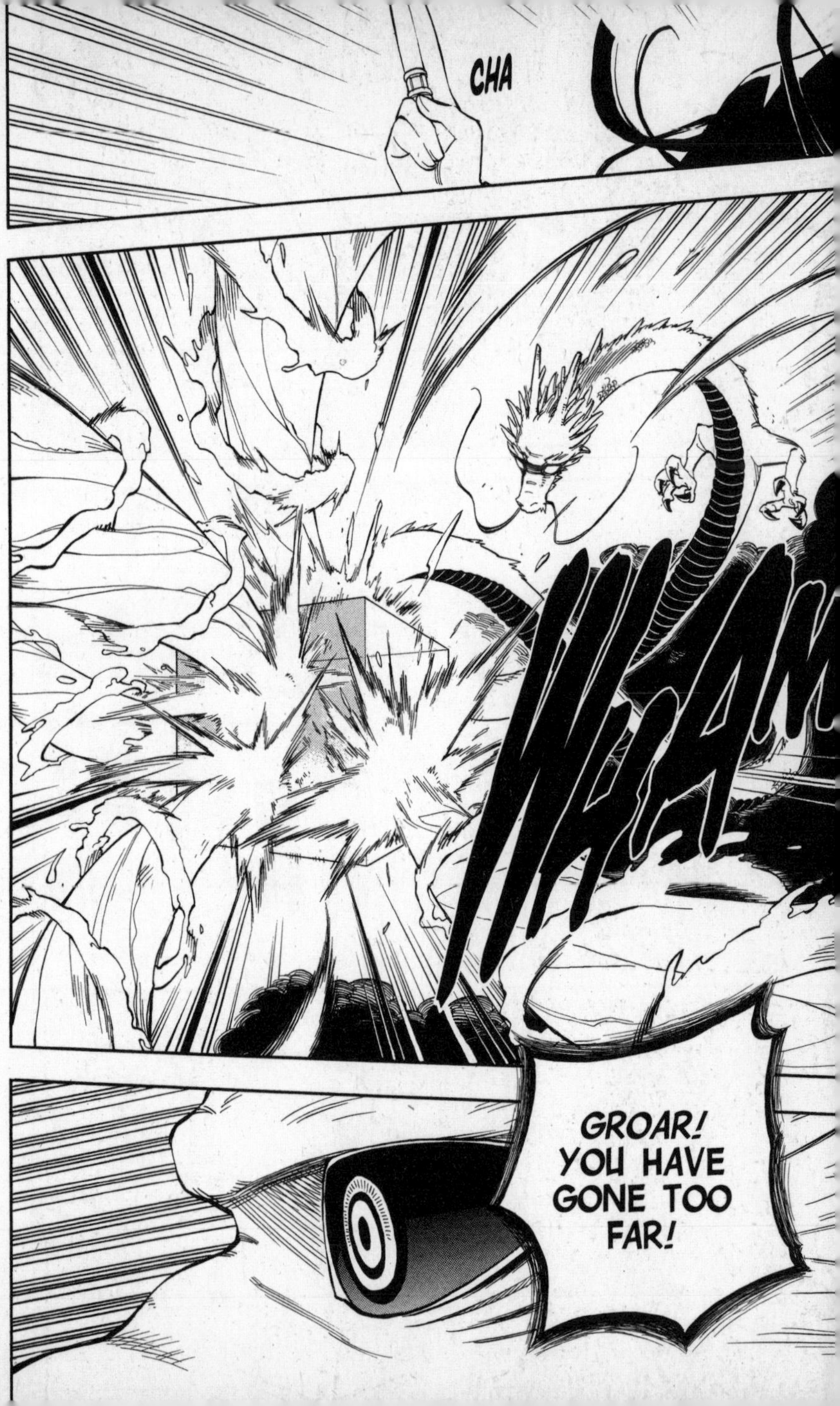
CHA
WHAM
GROAR! YOU HAVE GONE TOO FAR!

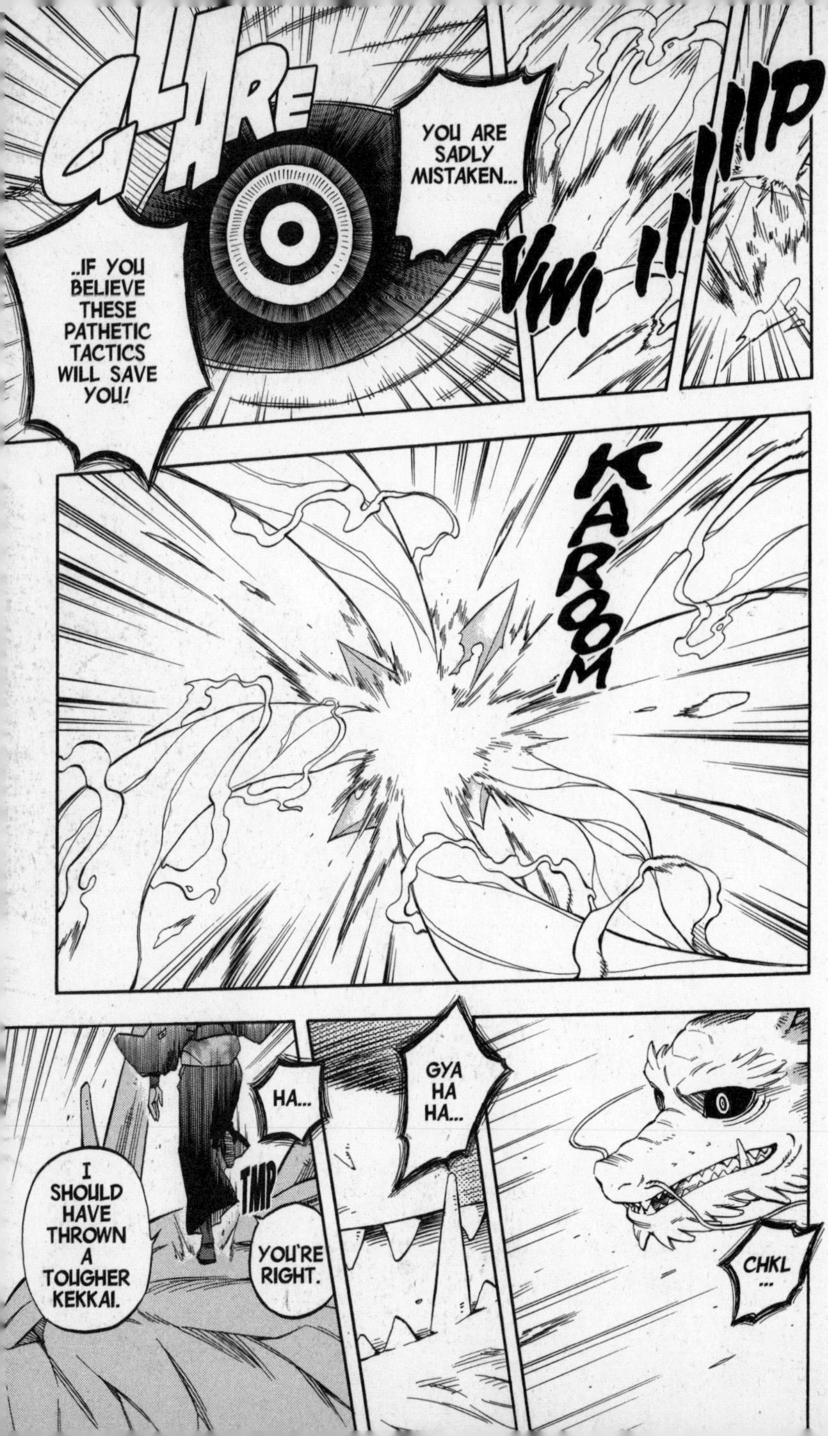
VWIIIIIIP
YOU ARE SADLY MISTAKEN...
GLARE
..IF YOU BELIEVE THESE PATHETIC TACTICS WILL SAVE YOU!
KAROOM
GYA HA HA...
CHKL ...
HA...
I SHOULD HAVE THROWN A TOUGHER KEKKAI.
TMP
YOU'RE RIGHT.

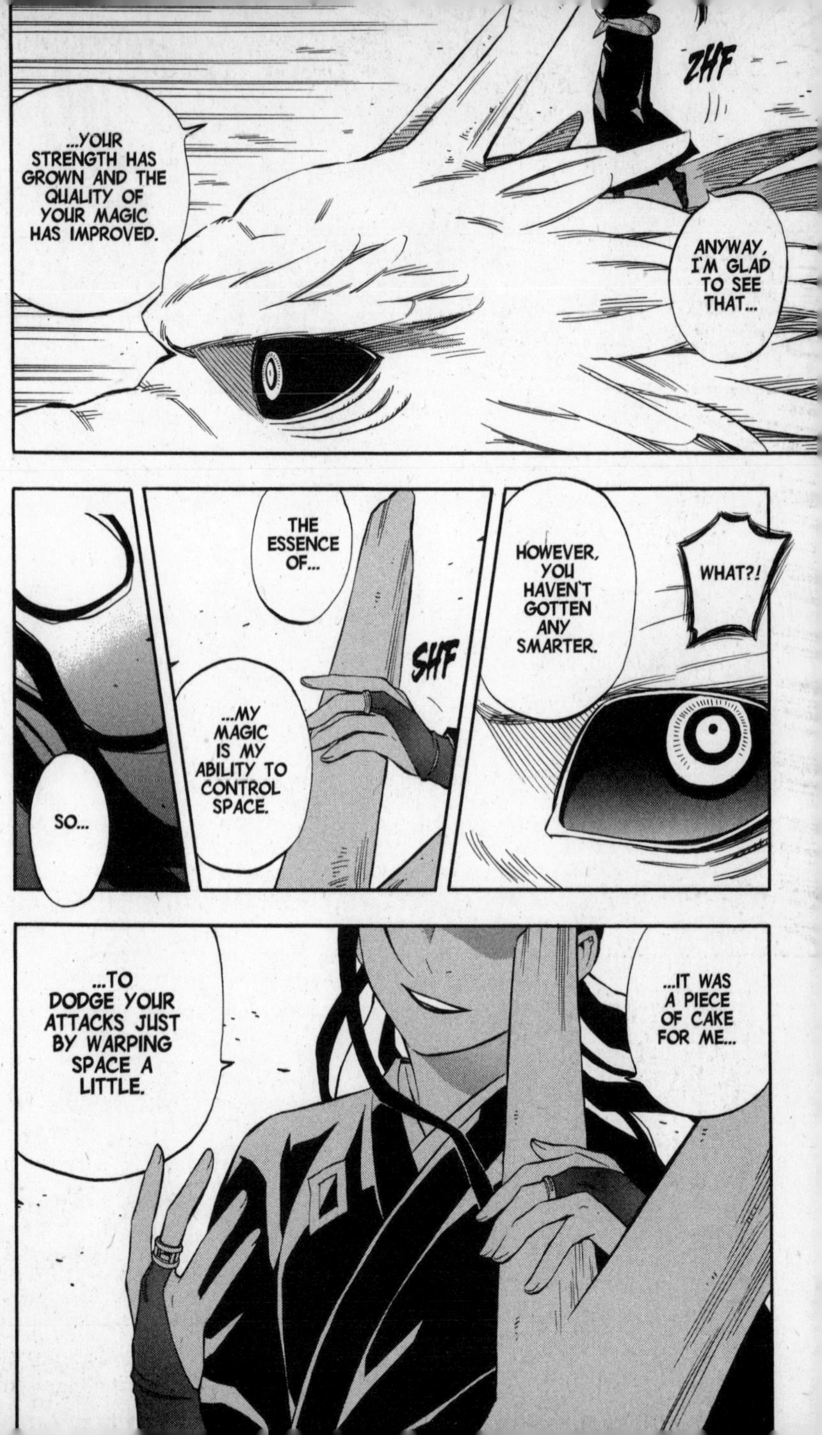
ZHF
ANYWAY, I'M GLAD TO SEE THAT...
...YOUR STRENGTH HAS GROWN AND THE QUALITY OF YOUR MAGIC HAS IMPROVED.
HOWEVER, YOU HAVEN'T GOTTEN ANY SMARTER.
WHAT?!
THE ESSENCE OF...
SHF
...MY MAGIC IS MY ABILITY TO CONTROL SPACE.
SO...
...IT WAS A PIECE OF CAKE FOR ME...
...TO DODGE YOUR ATTACKS JUST BY WARPING SPACE A LITTLE.

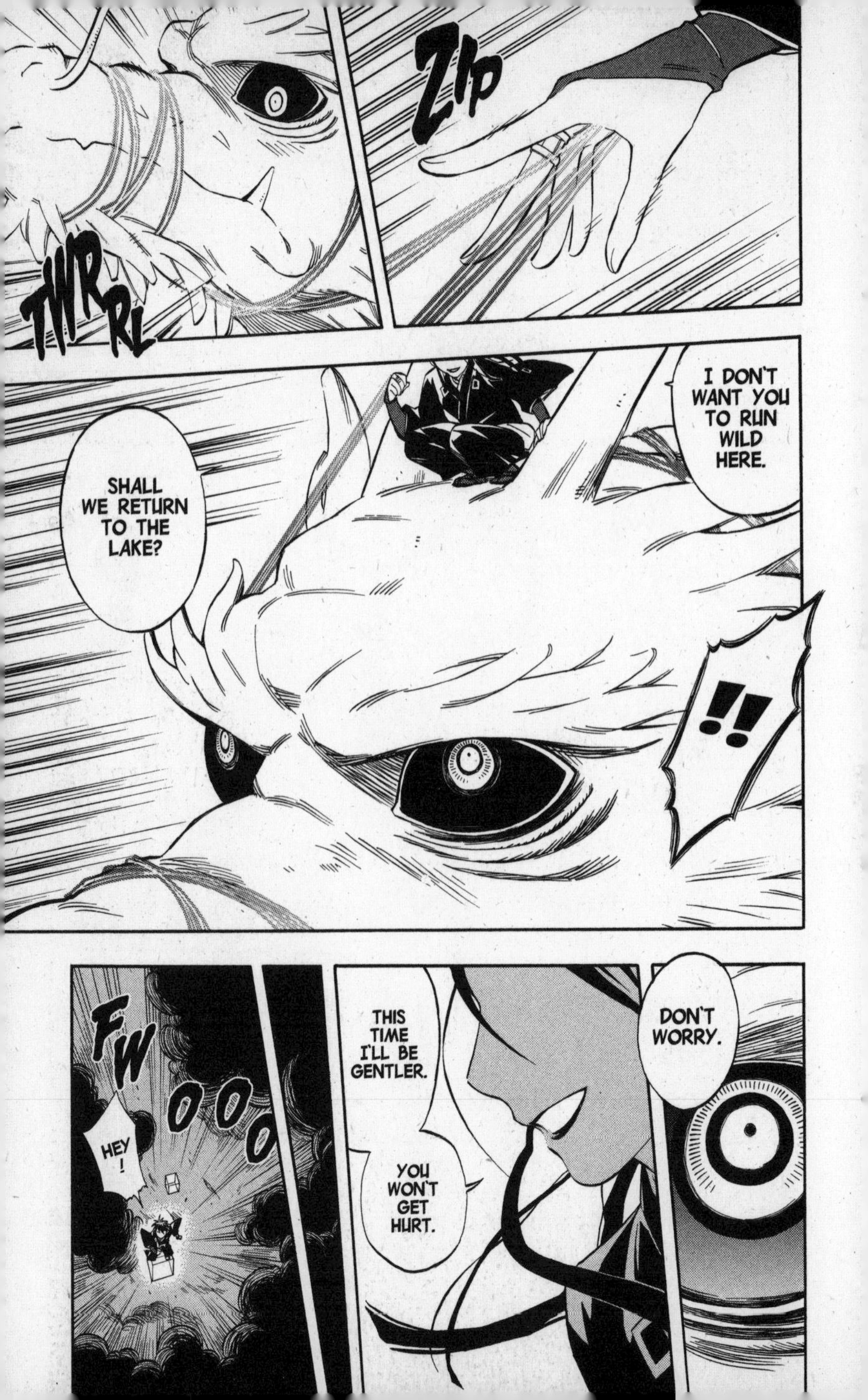
ZIP
TWRRL
I DON'T WANT YOU TO RUN WILD HERE.
!!
SHALL WE RETURN TO THE LAKE?
DON'T WORRY.
THIS TIME I'LL BE GENTLER.
YOU WON'T GET HURT.
FWOOOO
HEY!

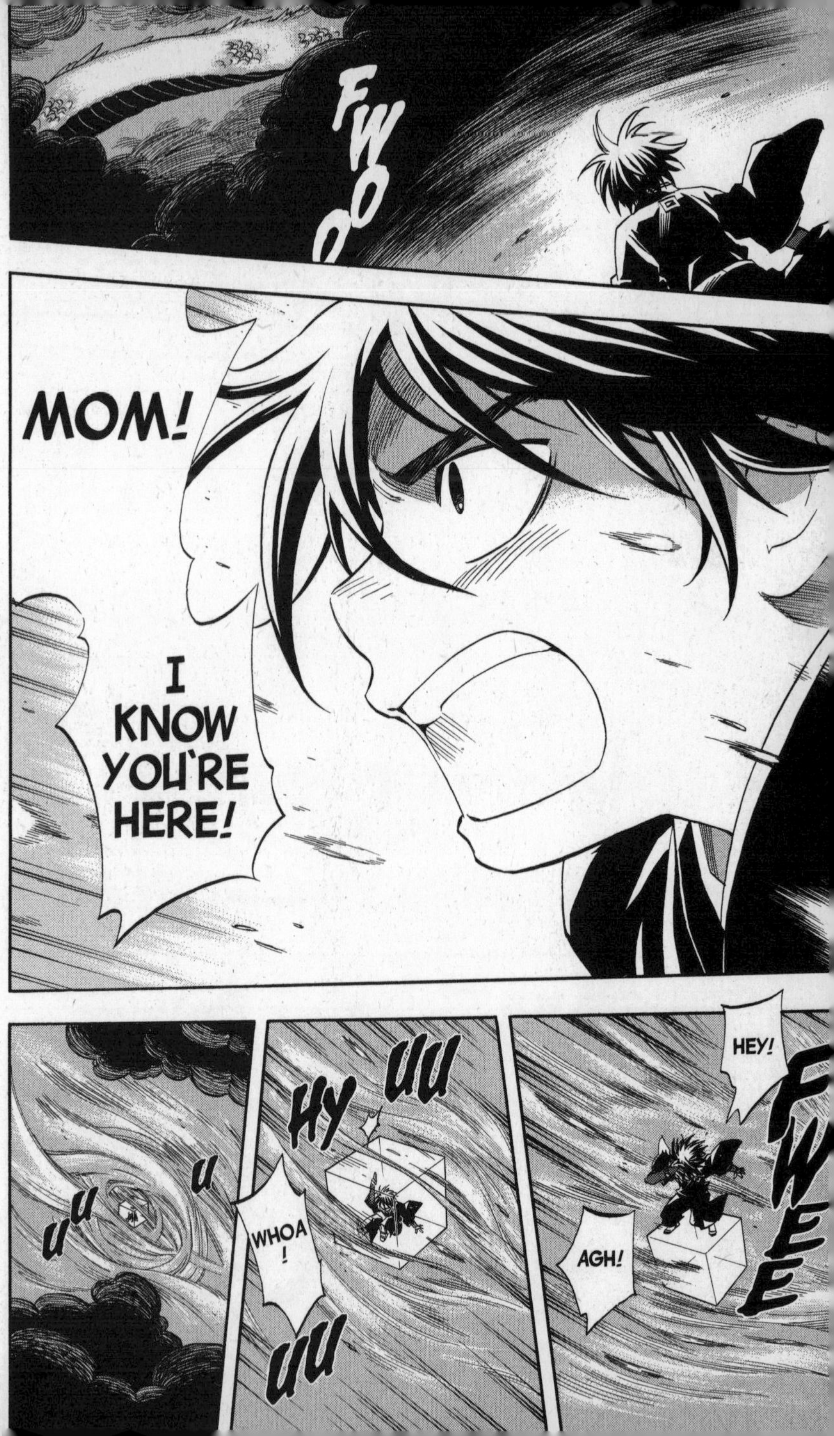
FWOOO
MOM!
I KNOW YOU'RE HERE!
HEY!
FWEE
AGH!
HYUU
WHOA!
UU
uUu
u

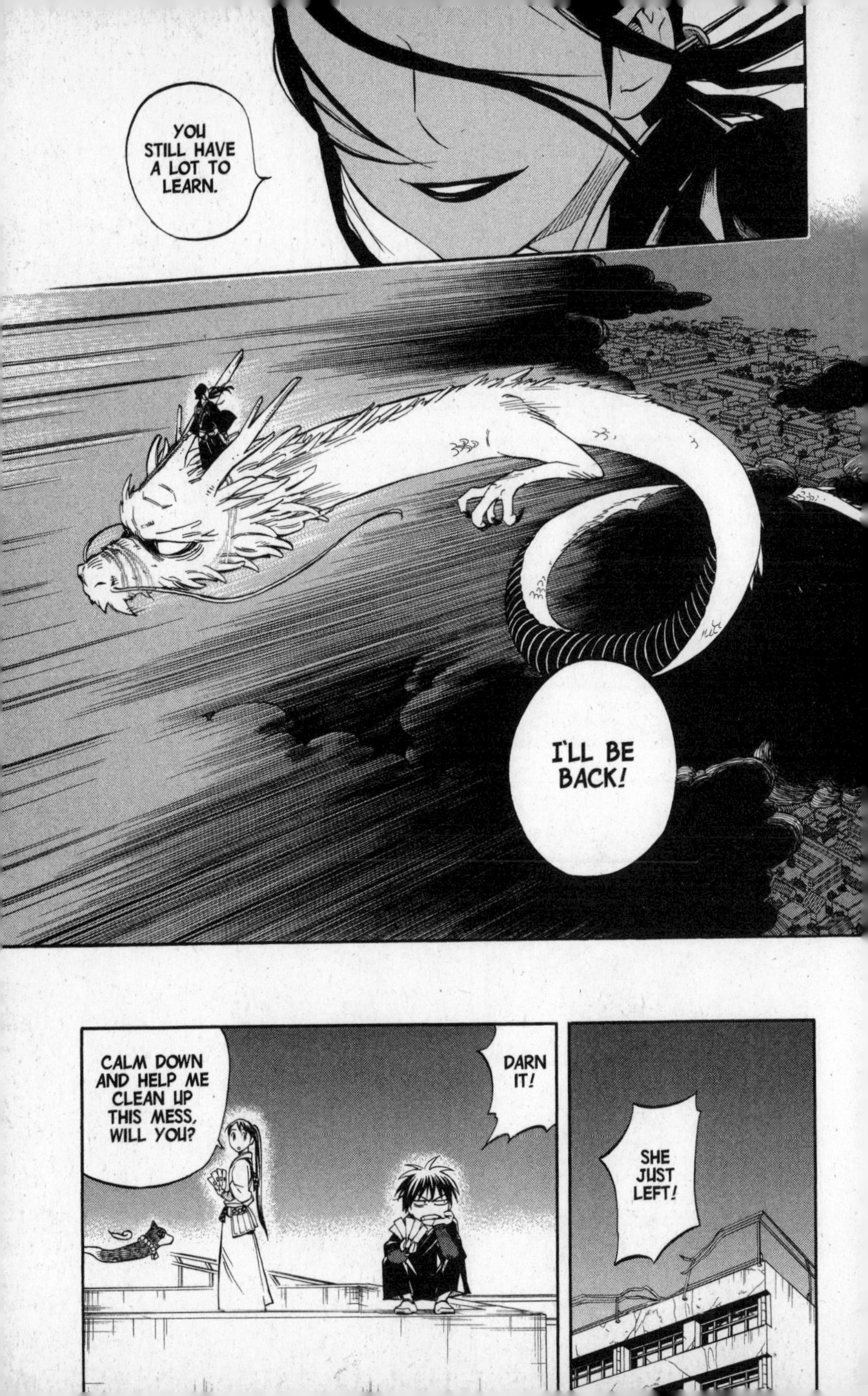
YOU STILL HAVE A LOT TO LEARN.
I'LL BE BACK!
SHE JUST LEFT!
DARN IT!
CALM DOWN AND HELP ME CLEAN UP THIS MESS, WILL YOU?

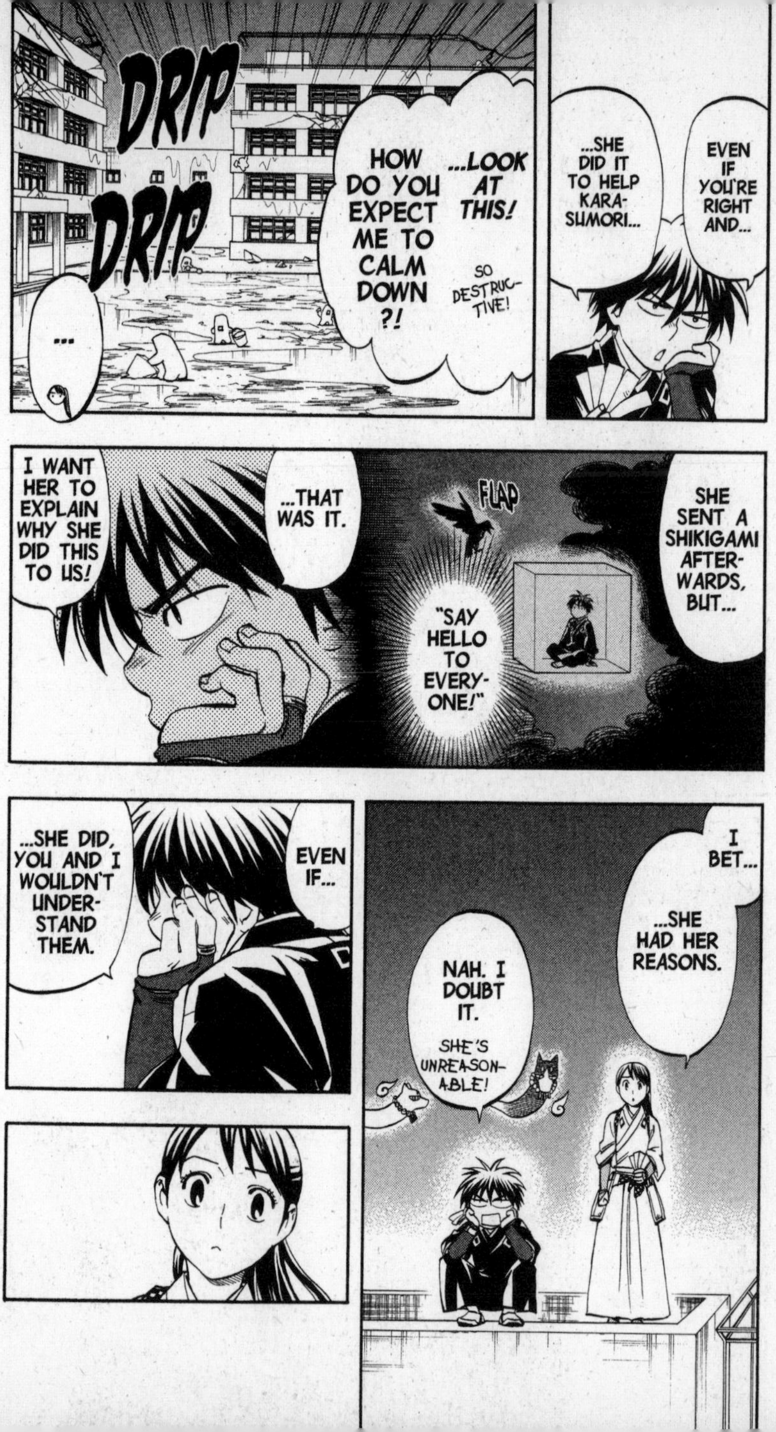
EVEN IF YOU'RE RIGHT AND...
...SHE DID IT TO HELP KARASUMORI...
...LOOK AT THIS!
SO DESTRUCTIVE!
HOW DO YOU EXPECT ME TO CALM DOWN?!
DRIP DRIP
...
SHE SENT A SHIKIGAMI AFTERWARDS, BUT...
FLAP
"SAY HELLO TO EVERYONE!"
...THAT WAS IT.
I WANT HER TO EXPLAIN WHY SHE DID THIS TO US!
I BET...
...SHE HAD HER REASONS.
NAH. I DOUBT IT.
SHE'S UNREASONABLE!
EVEN IF...
...SHE DID, YOU AND I WOULDN'T UNDERSTAND THEM.

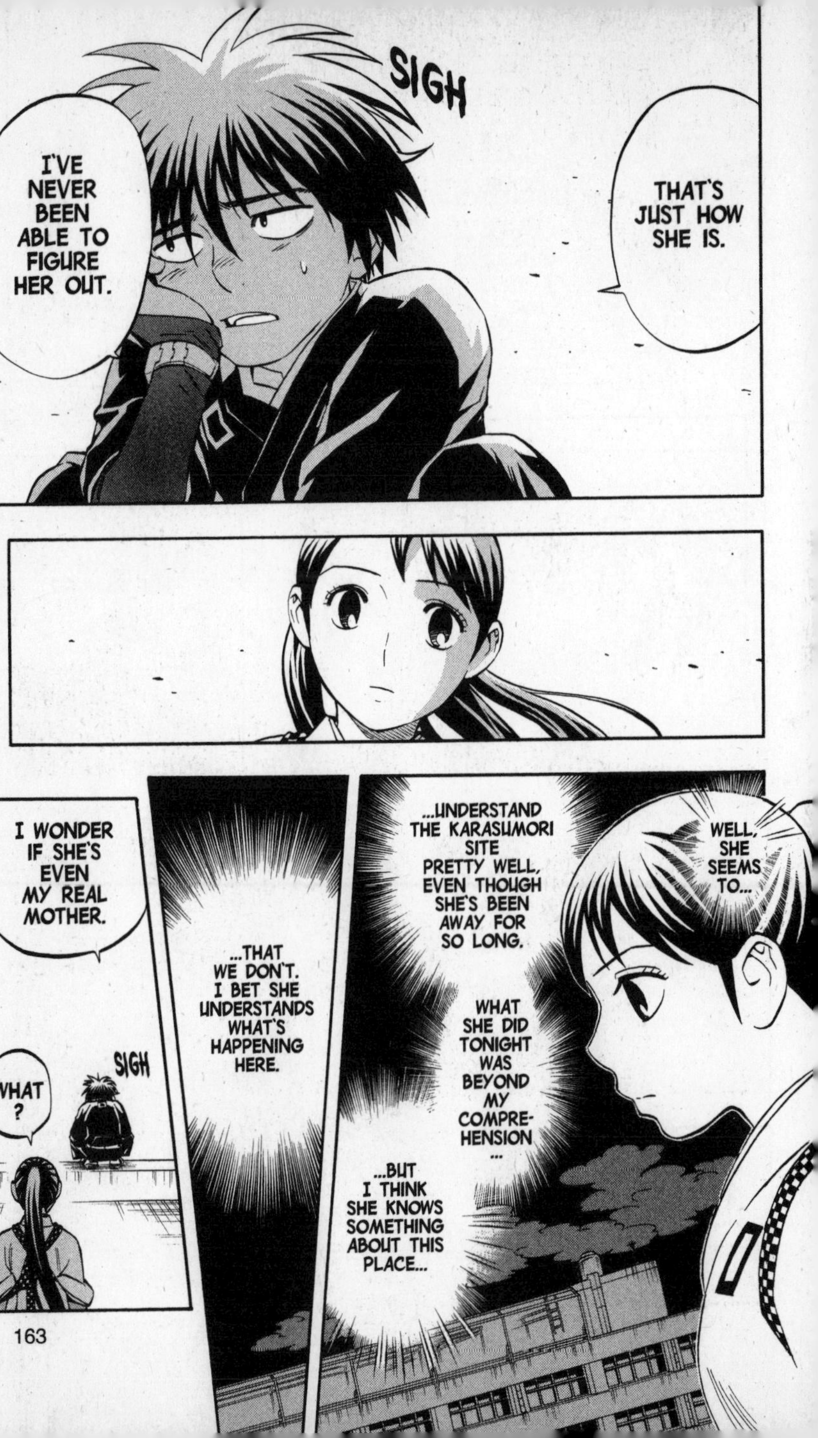
THAT'S JUST HOW SHE IS.
SIGH
I'VE NEVER BEEN ABLE TO FIGURE HER OUT.
WELL, SHE SEEMS TO...
...UNDERSTAND THE KARASUMORI SITE PRETTY WELL, EVEN THOUGH SHE'S BEEN AWAY FOR SO LONG.
WHAT SHE DID TONIGHT WAS BEYOND MY COMPRE-HENSION...
...BUT I THINK SHE KNOWS SOMETHING ABOUT THIS PLACE...
...THAT WE DON'T. I BET SHE UNDERSTANDS WHAT'S HAPPENING HERE.
I WONDER IF SHE'S EVEN MY REAL MOTHER.
SIGH
WHAT?

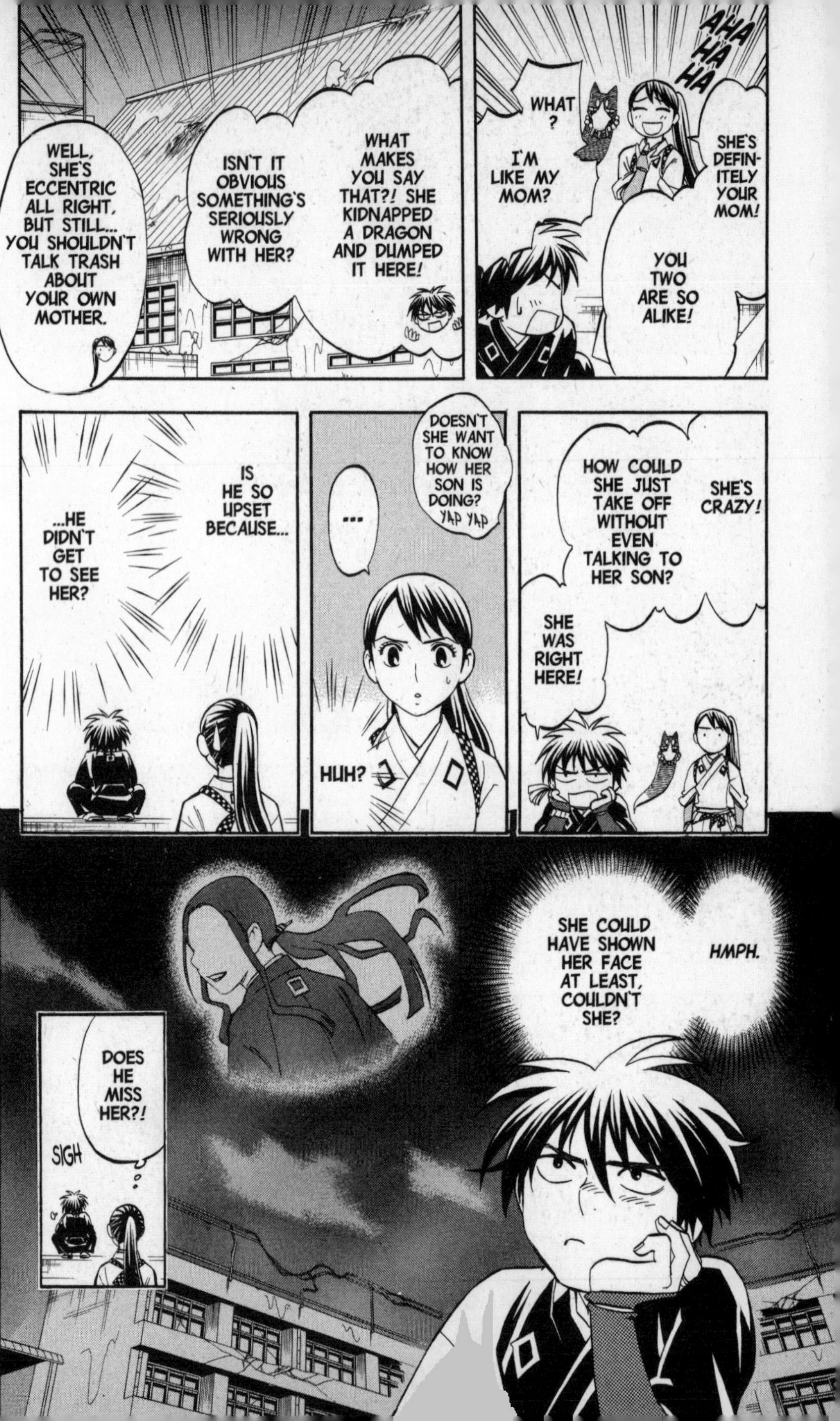
AHAHAHAHA
SHE'S DEFIN-ITELY YOUR MOM!
YOU TWO ARE SO ALIKE!
WHAT?
I'M LIKE MY MOM?
WHAT MAKES YOU SAY THAT?! SHE KIDNAPPED A DRAGON AND DUMPED IT HERE!
ISN'T IT OBVIOUS SOMETHING'S SERIOUSLY WRONG WITH HER?
WELL, SHE'S ECCENTRIC ALL RIGHT, BUT STILL... YOU SHOULDN'T TALK TRASH ABOUT YOUR OWN MOTHER.
SHE'S CRAZY!
HOW COULD SHE JUST TAKE OFF WITHOUT EVEN TALKING TO HER SON?
SHE WAS RIGHT HERE!
DOESN'T SHE WANT TO KNOW HOW HER SON IS DOING?
YAP YAP
...
HUH?
IS HE SO UPSET BECAUSE...
...HE DIDN'T GET TO SEE HER?
HMPH.
SHE COULD HAVE SHOWN HER FACE AT LEAST, COULDN'T SHE?
DOES HE MISS HER?!
SIGH

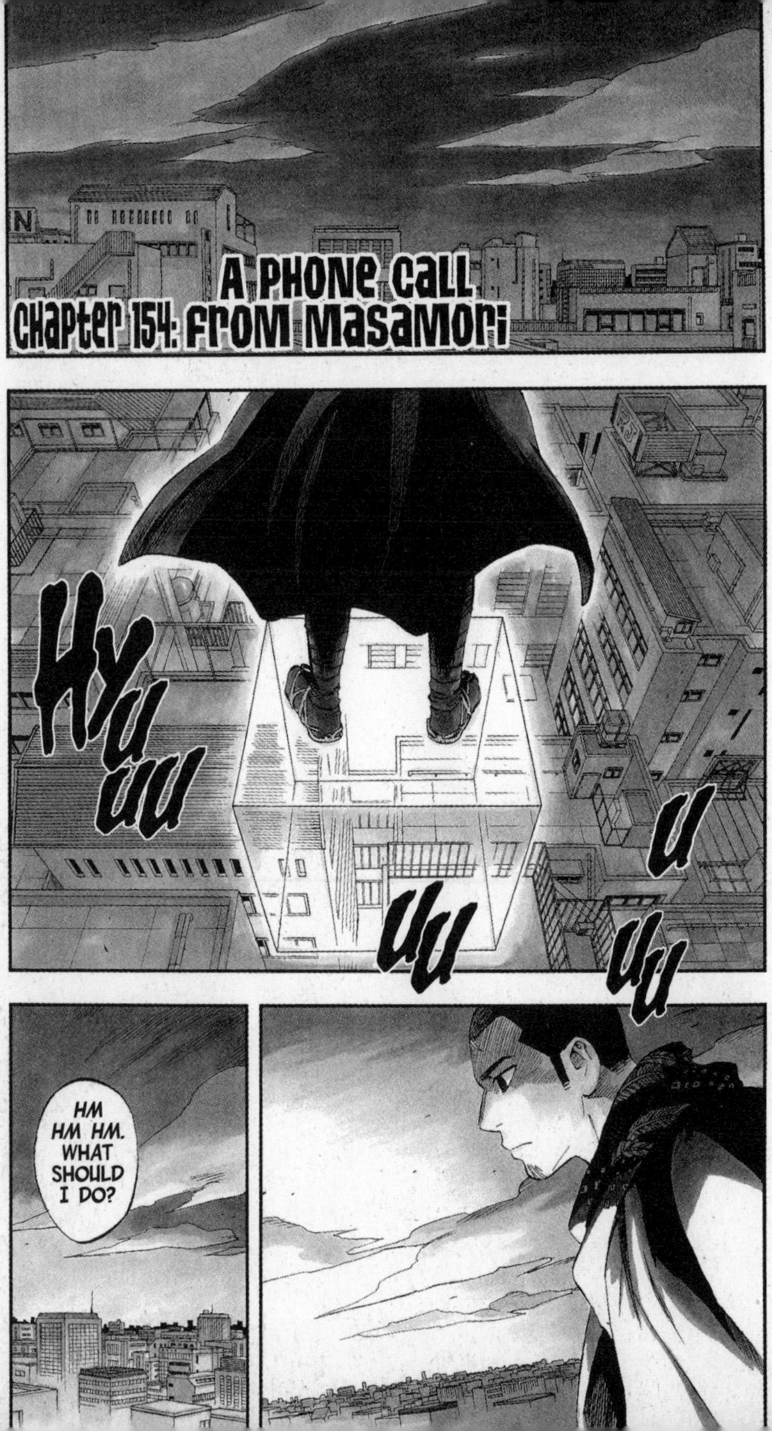
A PHONE CALL
CHAPTER 154: FROM MASAMORI
HYUUU
UU
U
UU
HM HM HM. WHAT SHOULD I DO?

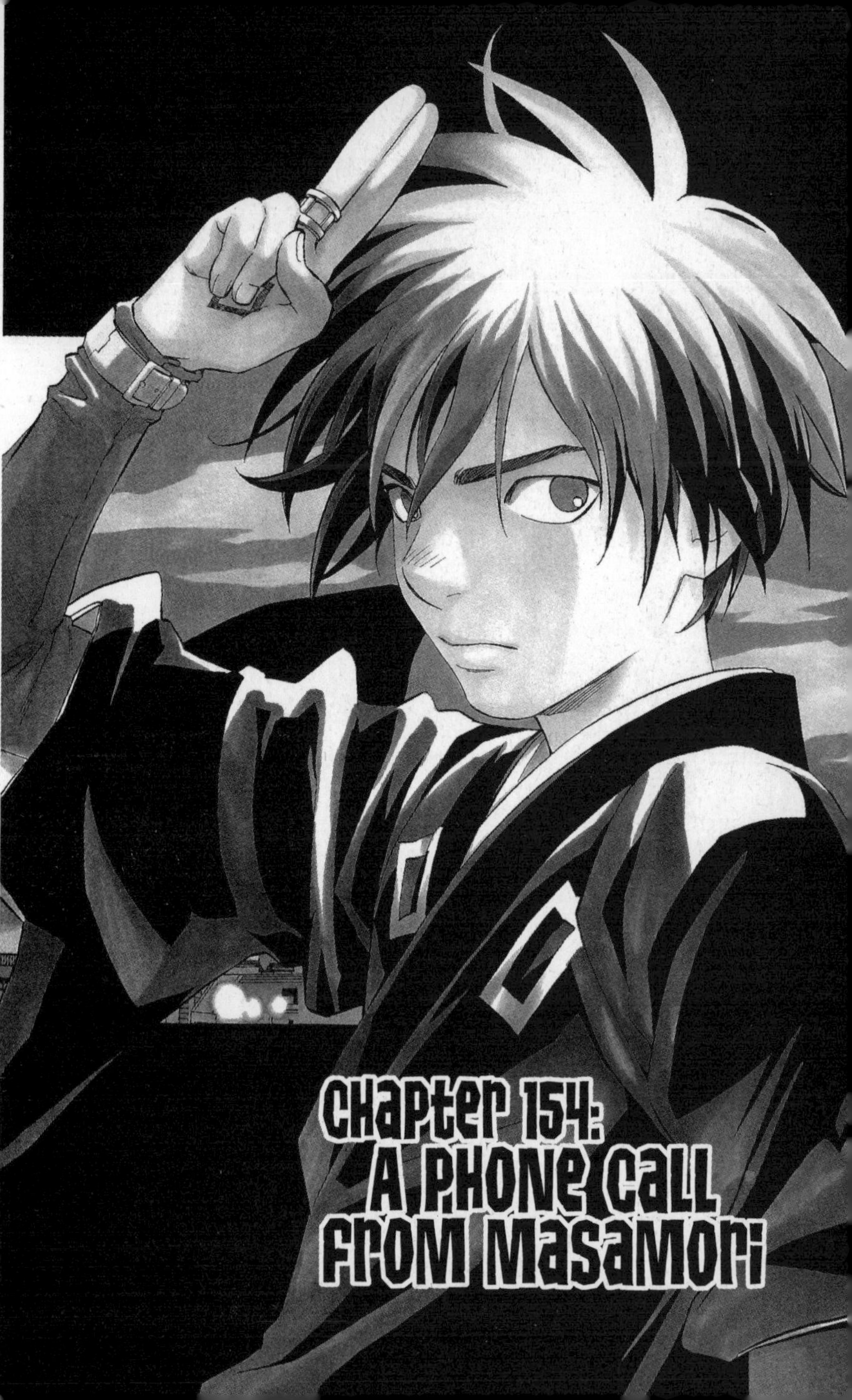
Chapter 154:
A Phone Call from Masamori

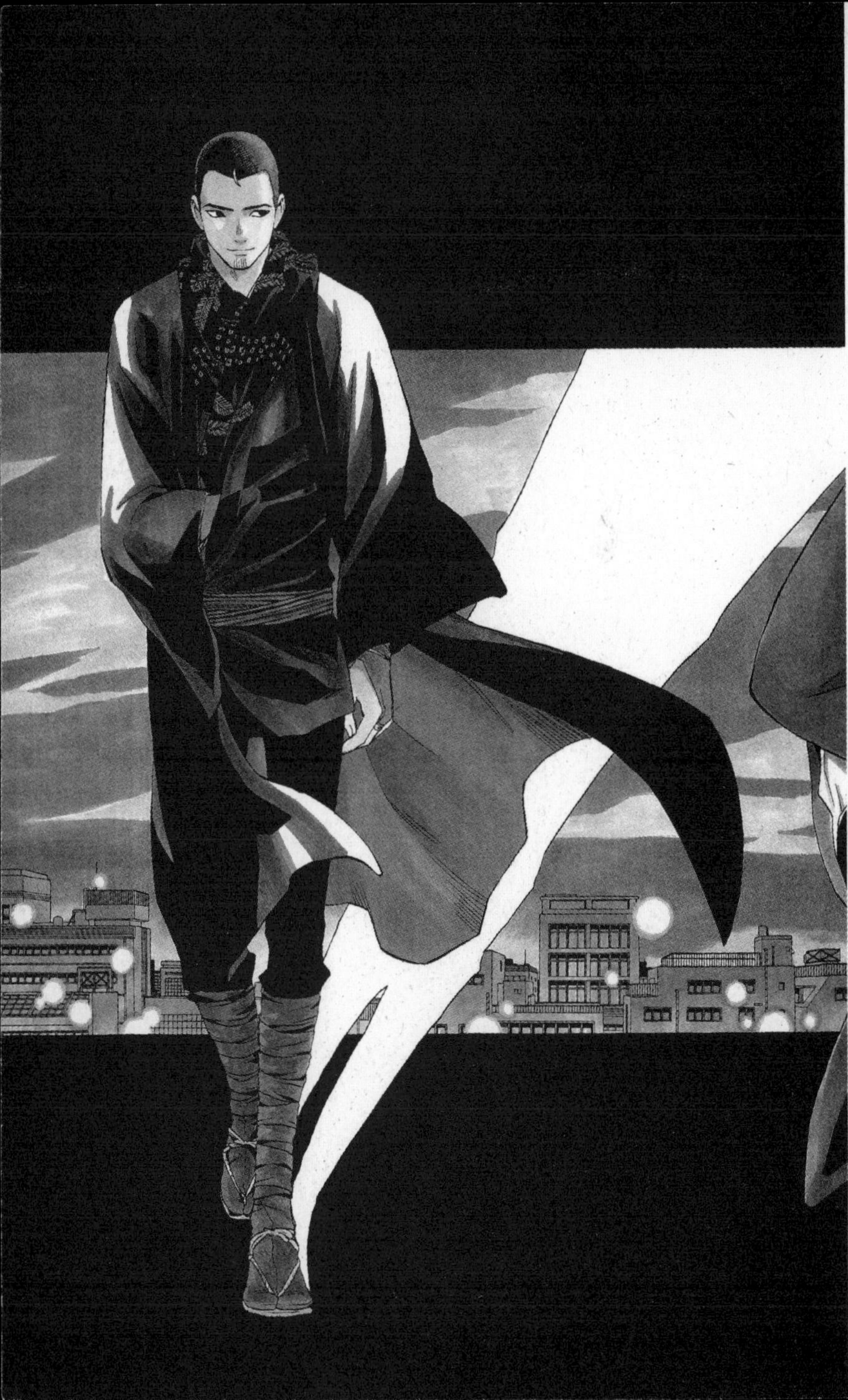

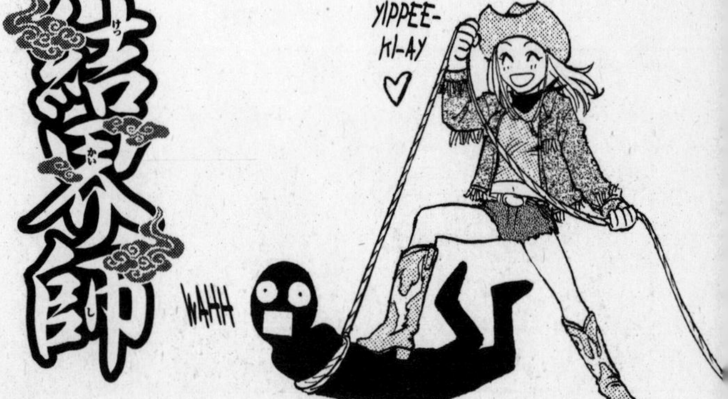
結界師
YIPPEE-KI-AY
WAHH

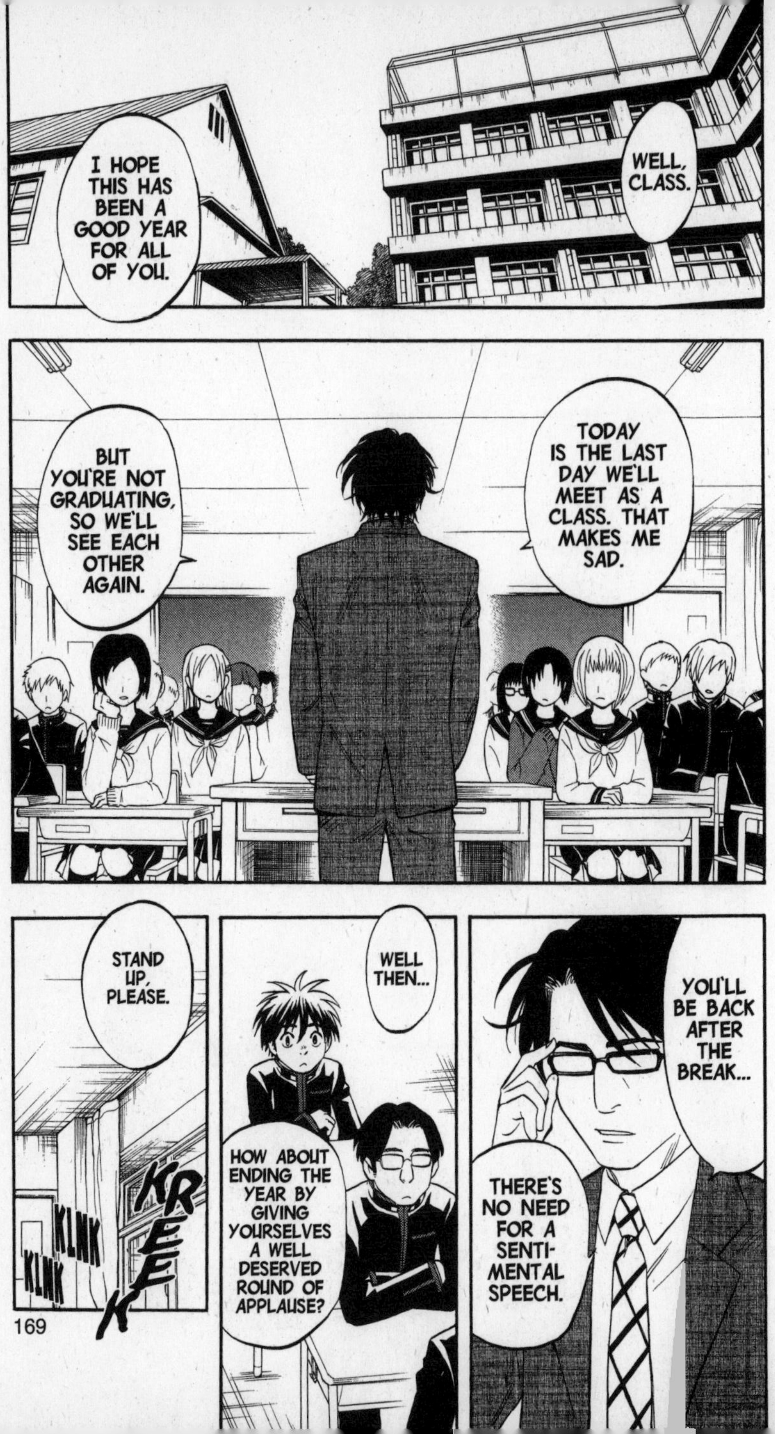
WELL, CLASS.
I HOPE THIS HAS BEEN A GOOD YEAR FOR ALL OF YOU.
TODAY IS THE LAST DAY WE'LL MEET AS A CLASS. THAT MAKES ME SAD.
BUT YOU'RE NOT GRADUATING, SO WE'LL SEE EACH OTHER AGAIN.
YOU'LL BE BACK AFTER THE BREAK...
THERE'S NO NEED FOR A SENTI-MENTAL SPEECH.
WELL THEN...
HOW ABOUT ENDING THE YEAR BY GIVING YOURSELVES A WELL DESERVED ROUND OF APPLAUSE?
STAND UP, PLEASE.
KREEK
KLINK
KLINK

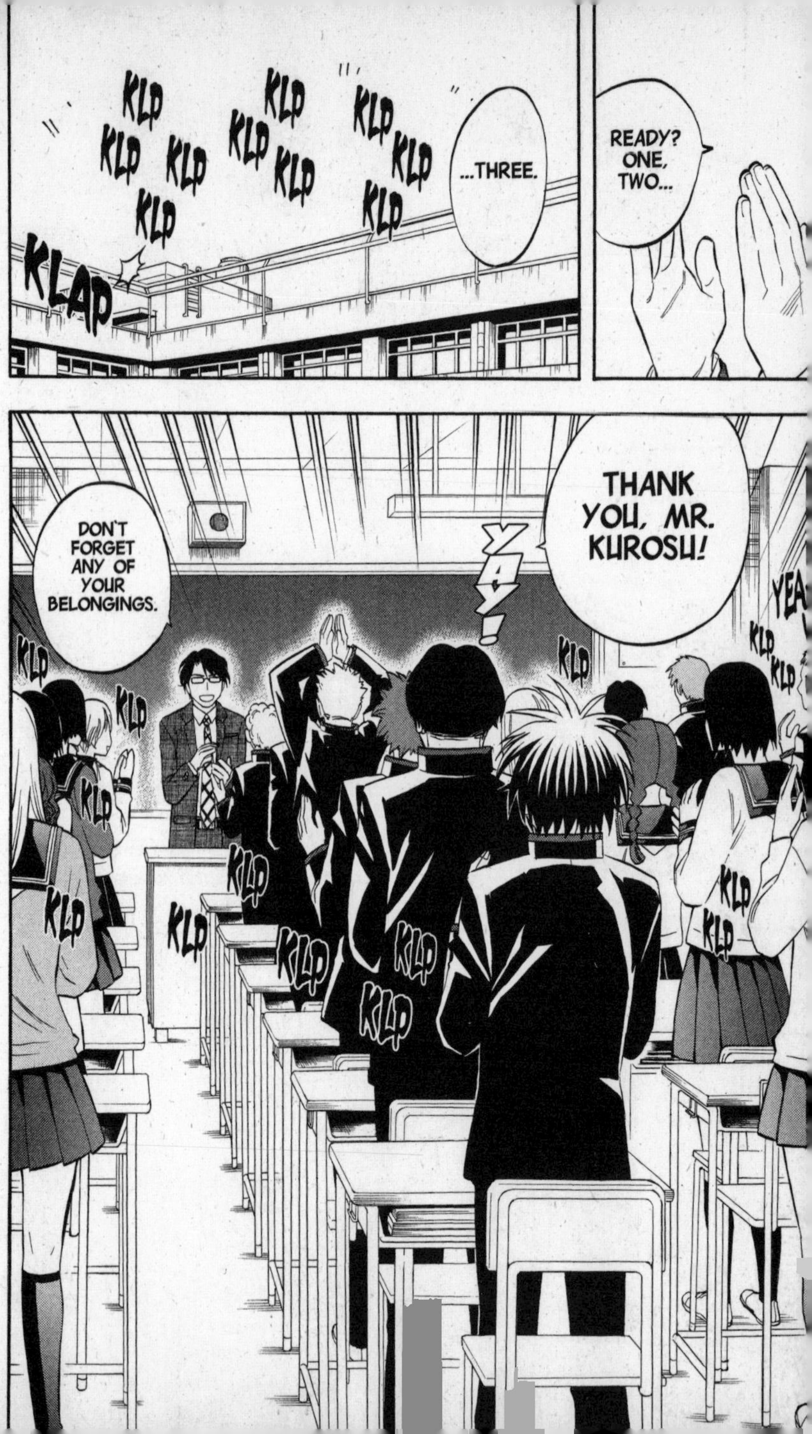
READY? ONE, TWO...
...THREE.
KLP KLP KLP KLP KLP KLP KLP KLP KLP KLP
KLAP
THANK YOU, MR. KUROSU!
YEA
KLP KLP
YAY!
KLP
DON'T FORGET ANY OF YOUR BELONGINGS.
KLP KLP KLP KLP KLP KLP KLP KLP KLP KLP KLP

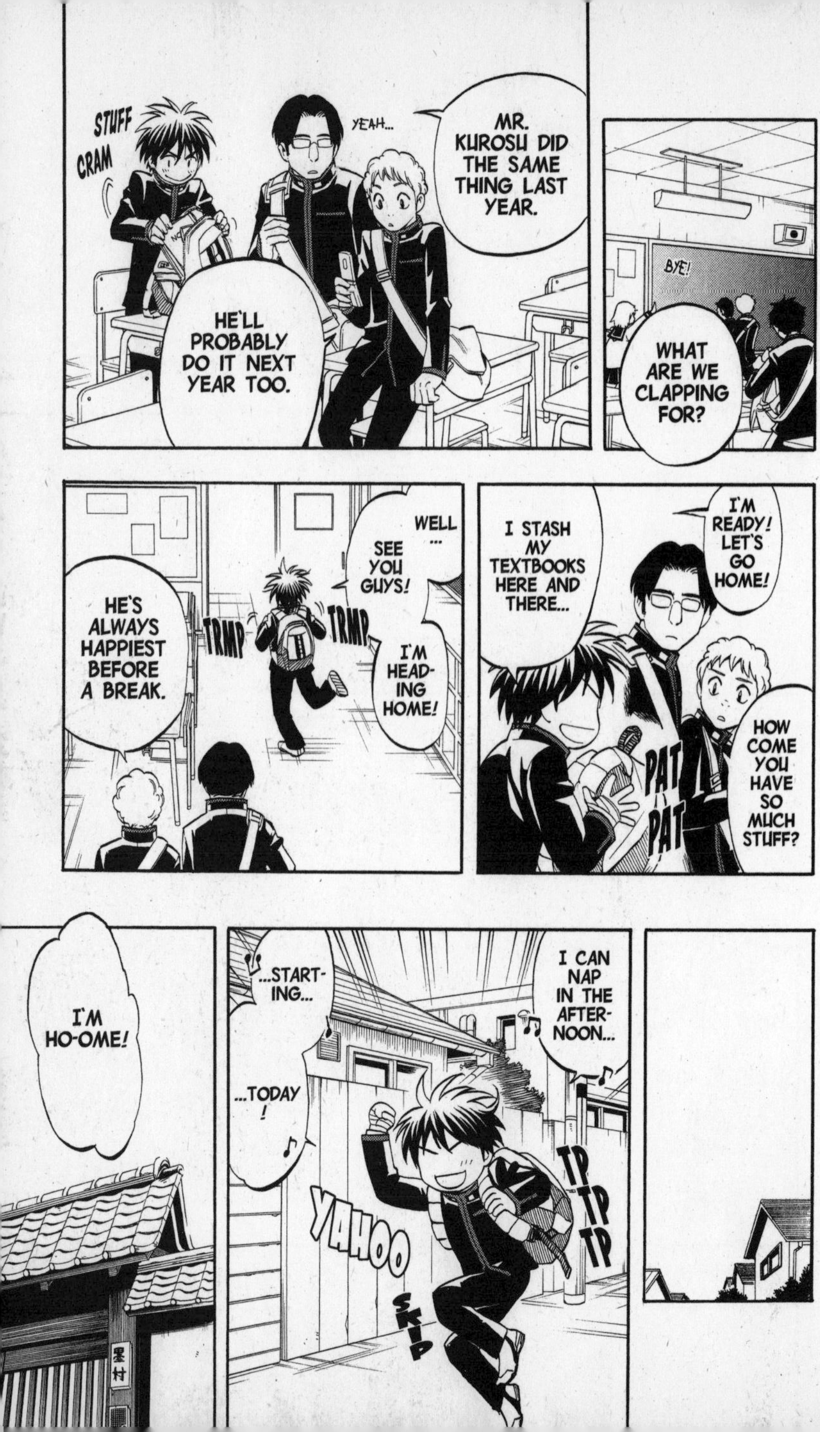
BYE!
WHAT ARE WE CLAPPING FOR?
MR. KUROSU DID THE SAME THING LAST YEAR.
YEAH...
STUFF
CRAM
HE'LL PROBABLY DO IT NEXT YEAR TOO.
I'M READY! LET'S GO HOME!
I STASH MY TEXTBOOKS HERE AND THERE...
PAT PAT
HOW COME YOU HAVE SO MUCH STUFF?
WELL... SEE YOU GUYS!
I'M HEADING HOME!
TRMP TRMP
HE'S ALWAYS HAPPIEST BEFORE A BREAK.
I CAN NAP IN THE AFTERNOON...
...STARTING...
...TODAY!
TP TP TP
YAHOO
SKIP
I'M HO-OME!
墨村

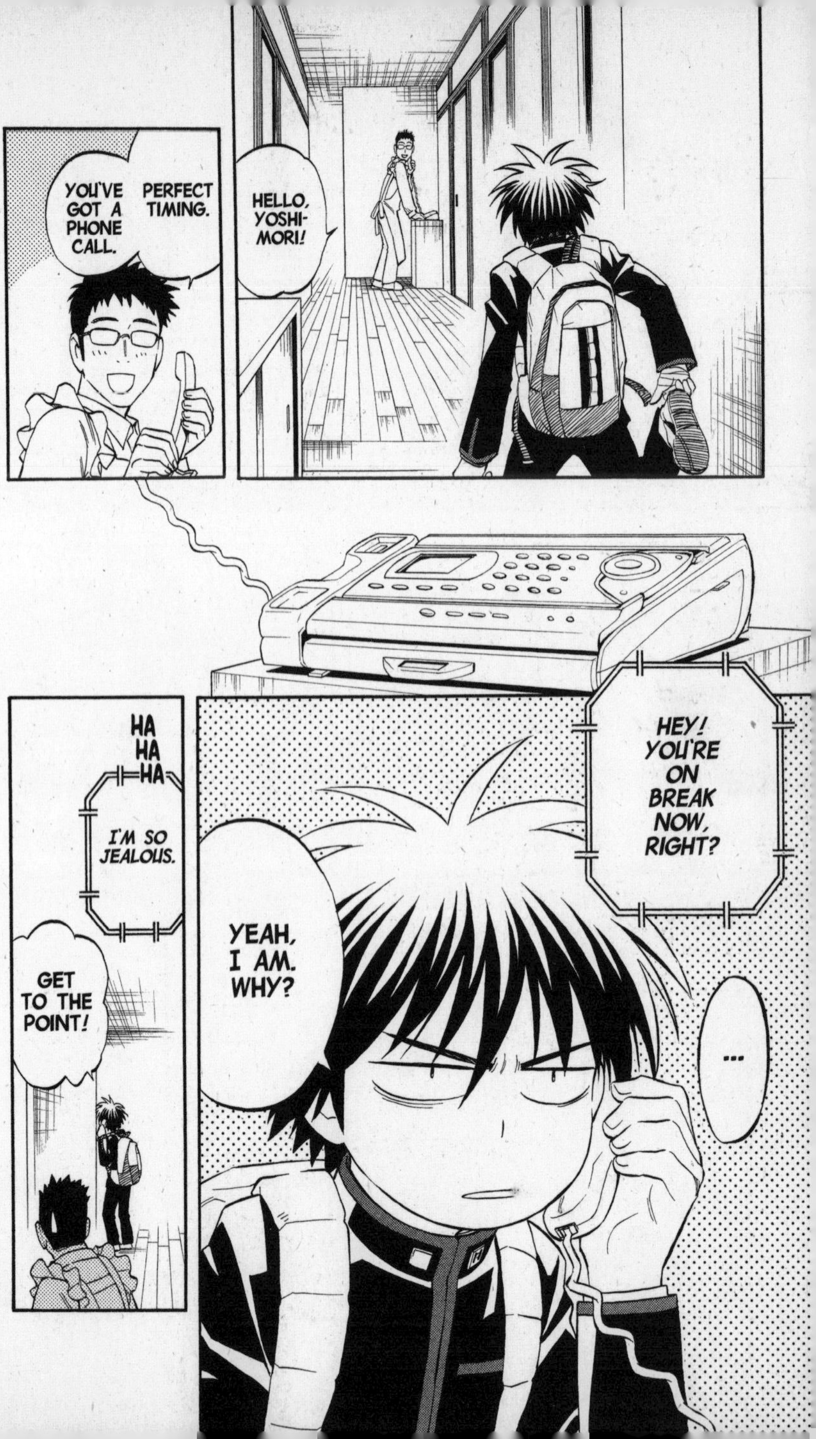
HELLO, YOSHIMORI!
PERFECT TIMING.
YOU'VE GOT A PHONE CALL.
HEY! YOU'RE ON BREAK NOW, RIGHT?
...
YEAH, I AM. WHY?
HA HA HA
I'M SO JEALOUS.
GET TO THE POINT!

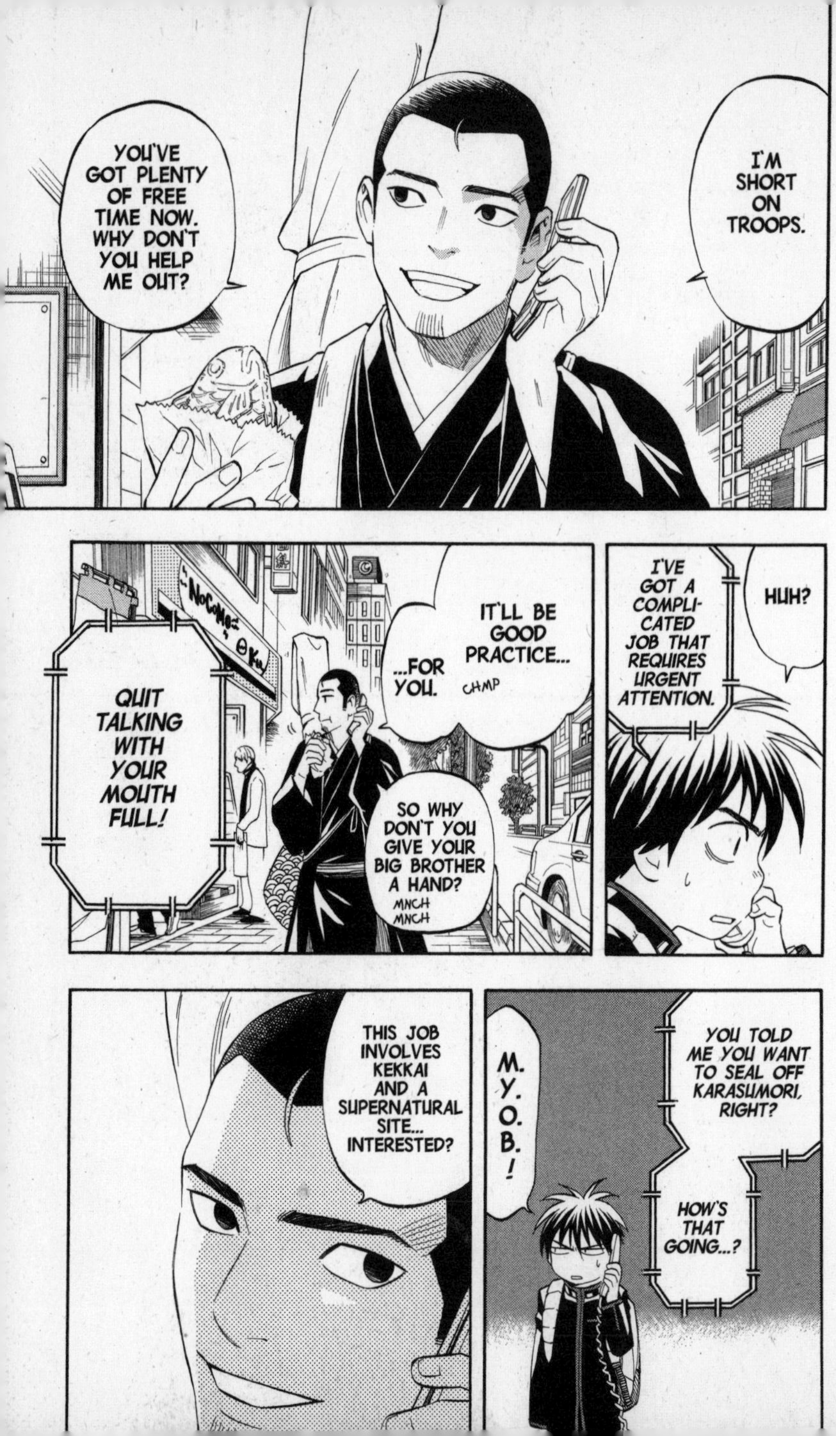
I'M SHORT ON TROOPS.
YOU'VE GOT PLENTY OF FREE TIME NOW. WHY DON'T YOU HELP ME OUT?
HUH?
I'VE GOT A COMPLICATED JOB THAT REQUIRES URGENT ATTENTION.
IT'LL BE GOOD PRACTICE...
...FOR YOU.
CHMP
SO WHY DON'T YOU GIVE YOUR BIG BROTHER A HAND?
MNCH MNCH
QUIT TALKING WITH YOUR MOUTH FULL!
YOU TOLD ME YOU WANT TO SEAL OFF KARASUMORI, RIGHT?
HOW'S THAT GOING...?
M.Y.O.B.!
THIS JOB INVOLVES KEKKAI AND A SUPERNATURAL SITE... INTERESTED?

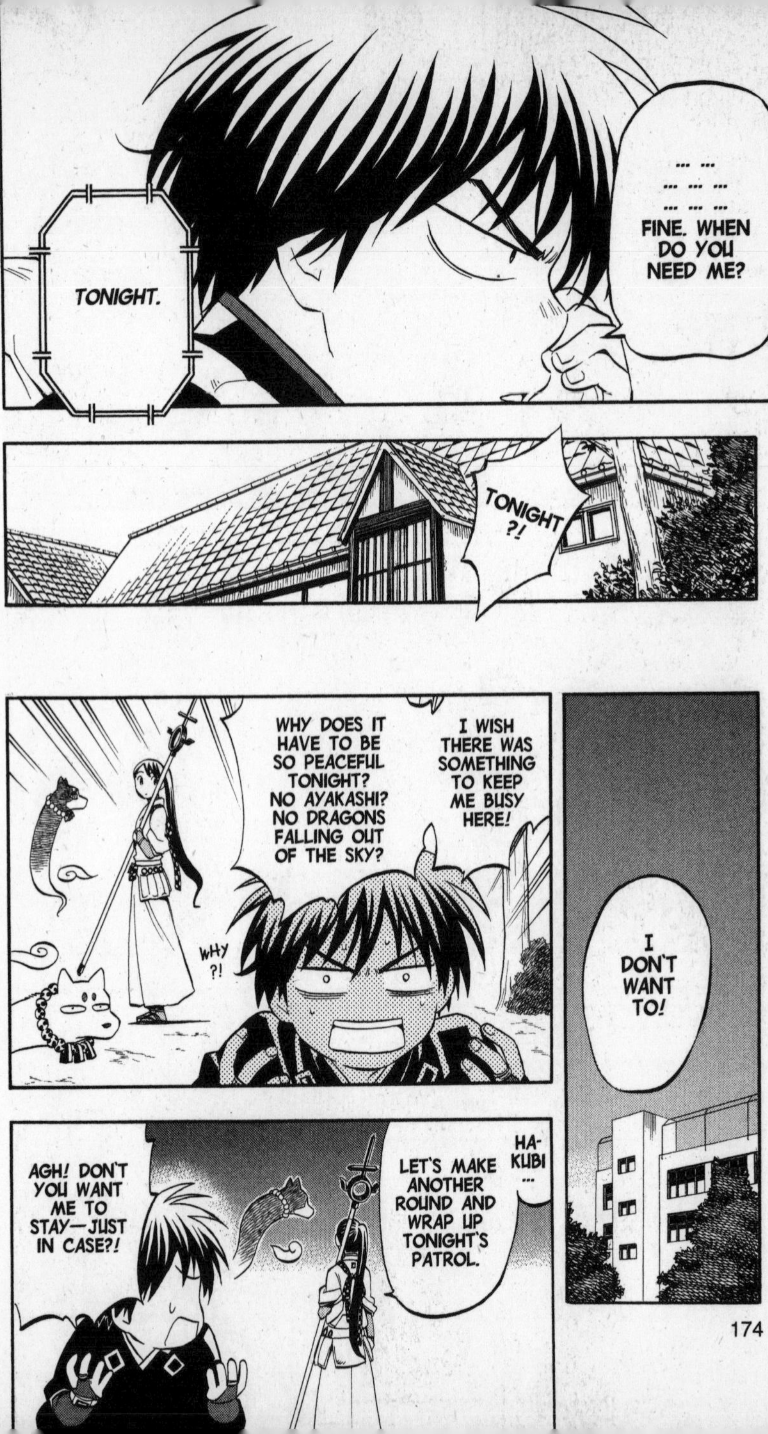

... ... FINE. WHEN DO YOU NEED ME?
TONIGHT.
TONIGHT?!
I DON'T WANT TO!
I WISH THERE WAS SOMETHING TO KEEP ME BUSY HERE!
WHY DOES IT HAVE TO BE SO PEACEFUL TONIGHT? NO AYAKASHI? NO DRAGONS FALLING OUT OF THE SKY?
WHY?!
HAKUBI...
LET'S MAKE ANOTHER ROUND AND WRAP UP TONIGHT'S PATROL.
AGH! DON'T YOU WANT ME TO STAY—JUST IN CASE?!

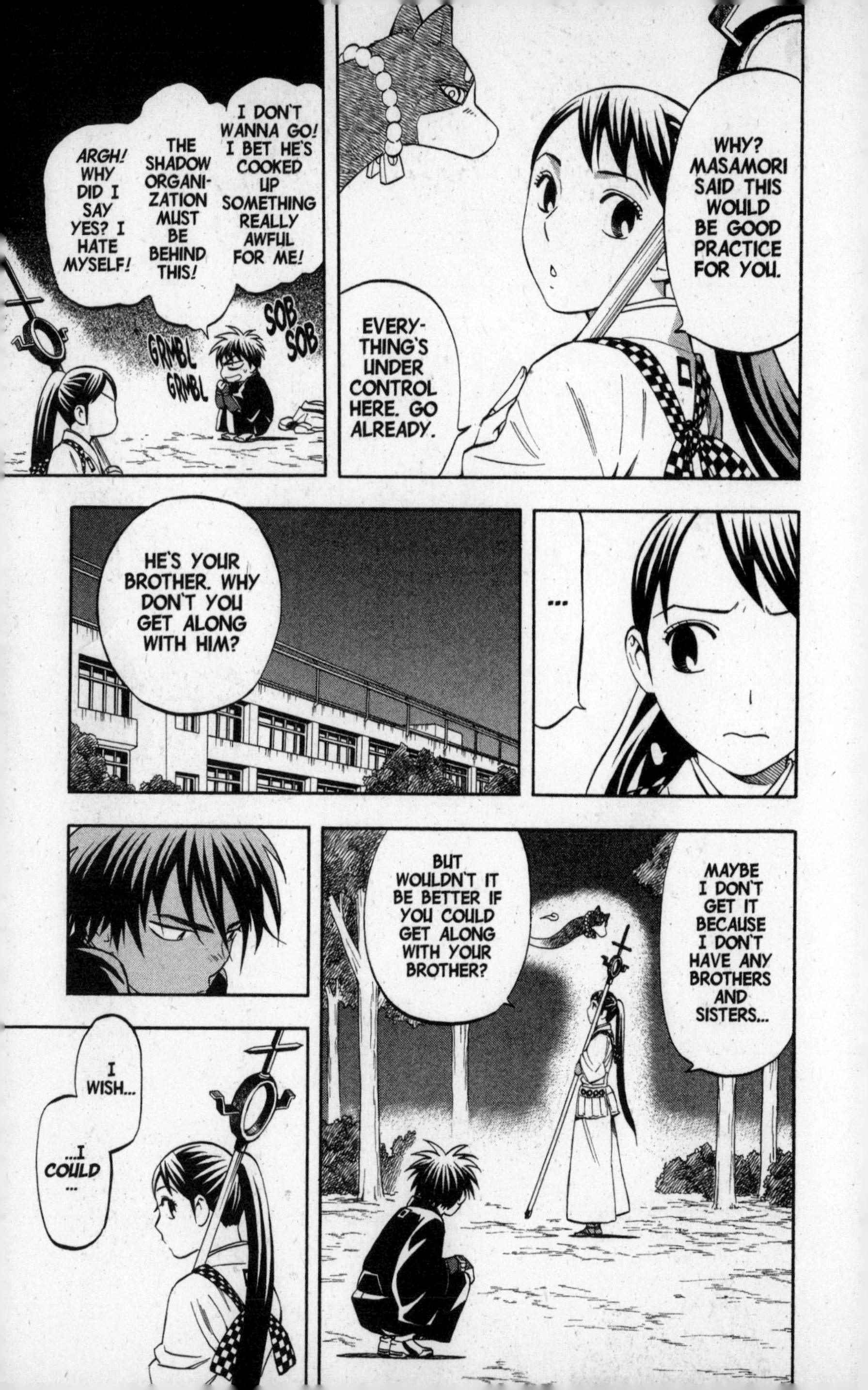
WHY? MASAMORI SAID THIS WOULD BE GOOD PRACTICE FOR YOU.
EVERY-THING'S UNDER CONTROL HERE. GO ALREADY.
I DON'T WANNA GO! I BET HE'S COOKED UP SOMETHING REALLY AWFUL FOR ME!
THE SHADOW ORGANI-ZATION MUST BE BEHIND THIS!
ARGH! WHY DID I SAY YES? I HATE MYSELF!
SOB SOB
GRMBL GRMBL
...
HE'S YOUR BROTHER. WHY DON'T YOU GET ALONG WITH HIM?
MAYBE I DON'T GET IT BECAUSE I DON'T HAVE ANY BROTHERS AND SISTERS...
BUT WOULDN'T IT BE BETTER IF YOU COULD GET ALONG WITH YOUR BROTHER?
I WISH...
...I COULD ...

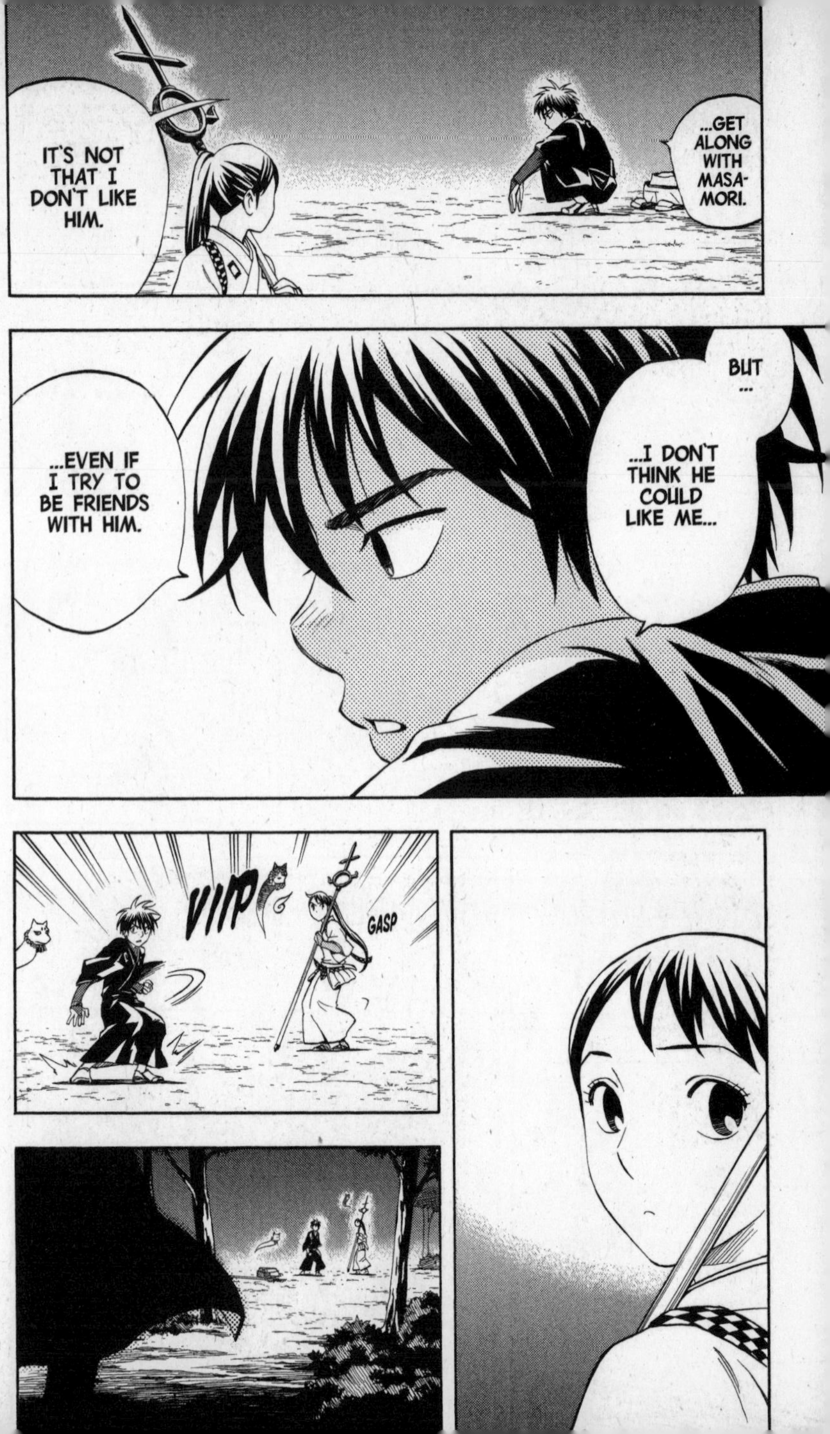
...GET ALONG WITH MASA-MORI.
IT'S NOT THAT I DON'T LIKE HIM.
BUT ...
...I DON'T THINK HE COULD LIKE ME...
...EVEN IF I TRY TO BE FRIENDS WITH HIM.
GASP
VIIP

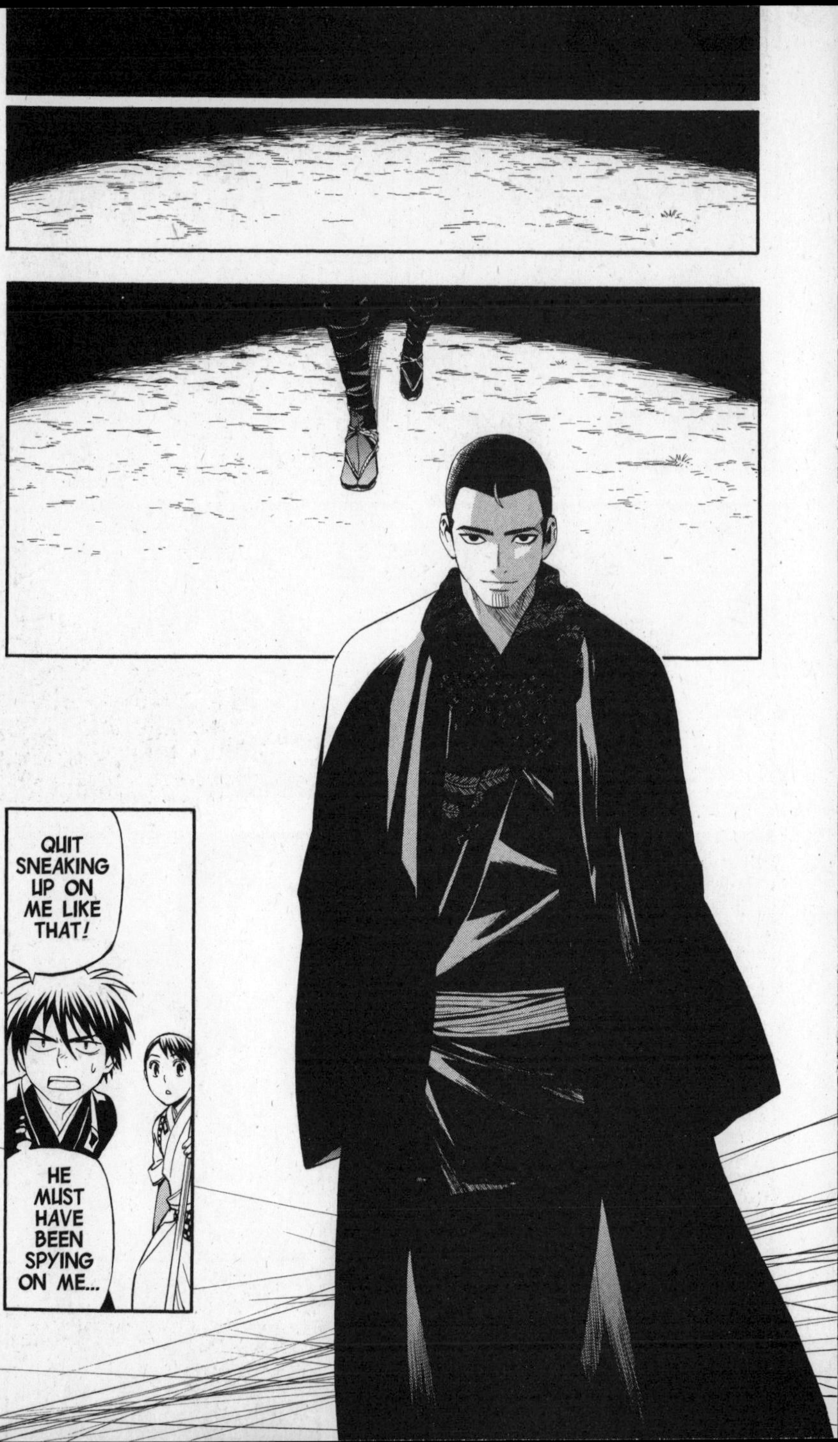
QUIT SNEAKING UP ON ME LIKE THAT!
HE MUST HAVE BEEN SPYING ON ME...

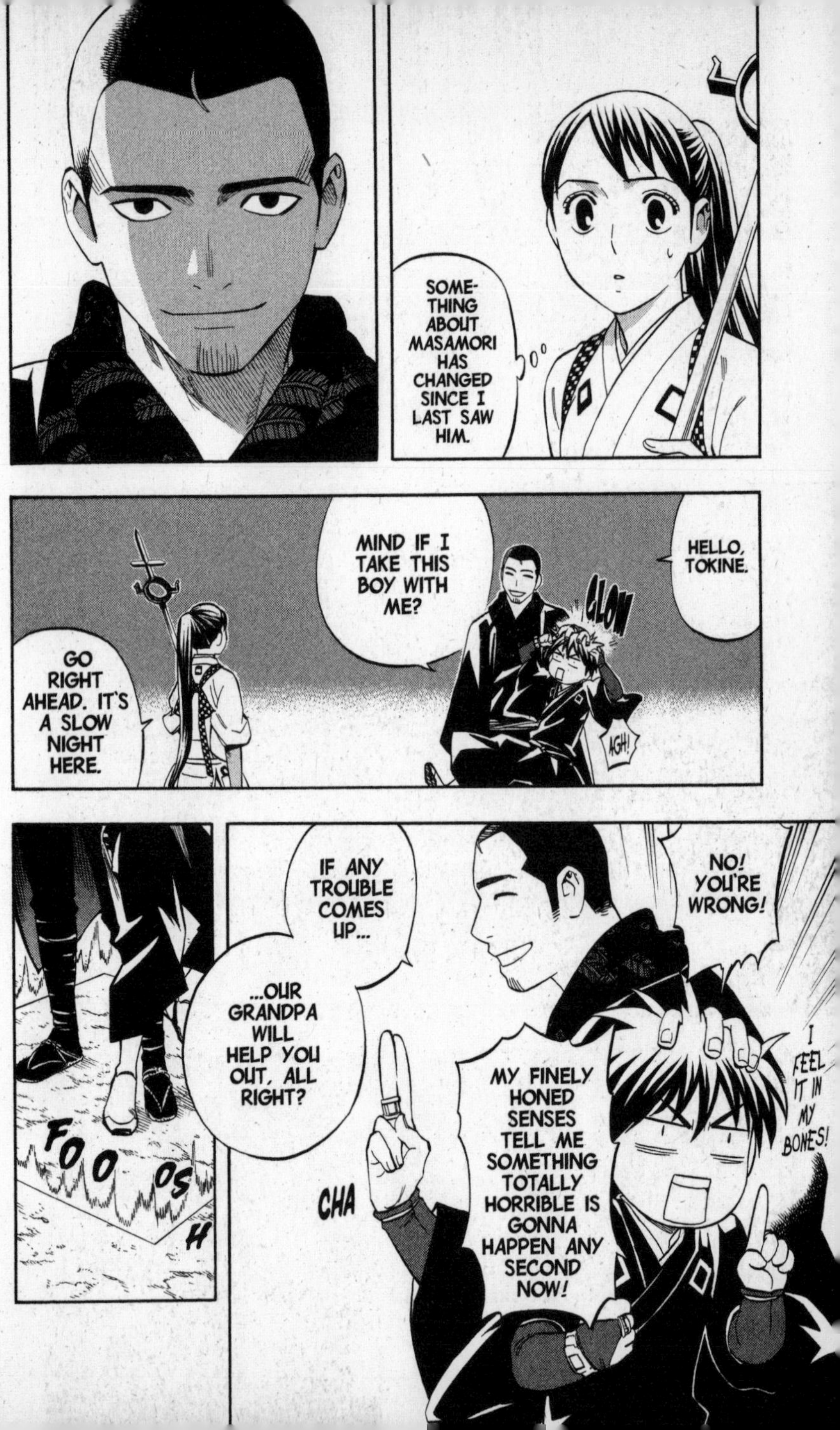
SOMETHING ABOUT MASAMORI HAS CHANGED SINCE I LAST SAW HIM.
HELLO, TOKINE.
GLOW
MIND IF I TAKE THIS BOY WITH ME?
AGH!
GO RIGHT AHEAD. IT'S A SLOW NIGHT HERE.
NO! YOU'RE WRONG!
I FEEL IT IN MY BONES!
MY FINELY HONED SENSES TELL ME SOMETHING TOTALLY HORRIBLE IS GONNA HAPPEN ANY SECOND NOW!
IF ANY TROUBLE COMES UP...
...OUR GRANDPA WILL HELP YOU OUT, ALL RIGHT?
CHA
FOOOOSH

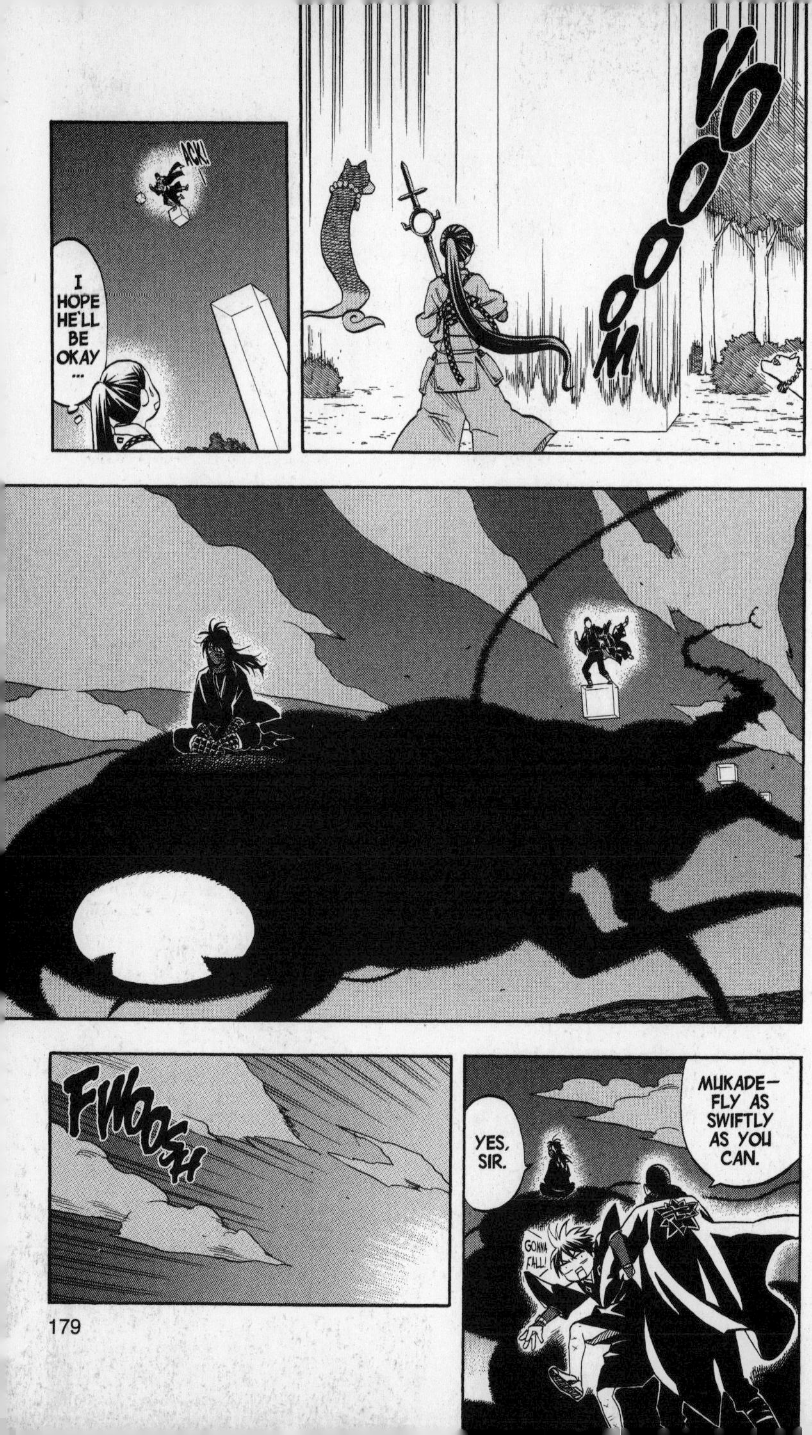
VOOOOOOM
ACK!
I HOPE HE'LL BE OKAY ...
MUKADE—FLY AS SWIFTLY AS YOU CAN.
YES, SIR.
GONNA FALL!
FWOOSH

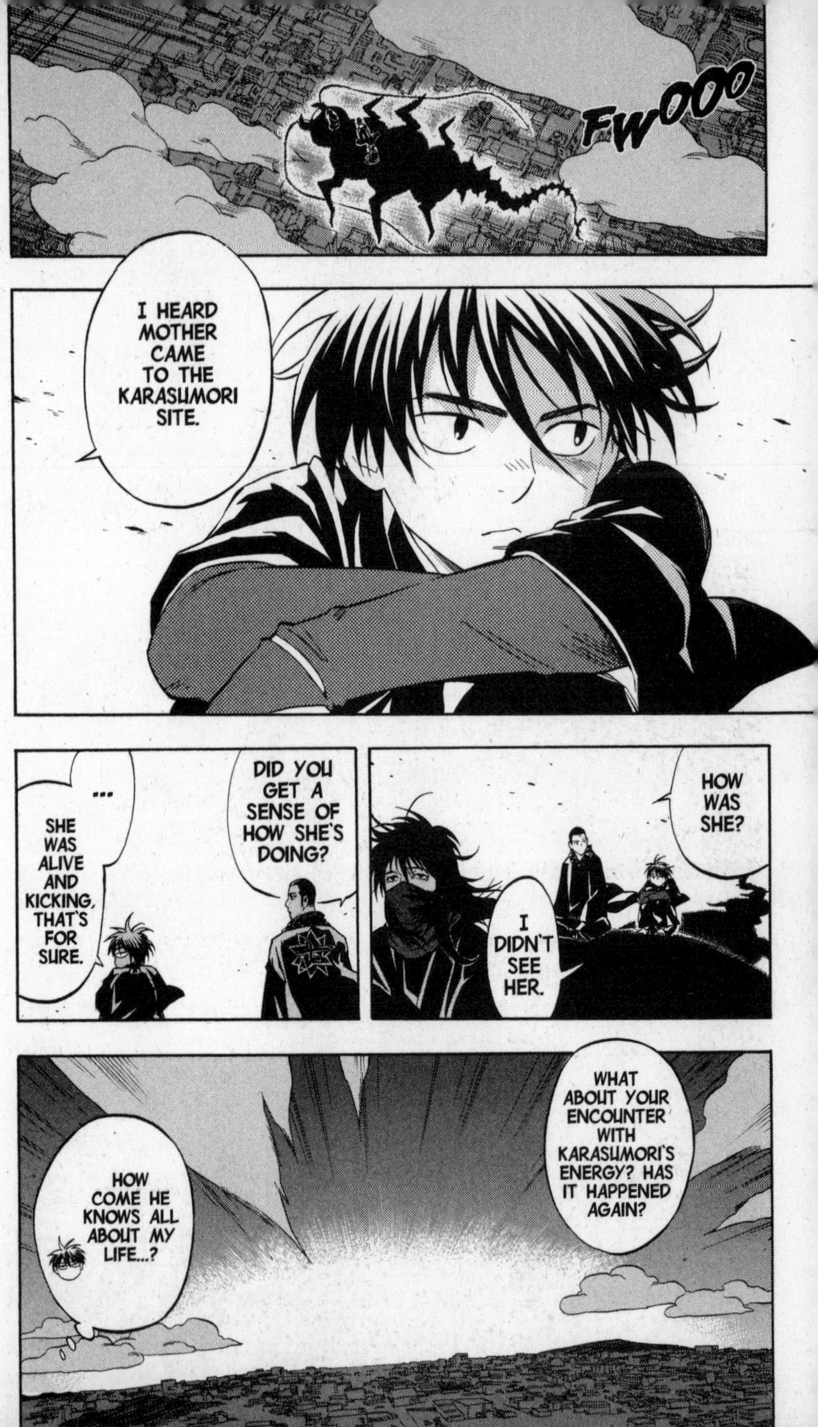
FWOOO
I HEARD MOTHER CAME TO THE KARASUMORI SITE.
HOW WAS SHE?
I DIDN'T SEE HER.
DID YOU GET A SENSE OF HOW SHE'S DOING?
...
SHE WAS ALIVE AND KICKING, THAT'S FOR SURE.
WHAT ABOUT YOUR ENCOUNTER WITH KARASUMORI'S ENERGY? HAS IT HAPPENED AGAIN?
HOW COME HE KNOWS ALL ABOUT MY LIFE...?

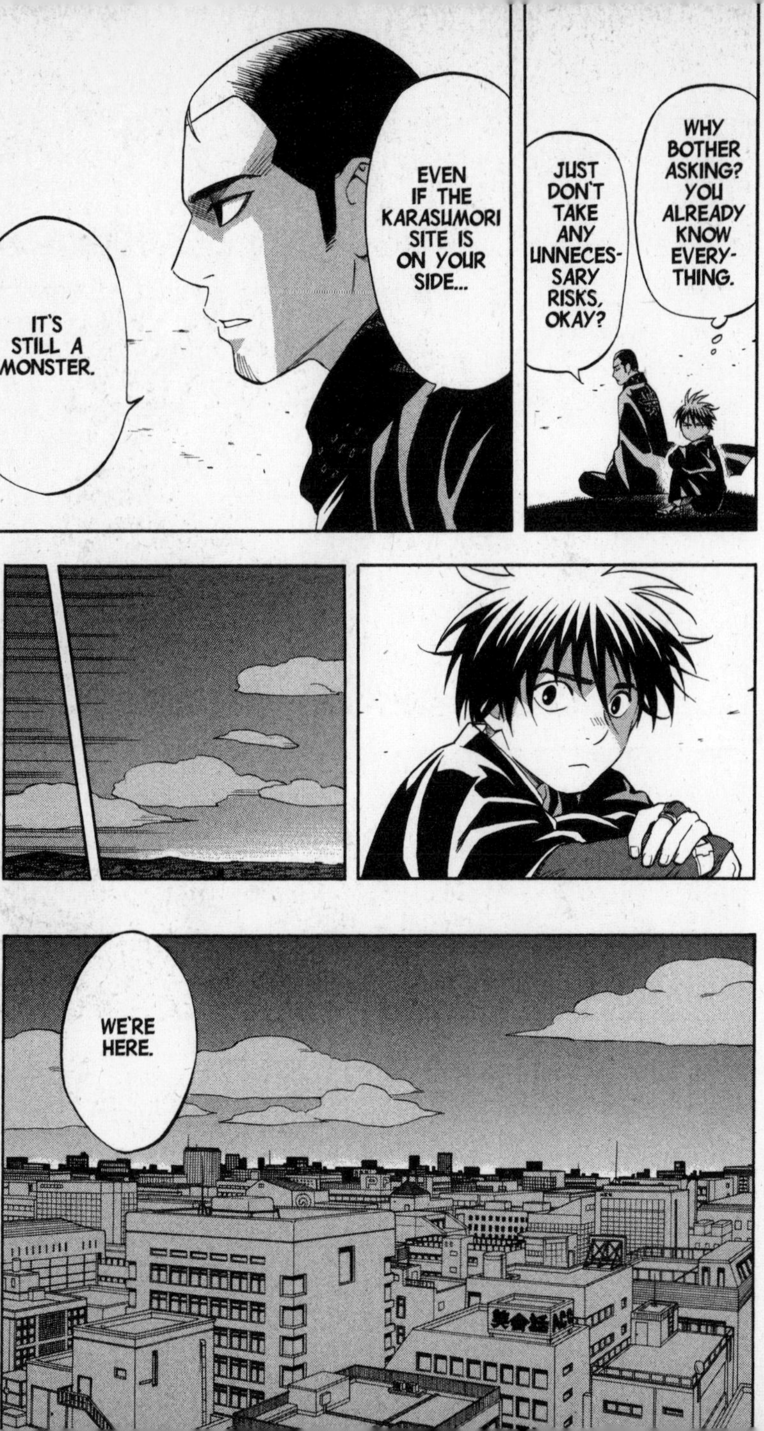
WHY BOTHER ASKING? YOU ALREADY KNOW EVERYTHING.
JUST DON'T TAKE ANY UNNECESSARY RISKS, OKAY?
EVEN IF THE KARASUMORI SITE IS ON YOUR SIDE...
IT'S STILL A MONSTER.
WE'RE HERE.

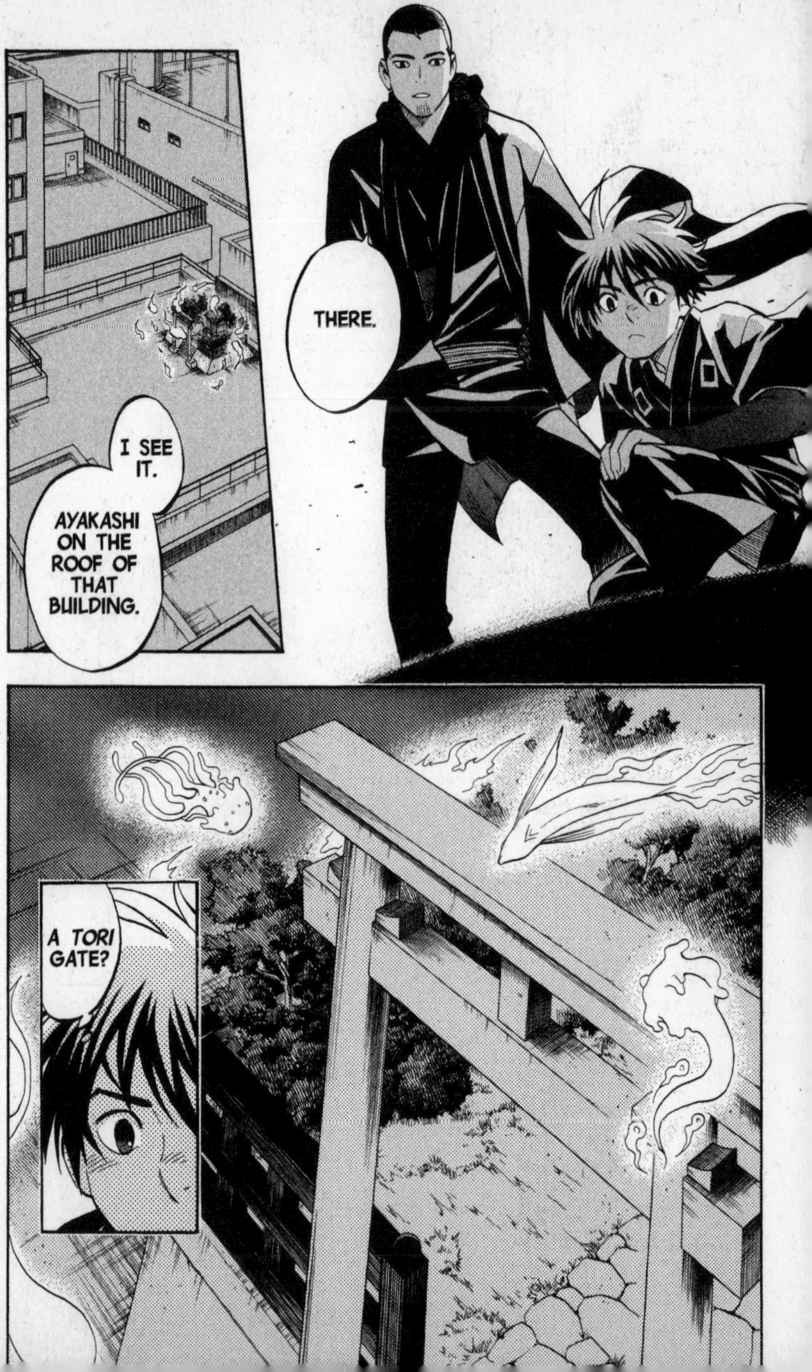
THERE.
I SEE IT.
AYAKASHI ON THE ROOF OF THAT BUILDING.
A TORI GATE?

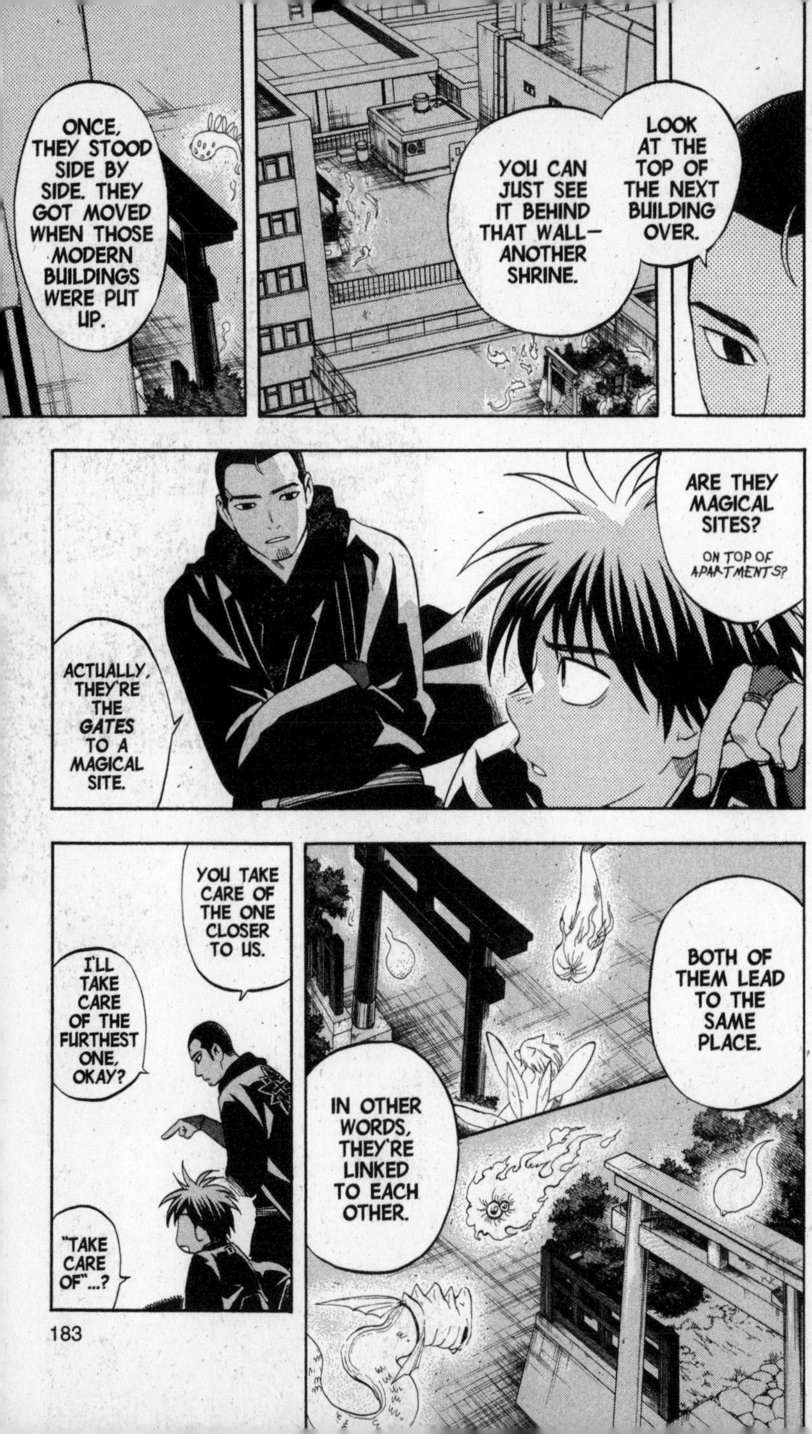
LOOK AT THE TOP OF THE NEXT BUILDING OVER.
YOU CAN JUST SEE IT BEHIND THAT WALL—ANOTHER SHRINE.
ONCE, THEY STOOD SIDE BY SIDE. THEY GOT MOVED WHEN THOSE MODERN BUILDINGS WERE PUT UP.
ARE THEY MAGICAL SITES?
ON TOP OF APARTMENTS?
ACTUALLY, THEY'RE THE *GATES* TO A MAGICAL SITE.
BOTH OF THEM LEAD TO THE SAME PLACE.
IN OTHER WORDS, THEY'RE LINKED TO EACH OTHER.
YOU TAKE CARE OF THE ONE CLOSER TO US.
I'LL TAKE CARE OF THE FURTHEST ONE, OKAY?
"TAKE CARE OF"...?

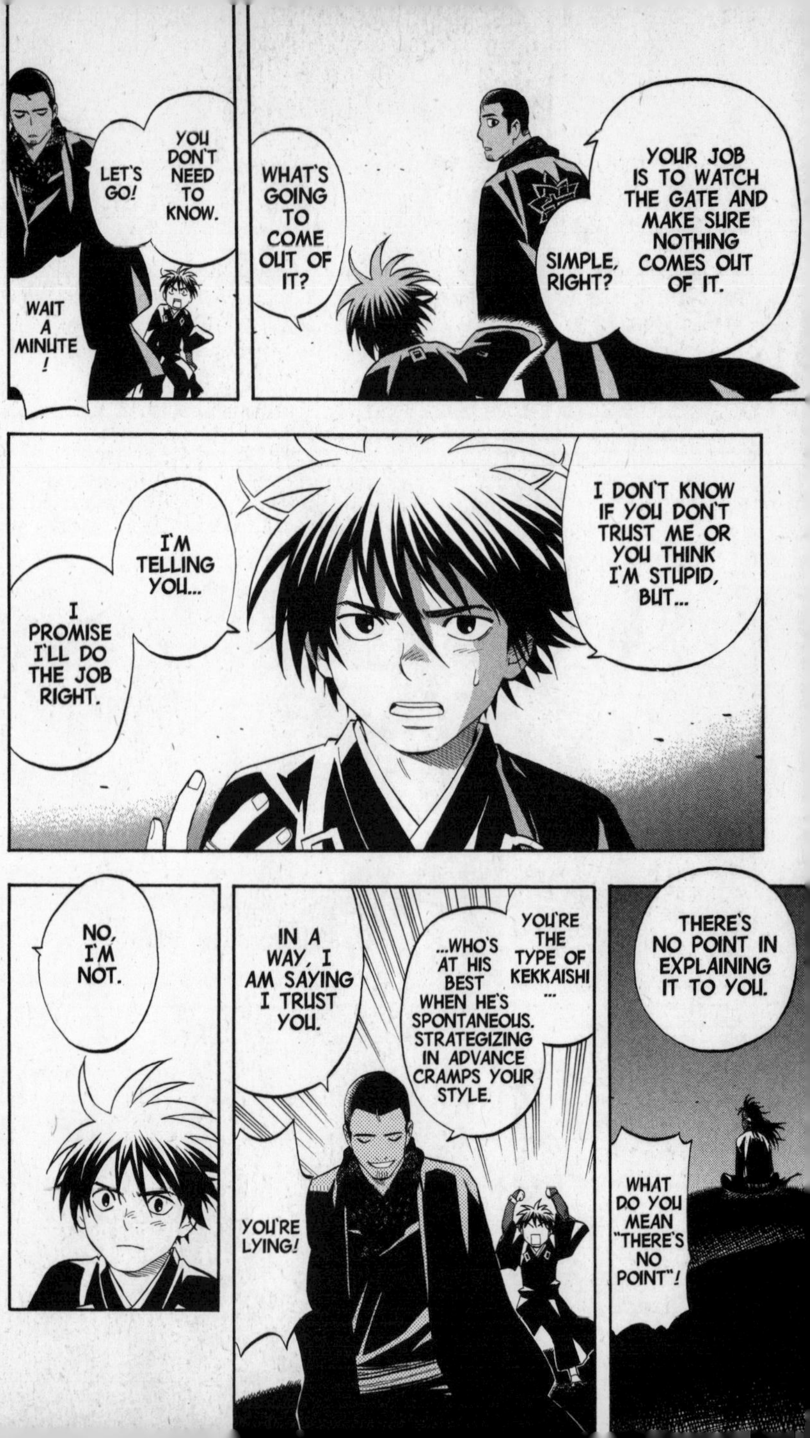
YOUR JOB IS TO WATCH THE GATE AND MAKE SURE NOTHING COMES OUT OF IT.
SIMPLE, RIGHT?
WHAT'S GOING TO COME OUT OF IT?
YOU DON'T NEED TO KNOW.
LET'S GO!
WAIT A MINUTE!
I DON'T KNOW IF YOU DON'T TRUST ME OR YOU THINK I'M STUPID, BUT...
I'M TELLING YOU...
I PROMISE I'LL DO THE JOB RIGHT.
THERE'S NO POINT IN EXPLAINING IT TO YOU.
WHAT DO YOU MEAN "THERE'S NO POINT"!
YOU'RE THE TYPE OF KEKKAISHI...
...WHO'S AT HIS BEST WHEN HE'S SPONTANEOUS. STRATEGIZING IN ADVANCE CRAMPS YOUR STYLE.
IN A WAY, I AM SAYING I TRUST YOU.
YOU'RE LYING!
NO, I'M NOT.

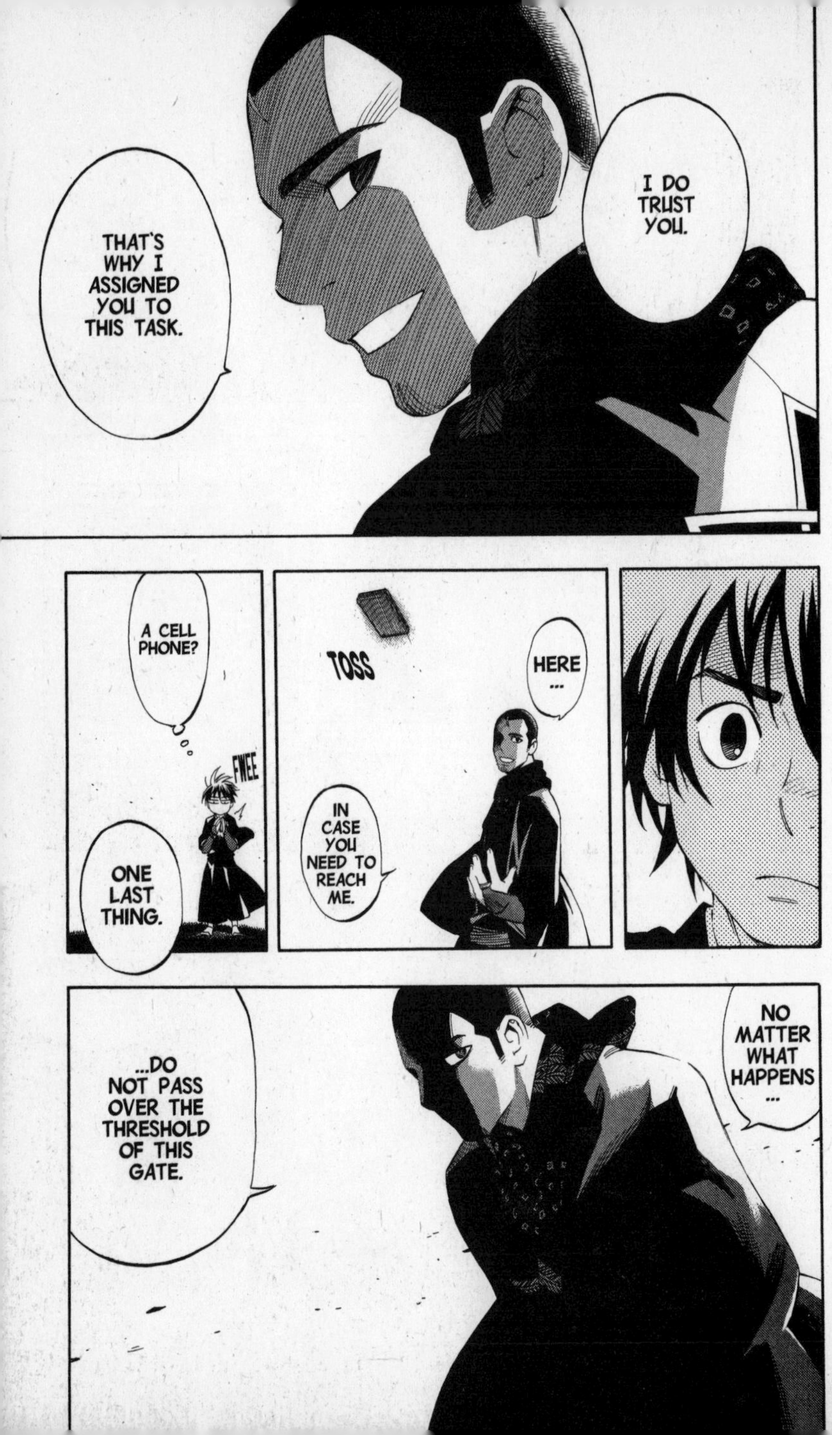
I DO TRUST YOU.
THAT'S WHY I ASSIGNED YOU TO THIS TASK.
HERE...
TOSS
IN CASE YOU NEED TO REACH ME.
A CELL PHONE?
FWEE
ONE LAST THING.
NO MATTER WHAT HAPPENS...
...DO NOT PASS OVER THE THRESHOLD OF THIS GATE.

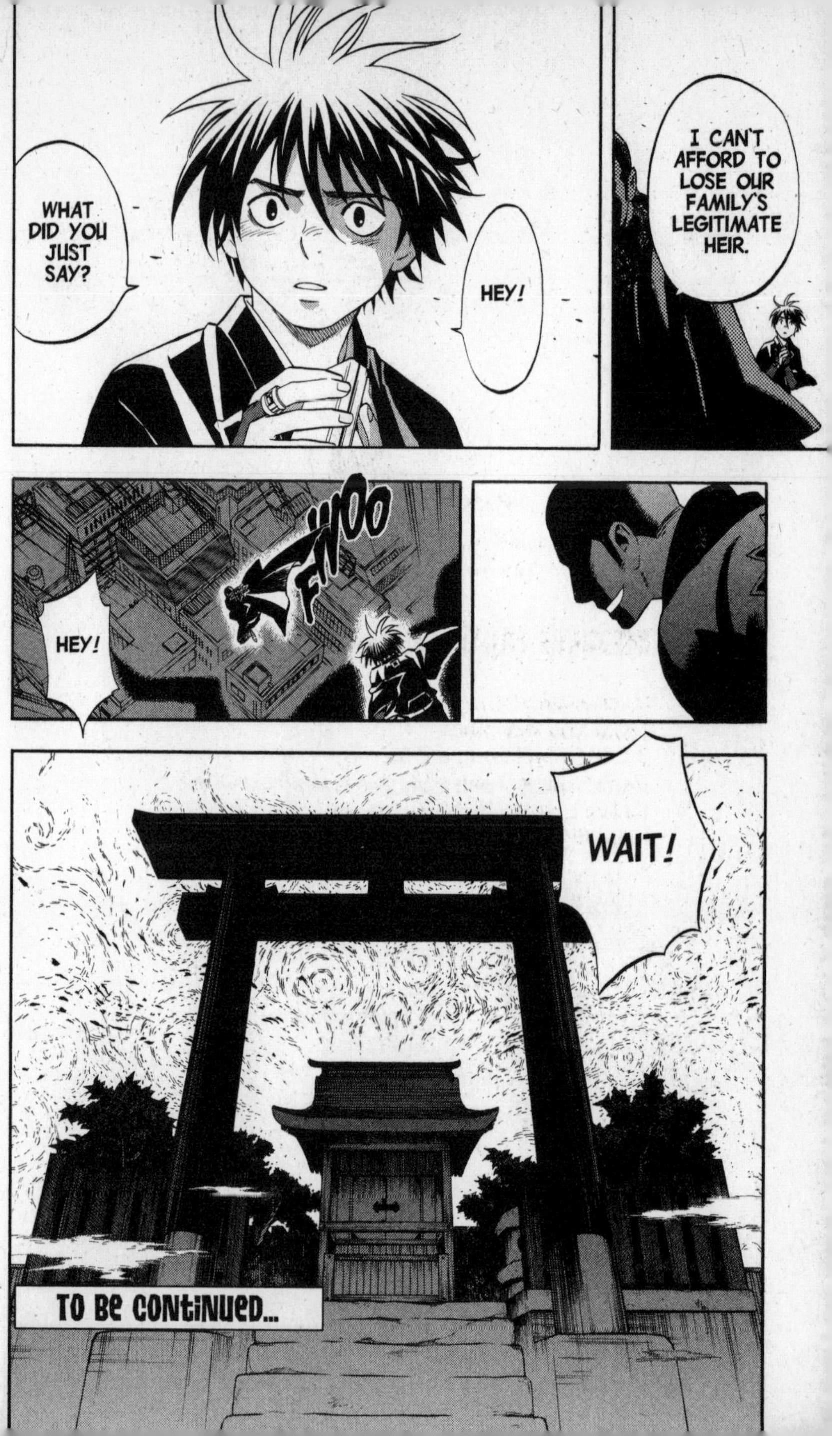
I CAN'T AFFORD TO LOSE OUR FAMILY'S LEGITIMATE HEIR.
HEY!
WHAT DID YOU JUST SAY?
FWOO
HEY!
WAIT!
TO BE CONTINUED...

This'll do... Won't it?

Makeshift Vase:
Jam Jar

MESSAGE FROM YELLOW TANABE

I was awarded the Shogakukan Manga Prize.
Thank you very much.
A lot of people sent me flowers.
Unfortunately, I only have two really plain vases.
I'd like to buy some better looking vases for all
these flowers.

KEKKAISHI

VOLUME 16
VIZ MEDIA EDITION
STORY AND ART BY YELLOW TANABE

Translation/Yuko Sawada
Touch-up Art & Lettering/Stephen Dutro
Cover Design & Graphic Layout/Izumi Evers
Editor/Annette Roman

Editor in Chief, Books/Alvin Lu
Editor in Chief, Magazines/Marc Weidenbaum
VP, Publishing Licensing/Rika Inouye
VP, Sales & Product Marketing/Gonzalo Ferreyra
VP, Creative/Linda Espinosa
Publisher/Hyoe Narita

KEKKAISHI 16 by Yellow TANABE © 2007 Yellow TANABE
All rights reserved.
Original Japanese edition published in 2007 by Shogakukan Inc.,
Tokyo. The stories, characters and incidents mentioned in this
publication are entirely fictional.

Printed in the U.S.A.

Published by VIZ Media, LLC
P.O. Box 77010
San Francisco, CA 94107

VIZ Media Edition
10 9 8 7 6 5 4 3 2 1
First printing, February 2009

PARENTAL ADVISORY
KEKKAISHI is rated T for Teen
and is recommended for ages
13 and up. It contains fantasy
violence.
ratings.viz.com

www.viz.com

store.viz.com

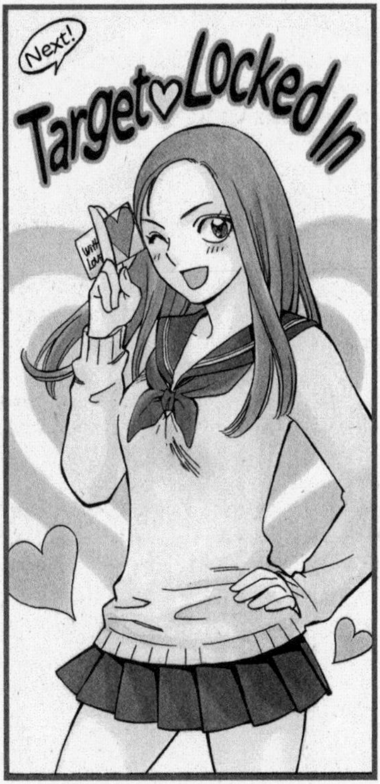
Next!
Target♡Locked In

LOVE MANGA?
LET US KNOW WHAT YOU THINK!

HELP US MAKE THE MANGA
YOU LOVE B